Women *in* Texas History

Women in Texas History
Sponsored by the
Ruthe Winegarten Memorial Foundation for Texas Women's History
Nancy Baker Jones and Cynthia J. Beeman, General Editors

The following individuals and organizations helped make
the publication of this series possible:
Ellen C. Temple
Leadership Women
Texas Historical Foundation
T. L. L. Temple Foundation
Devorah Winegarten

Women *in* Texas History

Angela Boswell

Foreword by
Nancy Baker Jones and
Cynthia J. Beeman

TEXAS A&M UNIVERSITY PRESS
COLLEGE STATION

This paper meets the requirements
of ANSI/NISO Z39.48–1992 (Permanence of Paper).
Binding materials have been chosen for durability.

Library of Congress Cataloging-in-Publication Data

Names: Boswell, Angela, 1965– author.
Title: Women in Texas history / Angela Boswell.
Other titles: Women in Texas history series.
Description: First edition. | College Station : Texas A&M University Press,
    [2018] | Series: Women in Texas history | Native American, Spanish, and
    Mexican women in Native American Texas — The Frontier South in the early
    nineteenth century — Creating an antebellum society in Texas — Civil War
    and Reconstruction — Making West Texas — Women's activism, 1870s-1920s
    — Women's work, 1890s–1920s — Depression and war — Accepting and
    rejecting conformity in the postwar decades — Taking charge: women to the
    end of the twentieth century — Conclusion — Notes. | Includes
    bibliographical references and index.
Identifiers: LCCN 2018028076| ISBN 9781623497071 (book/cloth : alk. paper) |
    ISBN 1623497078 (book/cloth : alk. paper) | ISBN 9781623497088 (e-book)
Subjects: LCSH: Women—Texas—History. | Women—Southern States—History. |
    Women—Texas—Social conditions. | Gender expression—Texas. | Texas—Race
    relations. | Texas—Ethnic relations. | Women pioneers—Texas. |
    Texas—History—Civil War, 1861-1865—Women.
Classification: LCC HQ1438.T4 B69 2018 | DDC 305.409764—dc23 LC record
available at https://lccn.loc.gov/2018028076

*Front cover clockwise from left: Courtesy of Museum of the Gulf Coast; Texas Woman's
University; TWU Libraries, Woman's Collection; Lockheed Martin Aeronautics Company,
Fort Worth; Texas Woman's University, TWU Libraries, Woman's Collection; Abilene
Photograph Collection, Hardin-Simmons University, Abilene, Texas; and Tarrant County
College District Archives, Fort Worth, Texas.*

Back cover: Courtesy of Kheel Center, Cornell University

Contents

Foreword

The publication of Angela Boswell's *Women in Texas History* is an important milestone in the historiography of Texas history survey texts: it is the first narrative synthesis of Texas history from precontact to the late twentieth century written from the perspective of women's experiences. In comparison, existing overviews often follow another pattern, focusing on political events—such as settlement and war—from predominantly Anglo, male perspectives, injecting women into the narrative to address social reform, and making "women" an index item because they have not been infused into the chronology.

As Boswell's title subtly asserts, women are, and always have been, *in* Texas history. But it took the emergence of women's history in general, and Texas women's history in particular, to make this volume possible. Texas women's history is relatively new, having emerged only in the late twentieth century after decades of persistence by women's movement activists, public historians, independent scholars, and academics. Through their organizing, researching, and writing over the years, they laid the foundation for *Women in Texas History*.

Historian Gerda Lerner's 1975 essay, "Placing Women in History: Definitions and Challenges," which is still an important reference, points out some of the key elements of women's history.[1]

- Women's history is the history of the majority of humankind.

- The true history of women is the story of their living in a male-defined world on their own terms.

- Women of different economic groups and cultures have different historical experiences. Their differing experiences also depend on whether their activity is male-defined or woman-oriented. Because

women are indoctrinated in a male-defined value system that generally subordinates them, they conduct their lives accordingly.

- Once women become woman-oriented, they begin to push for reform of social and political systems, sometimes to equip themselves
  for their traditional roles, sometimes for new roles. When they
  recognize their interests as a subordinated group, feminism emerges
  as resistance to subordination.

- Traditional histories have applied male-centered questions from
  political and economic frameworks to women. Social and women's
  histories focus instead on arenas in which women play large roles,
  such as family and reproduction, marital status, sexuality, work,
  community building, and social reform. The focus shifts from one
  on condition to one on experience.

- Women's history consults not only traditional resources but also
  those by and about women, such as diaries, letters, oral history, and
  autobiographies. Women's voices and points of view are considered
  not only legitimate, but essential.

- Women's history may not fit neatly into traditional political periods. For example, the American Revolution is generally character-
  ized as a boon to democratic principles and the formation of a more
  equitable society. Women of all classes and cultures, however, were
  not then considered citizens and could not vote.

Women in Texas History is informed by this intellectual legacy. As Boswell
states in her preface, the book is based on a simple premise: "what wom-
en did in the past is intrinsically worth knowing. Texas would not be Texas
without one-half of its population." In addition, however, the book is also
complex. Boswell describes its four facets as *Texas* women's history; Texas
women's history; Texas *women's history*; and as a history of *all* Texas wom-
en, acknowledging race, ethnicity, and class as inclusively as possible. Boswell pays attention not only to the diversity of Texan identities but also to
the differences in their experiences. Here readers will find not only Native
Americans, Tejanas, African Americans, Anglos, Germans, and Asians but
also discussions of what Boswell calls "categories that shape women's identity,
such as class, religion, political ideology, and sexuality." And, of course, the
concept of gender, which developed as cultures assigned meaning and value

to the biological and behavioral differences between men and women. "Understanding what it means to be a woman changed over time," Boswell notes, and her chronology attempts to demonstrate those changes.

The Ruthe Winegarten Foundation for Texas Women's History is proud to sponsor the Women in Texas History book series, published by Texas A&M University Press, in which *Women in Texas History* now appears. This groundbreaking book is a "first" in both its concept and approach to Texas history, just the kind for which this series was designed. As such it must also be understood to represent a beginning, not an end, and so we look forward to what follows.

—Nancy Baker Jones and Cynthia J. Beeman
Series Editors

1. Gerda Lerner, "Placing Women in History: Definitions and Challenges," *Feminist Studies* (Autumn 1975), 5–14.

Preface

This book is a narrative of Texas women's history. It is based on a simple premise: what women did in the past is intrinsically worth knowing. Texas would not be Texas without one half of its population.

The mythic narrative of Texas history has long emphasized the iconic cowboy taming the frontier, men fighting valiantly against foes to win glory for themselves and the state, and politicians engaged in debates in which personal and ideological differences played out, shaping the idiosyncrasies of state laws and economics. Such myth not only omits the women from those activities, it conceals the reality of women's lived experiences—their history.

Despite the mythic narrative that dominates our thinking about Texas' past, for the last forty to fifty years historians have been writing about Texas women. Women's historians in Texas began researching earlier, wrote more, and have advanced the knowledge about women in their state further than any other state in the country. This attention to women in history has come both from the continued insistence that Texas is unique and because the state's unique historical narrative leaves out women. The wealth of research and writing on women's history in Texas has made this book possible; the fact that the historical narrative still obscures women makes the book necessary.[1]

A narrative such as this one, covering hundreds of years of history, must omit more than it includes. As a result, some remarkable women in Texas —even ones who have done amazing things and changed the course of history—may not be mentioned in these pages. This book, however, will provide a framework for understanding women's actions and lives in the past. In attempting to accomplish that goal, I have concentrated on four major unifying guidelines.

First, this is *Texas* women's history. Although Texas women's history was shaped by and helped shape the major trends and events in regional and national women's history, this book concentrates specifically on when and how those forces affected women in Texas. For instance, industrialization and urbanization created changes in Texas women's work and roles at a far later date than that of their sisters in the Northeast, while some other economic changes occurred and affected Texas women's lives before their southern sisters experienced them. This narrative, therefore, does not examine topics and events of American women's history unless there is evidence that women in Texas affected or were affected by those forces.

Second, this is Texas *women's* history. It is about women, and therefore the topics traditionally covered in Texas history may not be mentioned or receive significant attention. Developments and events that occurred in the state are discussed in relation to their effects on women or women's effects on them. As a result, the periodization of chapters is not quite the same as traditional narratives of Texas history because war and politics did not always have a profound effect on women's lives the way technological innovation or patterns of migration did.

Third, this is Texas *women's history*. As such, it fits into the evolving field of women's history. Some of the first histories about women were "compensatory," in that scholars searched the past to tell the stories of some famous or infamous women. During the next stage of women's histories, researchers uncovered the stories of unsung women who had "contributed" to the traditional narrative, usually as forgotten or behind-the-scenes actors. Both contributory and compensatory histories, however, tended to celebrate the remarkable woman without leading to a historical understanding of most women's lives. When researchers began looking at history through women's eyes, concentrating on the spaces in which women spent their lives—such as family and reproduction, work, community building, and social reform—a fuller understanding of the history of women emerged. This text does celebrate remarkable women, but the overarching story is about how unremarkable women coped with daily life, acted as agents in their own lives, and participated in the historical changes that shaped women's future opportunities.

Fourth, this is the history of *all* Texas women—as inclusive as possible. As women's history has evolved, the field has become ever more cognizant that race, ethnicity, and class have an impact on all aspects of women's lives, from identity to expected social roles to the arenas in which they play large roles. Because of Texas' ethnic diversity, this book pays special attention to the differences in the lived experiences of Native Americans, Tejanas, African

Americans, Anglos, Germans, and Asians. Other categories that shape women's identity, such as class, religion, political ideology, and sexuality are also explored.

Another concept fundamental to this history is that gender is a social construct. Women's biology differs from men's in some key ways, but it is society that has assigned meaning to those biological differences. Nothing makes this clearer than studying the past and how gender constructions change. From the earliest years, different cultures in Texas constructed ideas of gender, and what gender means, differently. Understandings of what it means to be a woman changed over time. The chronological approach will demonstrate those changes even when a chapter does not explicitly explore gender construction.

The chronological approach of this book also allows an opportunity to understand women's history in each particular period while identifying change over time in fundamental matters, such as work, law, daily life, community involvement, familial roles and responsibilities, education, and politics.

At the heart of any discussion about women's history is feminism. "Feminism," a term coined in the early twentieth century, only came into widespread use in the late twentieth century to describe movements to expand the rights and freedoms of women. Some women fighting for suffrage in the early twentieth century used the term, but most preferred "woman suffrage" or, when the goal was more expansive than just suffrage, "woman movement." Beginning in the 1960s, a new concerted push for equal rights for women and an emerging "women's liberation movement" that pushed for more social and economic freedoms coalesced, claiming the term "feminism." As a result, "feminist" may be applied to any effort to equalize the gender hierarchy, and historians of the 1970s often retroactively applied the term to the women who won suffrage, referring to them as "first-wave feminists." In this book I will refrain from using "feminist" when discussing women before the 1960s, no matter how clearly they might fit our modern definition, because they generally did not use the word to describe themselves.

Terms referring to people of cultural groups have also changed over time and carry particular connotations. Like gender, race is a social construct. Because race has been used as a category historically, I do use the term "race" in this text, although I use it interchangeably with "ethnicity." Both "race" and "ethnicity" signify groups of people who identify themselves as sharing culture, biology, or background in common—or who are identified by others as doing so. The words are imperfect, but they allow me to discuss some significant differences among women. I use the terms "white" or "Anglo" to signify Americans who descended from cultures primarily dominated by English laws and culture and the term "Germans" to describe those descended from German-speaking provinces and areas of Europe. "Native Americans" and "Indians" signify those who are descended from and identify with those groups of people who occupied America before Europeans arrived. The terms "African Americans" and "blacks" are used interchangeably for those who were—or were perceived to be—descended from Africa. To signify those who identify with cultures of Mexican descent, I use the terms "Tejana/os," "Mexicans," "Mexican Americans," or "Chicano/as," depending upon the period and the terms these groups most commonly used to identify themselves at that time. "Asians" refers to any person descended from immigrants from southern or eastern Asia.

Chapter 1 explores prehistoric women, the Native American women who occupied the area that would become Texas, and the first Spanish/Mexican women to arrive in the area that was still controlled largely by Native Americans. Chapter 2 discusses the clashing of cultures and the primitive "frontier" conditions in the early nineteenth century as Mexican, Native American, Anglo-American, African American, and German women all settled in the state, negotiating coexistence with each other as well as with sometimes difficult environments. The third chapter traces the creation of antebellum southern cotton-farming culture in the eastern portion of the state, the resulting establishment of southern social classes and expectations, and the consequences of these developments for Anglo, African American, German, and Mexican American women. Chapter 4 explores the effects of the American Civil War and Reconstruction on women in all areas of the state, as well as the joys and results of freedom for African American women.

The fifth chapter shifts the focus of the narrative decidedly westward, covering ranching in West Texas and Southwest Texas, especially along the border. Chapters 6 and 7 both cover roughly the end of the nineteenth and the beginning of the twentieth century. The sixth chapter traces the growth of women's activism in this period, including in populist and progressive movements and the suffrage movement. The seventh chapter explores women's work on farms and in cities and how it changed in this period. Chapter 8 finds women working harder than ever before to support their families during the Depression, and then examines changing roles as men went off to World War II while women took higher-paying jobs in factories and began moving to cities in large numbers. After the war, while many women embraced domesticity and conformity, others began challenging the social order that oppressed many, including women. Women's roles in Cold War conformity, the civil rights movement, and the emergence of the women's liberation and feminist movement are addressed in chapter 9. Chapter 10 explores the powerful feminist movement of the 1970s, the backlash against it in the 1980s and 1990s, and its enduring legacy. Finally, the conclusion discusses twenty-first century events and the status of women now.

As a narrative of women's history, this book relies almost exclusively on the work of other historians. As mentioned above, scholars of Texas women have been extraordinarily productive and have produced abundant compensatory and contributory histories, as well as histories that focus specifically on women's lives and experiences. I have tried to bring together those hundreds of secondary sources and represent the prevailing interpretations of Texas women's history at this time.

Relying upon the published research of others presents multiple challenges, the most serious of which is the uneven coverage of some women and some topics. While some subjects, such as progressivism and suffrage, have received extensive research from a variety of perspectives, others, such as how Native American women coped with removal, lesbians' lives and fight for rights, and women's roles in emerging Asian communities, have only recently begun to receive historical treatment. Much more research needs to be conducted about women's history in Texas. I hope that many readers will wonder about topics barely covered or not mentioned at all in this book and go out and conduct new research: fill in the many missing pieces, interpret the meanings of women's lives in the past, and challenge past interpretations. My ambition in writing this book is to provide a broad narrative interpretation that will be an inspiration and a beginning—not an end—to telling the history of women in Texas.

Acknowledgments

This book has been over a decade in the making and has therefore accumulated more debts of assistance than can be sufficiently acknowledged. I never would have dreamed of embarking on such a project if it had not been for the idea and amazing support of former Texas A&M University Press editor in chief Mary Lenn Dixon. It took me much longer to finish than she hoped, but I am forever grateful for her patience and support, as well as that of her successor, Jay Dew. Without their faith in me, I would have quit well before the finish.

Many, many people helped in the research stage. This work depends mostly on secondary sources, and Katrina Rogers, interlibrary loan technician at Henderson State University's Huie Library, has worked very hard and brilliantly tracked down hundreds of books, theses, and articles, some quite obscure, assisted by her colleague Kim Hunter. Other Huie Library staff members have also been helpful, making sure I had access to necessary databases and support of all kinds. Thank you especially to Bob Yehl, former library director, and Lea Ann Alexander, current director. Several graduate students throughout the years have helped tremendously by flushing out and previewing sources for me: Nadia Malinowa, Joyce Powell, Cadra McDaniel, Regina Beard, Brian Lott, and Matthew Webber. I especially acknowledge the Ruthe Winegarten Memorial Foundation for Texas Women's History and its excellent website "Women in Texas History."

The colleagues assisting me in writing are so numerous as to make this, in essence, a group project. My writers' group at Henderson State University read and helped me revise the earliest drafts of each chapter, suffering through some of the worst prose and least-developed ideas. I appreciate their help in revisions and their moral support: Suzanne Tartamella, Pam Bax, Vernon

Miles, Kyle Jones, Melanie Angell, Martin Halpern, Matthew Bowman, and especially David Sesser, Travis Langley, and Mike Taylor, who have been assisting throughout nearly the whole project. I also must acknowledge the enormous emotional support provided by friends across the country who cheered on my progress via a social media support group.

Colleagues in Texas women's history have also been generous with their time, reading early versions of chapters, particularly Jessica Brannon-Wranowsky, Stephanie Cole, Judith McArthur, Rebecca Sharpless, and Jean Stuntz. Elizabeth Turner and Nancy Baker Jones read the entire manuscript. These wonderful historians have pointed out omissions, helped me correct mistakes, made wonderful suggestions for improvement, and have shaped the book. Despite their best efforts, I have undoubtedly persisted in making errors, and those mistakes are all mine.

I would also like to thank my institution. Henderson State University has supported my teaching, research, and writing, and I am very grateful for the administrators and colleagues who have helped me through the years. I would also like to acknowledge a few archives that I visited for this project: the Rosenberg Library in Galveston, the Woodson Research Center at Rice University in Houston, the Dallas History & Archives Division at the Dallas Public Library, and especially the Woman's Collection at Texas Woman's University in Denton, Texas. I am grateful to staff members at these institutions.

My family has been understanding and supportive of this long obsession of mine, especially Barb Boswell. She encouraged me to take on the project, became accustomed to "the book" as another entity in our household, and has been my greatest cheerleader in seeing it to the end. I cannot thank her enough.

Finally, I must thank the hundreds of historians who have written about Texas women's history—whether it be books, articles, paragraphs, or even sentences—especially those who have dedicated their careers to uncovering and understanding women of the past. Their work made it possible for me to even consider writing a narrative of Texas women's history. They continue to be my role models and inspirations.

Women *in* Texas History

Chapter 1

Native American, Spanish, and Mexican Women in Native American Texas

For thousands of years, groups of people historians have called collectively American Indians or Native Americans inhabited and controlled what is now Texas. Even for hundreds of years after the Spanish subjugated many American Indians in Central, South, and North America, and even after the English and French carved out settlements and areas of domination in North America, Native Americans remained in control of the culture and politics of Texas.

Women held significant and varied roles in the culture, politics, and survival of the peoples of Texas for thousands of years. Because written records do not exist, most of what is known about these women must come from archaeological sources and from what the Europeans observed when they arrived. When Europeans arrived in Texas, they brought with them multiple ideas about gender and women's roles that differed from those of the first inhabitants, but even those ideas were filtered and shaped by the scarcity of European women and the predominance of Native Americans.

The First Women of Texas

Descended from peoples who had moved into North America tens of thousands of years earlier, the first women migrating to Texas faced a frontier very different from today's Texas. At the time, lush grasslands covered western

Texas, and eastern Texas contained extensive forests with varieties of trees. This bountiful environment allowed the nomadic hunting and gathering bands to thrive and to multiply.

Archaeologists still disagree on when these first bands, which they refer to as Paleoindians, arrived in Texas. At the heart of this debate is the skeleton of a woman nicknamed Midland Minnie. Archaeologists discovered her skeleton in 1953 along Monahans Draw in West Texas. Some archaeologists have offered evidence that it might be as many as thirty-seven thousand years old, which would make her remains the oldest in North America, but most archaeologists believe she lived in Texas between ten thousand and twelve thousand years ago.[1] Minnie and other women who migrated with her were crucial to the survival of their families and bands. Paleoindian men might head out on hunts of days or weeks without women, but usually groups of men, women, and children, consisting of forty or more people, followed herds of large animals (such as mammoths), camels, small species of horses, and especially bison. Women probably did not often participate in the killing of the animals, but they assisted with butchering and preserving the meat, as well as preparing the hides by scraping and drying them. In addition to helping with the hunts, women gathered edible vegetation, such as roots, nuts, and berries, and trapped small game.[2]

About eight thousand years ago the large animals disappeared, and hunters turned to smaller animals such as deer, rabbits, turkeys, birds, and fish. During this period, the Archaic, they still followed game, but women's food gathering became much more important, and bands were more likely to travel according to the season to the best locations for gathering seeds, roots, nuts, berries, insects, and shellfish. Knowledge of plant life and plant cycles was crucial, as was understanding what parts of plants were edible and how to find these foods, especially roots that were hidden underground. Women gathered a diverse variety of vegetation, such as prickly pear, acorns, and mesquite beans, and prepared it by grinding it into powder, cooking it in rock ovens, adding water or other ingredients to it, or otherwise doing whatever was necessary to make it palatable. While men's hunting added meat to the diet, most of the foods eaten by these Archaic people were the fruits of women's gathering and preparation.[3]

Technological developments, such as spear-throwers and bolos, increased the amount of game that men could harvest, while ropes, mats, nets, and baskets increased the gathering abilities of women. Greater food supply caused the bands to grow in size and specializations. Whether male or female, those within a tribe with special knowledge and skills gained great respect. Women who gathered vegetation were probably the first to recognize the healing properties of herbs, and those who excelled at healing may have earned esteem. Men were more likely to have been admired as a result of hunting prowess or military leadership. However, because hunting and gathering required constant travel and because these focused primarily on subsistence—just finding enough food to survive—no one could accumulate much property.[4]

Archaeologists have learned much about these early hunter-gatherers, including some about the gendered division of labor and the importance of women to the survival of the bands. What cannot be known, however, is what the work meant to the women and men of that time. Was the division of labor somehow politically dictated? Was it socially enforced? Or did people merely engage in the activities for which they were best suited, discouraging women—who often had to care for infants and small children—from participating in the hunts? Did the nomadic bands' reliance on food gathered by women give them more political and social power? Because people kept no written records, historians will probably never be able to answer fully these questions. Anthropologist Patricia Bass's study of the oldest rock art in Texas—pictographs on the walls of caves in West Texas—notes both male- and female-associated art. This artwork cannot elaborate much upon gender roles, but the presence of images of vegetation as well as animals indicates that these Archaic peoples recognized the importance of the plant life gathered by women and complicates any assumptions that only men engaged in creative expression.[5]

Relying on gathered food entailed the need for people to understand their environment and predict changes in it. The bands traveled in search of not only bison and deer but also began regulating their movements according to the seasons when certain plants, nuts, berries, and roots would ripen or become available. Becoming familiar with a specific terrain helped the transition to agriculture, a process in which women played the dominant role. As early as AD 700 some women in northeastern Texas moved from merely gathering vegetation growing naturally to planting and cultivating small crops, such as sunflowers and squash. These foods did not provide enough nutrients for a complete diet and so served only to supplement hunting and gathering. However, establishment of these preliminary agricultural practices facilitated full-scale agriculture after trade networks with South America brought corn to North America. By planting and harvesting only the best seeds, women improved crop yields. When women sowed beans and squash along with corn, these plants began providing sufficient nutrition, and people began to settle down in villages. Women continued to gather food, and men continued to hunt, but no longer did they travel constantly to find food.[6]

Settling into villages probably changed the lives of women significantly. There were definite advantages to having more permanent homes and decreasing the amount of travel, especially for pregnant women and women caring for infants. However, feeding a large village through agriculture required more hours of work than hunting and gathering, with women performing a large share of that work. In looking at skeletal remains in North Texas, archaeologists have found differences in the type of repeated stress injuries found in skeletal remains, indicating that a clear division of labor by gender continued. The stress injuries in women's skeletal remains show that they exercised primary daily responsibility for planting, harvesting, and preparing the crops. Men, however, continued to engage in less-frequent, high-stress activities such as hunting, paddling, warfare, and perhaps clearing fields for planting.[7]

Village life did provide for enough leisure time for some individuals to engage in activities other than food procurement. Pottery became more plentiful and ornamental as well as useful, houses became sturdier and more permanent, and the tanning of hides and skins for blankets, clothing, and shoes became more refined. Northeastern Texas was not the only part of North America to experience these changes during the Archaic period. Much of eastern North America from Texas to Florida and north to Wisconsin began organizing every aspect of life, government, and religion around agriculture. Abundant food and specialization of tasks led to the ability to accumulate goods and to the desire to trade. Rivers linked this enormous expanse of villages, towns, and even large cities in a trade network. Not only were goods exchanged; so too were ideas and religious beliefs, forming a massive culture that archaeologists now call the Mississippian.[8]

The people of this Mississippian tradition sought understanding of their new sedentary situations and often looked to deities that were particularly earth- and crop-based. In the worship of these gods, people of the Mississippian tradition built large earthen mounds, and so archaeologists often refer to them as "mound builders." Although the priest-chiefs and other leaders in the mound-building societies appear to have been mostly male, women's control of the primary food supply probably elevated women's status and power in the society.[9]

On the other side of current-day Texas, the Mogollons in far western Texas also developed agriculture around the same time, perhaps even as early as AD 500. Like the people of eastern Texas, these Archaic people entered into trading networks that eventually led to their absorption into a larger culture by AD 1200. Until very recently, archaeologists referred to this culture of the North American Southwest as Anasazi, but they have recently begun using the term "Ancestral Pueblo." The Ancestral Pueblo depended perhaps even more heavily on agriculture than those of the Mississippian tradition to the east, and men gave up hunting to till the fields. Skeletons from this period show evidence that men regularly stooped, as they would have if working the ground with a hoe. Women's skeletons, on the other hand, indicate habitual kneeling, as would be necessary for grinding corn.[10]

For reasons that are still unclear, both the Ancestral Pueblo and Mississippian traditions had declined and disintegrated at least a century before Europeans entered Texas. In both regions strong cultures revived by the sixteenth century, but neither was as large or expansive as earlier. The later Pueblos continued agriculture and living in homes cut out of cliffs, but their influence did not return to Texas until after the Europeans had settled in America. The Mississippian tradition, however, left a much more permanent impression on Texas. The Caddos of northern and eastern Texas no longer built mounds but did continue similarly complex social organizations, religion, and, above all, reliance on agriculture.

American Women at the Time of European Explorations

One of the cultural traditions carried over from the Mississippians to the Caddos was matrilineal descent—that is, they traced descent through their mothers. Because groups of women planted, harvested, and even performed spiritual ceremonies to ensure good crops, most American agricultural societies found it important to keep together the women who knew how to work the fields and distribute the food. Therefore, when a couple married, the husband went to live with the wife's family—a practice referred to as matrilocality.[11]

Caddo women performed the significant share of work sustaining their village and thus exercised control over much of their daily lives. Women planted, cultivated, and harvested the crops. They also continued gathering foods from nearby forests and fields. When women collected the harvest— or when men returned from hunts with meat—women divided and stored

Figure 1.1. Approximate location of Native American groups during initial period of European contact.

the food. Meals were prepared communally in the household, which usually included a mother, her husband, her daughters and their husbands, and her unmarried sons. In the morning, under the supervision of the chief woman of the house, each woman would contribute to the day's meals from her family's private store. All the women would participate in the meal preparation: baking breads and preparing stews; boiling, roasting, or broiling meats and vegetables; seasoning food with bear oil; wrapping mixtures in corn shucks to be baked in ashes. Women ground the corn, beans, sunflower seeds, acorns, and nuts into flour in stumps of trees that they had burned out to use as mortars. They wove reeds into screens to sift flour, used grasses to make baskets for storing flour, and made large clay pottery jars to store the bear grease and water that they hauled to their homes. And, of course, cooking required firewood that the women chopped and carried.[12]

Men's primary responsibilities among the Caddos involved hunting and warfare. However, men also chopped trees for homes and firewood, built grass homes, and cleared the fields to prepare them for planting. Even when men and women worked on the same project, such as clearing fields or building a new home for a family in the community, they worked separately in gendered groups. Chiefs and priests were primarily men, and councils of men would make decisions about going to war. However, women also participated in many public ceremonies, and some ceremonies, including those performed before planting, involved women only. Even the male chiefs usually inherited their political and hereditary position through their mothers' lines.[13] And women directed the daily affairs of the households, where most decisions were made. A Spanish missionary once reported that he had arranged with a male chief to stay among the Caddos and live in the chief's household. The chief agreed, but when he told the women of the house his plans, they refused, and then, much to the surprise of the missionary, the chief heeded their wishes.[14]

Unlike Caddo women, the majority of Native American women lived in groups that did not rely on agriculture. Peoples such as the Atakapas, Jumanos, Karankawas, and Coahuiltecans ("Coahuiltecan" came to include many different ethnic groups in South and Central Texas) continued ancient hunting and gathering practices. In hunting and gathering societies it was more important to keep an experienced band of hunters together. Wives would go live with their husbands' families (patrilocality), and people were most likely to trace their descent through fathers (patrilineality). Because most hunting and gathering bands were small—about forty people—husbands looked for wives outside of the band. This meant that women not only left their families' homes but also left the band of their families.[15]

Patrilocality could greatly decrease women's chances of survival when taken to the extreme as it was periodically. When scarce resources contributed to warfare, as it did intermittently, some Coahuiltecan parents would kill their female infants so as not to waste food on children who would marry into bands of competitors and thus increase their strength. Among most Texans, however, the emphasis on hunting as the most important and esteemed activity did not decrease the status of women. Even Coahuiltecan women contributed significantly to the sustenance and survival of their people.[16]

A Coahuiltecan woman would carry her family's burdens on the frequent journeys, and when they stopped she would make a house by bending saplings and placing over them grass mats that she wove. In addition to weaving mats for the house, she wove baskets for gathering foods and for cooking. She carried water, wood, and animals that men had killed, hauling them into camp where she and the other women worked together to prepare and preserve the meat and tan the hides. She then sewed hides into blankets and clothing. Above all, she gathered the vegetation that made up the majority of the food in winter. To do this, she began early in the morning to search up to eight miles around the encampment for the sotol roots that were widely dispersed and hard to find. After digging sufficient roots, she dug a dirt oven and cooked the roots for two days. In addition to the mainstay of roots, she also gathered anything edible in the barren regions of southern Texas, such as pecans, prickly pears, and even insects.[17] Because bands were so small, the structure of government was not very rigid. Although men led the bands and chose whether or not to go to war, women still exercised considerable influence. Through chants, women could incite men to attack enemies. Women could also be the peacemakers, bringing bands into alliances.[18]

Karankawas particularly mourned the death of a young man because it represented a tremendous loss of potential livelihood to a band. Men fished in coastal marshes of the central portion of the Texas Gulf Coast, and they hunted deer, alligators, buffalo, and smaller game. Yet even though Karakawan society was patrilineal and patrilocal, marriage arrangements indicated the high value placed on women's contributions. The bride's parents arranged the marriage, and eventually the woman moved to her husband's band and lived with his family. However, because her family was losing a useful family member, the groom agreed upon a period of indenture; for a time after the marriage, all the game caught by the husband was given to the bride to present to her family. Her family would then return enough of the food to feed the bride and her husband until the agreed-upon time had elapsed. Like the Coahuiltecan women, the value of Karankawa women came from their important ability to supplement the diet by gathering acorns, pecans, prickly pear, blackberries, mustang grapes, and other plants, nuts, and berries. Karankawa women were also responsible for the house, including weaving mats out of rushes or tanning animal hides to throw over willow poles to make houses as well as packing and carrying the materials for the house on the frequent moves. They also hauled the water, carried the wood, prepared the foods, and tanned the hides.[19]

Not as much is known about the Jumano or the Atakapas women. The Jumano women cultivated some crops in good years, but the bands relied primarily on hunting and gathering. Jumano women gathered mesquite to make flour, agave bulbs to cook in dug pits, and prickly pears for their juice and fruit. Like the Coahuiltecans and Karankawas, the Jumanos relied primarily on hunted game such as deer and buffalo and so probably ordered their gender relations similarly. Because men were primarily responsible for warfare, Jumano women often served as intermediaries with other tribes, because women could act as neutrals. Located in South Central Texas and along the Rio Grande, the Jumanos dealt with other tribes frequently.[20]

As described above, most groups of Texas peoples fell into one of two categories: hunter-gatherers, who were patrilineal and patrilocal, and agricultural peoples, who were matrilineal and matrilocal. However, the Apaches did not neatly fit this pattern. Hunting was preeminent among the Plains Apaches of Texas, especially the hunting of buffalo. Chasing the buffalo herds left little ability for crop cultivation except for a little corn planted and left to fend for itself until the band returned to the area later in the year to harvest. Women's primary responsibilities, then, were to help with the hunt (by cutting and carrying the meat and hides back to camp, making the meat into jerky, and tanning the hides) and gather wild vegetation such as walnuts, acorns, piñon nuts, juniper berries, mesquite beans, and narrow-leaf yucca. Women made and carried the housing, hauled the water, carried the wood, and prepared the food. Although this was typical of all the other hunting-gathering societies, the Apaches were matrilineal and matrilocal. Each home—dried skins stretched across poles known as tipis—usually contained one nuclear family (a wife, a husband, and children). However, the tipis were located within clusters of related families traced through the mother's line. When a man married, he moved into the cluster of his wife and joined her family, promising to protect it and provide for it forever.[21]

Men were responsible for warfare and made most of the decisions for the band in a council. However, some Apache women were exempted from household duties and took leadership positions among the women. These women were also allowed to speak at war dances and chiefs' councils. The girl's puberty ceremony was such an esteemed occasion among the Apaches that they would often change war plans to celebrate it. Even though women were highly respected and even given influence and power in some situations, women were subordinate to men in many ways. For instance, a wife had to wait until her husband had eaten, and then she could eat only what he had left.[22]

The different societies in Texas had developed and changed over thousands of years, adapting social, political, and economic traditions to fit changing environments and to take advantage of material opportunities. As they did, gender ideals and roles adapted too. As they had for centuries, the people of Texas would change and adapt when a new environmental factor entered their world—this time the arrival of a new group of people, Europeans.

Arrival of Europeans

In 1528 the first Europeans to set foot in Texas—a small band of Spanish men who were ragged, naked, hungry, and desperate, survivors of the ship-wrecked Narváez expedition—certainly did not seem to have the capacity to affect the role and status of women's lives. In fact, the Spanish survivors, led by Alvár Núñez Cabeza de Vaca, did not mark the beginning of inexorable European conquest and occupation of Texas. Descriptions of Texas recorded by Cabeza de Vaca and other male explorers of the sixteenth and seventeenth centuries did not charm Spain, and early Spanish attempts to build relationships with the Natives of Texas, such as the Caddo, failed.

Native cultures in Texas eclipsed Spanish military and cultural control for nearly two centuries, but even the brief presence of Europeans, both Spanish and French, began transformations in those cultures. The most devastating of the changes were deaths and decreases in population due to disease. The Americas had not suffered the widespread epidemic diseases that Europe, Africa, and Asia had, and therefore its people had developed no immunities. Europeans, who had developed antibodies by previous exposure, might survive smallpox, cholera, influenza, typhus, and childhood diseases such as measles and mumps, but these decimated the peoples of Texas. After Europeans arrived there, Native Americans began dying. Shortly after the Narváez shipwreck, half of the people on Galveston Island died. And it was not necessary for Spaniards to even visit Texas for the diseases to spread. Once in the Americas, diseases were passed from person to person in the course of trade or via infected objects, such as smallpox-infected furs. In the sweeping epidemics that followed, thousands of people died. Between 1492 and 1900, the Native American population in Texas decreased by 90 percent.[23]

In addition to the loss of life caused by the diseases, the epidemics severely weakened some of the tribes' strength militarily and culturally. Fewer warriors could not protect the tribe from enemies as well as before. Shamans might die before passing down valuable religious and medical information. Women's important knowledge of herbs, plants, and roots might be lost, thus decreasing the ability of their people to survive. If a midwife died before training someone to take her place, all the women in the camp or village suffered. And all of these calamities made it difficult to remember and maintain social roles and expectations.[24] For instance, the stress of European interaction and disease probably strained the hereditary choice of male leaders. A woman, Santa Adiva, acted as the principal authority in one of the Caddo villages around 1768. However, disease did not decimate all Texas peoples. Some, such as the Comanches, did not contract European diseases until two centuries after the Narváez shipwreck.[25]

Like the European diseases, Spanish horses arrived in Texas ahead of Spaniards and drastically transformed lives. Horses escaping from numerous Spanish expeditions bred in the wild. These mustangs were perfect for use in hunting buffalo and greatly increased the number of animals that could be killed in one hunt. Yet killing buffalo on horseback was more an individual activity and less a group activity. A man with great skill could accumulate significant wealth in buffalo hides and earn higher respect among his people. Women did not have access to the greater status through the hunt, but men who were proficient in hunting needed more wives to process the additional number of hides, thus increasing polygyny. With horsemanship also came the ability to carry out war more effectively. As a tribe focused more time and energy on the traditional activities of men—warfare and hunting—women's traditional roles became less valued and respected. Even groups such as the Caddos, who did not rely upon hunting buffalo, were altered. Although they did not need horses for subsistence, they needed them to defend themselves after their enemies acquired horses.[26]

The Spanish affected the people of Texas for over a century before establishing residence there. But the effects were accidental, incidental, and not the result of purposeful imposition of Spanish will, authority, and culture. In fact, throughout the entire Spanish colonial period, the Native peoples of Texas would retain physical and cultural dominance over the Europeans.

Early Spanish and French in Texas

During the three centuries that comprised the Spanish colonial period (1500–1800), the Spanish exerted very little power in Texas and had only a small presence there. A century after Cabeza de Vaca passed through Texas, even missionaries did not find Texas very promising. In July 1629 a group of Texas Jumanos traveled to the well-established Spanish mission at Albuquerque, New Mexico, and asked for missionaries to be sent to live among them in Texas. Upon interrogation by the dumbfounded priests, the Jumanos told a tale about a "Lady in Blue" who miraculously appeared to them periodically as if out of thin air. According to their descriptions, the Lady in Blue was a European woman who taught the Jumanos about Christianity and told them to go to New Mexico to seek instructors in the faith. Through correspondence and visits to Spain, several church officials decided that the mysterious Lady in Blue must be Maria de Ágreda of the Order of Discalced Carmelites in Spain. While Maria had never actually left Spain, she had for years lapsed into trances during which she described herself as teaching people in a distant land. Her clothing and face matched that described by the Jumanos, convincing many of the faithful that this Lady in Blue was the first Spanish woman to walk among the people of Texas, even though she herself later repudiated this. As inspired as Spanish clerics and administrators may have been by their belief that a miracle had occurred in Texas, they still did not set up a mission among the Jumanos.[27]

Instead, the Spanish continued concentrating on northern Mexico and what would become New Mexico, especially the missions and settlements among the Tlascalans and Pueblos. When the Pueblos of New Mexico revolted and drove out the Spanish in 1680, many settlers escaped to a location across the Rio Grande River from current-day El Paso. The two thousand refugees from Santa Fe, over half of whom were women, expected Spanish military forces to quickly subdue the Pueblos. When this proved to be impossible, the refugee settlement at Ysleta became the home of some of the first women in Spanish-occupied Texas (although most or all of the women were Hispanicized Indian women, not Spanish women). During the sixteen years it took to reconquer the Pueblos, the women in these Spanish settlements helped to sustain the will of their families to resettle, and they worked at growing and providing food. When finally faced with the opportunity to move back to New Mexico, many women enthusiastically supported the endeavor despite the horrors of the revolt and fears of returning. Of the fourteen families comprising the El Paso refugees agreeing to return, four were headed by women. Two of these couched their decisions to return in political terms, stating that they "would go wherever his majesty would order" in order to increase the kingdom of Spain.[28]

About the same time as women refugees from the Pueblo revolt set up camp in western Texas, French women took part in attempts to settle in eastern Texas. René-Robert Cavelier, Sieur de La Salle, had explored the lands drained by the Mississippi and claimed them on behalf of France. In 1685, leading an expedition of three hundred, including women and children, to settle those lands, La Salle overshot the mouth of the Mississippi and landed on the coast of Texas at Matagorda Bay instead. Plagued by internal difficulties (including the murder of La Salle by his own men), the small group of settlers antagonized the local Karankawas, who attacked and killed all but a few children in late 1688. More is known about the deaths of the women at this brief French settlement than about their lives, but the aborted settlement was enough to convince Spain to attempt building a settlement among Native Americans in Texas.[29]

Spanish in Indian Texas

By the time Spain turned to settling Texas, the Spanish had centuries of experience conquering and settling frontier regions. During the four hundred years of the Reconquista—driving the Moors out of the Iberian Peninsula in Europe—Spain had developed a method of conquering and holding places and peoples. This well-practiced process assisted the Spanish in dominating some areas of the Americas. While military force might conquer a people and a region, controlling those territories required imprinting the area with Spanish culture, including loyalty to the monarch and the pope. With the use of the military to subdue an area initially, priests and lay missionaries were crucial to converting the people to Catholicism. Equally important was the establishment of civilian settlements already indoctrinated in Spanish culture. These three elements—military, religious, and civilian—worked together to assimilate the conquered persons into Spanish culture, thus insuring obedience to Spain and easing administration and control.[30]

The time-tested method of conquest, however, would not work in Texas for many reasons. The abortive French colony presented the threat of possible French incursions in Spanish territory, causing the Spanish to leapfrog over the Native American population in southern Texas and instead send soldiers and missionaries to the numerous and better-organized Caddos of eastern Texas, where the French had made contact and begun trade. Normally the Spanish advanced geographically so as to remain close enough to settled cultural areas to support the new outposts. The missions among the Caddos proved to be far beyond the support mechanisms in Mexico.[31]

The Spanish also suffered a serious disadvantage in establishing trusting relations with the Caddos because of the lack of Spanish women. Missionaries and soldiers sent to protect them were all male, an arrangement that severely handicapped the Spanish in the eyes of the Caddos, who saw this as bizarre. Male and female roles differed among the Caddos but they complemented each other, and the Spanish who tried to settle with and near the Caddos were seen as incomplete. Men without wives or other female kin had no status in a society organized along matrilineal clans. It was women's control over food production that made it possible for Caddo men to gain honor and show hospitality through the diplomacy of giving and receiving gifts. The Caddos could not conceive how the Spanish might continue to engage in such exchanges with no wives to provide for the men.[32]

When it became clear that Spanish men intended to stay permanently, the Caddos became disturbed by their presence. Spaniards without wives could not establish families and kinship connections that would make them trustworthy and contribute to the economic well-being of the community. The Caddo women could not interact socially and economically with the Spanish in traditional ways because there were no women with whom to interact. Unfortunately, interactions between Caddo women and Spanish men often turned into sexual assaults upon the women, which further soured relationships between the groups.[33]

The Spanish abandoned their first attempt at establishing missions among the Caddos, and a second attempt fared no better due to smallpox as well and the lack of Spanish wives. The Caddos evicted the Spanish in 1693 and, as the French threat had decreased, Spanish support for Texas missions dissipated.[34]

After another unsuccessful encroachment by the French, the Spanish turned their eyes again toward establishing permanency in eastern Texas. Because the Spanish had learned what was necessary to be successful in settling among the Caddos, the Spanish viceroy ordered that only men with wives be sent. Despite the order, it was difficult to convince families from Mexico to settle in so distant a land. The Spanish party that arrived in 1716 contained priests to establish a mission and soldiers to build a presidio to protect the mission, guard against hostile Indians, and intimidate the French. Only six of the soldiers, however, were married and brought their families. Another one hundred soldiers settled in 1722, only thirty-one of whom had families. With so few wives, the Spanish never integrated with the Caddos or influenced them, much less took control of the area. By the 1730s, the French threat was not as significant, the attempts at settlements had proven unsuccessful, and relationships with Native Americans in central and southern Texas seemed more promising. The Spanish abandoned their missions in eastern Texas and instead began concentrating in the area around San Antonio.[35]

A mission at San Antonio had been founded in 1718 as a midway point between the settlements in northern Mexico and the eastern Caddos. The wives of soldiers had preferred this mission to the isolation of the Caddo missions. In addition to having more women to share their burdens, it was closer to Mexico and its support systems, and the Indian peoples of southern and central Texas were seemingly more amenable to making alliances with the Spaniards. The spread of European diseases had exercised a much more devastating effect among the many different Native American peoples of central and southern Texas, leading to severe population declines. The encroachment upon their traditional hunting and gathering lands by aggressive Apaches had also led to internal social and political rearrangements. To cope with the changes, traditionally independent-minded and diverse hunting and gathering bands that spoke several languages formed confederations and came to be known as Coahuiltecans.[36] Because of the demographic pressures, Coahuiltecans were more willing to consider joining the Spanish missions. From the Native American point of view, the missions and presidios were logical places for the beleaguered Coahuiltecans and small population of Spaniards to come together for defense and food production. From the Spanish point of view, however, the missions and presidios or settlements built around each mission to support it were places where the heathen Indians could be "civilized" by becoming Christian in religion and Hispanicized in culture.[37]

The plans to imprint Spanish culture in central Texas and among the Coahuiltecans depended on women. In Mexico, the Spanish had successfully converted Indians through the process of intermarriage, and most of the families recruited to Texas came from other communities in New Spain, with the majority of immigrants coming from regions in northern Mexico, such as Coahuila. These immigrants brought with them Spanish culture already adapted to frontier conditions. And most of these families were mestizos—the descendants of Spanish and Indians, primarily Tlascalans. Intermarriage had been common and encouraged in colonial Spain, in large part because the number of men far exceeded the number of women immigrating to America from Spain. Intermarriage had the additional advantage of fostering assimilation. When a Spanish man married a woman among the conquered peoples, not only was she intimately introduced to Spanish culture and then and indoctrinated in it, but also their children were brought up in the Spanish culture, including religion and law. Within two generations, the cultural takeover was virtually complete. Yet even though intermarriage was encouraged, in Mexico the products of the unions were seen as lower in status than the "pure-blood" Spanish. A distinct social caste system developed in which *espanole* ("pure" Spanish) topped the list, and further distinctions were made down the line: *mestizo* (the children of Spanish and Indians), *mulato* (Spanish-African mix), *coyote* (Indian-mestizo), Indians, *lobo* (Indian-African), and *negro* (African or African American).[38]

Settlers in Spanish Texas were encouraged to intermarry with the Native Americans in order to speed up assimilation. However, the caste system that formed a crucial understanding of society faced severe challenges in Texas, primarily because the number of Spanish was too small to form an elite class that married only among themselves. Instead, mestizos could and did claim *espanole* status on the basis of wealth and community status instead of the basis of "pure" Spanish blood. Although not all mestizos were considered elite, that enough of them passed as *espanole* made the social system in Texas much more fluid than in other parts of colonial Spain. As a result, *espanoles,* and anyone claiming that status even if they were mestizos, rarely married Indians, preferring instead to marry among themselves, keeping their ability to claim elite status. Therefore, fewer Indians in Texas than in Mexico engaged in intermarriage with Spanish or even those of Spanish descent, although intermarriage in Texas did increase by the end of the eighteenth century. Mission Indians intermarried with people from different groups but usually among others classified as "Indian."[39]

Although formal marriages brought little mixing of Europeans and Indians in Texas, informal alliances arose between Indian women and Spanish or mestizo men. The practice of *barraganía,* or concubinage, was most common in frontier regions with a greater number of men than women, especially near military installations such as presidios. Men with claims to higher status due to Spanish blood who would not ordinarily marry Indian women could cohabit with them for long periods. The children of such a union usually took the father's name and became Hispanicized, including being baptized in the church as the father's "natural children."[40]

Through intermarriage, cohabitation, and the activities of the missions, local Indians might be adopted into the Spanish culture. For the priests, ideas about gender were central to successful adoption of European culture. Mission priests worked actively to ensure that these mixed families, as well as the Indian families within reach of the mission, adopted Spanish gender roles and the ideals of the patriarchal family. Women, therefore, were supposed to remain secluded within the home (where men could control their sexuality and reproduction). Women in missions prepared food and made clothing for their families, but they were excluded from their traditional roles—procuring food and materials for clothing—that had given them status. Missionaries attempted to redefine work in agricultural fields as exclusively a male role.[41]

Despite their attempts, however, Native traditions persisted. A shortage of male labor at the missions required the women to continue agricultural work (although alongside their men). Men continued to hunt; women continued to make clothing from the skins of hunted animals.[42] Even within mixed households, Indian culture continued to shape everyday life. Indian women passed down their knowledge of food preparation best suited to the Texas environment. For instance, all social classes used grinding stones to prepare corn for tortillas, just as the Natives had before European arrival. Basket weaving, mat making, and cloth preparation were accomplished according to Indian techniques and style. Indian pottery served as tableware for the majority of Texas settlers who could not afford to buy imported Spanish goods. The Spanish resisted the infiltration of Indian culture in highly visible male institutions such as religion, building construction, and even warfare. Daily female activities, however, were much more affected by the Native ideas and culture.[43]

Other practices within the mission complexes signified a continuance of traditional Native roles for women, many of which frustrated and horrified the male priests. Nuclear family units were not the patriarchal households upon which priests insisted but instead continued to serve as subunits of extended kin networks, many of which were matrilineal and in which women exercised power. In these extended networks, age rather than gender signified authority, and equality in courtship practices and divorce also undermined Spanish ideals of husbands ruling over submissive wives.[44]

While the missions in central and southern Texas endured in the eighteenth century, they had limited success at imprinting Spanish culture on the Indians and at convincing Spaniards and Hispanicized Indians to move to Texas. They had even less success in enticing Apaches, Wichitas, or Comanches to the existing missions or settling new missions among those powerful groups. The Spaniards throughout the rest of the eighteenth century engaged in continual warfare with these groups, and Indian females were often taken as captives. Many of these women and girls were made into slaves and servants in the missions and presidios. Other captives were traded and returned to tribes, and these women who could speak both languages acted as mediators. Because both Spaniards and Indians considered women to be symbols of peace, they played important roles in peace and negotiations.[45]

Spanish Texas

By the end of the eighteenth century, the Spanish were still culturally inconsequential and numerically inferior to the Native Americans in Texas. In the southern and central portions of Texas where missions and presidios had endured, however, there emerged a mixed culture much more heavily influenced by the Spanish culture than elsewhere in Texas. In these areas, women, most often descended from Indians from Mexico or Texas, continued traditional practices within the household, passing knowledge and expectations down from mother to daughter. The Spanish were more insistent on upholding ideas about traditionally male cultural activities, which were deemed more important due to the higher status that males held in Spanish society. Spanish society was patriarchal; it was assumed that men, by rights, should rule at all levels of society, especially as the head of the family. Women answered to their fathers until they married and then promised to obey their husbands. Fathers and husbands had tremendous control over the decisions and property of women in their families. A woman's greatest virtue was her chastity, and such was the double standard of society that a man could gain honor for himself and family through noble and heroic actions, but women's actions could never gain honor, only lose it.[46]

Colonial institutions, frontier conditions, Indian heritage, and even Spanish law, however, combined to give women greater power in colonial Texas than in most traditional patriarchal societies. The nature of colonial administration led to decentralization. The monarch might give orders to be carried out in the American colonies, but administrators had to modify those orders to comply as much as possible but also to make allowances for frontier conditions. This left a great deal of the governance up to local communities, especially those as far from the central colonial government as Texas. Thus the line of power did not descend directly down to the father of the family. Instead, the decentralization of the power in the family mirrored that of the colonial administration, as civil, military, and religious institutions all laid claims on individuals' obedience, including the obedience of women. For instance, the church often supported individuals' decisions, such as those involving choice of marriage partner, even if they conflicted with fathers' wishes.[47]

Spanish law also gave women far greater rights than women in many other patriarchal societies. Unlike English law and the Anglo-American law that later followed it, when women married under Spanish law they maintained ownership of their separate property brought into the marriage, including not only paraphernalia and other movable property but also real property such as land. During the marriage, husbands almost always controlled the property and made decisions about how it was used, but a husband could not sell, mortgage, or otherwise commit to the sale of the property without his wife's express permission. In addition to separate property, Spanish law considered marriages to be *ganancial* in nature—in other words, both individuals in a marriage expected to benefit from a partnership, and all property gained during the marriage belonged to husband and wife equally. Formed during the Reconquista, when Spain wanted to entice civilians, especially respectable women, to the frontier regions of Spain recently reclaimed from the Moors, this concept of community property recognized the important contributions of women to the economic benefit of the entire family. Although husbands usually controlled both community property and the property of a wife, a married woman still could renounce all laws favorable to women and take up the rights afforded to men to sue and be sued, make contracts, make wills, and even buy and sell property. Technically her husband was to sign all sales, but when challenged, if a court found that a sale was in the favor of the woman who signed the contract, it was upheld even if it did not have her husband's permission. A wife who disagreed with her husband's management could take him to court for wasting or fraudulently disposing of her (or their) property. Thus, the courts, like the church, sometimes intervened in matters of the family, diluting the power of the patriarch.[48]

Frontier conditions also gave women more power than they could have wielded in Spain or most of Europe. Many women accompanied soldiers to the new presidial settlements, where soldiers were often called away from home to perform their duties of defense and warfare. This left women in charge of the home. Frontier defense also often took the lives of soldiers, leaving widows to head families on their own. While few women welcomed the opportunity to exercise more power at the expense of their husbands' lives, it was the opportunity of widowhood that allowed many women in Spanish Texas to become quite independent and powerful. Doña María Robaina

Betancour, a member of one of the sixteen *espanole* families who relocated to San Antonio from the Canary Islands, became one of the first ranching women in Texas. But she was, by far, not alone. In 1770, a widow owned the second largest herd in Béxar. A listing of those legitimately engaged in ranching in the San Antonio area in 1793 showed that out of forty-five persons, ten were widows, a trend that seemed to hold true throughout the colonial period.[49] By 1798, Rosa María Hinojosa de Ballí had acquired about one-third of the lower Rio Grande Valley, 642,755 acres, and became one of the first cattle queens of Texas—all after the death of her husband.[50]

Widows were not the only women crucial in the building of ranching in Texas. Married women contributed significantly to the success of their ranches that, because of Spanish law, belonged to both the husband and the wife equally. Ranch headquarters were most often located in the homes, giving wives input into running the business and at the very least enabling them to see and understand the daily workings of the ranches. Women, of course, also contributed extensive labor to the family that enabled it to succeed economically. They were essentially in charge of keeping the family fed and clothed: cooking, cleaning, washing, sewing, mending, milking, and, of course, having and raising children.[51] On the frontier, food preparation alone was time-consuming and required great skill and energy. And, in the eighteenth-century Spanish settlements of Texas, women were mostly responsible for the agricultural production. This was in part due to the mestizo heritage of most settlers where women had been responsible for agriculture for centuries among the Native peoples. But the lack of economic incentive in farming also played a large role. Markets for agricultural produce in Texas were small, transportation was risky, and, above all, the threat of Indian invasions that would force settlers to leave made cattle that could be moved out of harm's way more desirable than crops that could not be moved. As a result, most economic gains came from ranching, not farming, leaving subsistence farming for family use primarily to women.[52]

In addition to assisting their husbands in joint enterprises, Spanish women, socially and legally, were allowed to enter into occupations. A royal decree in 1800 reiterated the right of Spanish women to work in whatever trade their decorum allowed. Most women who worked for wages were day laborers, as were most men. Women also worked as cooks, launderers, gardeners, cattle herders, dressmakers, tailors, midwives, healers, peddlers, vendors, and prostitutes.[53] Women also routinely gave testimony in colonial courts.[54]

While women were much more empowered in colonial Texas than is usually imagined, equality was not their reality. They still lived in a society that elevated men's functions over those of women. Men still held all political and religious positions of authority and made the laws. Women could not vote or hold public office. A social and legal double standard applied, in which women suffered much more severe punishment for adultery than did men. Adultery was legal grounds for a husband to divorce his wife, but there were no grounds for a woman to divorce her husband. The right to sue her husband for wasting her property could be jeopardized if a wife's honor was called into question. While outside institutions such as the court and the church might step into family matters to protect wives and daughters, they could also impose harsh decisions upon women. For instance, a woman could legally be forced to return to her husband or stay with him, even in abusive situations. Seemingly insignificant social customs also reinforced her inequality; tradition held that women served the meals to their husbands and then ate separately.[55]

Mexican Women

After a century of settling Texas, Spain had healthy settlements in San Antonio, Nacogdoches, Goliad, and on ranches along the Rio Grande. By the beginning of the nineteenth century, women had helped establish permanent settlements that eased some of the greatest difficulties of the frontier. Food still came from ranching and farming in the region, but the supply was more stable. Because of the Spanish emphasis on family and community, towns grew, offering opportunities for trade as well as support and protection. Even along the Rio Grande, the ranchero served as a place of community.

Beginning in 1810, an independence movement emerged in New Spain, leading to over a decade of turmoil and warfare and then Mexican independence from Spain in 1821. Although most of the war took place outside Texas, fighting erupted in Laredo and San Antonio. Women sometimes actively participated in the war. Doña Maria Josefa de la Garza patriotically donated ten head of cattle to feed royalist soldiers. On the other hand, royalists confiscated everything Doña Luisa de Luna had, including her house, because her husband fought on the side of those wishing independence.[56] Although women who actively assisted the insurgents by spying, nursing, or soldiering had the most to fear, civilians could be swept up in the violence too. After the Battle of Medina, Spanish soldiers occupied San Antonio, executed rebels, and imprisoned women suspected of being related to revolutionaries.[57]

Many women were left widowed due to the high number of men killed in the uprisings and reprisals. Overall, the population of the region decreased from nearly 4,000 in 1803 to only 2,240 when independence was achieved, with slightly more Mexican women than Mexican men, especially in towns.[58] Much of the progress in building stable, trustworthily supplied settlements was reversed. The Mexicans in Texas found themselves vastly outnumbered by hostile Indians, while much of the infrastructure and population was destroyed. Political independence did not change the lives of most women—or men—in Texas except that they were now Mexican instead of Spanish. After the war, Mexican communities set about rebuilding and gradually increased in population and scope.

Mexicans continued to accept intermarriage, although few intermarried with Indians in Texas. By the nineteenth century, almost no full-blooded Spanish lived in Texas, and the upper caste of society, who referred to themselves as *espanoles*, or full-blooded, were actually descendants of Spaniards who had intermarried with mestizos. As a result, the racial caste system in Mexican Texas operated more as a social class system than an actual racial class system. Intermarriage between mestizos and full-blooded Indians was very rare even before Mexican independence and almost nonexistent afterward. Previous intermingling and coping with frontier conditions, however, meant that Mexicans on the Texas frontier continued to use ideas adopted from the Native Americans when it came to surviving on the land, especially in the areas of diet and preparation of food. From their Spanish heritage, Texans continued to recognize the legal and property rights of women who were crucial in building European-style societies on the frontier.[59]

A woman's work was very hard, with much of her time involved in subsistence activities: clothing the family, raising gardens for food, grinding corn with the traditional Indian tool, the stone metate, and constantly cooking. The growing community helped ease the workload—or at least make the work more enjoyable. Women would gather together to grind corn or to make blankets and clothing. In areas along rivers such as the San Antonio and Goliad, women gathered on washday. An incredibly backbreaking and onerous job was thus turned into a social occasion. In addition to washing their clothes, women took this opportunity to bathe. In the heat of a Texas day, after scrubbing and hauling laundry, a dip in the cool water must have felt good, and the Mexican women had no social compunction against stripping naked for their swimming and frolicking. Even when men were present as bathing participants or observers, women were not ashamed of being naked in the water—to them bathing was a perfectly innocent and wholesome affair.[60]

Another popular form of entertainment met with mixed social reactions. Fandangos were held in halls or on plazas, and women exerted a great deal of control in the dance: when the music began, women chose their dance partners from a line of men. The rhythmic music and sensuous dance movements scandalized Anglo observers and apparently some of the Mexican upper class as well. Although the dance was extremely popular among the lower classes, officials in some places tried to outlaw the fandango, while those in other locations, such as San Antonio, limited the number of dances and raised money for the city by placing taxes on fandangos.[61]

The most marked long-term change in the lives of women, however, would come because of a new immigration policy that allowed Anglos from the United States to move to Texas as long as they became Mexican citizens and converted to Catholicism. Americans had slipped across the border into Texas for hunting, gathering mustangs, filibustering, and even participating in the revolution for years before the government granted empresarios such as Stephen F. Austin permission to settle American families in Texas. The emphasis on families was important to the new Mexican government because families' farming or ranching was the surest way of protecting against encroachment on territory by foreign countries or by hostile Native Americans. The importance of creating families overrode any considerations of racial purity, and Spanish law that had always encouraged intermarriage between Indians and Spanish, also allowed intermarriage between Anglo and Spanish. In fact, land grant laws absolutely encouraged it. Not only did a man receive more land if he was married, he also received one-fourth more if he married a Mexican woman.[62]

Anglo-American culture, on the other hand, discouraged intermarriage. From the initial founding of English colonies in the seventeenth century, Anglos had disdained intermarriage with the Indians. In stark contrast to Spanish colonies that encouraged marriage with and living among the Indians, English colonies passed laws against intermarriage and attempted, above all, to remove the Indians from their presence. This belief in their own cultural superiority also carried over to their relations with other groups, such as Africans and Mexicans.

Many Anglo families who came to Texas kept themselves apart from the Spanish-Mexican population already in Texas, congregating instead in land grant colonies. Anglo women, especially, would have had little contact with Mexican men or chance to intermarry. Anglo men, on the other hand, found incentives to reconsider their prejudices. The Mexican law providing more land for men who married Mexican women proved to be a powerful financial incentive. Also, there were more women than men in Mexican settlements, while among the Anglos the situation was reversed. Anglo men outnumbered Anglo women by some margin until the 1860s, and in frontier counties the margin was sometimes significant. For these reasons, many Anglo men put aside their dislike of intermarriage and married Mexican women. Usually they justified their actions by making a distinction between the elites, with more European ancestry, and the lower classes, with less. By choosing the fairest and purest-appearing daughters, they also reinforced the Anglo ideal of beauty instead of challenging it.[63]

The motivations of the Mexican women who married Anglo men are not well-documented. The cultural acceptance of intermarriage in the Spanish frontier tradition provided no social obstacle to marrying someone from a different ethnic or racial background. Even with the acceptance and prevalence of intermarriage with Indians, the elite tended to emphasize that their blood was purer Spanish, thus setting them apart from the lower castes of more obvious mestizos. Although Anglo, American men could at least claim European bloodstock, more prestigious than Indian even if less prestigious than Spanish. Also, in many areas nearly every elite family was related, thus providing another incentive to look outward. After the Texas revolution, when Anglos took control of the Republic's politics, wealthy Mexican families saw political advantage in marrying their daughters to prominent and powerful Anglo men. The cultural traditions of supporting the good of the extended family would certainly have encouraged young Mexican women to entertain such courtships and marriages. Finally, historians should never rule out the strong incentives of such indefinable emotions as love—some Mexican women fell in love with their Anglo suitors and might have married with or without the family's blessing.[64]

The children of these mixed marriages could straddle the two cultures. After Texas's independence, as the Anglo population and racism against Mexicans grew, the children were more likely to be Americanized. They took their fathers' names, Anglicized their given names, lived increasingly among American families, attended schools that aided in the assimilation process, and eventually married non-Mexicans. Yet the influence of the Mexican mother and her family was still very important in the children's lives. Both Mexican and American families charged women with the religious training of children, and so, in these families, the Hispanic Catholic tradition prevailed. The mother's influence over religious matters in the children's lives was bolstered by the strong reliance on family and friends, especially the practice of godparents.[65]

In both cultures the most stable and secure relationship and the most socially acceptable one was marriage. However, not all women took that option, by choice or circumstance. Some financially strapped unmarried women turned to prostitution, especially in the towns with military garrisons that had an excess of unmarried men or married men separated from their families. Other Mexican women entered into informal relationships with men of higher classes who would not marry social inferiors. This practice of *barragánía* was well established before Anglo men arrived in Texas in large numbers, but the Anglo men were quick to adopt it. Mexican women who were not of the upper class often had mixtures of Indian or African ancestors (or both). Like upper-class Spanish men who had not seen fit to marry mestizos, Anglo men also found it easier to justify only a sexual relationship with these women in the absence of suitable Anglo marriage partners. One notable difference arose, however, between the *barrangía* as practiced by Mexican men and that practiced by Anglos. Church records show the baptisms of "natural" children of Mexican men who accepted the paternity of and responsibility for children born in these unions. However, few children of Anglo men and Mexican women received such recognition. Mexican men usually lived with their partners and children as a family, and the children were given their father's surname, while Anglo men usually maintained separate housing from their mistresses, and their children assumed their mothers' names. Unlike the children of mixed marriages who became Anglicized, the children of these long-term but legally unrecognized unions generally became thoroughly Hispanicized.[66]

Conclusion

For tens of thousands of years, the women of Texas lived in diverse societies, developing and adapting vastly different gender ideals and roles for women than those the Europeans would bring with them. Even for three centuries after Europeans had contacted, explored, and even conquered other parts of the Americas, Native Americans remained physically and culturally dominant in Texas. Women continued to maintain social and economic roles that were different from, but complementary to, the roles of men, rather than adopting Spanish ideals in which women played subservient roles. The European presence, nonetheless, had an impact on women, as changing economies and disease began to alter women's roles within their societies. By the early nineteenth century, Spaniards had made a few permanent settlements in southern and central Texas, where the women of Spanish and Indian descent adopted some of the Spanish ideals regarding women's roles. But the majority of the inhabitants of even these missions and presidios mixed traditional ideas with new European ideals, allowing women continued independence, influence, and power over the culture and formation of Texas. The first Anglos to arrive, predominantly male, then adapted the Spanish and mestizo practices. As a result, even as late as the 1820s, Native American women's work and culture permeated human settlements in Texas.

Chapter 2

The Frontier South in the Early Nineteenth Century

In the early nineteenth century, Texas remained borderlands—regions where groups of people and cultures overlapped. Before Mexican independence, Native Americans and the Spanish negotiated the borderlands through times of war and peace. Women played central parts in those interactions and the changing of gender roles that occurred as a result. While Native peoples and the Spanish were still evolving new communities and ideals in South Texas, new groups of people entered East Texas, creating yet more borderlands.

After Mexican independence, immigrants from the US South flooded into Texas, expanding the cotton-growing region and imposing their culture upon the landscape. Just as most Euro-Americans saw the western portions of the continent, southerners saw the prime farmland of Texas as desolate and unused, despite the presence of Caddos, Karankawas, and others with ancient claims. Instead of viewing the area as borderlands of existing peoples, they insisted that it was the "frontier," or the edge of civilization, and thus it was their right, and even duty, to settle and tame the land, not only sustaining their families but also making profits. As thousands of Anglos expanded into the region, they brought their beliefs about slavery as well as African Americans as slaves. Anglos from the United States, as well as a sizeable number of German immigrants, contributed to the development of a unique but clearly southern frontier culture in East Texas.

Women in this region faced physical and emotional hardships as they tried to adapt their new environments to their ideals about gender, society, and civilization. They were resilient, and their arduous work transformed the area. Southern Anglo women played a critical role in imprinting their culture and ideals on Texas. German women and African American women also preserved ideals and aspects of their cultures despite physical adversity and living among the dominant group of white southerners.

Women of the Borderlands in Mexican Texas

Spain had attempted to settle Texas with families sporadically and with very limited success for nearly three centuries. After Mexico won independence from Spain, Mexico took up the task. Permanent settlements with families were the key to holding the region against the encroachment of the increasingly powerful Comanches as well as other Native Americans who still claimed the land. Additionally, the rapid expansion of Americans westward threatened Mexico's hold on the territory.

Anglo-American men had been slipping into Texas well before Mexican independence from Spain, causing difficulties for the Spanish government, and this was a challenge for the Mexican government too. Men on filibustering adventures had been interested in rounding up wild mustangs, fomenting rebellion with the hopes of detaching Texas from Spain, and participating in the Mexican independence movement. Only a few Anglo-American women, the most famous of whom was Jane Long, accompanied these adventurers. She came from Mississippi with her husband, James Long, to Texas in 1819. In 1821, he left her at Bolivar Peninsula to lead forces attacking the Spanish at La Bahía. During a very harsh winter, the other civilians departed, but, along with her slave woman, Kian, Long remained at the fort, giving birth to a daughter. After learning of the death of her husband, which transpired in the spring of 1822, Long moved to Louisiana, but she later returned to Texas. The Anglocentric society that emerged after Texas independence dubbed her "the Mother of Texas" because she claimed to be the mother of the first Anglo-American child born there. Other Anglo-American children had been born in Texas earlier, not to mention thousands of non-Anglo children, but the name stuck. Long came to be one of the living myths by which Anglo-Americans marked their takeover of Texas.[1]

With Americans pushing their way into Texas and the reluctance of Mexican families to locate there, the Mexican government gambled that American

and other immigrants settling in the territory would discourage filibuster-
ers or other countries from encroaching upon Texas. Settlements of Anglo
families would also assist in pushing back enemy Indian groups such as the
Comanches, making it more attractive for Mexican families to move there.
The Mexican government authorized Stephen F. Austin and other American
empresarios to set up colonies of Americans who would receive land in return
for living on the land, farming, becoming Mexican citizens, and following
the official religion of Catholicism. Single men did come into Austin's and
other empresarios' colonies (and some lived together in order to claim larger
land grants), but the government emphasized recruiting married men who
would bring wives with them. As incentive, married men could each obtain
up to 4,605 acres of land for farming and ranching, while each single man
could patent only 1,476 acres.[2] By 1820, only 8 of the 150 men in Austin's
colony had brought their wives, but Austin claimed that most of the 150
were married and intended to have their wives join them as soon as they
made living arrangements. By 1825, eighteen hundred Anglos lived in Austin's colony, and, though the Mexican census did not enumerate women, the
majority of the men were married.[3] While these families came from all over
the United States, most were immigrants from southern states.

Anglo immigrants were the largest group in the period of Mexican rule of
Texas, but a significant number of Germans also came. Even before Mexican
independence, businessmen in the German-speaking provinces of Europe
(Germany was not yet a country) had opened markets in Spanish Mexico,
leading many Germans to move to Mexico. Only a few of these lived in
Texas until the immigration policies of the independent Republic of Mexico
encouraged the settling of Texas for farming. Under the leadership and
recruitment of Baron de Bastrop and Johann Friedrich Ernst, the German
population in Texas grew. Like the Anglo-Americans moving to Texas, the
Germans valued family, and the Mexican government gave preference to
families as well, thus encouraging and offering opportunities for German
women. Also like the Anglo-Americans, however, many more men than
women ventured to the new territory. As late as 1840, women comprised
only 40 percent of the German immigrants to Texas, but this was a vast increase since the Mexican period.[4]

The number of African Americans also grew, through both reproduction
and immigration. African Americans had been in Texas much longer than
Anglo Americans, maybe as early as 1600. Although most black women had
been brought to Texas by the Spanish as slaves, not all black women in the

Spanish period were or remained slaves. Even those who were slaves knew about courts and had access to them. For instance, in 1791 Maria Simona de Jesus Moraza filed and won a court case seeking her right to a change in owners due to mistreatment. The fluid nature of Spanish slavery, with limited but important rights protected by the courts, allowed many women who came to Texas as slaves during the Spanish period to work their way to freedom. Then, as a condition to recognition of Mexican independence, Mexico declared all slaves free. Thus, by the Mexican period, quite a few black women lived in Texas freely.[5]

The Anglo-Americans quickly filling East Texas had been attracted primarily by inexpensive farmland—land that was indeed suitable for growing a large-profit crop, cotton. Because most of the Americans came from the southern states and were accustomed to slavery, because cotton profits made the purchase of slave labor cost-effective, and because the availability of inexpensive land drew people interested in establishing their own farms, the Americans clamored for, and received, exceptions to the Mexican prohibition of slavery. When the Mexican government later rescinded these concessions, American immigrants used the subterfuge of indentured servitude to continue importing slaves. So, although slavery was never very secure under Mexican rule, thousands of slaves came to Texas. Slaves very rarely were given a choice whether or not to migrate, and so women who might be reluctant—like those in the Anglo and Germanic immigrations—could not refuse. As a result, the ratio of African American males to females was much more even than in those other populations.[6]

By the time Texas won its independence in 1836, people of different races and distinct cultures lived in Texas, speaking several different languages, coexisting precariously in this area of many borderlands. The women in these settings before and after independence often lived in frontier conditions marked by violence, isolation, crude and rudimentary housing, new, difficult, and unrelenting work, and frequent moves. Through their physical hard work and their adaptation to the environment, they would help build the future of Texas, reshaping their new communities to resemble as much as possible the ideals of their old ones.

Violence

The greatest fear women faced in any Anglo frontier of the nineteenth century was violence by Indians on whose lands they were encroaching, and Texas was

Figure 2.1. Cynthia Ann Parker nursing her daughter Topsannah (Prairie Flower). Courtesy of Abilene Photograph Collection, Hardin-Simmons University, Abilene, Texas.

no exception. One impetus for the Mexican government to allow Anglo immigration was that Spanish settlements, so far beyond the reach of armies and so sparsely populated, had been unable to attract settlers to areas vulnerable to Indian attacks. Settlers in Austin's colony clashed with Tonkawas, Wacos, Tawakonis, and the especially feared Karankawas. Although Indians killed few Anglo-Americans in the colony, the fears were real. The Karankawas would look for small groups of whites to kill and plunder. Comanches, however, would prove to be the most fearsome, since they plagued the Anglo colonies even into the 1850s. Comanches raided American farms for horses, goods, and captives, particularly women and children. In 1836 Comanches attacked a fort near Groesbeck, stealing horses, killing most of the inhabitants, and taking five captives. One of those, nine-year-old Cynthia Ann Parker, would spend twenty-four years with the Comanches, eventually marrying a member of the group and giving birth to Quanah Parker, who would become the chief of the Comanche Nation.[7]

While Anglo settlers had good reason to fear Indians, interactions between Anglos and Indians could be friendly and based upon trade, as in the case of Mary Helm, who, after initial horror on her part, befriended some Karankawas in Matagorda. Such interactions might avoid violence, but the threat was there. Henrietta King was baking on the Santa Gertrudis ranch in South Texas when she looked up and found an Indian holding a club to her infant. When he pointed to the bread, she allowed him to take all that he could carry, thus sparing her child. After several encounters with nearby Indians, Mary Rabb, near La Grange, would spin all night when her husband was away—to drown out the sounds of any prowling Indians. The spinning had no effect on the Indians, but it helped keep Rabb from a constant state of fear at every noise she heard outside.[8]

Wild animals, such as alligators and snakes, also posed a significant threat. Bears were plentiful enough in East Texas that men hunted them frequently for meat for the family. Outlaws and bandits also increased the risk of violence to women on any frontier. While Texas was not the home of western gunslingers and shootouts, the sparseness of settlement made law enforcement difficult. Bands of raiders would occasionally roam the countryside, attacking homes and taking belongings. Desperate outlaws might make themselves at home, caring little about the safety and welfare of women.

Women's relative isolation on farms and plantations in East and South Texas heightened their endangerment. Men had to leave to conduct business, gather supplies, hunt, or fight in wars. After Mary Rabb's husband moved his family, he went back to his old tract to grow crops, leaving her alone for weeks at a time. Disease, injuries, and warfare took the lives of many men, leaving women as widows. When her husband died, Laura Ann McNeill shouldered her husband's shot bag and hunting rifle to protect herself and her small children. Other women did not wait until their husbands' deaths to take up the shotgun. Mary Rabb remembered that she "went many times and took my gun and lay in the corner of the fence and helped . . . watch for Indians."[9]

Texas Revolution

For women on the Texas frontier, fear of violence did not arise exclusively from Indians, outlaws, or wildlife. As difficulties between Mexico and its province of Texas escalated into the Texas Revolution, women were caught up in the war. They played a role in encouraging and supporting the Tex-ian Army. Ann Raney Coleman remembered that she and other women in Brazoria molded bullets. Some women served as spies, while others donated clothes and other supplies, made banners and flags, and encouraged their husbands to join the army. Of course, some husbands went to war more will-ingly than others did. After Harriet Ames's husband lost almost everything they owned gambling and spent what little money left to buy provisions to join the army, Ames was very happy to see him go and wrote to him express-ing the hope "that the first bullet that is fired will pierce your heart."[10]

Susanna Dickinson, the only Anglo survivor of the Battle of the Alamo, is one of the most celebrated women in Texas history but she was not the only person to survive the two-week siege by Mexican troops. In addition to Dickinson, Tejanas Juana Navarro Pérez Alsbury, Andrea Castañon de Villanueva, Concepción Charli Gortari Losoya, and Ana Salazar de Espar-za were among the women who endured the constant bombardment, fear, shortage of food, and unbelievable carnage. Although the military defend-ers, both Tejano and American, were killed when Mexican forces took the Alamo, a dozen or more women, children, and slaves were allowed to live, go free, and tell their stories.[11]

As Dilue Rose Harris remembered later about the revolution, "every man and boy that had a gun and horse went to the army, and the women and children were left." When the Alamo fell and Mexican troops turned east, most Anglo women, like Jane Hallowell Hill, feared that the Mexican army "would over-run the whole country, sparing none." Some men left the army temporarily to help the women flee, but mostly women and children loaded as many provisions as they could on sleighs, carts, wagons, and oxen, and joined a mass migration eastward known as the Runaway Scrape.[12]

Women, children, and slaves traveled for miles "through mud and water, as it rained most of the time," Jane Hallowell Hill remembered. Ferryboats were the only way to cross rivers swollen from the rains. Even waiting for an opportunity to board a ferry could prove dangerous. Dilue Harris's party camped for three days before traversing the San Jacinto because "there were fully five thousand people at the ferry . . . every one was trying to cross first, and it was nearly a riot." On the overland portions of the voyage, mud caused wagons to get stuck in the lanes that counted as roads, and carts that tried to go around would also get stuck. Panic, camping in wet conditions, and the dangers of such a hasty move were too much for some women and children who died from disease, drowning, and other accidents. So many women went into early labor that quite a few children were born—and many died—in the Runaway Scrape.[13]

When word reached the travelers that Sam Houston and the Texian Army had defeated the Mexican army at the Battle of San Jacinto, many could not believe it. Some continued eastward to the United States, never to return. Those who did return found that the chaos of the evacuation, the presence of armies, and the opportunism of thieves had destroyed much of what they had painstakingly built in their frontier communities. Having taken little with them, Jane Hill's family was distraught to find that the supplies at home were gone and only most of the books remained. "The Mexican army had camped within five miles of our house and burned the fence rails to make their fires," she later recalled.[14]

Even after the war was over, fears remained since Mexico continued to claim Texas as a province and threatened to reestablish control. In 1842 a Mexican army invaded San Antonio, and women continued to fear the potential violence of war for years to come. Some women, such as Mary Holley and two of her friends, picked up rifles and practiced in case of an attack, and some became expert shots.[15]

Moving

Despite the fear of violence, the opportunity to own land continued to appeal to many before and after the war for independence. Not surprisingly, the beckoning of Texas with its dangers called much more often to men than women. For men, moving west offered opportunity, excitement, and the chance to exert independence. For women, moving west threatened to break family ties and remove them from the help and support of established communities. While many single men were willing to take the risk of leaving everything behind and trying new economic opportunities in Texas, very few single women similarly volunteered. Although these decisions would create a gender disparity in Texas, the vast majority of American immigrants arrived in families, in part because the Republic of Texas copied the Mexican rule of favoring them over single men.

In nineteenth-century American families, the husband was the head of the household legally and socially, and he made the major decisions affecting his wife, children, and any other dependents. Gender roles dictated that men held the responsibility for the financial well-being of the family. Thus, the decision to improve a family's fortune by moving to Texas ultimately lay with the husband. Many women complained bitterly of their husbands' decisions to move westward, and many felt helpless in the face of the decision. Yet not all women traveling to Texas were merely submitting to their spouses' will. Husbands might have the final authority, but most probably at least consulted with their wives. Some women undoubtedly talked their husbands out of the drastic move. At least some just refused to move to Texas even though their husbands did. For instance, in 1840, John Hope won a divorce from his wife because she refused to come with him to Texas.[16]

But many women embraced the move to Texas, recognizing along with their husbands the opportunities for their family. Mary Rabb's reminiscences about her move to Texas recounted her hardships but also her desire to improve her family's standing: "Now my children and grandchildren, I am going to try to tell you something about the way your pa and me had to do to get land for you." Even some single or widowed women claimed land: 176 (or 4 percent) of the headrights that the General Land Office of Texas granted to those who had settled prior to independence went to unmarried women.[17]

Once the decision was made, the journey to Texas was not as long as the overland crossing to places in the Far West such as Oregon, but it was difficult and dangerous nonetheless. Some families arrived in Texas by boat. As complex and time-consuming as some of the arrangements to get them to New Orleans might have been, the trip by boat from New Orleans to Galveston was often the most dangerous leg of the journey. In favorable weather, ships usually made it in a week. However, hurricanes and other storms could wreck or delay ships on the Gulf, leading to hardships for the passengers. Lack of wind could also cause the trip to take longer. Mary Helm suffered from hunger and thirst when the sixty passengers on the ship she took to Texas ran out of food and water: "After our cooked provisions had given out, crackers and hard sea bread sustained life; but when the water gave out, then real suffering commenced."[18]

Most moved to Texas overland. On this trek, the wealthiest and luckiest women rode in carriages with other women and children while wagons carried their belongings. Other women rode in wagons, sitting on top of everything they owned. Many women, however, walked up to fifteen miles each day. Mary Rabb traveled to Texas by horse with a special sidesaddle that carried her and her child plus "a pretty good pack." These trips, of course, were exhausting and even dangerous. Women often helped men perform difficult work such as driving wagons and watching the stock. They also had to help at river crossings and to pull stuck wagons out of mud. The usual female duties of washing, cooking, cleaning, and taking care of children were even more strenuous on the trail. James Holt remembered how his mother walked from Georgia to Alabama and then from Houston to Columbus, Texas, carrying a five- or six-month old baby the entire way.[19]

The move to Texas was hard enough, but Americans who moved westward, whether to Texas or elsewhere, often did not move just once. Families who made the decision to move in search of better opportunities might try two, three, four, or even more locations until they became satisfied that they had found the economic situation that suited them best. Nineteenth-century census records illustrate this pattern well: the children of many Texas families were listed as being born in different states along the path to Texas. But even once settlers reached Texas, their moving days were not necessarily finished. Mary Rabb's family relocated many times once she arrived in Texas. Her husband decided to move them from their first home after Indians stole their horses and he no longer felt safe. Thick mosquitoes and flies, then the lure of better land elsewhere, then utter isolation prompted three more moves.[20]

Living Conditions

It is impossible to know for certain how many women like Mary Rabb followed their husbands from one place to another trying to find the ideal location. At least some men went to Texas ahead of their wives to establish the homestead first.[21] Women who moved at the same time as their husbands or joined them shortly afterward coped with primitive living situations. The first priority of the new settlers was to clear land and plant crops to sustain the family in the coming year, and only after that did they concern themselves with improving their shelters. During these initial months (or sometimes years), women lived in tents or makeshift cabins. After moving to a new location, Mary Rabb put up a quilt and a sheet for a tent for a few weeks, then they built a small shelter, and finally, "before right cold weather," they set up a "camp covered with boards."[22]

Even after moving out of the tents, the first hastily built homes were incredibly small. Mary Rabb's husband built their first Texas home in a week. It was made of logs and had an earthen floor. In one corner was a chimney through which baby pigs would crawl. Rabb shucked corn at night for the little pigs to eat and then swept out the remains in the morning. Mary Helm's

Figure 2.2. Log cabin in Tarrant County, similar to what frontier families in Texas built after establishing themselves. Courtesy of Tarrant County College District Archives, Fort Worth, Texas.

first home was fifty feet square, and "the whole building [was] without joists or tennents, but simply forked sticks drove in the ground to support poles on which cross-poles were laid." Without material to build a new home, her family erected a tent within the house because the "fort let in much water in hard storms."[23]

Some of the largest drawbacks to the crude housing were the insects. Mosquitoes and "sand gnats" were so bad that the Rabb family abandoned their camp to sleep in the sand on the beach of the Brazos River. In her small, makeshift home with no amenities, Helm's two beds each had a mosquito net, "a thing quite indispensable."[24]

Even once the first permanent homes were finally built on the Texas frontier, they were not the substantial houses to which women in the East were accustomed. According to one of the more elite women of the time, even "most of the wealthy planters lived" in nothing more than "a double log cabin with an entry running through the middle. . . . To make money was their chief object, all things else were subsidiary to it."[25]

Work

Rudimentary housing was one of the many reasons that women's work was even more difficult on the frontier. Sweeping out the remains of corn in the morning was only one part of keeping earthen floors clean. Rarely were families able to bring with them the kitchenware that would have made life easier for women who cooked for large households. The absence of stoves required that women learn to prepare meals over open fires with a minimum of utensils. Noah Smithwick wrote of visiting a family on the San Bernard River near Columbia, who "showed in their every manner the effects of gentle training," although, when the wife served supper, the family and guests "sat on stools around a clapboard table, upon which were arranged wooden platters. Beside each platter lay a fork made of a joint of cane. The knives were of various patterns, ranging from butcher knives to pocketknives. And for cups, we had little wild cymlings [a type of squash], scraped and scoured until they looked as white and clean as earthenware."[26]

By its very definition, the frontier meant that women lived in remote places unconnected by roads to towns where items could be purchased. The difficulty of getting store-bought items led to the kinds of inventive solutions that Smithwick observed. Southern women had always played a valuable role in the economic production of the household, but on the frontier their resourcefulness was ever more important as they continued to raise gardens, preserve meat and vegetables, make soap and candles, and prepare meals. Men were primarily responsible for the corn crop, which women then would grind with hand-mills to make into porridge or cornbread. Nearly all other vegetables were the products of women's gardens. In fact, women produced nearly everything the family ate, including butter, cheese, bread, chicken, and eggs. Because beef and pork were scarce and expensive, men hunted deer, and women learned new techniques to dry venison.[27]

The lack of stores also required women to produce all the clothing from raw materials, meaning that many frontier Texas women engaged in home spinning and weaving to a much greater extent than their southern sisters to the east. Mary Rabb moved her spinning wheel to each of the many frontier locations she and her family inhabited. She spun under trees; she spun under the quilt and sheet they had erected for a tent; she spun to drown out the noise of Indians stirring around the house at night when she was alone. In a makeshift camp where mosquitoes were so thick they could only travel at night, she "spun enough thread to make forty-six yards of mosquito barring," and on a handmade loom she "wove it out in the open air and sun without any covering." When she and her family left that location for a better one, she lamented leaving the "house and loom and garden potatoes."[28]

While Mary Rabb and other frontier women prioritized their spinning wheels and looms, most frontier women could not spin enough thread and weave enough cloth to keep their families clothed. With no way to buy fabric, these women often were forced to find shortcuts that would have been socially unacceptable in their former homes. Seaborn Stapleton remembered that he was seven or eight years old before he got his first pair of pants. Women would sometimes make clothing out of animal skins. The genteel frontier family that Noah Smithwick visited and admired all "were dressed in buckskin." Many Texas women made clothing out of skins but only for male family members. There was a point beyond which women would not bend their social expectations.[29]

Women, of course, also continued the work of reproduction, giving birth frequently, while caring for large and growing families. Pregnant women who lived far away from the support of other women especially feared childbirth and childrearing, especially with the shortage of midwives and doctors. Infant mortality was generally high in the nineteenth century, and maternal mortality was common. Whenever possible, women would travel to more populated areas shortly before birth to be with other women when the event occurred. Large and growing families held the promise of assistance with work and chores as the children aged, but most frontier families were young, creating more work for an already overworked mother.[30]

As difficult as it was for women to carry on their usual responsibilities in frontier conditions, wives were often called upon to do much more. In young families, a wife was often one of only two adults and so had to assist with traditionally male duties that were too numerous for one man alone. Land had to be cleared and crops planted and eventually harvested. Although men were expected to build the homes, there was so much work to do to ensure good crops and a future food supply that women had to help.[31]

Southern women who were lucky enough to have slaves fared better and probably did not have to work as hard, but even these white women were far from exempt from the difficulties of the frontier. Most slave labor on the frontier, whether male or female, was directed toward clearing land and planting and harvesting crops. Women were very unlikely to have assistance in the household production, and with slaves they also had more food to prepare and more clothing to procure.

Black Women on the Texas Frontier

A small number of black women had lived in Texas under Spanish rule, during which time they took advantage of opportunities to purchase or earn their freedom. In that same period, Texas had also attracted some free and runaway slaves from the American South. When Mexico won its independence from Spain in 1821, slavery was abolished by decree, setting free the small handful of black women in Texas still held as slaves. At the same time, however, Mexico began allowing immigrants from the United States to form colonies in Texas. East Texas contained prime land suitable for cotton, and many immigrants wished to start farms and plantations growing cotton as they had in the southern United States. Thus, as noted above, they pleaded for—and received—exceptions to the laws prohibiting slavery, and very quickly the majority of black women living in Texas were held as slaves and would continue to be so until after the American Civil War.[32]

Granted the right to keep slaves, the empresarios of the Anglo settlements enacted slave codes similar to those of the states of the US South. However, the uncertainty over Mexico's commitment to continue allowing slavery made many settlers fearful of bringing many slaves, and changes in government policy convinced some to take slaves back to the United States. As a result, the population of slaves did not grow as quickly as the availability of inexpensive cotton lands might have allowed, and very few settlers brought more than twenty slaves, with most slaveholders claiming only a few. After the Texas Revolution, the new government enacted laws allowing slavery in Texas, and the slave population increased significantly, but the majority of slaves in the frontier areas continued to live on small farms with few slaves.[33]

As was the case for white women, the move to Texas caused many difficulties and hardships for black women. Women were torn from homes, communities, and families. Unlike white women who could exert some influence in the decision, slave women had no control over whether or not they moved. And, as was not the case for white women, the move to Texas signified the probability that they would never see or hear from loved ones left behind. Although white women kept connections alive through writing letters and even visiting, slave women were not taught to read or write. Millie Forward of Jasper came to Texas with her mother, who was separated from her husband by the move: "Dey lef' pappy in Alabama, 'cause he 'long to 'nother massa." Likewise, Rosanna Frazier of Tyler County described the separation of her family from her father as if a death had occurred: "My daddy name Jerry

Durden and after I's born they brings us all to Texas, but my daddy belong to de Neylands, so we loses him."[34] Slave women who relocated with their masters to Texas had a higher chance of maintaining relationships with family members; some southern slaveholders brought all of their slaves to Texas. Even these slaves, however, probably left behind family and friends who were claimed by other slaveholders. The slaves who were sold from other southern states and bought for farmers in Texas, however, were unlikely to have been able to relocate with any other family or friends. And this type of trade was brisk, with slave markets in Galveston, Houston, and elsewhere.[35]

Whether they were brought with families or bought in slave markets, slave women came in numbers equal to the number of slave men. By 1850, five years after Texas statehood, 50.6 percent of the slaves were female, similar to other southern states. While some would reason that male slaves would be more useful in a frontier society—for clearing and planting land and building houses—slaveholders themselves had multiple reasons for bringing as many women as men. Black women were thought suitable for hard labor, and although it was generally accepted that slave women would not produce as much as slave men, they could still be assigned to the same tasks in the fields such as hoeing, chopping, weeding, picking, and even clearing land. On the other hand, almost no male slaves would have had the domestic skills of women. Besides fieldwork, slave women could also spin, weave, sew clothing, and produce and prepare food. With a shortage of white women in Texas (as late as 1850, only 45 percent of the white population was female), these domestic skills were in short supply and as valuable as slave women's field labor.[36]

Larger slaveholders were also very purposeful in trying to bring equal numbers of slave women and men so that the slaves could have families, thus increasing the wealth in slave property through children. Charles Tait wrote to his brother who was relocating to be near him in Texas and asked him to bring a slave woman who would be a suitable mate for one of Tait's male slaves. Small slaveholders also had incentives to bring more women. An initial investment in slaves was significant, and a new settler desiring to purchase a slave (or two) for the first time could better afford a slave woman, whose purchase price would be significantly less than a slave man. Samples of census returns indicate that those who claimed fewer than five slaves were much more likely to hold only women than they were to hold only men.[37]

Perhaps the shortage of white women caused white slaveholders to prefer to bring or purchase slave women for another reason—or perhaps the presence of slave women coupled with the shortage of white women merely encouraged the higher incidence of interracial relationships on the frontier of Texas. Although the legislature passed some of the harshest laws punishing these relationships, the fluidity of frontier society allowed greater possibilities for these intimate relationships to form. No laws recognized the rape of a slave, so slave women had no legal recourse to prevent sexual intercourse with their masters. And undoubtedly at least some of the even long-term relationships were not by the women's choice. Abolitionist Benjamin Lundy wrote about two brothers named Alley who were "industrious immigrants from the State of Missouri. They have never married. They purchased, however, a handsome black girl, who has several fine-looking partly coloured children—specimens of the custom of some countries." Years later, after emancipation, the children of William Alley sued in court to be recognized as rightful heirs to his estate, prompting testimony to the effect that Alley never tried to free the mother and never acknowledged the children as his.[38]

On the other hand, at least some of the interracial couplings were based upon affection, taking advantage of the frontier conditions to live together and raise families. A slave woman named Puss began a relationship with a neighboring white man that led to her pregnancy. John Webber bought Puss from her master, and they set up a home in an unsettled location that became known as Webber's Prairie. John's friend Noah Smithwick noted that the Webbers "were constrained to keep to themselves" because they could mingle neither with whites nor blacks. However, due to the kindness and generosity of Puss Webber, they "merited and enjoyed the good will, and, to a certain extent the respect, of the early settlers." Other interracial couples moved specifically because frontier Texas offered more opportunities to live as families than did the southern states to the east. After moving to Nacogdoches from Georgia, David Town freed his slaves, who were actually his wife and children. Other early settlers such as William McFarland, William Primm, and Monroe Edwards were all recorded as living with black women.[39]

Most slave women who formed families on the frontier, however, did so with other slave men. White masters encouraged the formation of families by granting permission to their slaves to "marry abroad," by marrying someone claimed by a different master on another farm. Some masters went beyond encouraging and supporting slave marriages to choosing mates for slaves themselves. Whether by choice or coercion, southern slaveholders expected a 5 to 6 percent increase in wealth as a result of natural increase among their slaves. Texas law did not allow slaves to marry, and so such partnerships were always precarious. Even when masters recognized slave marriages and wished to keep families together, the financial difficulties of making a living on the frontier might force the sale of slaves. High death rates also spelled separation to many slaves when their masters died and courts equally distributed the slaves to heirs who might not live in the same location or even the same state. Because most slaves lived on small farms, they were most likely to marry a slave from another farm, and, with the frequent moves during the frontier era, when a slaveholding white family relocated to a better location, slave husband and wife might thus be separated.[40]

Despite the obstacles, slave women continued to seek and form families, from which they drew great strength and comfort. Although their marriages were not recognized by Texas law, slaves in the community recognized the marriages and the families. As in the southern United States, the ideal family among slaves was the nuclear family. Even if the husband was not always able to live with the wife because they were held by different masters, the husband was expected to perform his spousal and parental duties on visits. Neither fathers nor mothers had complete control over their children, since the master could interfere and arbitrate family matters at any time. Most slave parents, however, exercised a significant influence on raising their own children.[41]

German Women on the Frontier

German women began arriving as part of the earliest immigration of Europeans to Texas in the Spanish and Mexican periods, and they continued to arrive after the Texas Revolution. German women faced much longer journeys than American women, journeys that could be much more dangerous. Rosa Kleberg's ship from New Orleans to Texas shipwrecked off the coast of Galveston in 1834, and passengers made rough huts out of salvaged timber to await rescue. The difficulty and expense of the journey also meant that the opportunities to return home for good or for a visit were remote. Even more than with American women, German women's decisions to immigrate were made predominantly by their husbands or fathers.[42]

Very few women came to Texas alone, whereas many German men chose to immigrate without their families. Some men were married and intended to send for their wives later, but others were single and confronted a population where men greatly outnumbered women. Between 1836 and 1840, only about one-third of the German immigrants were female. After the 1840s,

the ratio improved a bit and women made up 40 percent of the newly arrived immigrants. The uneven gender ratio, however, made women valuable
in these frontier conditions, and even into the 1850s single German women
might receive marriage offers as soon as they disembarked in Galveston.[43]

Many of the same frontier conditions that plagued Anglo and African
American women—crude housing, lack of supplies, and hostile inhabitants
—created hardships for German women. As Louise Ernst Stohr, one of the
German women in Stephen F. Austin's colony, wrote, "There we sat, at the edge
of civilization; just to the west lived the Indians. And so we lived all alone in the
wilderness; it even seemed lonely for the Indians. They would bring back horses
and cows that strayed away, in exchange for milk and butter." Mathilde Herff,
who immigrated several years after her husband, chastised him for not telling
her the truth about the hardships and privations of Texas.[44]

Additional obstacles for them were the language and culture, since they
were a minority among Anglos. For the earliest German immigrants, assimilation was more likely because they lived close to American settlers and had
to adapt to American politics, customs, and even agricultural practices. Early
German settlers lived in Texas for many years before building churches and
schools. As a result, the home became the primary sanctuary of a continuing
German culture, and women were a crucial component of that. They continued to educate their children in German and to participate in religious
instruction.[45]

German women of the upper class especially worked hard to bring culture
to the frontier. Even though living in camps without proper housing, Valeska
von Roeder insisted on having her piano shipped to Texas. The frontier, however, claimed von Roeder's life before the piano arrived. Her sister inherited
the piano and used it to play German music in Harrisburg as early as 1835.
It would be a decade before another piano arrived in the German settlement
at Cat Spring. Even without pianos, women continued to carry on and pass
down the musical heritage of their homeland by giving voice lessons and
singing with the accompaniment of guitars.[46]

The German family was traditionally patriarchal, and the husband made
decisions for the entire family, but German women who adapted to the frontier were extraordinarily strong. They were just as interested and involved in
promoting the economic well-being of the household as their husbands. The
Texas frontier could embolden women to oppose their husbands if they felt
it necessary to protect the family, although this was probably rare. Margaret
Zimmerschitte took the extraordinary step of filing for divorce from her hus-

band in order to wrest control of the family finances from him because, she wrote, "[He] has been and still is waisting [*sic*] away in intoxication and dissipation all the property that he can possibly so dispose of and that to no advantage to himself or family." When her husband agreed to put the property in the hands of relatives, she dropped the suit. Her actions were rash and not without consequences. As she wrote to her daughter, "I know well if murderers had shot me, my family would shed few tears." However, the financial well-being of her family was more important: "If I had let my husband do as he wanted, I would have had no quarrels and would have had none with you either. Then you would not have had a foot of land nor would I either."[47]

Women and the Law

As Anglo southerners had gradually moved west, lawmakers in the frontier states had passed more and more liberal laws, especially regarding women, than the southern seaboard states. Some have theorized that men wanted to reward the women who braved the dangers of the frontier with easier divorces and even property rights. Mississippi, in fact, was the first state of the Union to pass a married woman's property act in 1839. Combined with this tendency for more liberal laws in the frontier states, Texas also inherited certain crucial concepts about property from Spanish and Mexican law under which it had operated before independence in 1836. Upon winning the revolution, Texas lawmakers at first attempted to establish English common law before realizing how ingrained certain property rights already were within the region. They then made a few exceptions to English common law, including provisions to continue Spanish law homestead protections, married women's property rights, and community property rights.[48]

Sometime before 1837, Joannah Dunlavy and her husband John relocated to Texas with their children. A free headright granting a league and labor of land (over 4000 acres) would have supported the Dunlavys and their children well, and, according to the Spanish law of community property, the wife would have had the rights to one-half of the property. Within a mere few months of moving, and before John Dunlavy could claim the land, John died, leaving Joannah alone on the frontier with nine children to feed. Although some women in Joannah's situation patented and obtained land themselves as heads of household, Joannah chose instead to remarry. Remarriage was the most common route for widows on the frontier. Since

men outnumbered women, widows had good odds of finding new husbands. With the difficult work of making a living for themselves, much less
for nine children, remarriage added an adult male to the household to help
build a farm and maintain sustenance for the family. Texas law also allowed
women to keep any property that they brought to their marriages in their
own names, so Joannah would have forfeited no property rights by remarry-
ing. Unfortunately for Joannah, her new husband Joe McCrabb lived only
a month after their marriage, just long enough to get her pregnant with her
tenth child.[49]

Not surprisingly, Joannah again remarried quickly. This time she brought
with her movable property inherited from two husbands as well as any she
had accumulated. The need for a quick remarriage, however, caused Joannah
to choose unwisely, as no doubt many women on the Texas frontier did. According to her divorce petition three years later, within three months of the
marriage William Dunlap tried to force her to give him all of her money and
other articles of value. Under Texas law, Joannah was not required to give her
husband any of her property, and she refused to do so despite the fact that he
became cruel and violent. After failing to take her valuables, William Dunlap
confessed to Joannah that he was already married to two other women, and
he then deserted her.[50]

In 1840 Texas would pass one of the most liberal divorce laws in the
southern United States, but when Dunlap deserted Joannah in 1837, Texas
had not yet made provisions for divorce. Without proof that her husband
was married polygamously, Joannah could not remarry, and she had to set
about finding a way to provide for her ten children. Texas laws regarding
property had been patterned on both English and Spanish law, and thus they
carried within them both traditions. Spanish law gave married women significant property rights yet restricted their rights to actually control the property
by leasing, selling, or otherwise improving it unless they renounced all laws
favorable to women. English common law had little recognition of a wife's
separate property, and recent legislation in Mississippi had given married
women the right to have property in their names but for this property to be
controlled by their husbands. In other words, it was unclear whether or not
Joannah had the rights to sell, trade, or lease her own property as long as she
was married. And as long as she was married, technically any contract she
entered into had to be approved by her husband.[51]

Joannah, however, began selling her property and investing in town lots,
for which she sometimes signed promissory notes. Her business sense and

shrewd investment in property enabled her to support her ten children. When Texas passed its divorce statute in 1840, Joannah was quick to take advantage of it. The grounds for divorce were very liberal: adultery, abandonment, or cruelty; Joannah charged William Dunlap with all three. Joannah won the first recorded divorce in Colorado County and married the justice of the peace, Jacob Tipps, the next day. Joannah fortunately had a long marriage with Jacob. However, they became entangled in legal battles over some of the promissory notes she had signed while still married to Dunlap. The Tippses tried to escape the payment of at least one of these notes, citing the fact that Joannah had been a married woman when she signed the note and therefore legally unable to make contracts. However, this legal maneuvering failed; the courts recognized that sometimes married women on the frontier acted as their own legal agents.[52]

There were other married women on the frontier who, through their own initiatives or the forces of circumstances, acted as if they were independent traders. Frontier conditions created situations in which married women had to act on their own behalf. Men had greater opportunities to pick up and disappear in the West, as Joannah's husband did. But on the frontier, men also often had to leave temporarily to conduct business, whether they were driving stock, going to town to get supplies, or fighting in battles against Indians or Mexicans. Although specific legislation was never passed to recognize the many married women who conducted their own business, frontier era courts upheld their right to make such decisions.

The frontier also created the circumstances that led to some women choosing to end their marriages legally. On the frontier, women had few economic options outside of a family farm. Therefore, they were reluctant to file for divorce for any but the direst circumstances. As a result, the most common reason women wanted to end their marriages in early Texas was abandonment; divorce allowed the women to remarry. Abandonment could only be claimed as grounds for divorce if the spouse had been abandoned for three or more years, however. Women who wanted to remarry more quickly most often cited other grounds, especially cruelty, in their petitions to win divorces. After all, leaving a woman alone on the frontier with children could definitely be seen as cruel.[53]

Women in frontier Texas, therefore, by legislation and liberal interpretations of the law by the courts, had far greater rights than their sisters in the United States. Most frontier women, however, never needed or wanted to take advantage of these expanded rights, as most women married early and did not divorce, and their husbands continued to make financial decisions for their wives and their property.

Conclusion

Anglo settlements in Mexican Texas and after independence would significantly change the shape of women's lives in Texas and lead to a large number of Anglo and African American residents. Anglo women survived war and violence, loneliness, constant moves, crude living conditions, and backbreaking, constant work in order to establish a southern society in East Texas.

A system of African American slavery that would not end until the Civil War was the tragic result of refashioning East Texas into the edge of the cotton-growing, southern frontier. The profitability and growth of slavery often caused women to be separated from their families as they were forced to move to Texas. African American women fought loneliness caused by the sparseness of population and coped with incredibly harsh living environments to perform fieldwork as well as extremely valuable domestic work.

The imprint of Spanish and Mexican traditions continued, however, allowing some fluidity regarding relationships between whites and blacks and even freedom for some African American women. Policies under the Mexican government also induced the growth in numbers of other European settlers such as Germans. German women negotiated both the harsh physical environment and a foreign culture and legal system, using them when they could to their advantage to protect and serve their families as well as preserve their own culture within households.

No matter what their origin, the women in this early period faced primitive living, social, and legal conditions compared to those they had formerly known. Women's hard work in such unfamiliar circumstances made the growth and increased settlement of Texas possible.

Chapter 3

Creating an Antebellum Society in Texas

Texas remained a land of moving borderlands, and some part of Texas could be considered a frontier through the end of the nineteenth century. Those who lived through a frontier era in any location were affected by that experience for life. In any one county or region, however, the frontier never lasted long. After initial families settled their land, others moved into the area, usually within a decade, forming systems of protection, society, and law. Southerners dominated in these new migrant groups, and the communities they created in the rapidly expanding cotton farming economy soon became distinctly southern. This transformation had a particularly significant impact in East Texas, altering the lives of both white and black women there, but the increased population of the state with its growing Anglo-American majority affected other regions as well.

Southern women created new societies based on social and racial hierarchies of the East, which they accepted as right and natural. White women did not question the institution of slavery that elevated their status, and elite white women worked to establish social distinctions among white women that justified their wealth and special privileges. To gain those benefits, women also accepted the hierarchy that placed all men above women. These ideals, reinforced by religion and law, as well as by other women, required women's submissiveness to men in return for male protection and status based upon family position. African American women in these new southern communities of Texas did not submit to male authority and female social orders due to religion or social ideals but instead due to laws that gave white masters (and mistresses) power over their time, labor, and even social arrangements. Despite this, African American women continued to foster families and form communities based on their own cultural ideals and desires.

At the same time that southern women were successfully building southern societies in East Texas, other groups of women not common in the rest of the South were establishing strong and vibrant communities of their own. In Central Texas, German immigrants built settlements away from the pervasive presence of southerners, and here women played a role in reproducing cultural practices. Tejanas persisted in their old traditions in South Texas. They had to adapt, however, to accommodate to Anglo laws and the increasing number of people who moved into the region. In some communities, the Anglo presence transformed culture and ideals, while important cultural aspects continued in other communities, especially in the areas of women's greatest influence, the home.

As women negotiated the changes occurring as the frontier faded, they created an antebellum society patterned after that in other southern states but unique because of its continued westward growth and large populations who ascribed to different ideals. The passing of the frontier assured women safety and community, but the growing rigidity of social and legal practices reduced women's opportunities.

Population Growth

The acceleration of migration into the state helped prevent the isolation and loneliness that women who initially settled had faced. In thirteen years, the state gained 462,215 people: the population grew from 142,000 in 1847 to 604,215 in 1860, and most of the new immigrants were families from southern states. Southerners made up approximately 75 percent of the population of Texas in 1850. New migrants could choose to settle in more populated areas to be near the conveniences of communities or to settle in frontier regions that might still have better land available. Even as early as the 1830s, empresario Stephen F. Austin suggested that his sister, Emily Austin Perry, and her family settle at Peach Point because the area was already populated. Her husband, James, however, at first chose better land in a more isolated area, but within a year they moved to Peach Point to be closer to people.[1]

Emily Austin Perry's move also highlights another pattern that helped prevent isolation for women: settling with or near relatives. The initial settlers

Figure 3.1. Key locations mentioned in chapters 2 and 3.

wrote to siblings, parents, and others encouraging their migration and offering to find land, help with housing, and provide other services to make the transition easier. While many women were reluctant to move because it meant severing familial ties, other women saw moving to Texas as an opportunity to reunite or keep their families together and thus supported relocation. Emily Austin Perry's husband might have made the decision about where in Texas to settle, but she was the one who convinced her husband to move to the state so that she could reunite with the extended Austin clan.[2]

Antebellum women migrants were more likely to move in groups that would ease the isolation that individual women had felt on the frontier. Extended families in the South often made the decisions to migrate together, and thus parents with several adult children, their spouses, and their children might all move together, thus reforming a tight-knit, related community. Sometimes joint decisions to relocate extended beyond kin. A large group of settlers from a community in Tennessee moved to Texas and formed the Osage community.[3]

With the influx of new settlers, concentrations of population allowed for the establishment of communities, towns, and institutions. Southerners' ideas about society and culture formed the basis for founding churches, schools, and government in antebellum Texas. Southern immigrants also replicated their ideals about class and social ranking, and they instituted activities that reinforced those principles.

Social Ideals

Even the earliest southern Anglo women to move to Texas had brought their ideals about their proper place in society, although frontier life had forced them by necessity to stretch and bend those concepts. With the increase in population, women were more likely to be relieved of what they considered to be male roles in the field or in court and were better able to uphold what they believed to be their place at home and in society.

As historian Barbara Welter has described, a "cult of true womanhood" emerged in nineteenth-century popular northern literature. In this pervasive ideal, society expected women to live by four central virtues: piety, purity, submissiveness, and domesticity. Although southern women led lives very different from those of women in northern industrializing states, the upper-class southern women especially imbibed these ideals through national literature such as the incredibly popular monthly *Godey's Lady's Book* and other magazines and novels, as well as through national religious literature and churches.[4] Elite women's adherence to these ideals took on special meaning in the South, where their submissiveness and dependence served as a key component of a social order in which whites asserted authority over blacks, and men asserted a different type of authority over women. Challenging the authority of men in the family could bring into question the legitimacy of the authority that slaveholders had over their slaves. As a result, white southern women measured their own successes by the extent to which they exhibited those fundamental traits that preserved their reputations, their families' reputations, and therefore their men's right to rule, whether it be as elites in the community or over slaves.[5]

Social functions served as a place for elite white women to establish their own and their families' reputations through public displays of grace and charm. As communities and towns grew, so did the number of social activities, including increasingly elaborate balls and dinners, and these served as opportunities to judge the honor and worthiness of people and families. At the Matagorda City Ball, the event's managers turned away the visitor Jane McManus. In New York, McManus had been friends with Aaron Burr, who had divorced in a well-publicized scandal. Rumors about the nature of her connections with the scandal made her unfit for respectable society in Matagorda. In southern fashion, the patriarch of the host family, Ira Lewis, issued challenges to duels in attempts to protect McManus's honor, but the damage of the rumors and the social snub were too severe. McManus left town, giving up a legal claim to land as well.[6]

McManus had failed the claim to purity, but she also failed the claim to domesticity and submissiveness. Instead of being submissive to her husband, William, and spending her days providing domestic tranquility for her family, McManus had separated from him and pursued an individual livelihood. Often writing under a pseudonym, McManus was an author, journalist, unofficial diplomat, and a promoter of westward expansion. In an article in the *Democratic Review*—which included no byline and thus has been commonly attributed to the editor John O'Sullivan—she coined the famous term "manifest destiny." According to the southern elites in Matagorda, however, a "proper" woman contributed to the family economy by her domestic endeavors and submitted to the male head of that family, which McManus did not do.[7]

Social class made a difference in the lives of these southern women. Social functions, church seating, and rounds of visitations ascertained those who were considered upper class in a community. Middle-class and upper-class white women were reluctant to mix with women of lower status, even more so than men, who often shared activities in town across class lines, such as attending court days, frequenting general stores and taverns, and drilling in volunteer militias. Wealth, and often slaveholding, was only a first determinant in upper-class status; a good family reputation was also crucial. Therefore, a woman's lack of adherence to social ideals, such as was displayed by Jane McManus, could get her banned from elite society.

Likewise, white women who were not upper class had expectations that further divided them. The majority of white women were members of families who owned farms (often referred to as yeomen) but had few to no slaves. They also judged each other by their devotion to their families and their ability to uphold the ideals of "true womanhood." The wives of yeomen, however, were more likely to engage in field work at certain times of the year

than middle-class and upper-class women, had less time to spend on domestic matters, and were less likely to read the literature urging such ideals.
Nonetheless, yeoman women were proud to be part of landowning families
and looked down upon less respectable white women whose families owned
no land at all. And, of course, they greatly distinguished themselves from
slave women, who lacked even the property of their own bodies.[8]

Women's lives were intricately enmeshed in the reputations, class, and
connections of their families. One of the most important family connections
derived from a woman's role as mother. Unlike their northern sisters who
were limiting reproduction, Texas women of all social classes bore and raised
many children, in part due to the ability of farms to support large families,
a lack of knowledge about contraception, and the continued prestige men
gained from fathering children. Southern mothers doted on their children,
and parents were careful to ensure that children at least maintained their
status in society. Families of yeomen prided themselves on their ability to
pass down land to sons and moveable property to daughters to enable them
to replicate their parents' farming and landowning lifestyles. Elite families
worked hard to guarantee land to their sons and moveable property to their
daughters, most often in the form of slaves.[9]

Elite families also had to ensure that their daughters had reputations of
being genteel and respectable. One manner of promoting this was through
providing education to both their sons and daughters. By the 1850s, the
most populated areas had numerous schools that offered rigorous academic
courses for girls, including math, science, English, and foreign languages,
as well as subjects such as piano, drawing, and sewing that were necessary
for developing gentility. Because these private schools were dependent upon
tuition, the best ones were attended almost exclusively by girls from elite
families, although some schools were flexible and charged low enough tuition
that a few children of yeomen might also attend. Among others, women
religious from the Ursuline and Incarnate Word orders in Europe and New
Orleans migrated to Texas to establish affordable Catholic schools for girls
in Galveston, San Antonio, and Brownsville for those elite and yeomen alike
who could spare their daughters the time to pursue an education.[10]

A genteel education prepared a young woman for her elite status in society, making her proper and sociable and making it possible for her to begin
her children's education at home. One of the reasons so much of her education focused on arts and homemaking was to make her an attractive prospect
for marriage. A young woman was allowed to choose her own suitors and

eventually husband, giving her the most power she would probably ever exercise. Because so much of a woman's happiness, comfort, and status rested on her ultimate decision, parents and other family members assisted by offering advice, asking into the background of potential suitors, and presenting opportunities for her to meet eligible and suitable men. In the end, however, the choice belonged to the young woman. According to Lizzie Neblett, her father so disapproved of her courtship with her future husband, Will, that he threatened to whip her with a cow hide and cut her off. Although Lizzie broke off the engagement twice, she eventually did marry Will, and her father neither beat nor disinherited her.[11]

Men of the yeoman class generally looked for potential wives who had strong domestic skills and were not afraid of work. Men of the upper classes, however, looked for women who were genteel, well-groomed, and respectable and therefore would maintain the family's position in society. Elite women looked for men who could provide the best lifestyle possible for them financially, but they also looked for love and companionship. In fact, both men and women anticipated and promised romantic love, not just economic fortitude. Women expected to submit to husbands, but they wished to find husbands who would treat them with tenderness and affection and solicit their opinions on matters of the family and heart. Courtships among the elite, therefore, were usually lengthy, giving all family members the opportunity to check out the potential mates and for women to test the true nature of their suitors.[12]

Religion

The growing population of Texas provided the foundations for the establishment of churches, and women were instrumental in their building and support. These churches offered valuable spiritual and social outlets for women, and religion shaped most women's perceptions of themselves and their world.

While women could not serve as ministers or deacons in antebellum Texas churches, women's support of the churches was crucial for their success. Even though a minority in the general population, women made up the majority of members of the churches. As parishioners, they exerted several kinds of formal and informal power within the congregations. Formally, both Baptist and Methodist churches allowed their female members to vote on a variety of measures regarding the health of a church, from the amount to be spent on missions or refurbishing church pews to whether members should

Figure 3.2. Bascom Chapel Methodist Church, Palestine, around 1850. Courtesy of Palestine Public Library.

be allowed to dance. As the majority, women held some weight. Additionally, evangelical denominations, such as Baptists, Methodists, and Presbyterians, often appointed women to disciplinary committees, which had the power to recommend punishments and even dismissal from a church. In these churches, women also served as founding members and signed foundational documents.[13]

Informally, women exercised considerable influence in the formation of churches. Private homes sometimes served as places of worship until people could construct or purchase church buildings. Nancy Jane Cochran of Dallas County hosted the first formal worship in the area in her home in 1844 and donated land for a building in 1856. Sarah Cockrell and a Mrs. Bullington also donated land in Dallas to their respective organizations to construct church buildings.[14]

Ministers often found themselves dependent upon women church members. Not only did women make up the majority of congregants, they were also the ones who took responsibility for hospitality. They could make the clergy's lives much more—or much less—pleasant. Women fixed up rooms or parsonages, cooked meals for single or traveling ministers, and otherwise insured their comfort. In these ways, women could encourage ministers they liked. Women could just as easily discourage the ones they disliked from staying by providing less frequent meals and less comfortable housing, as well as by staying home from church and expressing their opinions to others about one's lack of suitability—in other words by exercising the powerful tool of gossip.[15]

Women formed crucial auxiliary organizations that carried out the goals of the church, such as "ladies' aid societies" or "sewing societies." In her diary, after her arrival in Columbus, Fannie Darden described "the meeting of three ladies, Mrs. Mackey, Mrs. Foshey and myself for a sewing society. We met in faith and love, had nothing to work with but a few hands full of scraps. But the Lord blessed our efforts."[16] These societies often assisted by furnishing a church, ministering to the needy, or raising funds for church needs, such as repairs or new buildings. For instance, the "Sewing Circle" of the Christ Episcopal Church in Houston suggested "certain repairs and improvements" to the church building and offered the church's all-male governing body the $130 they raised for that purpose. Through their control of the money, the women were able to get the repairs that they deemed necessary without power being ascribed to them in the governing structure.[17]

Church and auxiliary organizations gave women critical opportunities to socialize. Even as the frontier faded, rural women in the state, as in the rest of the South, lived on large farms and plantations distant from one another. Sunday services and organizational meetings provided opportunities to leave the farms and visit with many different people. Even for the women who lived in the increasing number of small towns, religious services and organizational meetings offered society and companionship and broke the monotony of home life.[18]

Despite the religious nature of the gatherings on Sunday mornings, these social occasions were also opportunities for women to exert their class ideals. Elite women preferred to sit together and socialize together before and after church, and social conventions indicated their status in the society. As a grown daughter from an elite family in Brazoria County, Sallie McNeill felt a social slight so significant she recorded it in her diary. After McNeill invited the preacher's wife to visit with her after church services, another parishioner also invited the woman. The preacher's wife "decided to accompany Mrs. W without the slightest apology or excuse to me." McNeill felt insulted and that her "invitation at least deserved some notice."[19]

While the number of churches grew during the antebellum period, there were not always enough clergy. Women often waited weeks for the itinerant minister of their particular denomination to visit their communities and preach. In the intervening weeks, parishioners would sometimes have meetings without a preacher. Many, however, would attend a church service where a preacher was present, even if he was of a different denomination. By 1856 in Dallas, ministers of different Protestant faiths took turns preaching in the Masonic Hall, so every Sunday the residents of the town could attend a service.[20]

The absence of full-time clergy of their particular faith meant that many women did not develop strong attachments to a particular denomination.[21] The shortage of other social opportunities also meant that female parishioners sometimes treated Sunday morning services primarily as social events. Nonetheless, women's faith played a significant role in shaping their lives, their ideas about themselves, and their roles in society.

Throughout the country after the Second Great Awakening of the early nineteenth century, the Protestant religious revival, women began exceeding men in church membership and attendance. An idea arose that women were more moral than men and significantly contributed to the "true womanhood" ideals. Women's greater "natural" piety was celebrated as the means by which other family members would be brought to God. By being good examples and using moral influence, women could persuade husbands and sons to walk paths of righteousness. More than one preacher told stories of a pious mother whose influence reached into her son's life as an adult. In some he never touched a drop of alcohol because of her influence, in others he requested a deathbed conversion after years of irreligious activity, and in still others he credited her example for raising his own strong Christian family. While celebrating a woman's influence, the religious ideals also demanded her submissiveness. In her submissiveness to Christ, to her father, to her husband, to the church, and to trials and tribulations, a woman was to fulfill her true Christian calling and, in doing so, gain the respect to influence her family. As a result, southern Christian women struggled between being called to use their supposedly superior moral abilities to lead their families to Christ and submitting passively to their male members.[22]

These struggles appeared in the diaries, journals, and letters of literate antebellum women. Lizzie Neblett of Grimes County, while anticipating the dangers of childbirth, wrote that she was "content, for I believe god to be all wise, merciful and good, and have sufficient faith to think and believe that 'he doeth all things well.'" However, she mused whether her death in child-birth might finally cause her husband "to repent of his sins, and become an heir to the Kingdom of Heaven."[23] Henrietta Embree of Bell County struggled nearly every Sunday with alternating feelings of commitment and failure. One Sunday she was determined "let come what will . . . to serve the most High God." On the next she fretted, "Another Sabbath day has closed and how has it been spent by me? as it should? I greatly fear not." A week later: "Why is it I feel so bad every Sabbath night?" While her faith was a source of comfort, it was also a source of feelings of disappointment. Although she strove to do her duties to her family and "especily to my God," she felt "at times over come" because she felt insecure in knowing what was right.[24]

Likewise, Sallie McNeill exhibited the contradictory impulses of passivity and active authority. In her diary she prayed for a spirit of submissiveness: "O God, may I feel my dependence on thee and ever look upward for Thy aid." Yet McNeill quite actively used her religion as a source of validation for her decision to remain single: "I look forward to a lonely life with no apprehension, since if 'God' wills it is all for the best." She maintained it was "a sin to marry one unsuited."[25]

Thus, religion served as a major force in women's lives, both in socializing and as a source of personal meaning. Even women who were less religious than others found themselves a part of a society in which evangelical notions heavily influenced ideals about women's proper roles and place.

Work

Two major changes from the frontier period altered the character of women's work in antebellum Texas: the greater population and access to store-bought goods. On the frontier, it was common for a husband, wife, and small children to build a homestead out of uncultivated land by themselves. This meant that the wife had to take on numerous ostensibly male duties. However, as more people moved to any particular area, families more often had kin and neighbors to assist. Men might gather together for barn raisings, and women for quilting bees, allowing women to concentrate more of their labor on traditional women's duties. The greater population also meant that there were more men to hire to help with small jobs. And the increase in slaves benefited not only the women in families who owned slaves but also those in families without, because non-slaveholders often borrowed or leased slaves for help. As frontier families aged, they not only saw an influx of set-tlers, their own children also became old enough to work on the farms and plantations.

Although women concentrated more on domestic or traditionally female duties in the antebellum era, their work was far from light. They were re-sponsible for growing, preserving, and preparing most of the food that their families consumed. Women planted, cared for, and harvested vegetables in large gardens next to their houses and tended and harvested fruit and nuts. As the vegetables and fruits were harvested, women engaged in continual processes of food preservation usually from June to September. They also

Figure 3.3. Ad from *Dallas Herald,* October 27, 1858. Courtesy of University of North Texas Libraries Portal to Texas History.

assisted with the butchering of pigs, cattle, and game, preserving all parts of the animals and tending the smokehouse for drying most of the meat. They raised chickens for eggs, milked cows, and then turned the milk into butter and cheese. Preparing the food for meals was arduous work, over open fireplaces or even outdoor fires, requiring much practice and expertise. With more families, more stores, improved roads, and more reliable mail service, women had greater access to cooking utensils, which made cooking somewhat easier, but only the wealthiest families had much more than the bare essentials. The construction of local mills eliminated the need for many to grind their own corn or other grains by hand. Wealthier families were also able to purchase extra foods and spices to vary their diets.[26]

Even more than feeding the family, the work that preoccupied most women's time involved clothing. Stores and improved transportation increased the ability of families to buy cloth rather than make it. Newspaper ads promoted newly arrived shipments of fabric and other goods, but since retail stores were still male domains in the nineteenth century, women instructed men on what to buy. Despite the increased availability of cloth for purchase, many families could not afford to buy enough for all their needs, and thus women continued to spin and weave at home. Others at least continued spinning, if not weaving, to make socks and other knitted items. Spinning was a time-consuming, laborious task that women were eager to teach their daughters, both to pass down the skill and gain help for the ongoing chore. Spinning usually took place at night by candlelight, and getting and keeping enough light was always a concern. (The tallow candles that were made to last as long as possible were increasingly store-bought during the antebellum era, but women still made many of these at home.) In the small proportion of slaveholding families, slave women often assisted in the production of thread and yarn by spinning at night after working in the field all day. Only a tiny portion of the population living on the largest plantations had slave women dedicated to producing cloth, but those women sometimes developed renowned expertise in spinning and weaving.[27]

Thread and yarn used for cloth or knitted items had to be dyed, and the greater access to country stores gave women the opportunity to buy commercial dyes that gave their clothing variety. For everyday and slave clothing, however, most women continued to use natural dyes made from the likes of indigo, sumac berries, and plum roots. After dying the thread, women wove fabric before making clothes. Even women who took advantage of store-bought goods still had to make or repair clothing for their large families.[28]

As time-consuming as making and repairing clothing was, the worst part about keeping a family clothed was keeping the clothing clean, according to women on Texas farms. Performed mostly outdoors, laundering required many gallons of water that had to be carried, soap that the women had to make with lye and grease, and fires that had to be stoked and fed with logs that also had to be carried. Women scrubbed clothes on rocks or a rub board, stirred and "punched" them as they boiled in water, and then transferred them by hand to a vat of rinse water. The clothes then had to be blued and starched and ironed before they could be worn.[29]

Preparing food and making clothing contributed to a family's home economy as surely as did planting and harvesting the major money-producing crop, whether it was corn, cotton, or sugar. In a period where all work was performed at home, there was much less distinction made between working for wages outside the home and working at the home or farm. Everyone on farms and plantations—men, women, and children—worked. However, men held nearly all the occupations that earned money outside the family farm structure. From doctor to politician to lawyer and teacher, men held most professional positions, and women rarely, if ever, pursued an outside career. On the census returns of one county (Colorado), as late as 1860 only 6 percent of adult women listed occupations, and the majority were widows continuing farms after the deaths of their husbands. The few who did list "occupations" outside the family or farm structure included one seamstress, nine servants, and four teachers. Other types of work that women performed to bring additional money into their families were not seen as occupations. These included taking in boarders, washing or making clothes for others, selling the products of gardens and orchards, and, above all, making and selling butter, cheese, and eggs to neighbors and local stores.[30]

While all white women had tremendous work responsibilities, class status affected the type and amount of work they did. Elite plantation mistresses, for instance, had the responsibility of making sure a much larger number of people on the plantation were fed, clothed, and given medical attention, but they were much less likely to engage in manual labor themselves and more likely to oversee slaves performing the work. Wives of yeomen with some slave help could concentrate on their domestic duties with occasional help from slaves, who were more likely to spend most of their time in the fields. Such women with no slaves, however, not only performed the arduous domestic duties themselves, at certain times of the year they would often be needed to assist in the fields as well.

African American Women and Slavery

Slavery was a distinguishing aspect of the antebellum era in Texas. Prime cotton fields in East Texas encouraged the extension of the southern plantation system, especially after the state government ensured legal continuation of slavery. The ability to grow and produce sugar along the Brazos River stimulated very large plantations in that region. Slavery fueled economic growth and provided the basis for social stratification, ensuring that the state was in every way a slave society.

Slavery was woven into the fabric of antebellum Texas even though only a portion of the population owned slaves. In 1850, 30.1 percent of white families held slaves, and only 2.3 percent held twenty or more (usually the minimum amount of slaves for a farm to be considered a plantation). Over the next ten years, the number of slaves increased 214 percent, while the stratification increased, with only 27.3 percent holding slaves but 3 percent holding twenty or more. In other words, a smaller percentage of white families owned slaves, while a larger percentage owned more than twenty, mirroring a trend in the other southern states.[31]

Plantation women whose families owned twenty or more slaves benefited directly from their labor. These white women were less likely to perform manual work such as building fires, cooking food, and even spinning and weaving, although they still oversaw the running of large households and ensured the feeding and clothing of dozens of people. These women were more likely to have leisure time to keep diaries, write letters, and read the national and religious literature that counseled them on how to behave. Slavery also gave them elevated status in society and a claim to better treatment in law.

Women of families that owned few or no slaves also benefited from the system of slavery, although much less so than their elite counterparts. As white women, they automatically had a claim to a higher status than the lowest class, no matter how poor they might be. Additionally, although a smaller and smaller percentage of families could afford to purchase slaves, the slave leasing system was vibrant. Those who needed extra labor for short periods of time could lease slaves from other farmers or from planters for a few months or even for an entire year, an especially common arrangement made by slaveholding widows who decided not to continue running their own farms.

The institution of slavery, of course, affected one group of women far more than any other: African Americans. As the influx of immigrants from southern states arrived in Texas, bringing with them attitudes about slavery, the institution was firmly ensconced in law and society. The slight fluidity in race relations that had been allowed in the frontier period evaporated. A series of Texas laws enacted beginning in 1836 made it increasingly clear that all African Americans were to be treated as slaves. State legislators went so far as to enact a law in 1858 requiring every free black person to choose a master and become a slave or leave the state. Socially, all transgressions of the racial line were severely punished. John and Puss Webber (see chapter 2), an interracial couple who had found a space on the frontier to live and raise children, were so threatened by new arrivals with "bitter prejudice, coupled with a desire to get Webber's land and improvements," wrote early settler Noah Smithwick, that they left the state and moved to Mexico.[32]

While the increased immigration of southerners to Texas fastened the shackles of slavery ever more tightly on African American women, the greater population did provide one benefit: the greater likelihood of finding mates and raising families. The number of slaves on each farm and plantation increased during the era. In 1850, the US census for Texas indicated that 38 percent of the state's slaves lived in households with fewer than ten slaves each, and by 1860 this had decreased to 29 percent. Not only did this make it more likely that slaves could find partners on the same farm or plantation, but also with the general increase in the slave population came the greater possibility of finding stable relationships with persons on neighboring farms (known as marrying "abroad"). Slaveholders encouraged the formation of families by giving permission to marry abroad, by celebrating marriages, and sometimes by overt interference. Sarah Ford reported that her mother "say de white folks don't let de slaves what works in de field marry none, dey jus' puts a man and breedin' woman together like mules. Iffen the women don't like the man it don't make no diff'rence, she better go or dey gives her a hidin'."[33]

Marriage between slaves was still not recognized by law, but the increasingly cohesive slave communities enforced certain expectations socially. Fidelity to one's spouse was expected, but when a couple was separated by sale or relocation, something that continued to happen despite the greater stability of population, their marriage was considered terminated. In addition to separation, other factors could lead to the end of a slave marriage. Abuse, constant conflicts, and even just falling out of love sometimes led to mutual splits recognized and accepted by the slave community. Although these divorces were acceptable, most people in slavery preferred and were able to maintain nuclear households. In the 1930s, when the Works Progress Administration interviewed former Texas slaves, most of whom had been young children before emancipation, 60 percent remembered living in a household with both parents. Another 9 percent lived with parents in marriages abroad, staying with their mothers while their fathers lived nearby.[34]

Slave women, even in nuclear families, however, could not focus exclusively on domestic roles. Whereas white women were not expected to perform heavy field labor, this type of work occupied the majority of most slave women's time. Whenever possible, work was segregated by gender. Women hoed, picked, weeded, thinned, ginned, and pressed cotton into bales, grew food, tended livestock, and formed all-female gangs to clear out trash, while men did most of the plowing and fence-tending, as well as picking, weeding, and ginning. Irella Battle Walker, like many young women, was put to work early: "When I still little I went to de fields. . . . I could pick about a hundred fifty pounds a day when I's twelve."[35]

After work in the field, women also were assigned to the white family's household work such as cooking, sewing, or spinning. After waking to go to the fields at 4:00 a.m., then working all day, the women in Emma Taylor's family had "to spin four cuts of thread every night and make all de clothes." Taylor said, "Some has to card cotton to make quilts and some weave and knits stockin's. Marse give each one a chore to do at night and iffen it wan't did when we went to bed, we's whipped." Although many slave women took pride in their work and their ability to do much of it, the primary motivation for most of the work they performed was fear of discipline. In order to keep slaves working, whites used a variety of punishment, the most common of which was the whip, which was used liberally by both masters and slave patrols, whose duty it was to capture and punish any slave away from his or her farm without a pass. As Sarah Ford acknowledged, "And even does your stomach be full, and does you have plenty clothes, dat bullwhip on your bare hide make you forgit de good part, and dat's de truth." On the farm, the law allowed masters great freedom in punishing slaves however they might see fit, and the courts barely enforced the few laws against cruel treatment of slaves. In addition to the whip, slave women as well as men endured other forms of corporal punishment, but non-corporal punishments were also common: reduced food rations, withholding passes to church or visitation of family members, and the threat of sale and separation from loved ones.[36]

The main incentive to work for the master might have been fear of punishment, but slaves usually had some time to work for their own families. Most received half day Saturday and all Sunday except during cotton-picking time. Within their own households, usually small cabins containing one nuclear unit, women and men had separate responsibilities. Men hunted and fished and did repairs. Slave women prepared meals and made clothing. They often worked with their husbands to plant and tend garden plots in which they grew food to supplement the meager cornmeal, molasses, and pork provided by their masters.[37]

The legal institution of slavery endeavored to turn human beings into property, but slave families, vibrant communities, and religion gave slave women solace and sense of self-worth. As a result, slaves did not necessarily internalize their inferior status, and evidence abounds of resistance to bondage. Murdering masters or mistresses and running away were at one end of a spectrum of resistance, while at the other end of were negative personal opinions shared with children in the slave quarters. In between were thousands of acts of passive rebellion, from slowing down work to feigning illness or pregnancy, a tool especially used by women against masters who were reluctant to risk a future slave child.[38]

Although rarely recognized, African American women's contributions to the growth of the Texas economy and society were significant, even if coerced. The rapid settlement of the state and the extension of the cotton economy were made possible by the productive and reproductive work of slave women.

German Communities

Even though Anglo and African American southerners quickly became the majority in the population, thus making it an extension of southern society, other ethnic groups called Texas their home. In particular, German-speaking peoples continued to live in the state, and after the revolutions of the 1840s in Europe the number grew even larger. As with the Anglo settlers, the lives of German women changed in the antebellum era as the frontier receded. New migrations increased the population and better allowed immigrants from Europe to set up communities with concentrations of people who shared the same language and religion. Founded by nobles in Europe in the 1840s, the Adelsverein, or German Emigration Company, encouraged more than seven thousand people to relocate to Texas. These augmented the populations of existing communities, including Galveston and Houston, as well as several small towns in Austin and Colorado Counties. Additionally, they founded new towns such as New Braunfels and Fredericksburg in Central Texas.

Figure 3.4. Betty Holekamp immigrated with her husband to the Texas Hill Country in 1844 as part of the German Emigration Company.

With increased population, building churches and schools became possible and a priority in these German immigrant communities. While a minority of intellectuals who escaped the civil wars in Europe were agnostic, church was central for the majority. Mathilda Wagner remembered that her entire family went to church every Sunday: "Almost everyone who was well went Sunday morning, young and old." Women helped raise money for, attended, and otherwise helped support the churches. The Lutheran, Catholic, and Methodist churches' ministers, however, were men. Following both the traditions of their home country as well as the southern traditions of their adopted country, nearly all of the schoolteachers were also men. The primary responsibility for teaching and conveying culture, therefore, shifted from women in the home to these male-controlled institutions, although women continued to reinforce the learning, particularly regarding culture, at home.[39]

Upper-class women continued to play a central role in patronizing and supporting the arts, especially music and painting. Women continued to give and take music lessons; Emilie Schuletze and her brothers formed a traveling singing quartet. With the increased settlement, Germans were able to turn their endeavors toward more than just subsistence and built halls for dancing, including one added to a home near La Grange in the late 1850s. Women organized dances, fund-raisers, and other cultural events in these halls and participated alongside men in literary societies that met there. Unlike their Anglo southern sisters who saw such behavior as immodest or shameful, German women also performed, both onstage and off, in professional and amateur theatrical productions.[40]

Women helped their communities preserve significant parts of their culture and traditions, some of which still continue in many areas of the state. These Germans were living in the US South, and they adopted many southern practices and much of the culture. They had to operate within the US economic and legal system. Women took advantage of Texas laws that granted them more rights than perhaps they would have been able to exercise in Europe, including the right to own property in their own names, the right to community property, the right to administer deceased husbands' estates, and the right to divorce. Some women even recorded cattle brands in their own names.[41]

Germans also became enmeshed in the economic system of the state and region, with consequences for women. They introduced no significant crops from Europe, tending instead to adopt the southern formula for success, planting corn and cotton, and, relying upon cotton as a cash crop, they needed workers. They maintained a general distaste for slavery and preferred to hire other immigrants who needed work. Some of these workers were women, and as a result the census-takers listed some German women as "laborers," a designation virtually unknown for Anglo women, no matter how much work they performed.[42]

Despite German immigrants' broad cultural dislike of slavery, some nonetheless invested in slaves to make profits on cotton like their neighbors did. Seemingly, more families, however, purchased slaves to work as house servants than for work in the fields. Women found it difficult in the United States to find "good help" as they were accustomed to in their home countries. Once lower-class German women migrated, they no longer had the proper and completely deferential attitudes they had exhibited in Europe, and, according to those hiring them, these servants were unwilling to work as hard as they had in Europe. Upper-class German immigrant women then turned to slaves for domestic service. Because they saw slaves as replacing the European ideal of the house servant, there is evidence that the women treated their slaves less like property and more like free servants.[43]

Overall, women were an integral part of a cultural milieu within the German settlements in antebellum Texas. They contributed to preserving significant portions of their own cultures while adapting to and becoming part of the wider antebellum southern culture.

Tejanas

Unlike the German-speaking peoples that migrated to Texas and adapted to the prevailing southern culture, the people of Spanish and Mexican descent had settled and developed a distinct Tejano culture well before the influx of Americans. In the antebellum period, women played a crucial role in preserving that culture despite the Anglos' growing numerical superiority and seizure of political power.

Although many Tejanos had fought for independence from Mexico in 1835, Anglos increasingly expressed suspicions about the loyalty of all Mexicans. Annexation to the United States in 1845 and the ensuing war with Mexico gave rise to even greater hostility to Tejanos and their families. For many this led to exclusion from politics and government. For some it entailed exile, as it did for the former mayor of San Antonio, Juan Seguín, whom white Texans suspected of disloyalty. To nearly all it meant the development of negative stereotypes and the hardening of negative attitudes, which could lead to violence, harassment, and unfair treatment. In many of the Anglo-dominated areas, Tejanos lost all power, and in some they were forbidden from residing.[44]

Even in the parts of the state where Tejanos continued to be a large portion of the population, particularly San Antonio and South Texas, non-Tejanos became more powerful and influential. Americans and European immigrants alike saw opportunities to increase their fortunes through large-scale dispossession of land formerly owned by Tejanos. Fraud and violence played a major role in transferring thousands of acres of land, although the market forces of a vibrant US economy probably also played a role.[45] Yet another significant way land ownership transferred from Tejano to Anglo hands was through intermarriage. Traditionally, Mexican daughters of landowners inherited land (whereas Anglo Americans tended to will their daughters moveable property rather than land). The practice of Anglo men marrying Tejanas continued from the frontier era into the antebellum period—primarily in regions numerically dominated by Tejanos—thus offering another avenue for Anglo men to accumulate land.[46]

Even with the Anglo takeover, Tejanas retained active economic and legal roles within the family and society, more reminiscent of the Spanish and Mexican tradition than the Anglo-American tradition. Tejanas still regularly exercised control over property and participated in economic endeavors, including loaning money, running businesses, and leaving wills in which they dictated the distribution of their wealth. The widow Patricia de la Garza de León not only took care of the physical and spiritual needs of her children and grandchildren, she also made financial and economic decisions, including petitioning the court in their best interest. In 1847 de León petitioned the Victoria County court to sell real estate for the benefit of her grandchildren: "She has been placed in charge and care of Pilar, Libriata [*sic*], and Matiana for the last four years and six months. Support of said children has come from her own purse. During the whole period of her said charge she has received nothing from the estate except $100 and a small amount of clothing and necessaries." Upon her death, de León continued making her own decisions about money and willed her money and property equally to her daughters, forgiving debts they had to her. But she left nothing to her son, even refusing to forgive his debt: "to each of my children equal portions of the $1000 that Fernando borrowed from me to pay debts." A woman of property such as de León owed respect and obedience to her father and her husband, but upon their deaths she ascended to become matriarch of the family, with the expectation that her children, including her sons, would respect her.[47]

Many Anglo and European men respected the economic traditions of their wives. When John Young married Salomé Balli, he treated her as his business partner in the accumulation of land. Balli, in fact, had begun buying land before meeting Young, and the money that he brought to the marriage made it possible for her to reassemble nearly the entire Santa Anita tract that had been granted to her forbears. Other Tejanas in relationships with non-Tejanos continued to make wills, record separate cattle brands from their husbands, and otherwise take advantage of laws and customs that gave married women greater rights than women under English law traditions.[48]

Within other mixed marriages, Anglo men exerted political and probably economic control of the family, but almost all left the raising of the children and particularly the imparting of religious ideas to the women. Although some Tejanas converted to Protestantism, most remained devout Catholics and raised their children in the Catholic faith. For instance, Petra Vela, who married the Anglo Quaker Mifflin Kenedy, took the responsibility for the education of and the spiritual guidance of their children. She taught her children at home but sent them to Catholic schools when possible, even though it sometimes meant sending them out of state.[49]

Religion remained central in the lives of most women, no matter whom they married, and Tejano society often equated women with piety.[50] Women created altars in the homes and decorated them with pictures or representations of saints. They instructed their children and led family prayers before the altars, especially in times and places when there were a shortage of priests. Women also took an active role in founding and supporting Catholic churches. They participated in planning and celebrating holy days, they raised money for activities of the churches, and they contributed significant amounts of money. In their wills Tejanas such as María Concepción de Estrada of San Antonio first made contributions to the church or its missions. Estrada left traditional amounts to the church and an additional three pesos for "widows and orphans who died defending the just cause." Women were more likely than men to ask for masses to be said for them and have other specific requests for their funerals. Wills also indicated that women were more likely than men to own religious objects and maintain their prerogative for dispersing these among their heirs. Even in families such as Petra Vela's, where the head of the household was a Protestant, women exercised considerable influence and insisted on contributions to the church.[51]

Whether on ranches in Tejano-dominant areas such as South Texas and along the Rio Grande or on farms and small towns within Anglo-dominated areas of East Texas, Tejanas' work resembled that of southern women. They were responsible for food and clothing production, thus making significant economic contributions to their families. Tejanas continued, however, preparing traditional foods that differed from their southern sisters, especially frijoles and corn tortillas. Well into the late nineteenth century, every kitchen had a metate to grind corn, and women cooked tortillas at every meal.[52] Women of all classes continued to spin and weave cloth, although most women did so with very limited resources. Even so, the blankets that El Paso women might take five or six months to weave were long-lasting and able to protect their wearers from rain and wind.[53] One other difference from southern white women marked Tejanas' lives: they probably dreaded washday much less because it continued to be treated as a social occasion in areas with large Hispanic populations. Women brought their children and dirty clothes to the rivers and streams, washing together, enjoying each other's company, and cooling off by taking dips in the water. As Anglo culture came to dominate an area, however, traditions such as sunbathing began to be curtailed. By 1859, the Board of Aldermen in Laredo began passing ordinances forbidding many previously culturally acceptable activities, limiting the business hours of saloons, requiring licenses for fandangos, and restricting the bathing areas along the river, among other things.[54]

Conclusion

After Texas won independence from Mexico and then became a state, its population increased rapidly as it attracted more settlers from southern US states as well as from the German-speaking provinces of Europe. As more southern families arrived, women worked with men to transform eastern portions of the state from a frontier into an extension of southern society, complete with ideals about class, gender, race, and slavery. White women benefited from the system of slavery that brought black women to the state in large enough numbers to promote families and cultural traditions of their own. German women also continued to arrive, building stable communities in Central Texas that were influenced by southern culture but not subsumed by it. Tejanas, meanwhile, coped with the influx of southerners and their assumption of political power, while continuing their social, and even legal, traditions. While the transformation of the frontier took place at different times in different places, East Texas and much of the central and southern portions of the state established economies, societies, and cultures that both supported and constrained women's lives and opportunities.

Chapter 4

Civil War and Reconstruction

By the end of the antebellum era, southerners comprised the majority of the population of Texas. They controlled most of the businesses, newspapers, and, most importantly, political positions. Thus, it was not surprising that Texas seceded along with the ten other southern states in 1861 and joined the Confederate States of America. White women in the state experienced the war caused by this secession much like other white women throughout the South. The new adversity during these four years altered their roles, expectations, and daily lives in previously unimaginable ways, but they faced those trials while clinging as tightly as possible to the antebellum ideals of themselves. Also as in other southern states, African American women both challenged their bonds of slavery and suffered more in those bonds during the war. The stories of southern women in Texas, black and white, are part of broader southern women's history during the Civil War. They highlight the changes in society, the power of ideals even in tumultuous times, and the ability of women to continue families, households, livelihoods, economies, and society in the most adverse circumstances. However, not all women in Texas were southern women. German women, Tejanas, and even northern or pro-Union women experienced the war very differently. They too overcame tremendous personal hardships and threats of physical violence.

After the war, as politicians endeavored to reconstruct the political status of Texas, women worked with men to rebuild and create new social and economic systems. While white southern women attempted to reestablish the prewar society that gave them special privileges, black women sought to create new social orders that would give meaning to their emancipation from slavery and accord themselves control over their lives and within their families and communities.

White Confederate Women

After the election of Abraham Lincoln and the secession of South Carolina, Texas men clamored for the right to boast that Texas "got out of the Union before Lincoln got into power."[1] The refusal of Texas governor Sam Houston to call a secession convention delayed the consideration, but women were not silent witnesses to the onrush of events that followed. The majority of white women held southern ideals about society and its hierarchical makeup. Elite white women advocated strongly for secession as the means to protect slavery and thus the elevated social status slaveholding conferred upon them. Caroline Darrow, a visitor to Texas in 1861, recorded, "Late in January was held the election for delegates to a State convention which should consider the question of secession. San Antonio was crowded. Women vied with each other in distributing the little yellow ballots."[2]

In Refugio County, a Miss Adams took to the podium when it appeared no one else might and said: "Sons of Texas, it is not in the sphere of a lady to address a political assembly; but when the honor of her sex and the freedom of her country are at stake; when men are either deterred by danger, or slumber in indifference, it is her duty to raise her voice. The time for deliberation is passed, the time for action is come."[3] On February 2, convention delegates finally met in Austin to vote for secession, and when the roll call vote was affirmative, boisterous celebrants snaked their way up and down the aisles of the chambers, including numerous women who had been there observing from the galleries.[4] A month later, the *Colorado Citizen* in Columbus ran a story about the Williamson County delegate, one of the few to cast a vote against secession. According to the article, he had returned to Austin and asked permission to change his vote after he went home and "his wife wouldn't let him in at the front door!" The editors of the same newspaper boldly proclaimed: "That cause can never perish which is sustained by the smiles and approval of our noble Southern women!"[5]

While editors of antebellum Texas newspapers earlier would not have celebrated women's political involvement as these did during the secession crisis and at the beginning of the Civil War, but their change in tone did not mean editors had come to endorse a shift in gender roles. Newspaper editors, like Texas society at large, saw the potential war as an opportunity to reaffirm the differences between men and women. Women expressed their support of men and encouraged them to take their proper places as defenders of home, property, and womanhood. Men, on the other hand, were supposedly the only ones who could and should take up arms to protect their homes and their women. A woman writing under the pseudonym "Helen" in the *Colorado Citizen* expressed sentiments similar to many Texas women at the beginning of the war when she bemoaned that she could not go to war: "If my sphere permitted me to go to the wars, I should have taken delight in going some time ago, and nothing could have prevented me from going." In diaries and letters, women across the South expressed helplessness at their femaleness at a time when their country needed men.[6]

Although women could not volunteer to fight, they could encourage the men of the community to do so. Women participated in planning and conducting elaborate sendoffs for their valiant soldiers. Members of "ladies' aid associations," formed to make clothing for the soldiers, also made flags for each company, and at the sendoff celebrations, beautiful young girls or women were chosen to present the flag. For instance, the editors of the newspaper in Marshall described the qualities of one such presenter: "Miss Smith was beautifully and tastefully attired, and rode an elegant milk white steed. She presented a model of ease, grace, and loveliness, and as, accompanied by her escort, she took her position, a thrill of admiration pervaded the concourse assembled to witness the scene." At most celebrations, a "lady" merely presented the flag, but at some, as at the one in Marshall, she also gave a short public address in which she pledged women's support of men's gallant defense: "In behalf of a thousand bounding and exultant hearts, in behalf of the tender mothers, wives, sisters, loved,—and it may be betrothed, ones—you leave behind; in behalf of the more than ten thousand female hearts who this day pray God speed your patriotic toils, I come to present you this pledge, a pledge designed by patriotic hearts and wrought by patriotic fingers, that they will neither forget nor forsake you; our prayers and our contributions shall follow you."[7]

Communities were expected to celebrate men who volunteered to fight, and women, by being stoic in the face of possible death of their loved ones, could encourage those in their families to join the war. If family and community celebrations of volunteers were not enough, women could exert other forms of pressure, such as shame. The editorial mentioned above by "Helen" continued to suggest that "all the young men that won't go to the wars, ought to put on hoops and long gowns." If they thought that they might "stay at home and marry while the choice young men are gone to the wars . . . they are much mistaken! A man that won't protect his country won't protect his wife." Groups of young ladies would sometimes deliver hoop skirts directly to healthy young men who refused to volunteer. The men drumming up support for the war encouraged such behavior by women and placed stock in women's ability to motivate family members. John Shropshire, an officer in the Confederate army, wrote to his wife, asking her to tell her sister "that if she had the pluck of our ancient mothers she would hen peck Ben like the devil if he did not leave soon for the wars."[8]

At the beginning of the conflict, then, women used their influence rather than power or authority of their own to assist the war effort. They motivated men to enlist as soldiers and provided such a unified show of support that other women dared not criticize the South or the war. Neither men nor women predicted significant challenges to their proper spheres or gender expectations. Texans did not anticipate the war would last long, and they expected the coping mechanisms that women used before the war whenever their husbands might be absent on business would continue to work. Antebellum plantation mistresses and farmwives alike had continued farming in the temporary absences or the deaths of spouses. With the help of grown sons, nearby male family members, and other men in the community, wives had conducted the agricultural business until husbands returned or until estates were settled and other arrangements could be made.[9]

In their early letters home, husbands serving in the army continued to direct the activities of their businesses and plantations. They also urged their wives to rely on other men. Theophilus Perry instructed his wife, Harriet Perry, of Marshall, to "consult Papa in every thing," and John Shropshire asked his wife, Caroline, of Colorado County to forward his instructions regarding baling cotton and paying debts to her father, writing, "I rely upon him entirely and feel satisfied that he will act entirely for the best."[10] However, the war was not short, and mail service quickly became unreliable. By the second year, husbands on faraway fields of battle and dealing with the drudgery of camp life knew increasingly less about the economic and agricultural situations at home, and their letters included fewer instructions to their wives. As more men volunteered and the Confederate government began conscription in 1862, fewer men remained at home. Wives were increasingly forced to make decisions about planting, harvesting, selling, and other business matters on their own.

Antebellum laws that allowed husbands to act on behalf of their wives in law or business but not vice versa. These laws did not change during the war, but both businesses and the courts relaxed restrictions. It was not unusual for women to rent, lease, and sell personal and real property on behalf of themselves and husbands. Some men signed powers of attorney to clarify their wives' legal powers, but most did not. Without a legal power of attorney, Helen Le Tulle signed promissory notes acting "in the capacity of agent for Le Tulle and Co.," her husband's store. Michael McLemore signed a power of attorney to grant his wife, Mary, the right to sell property and conduct business. This led to an awkward situation: after she signed her own and her husband's name to a deed, the county clerk still had to attach his certification that he had examined her privately and apart from her husband to ensure that she agreed with her husband's sale of the property. Although the practice was irregular, courts upheld the business conducted by wives in their husbands' absence during the war.[11]

Very few women relished the opportunity to continue performing their own time-consuming work as well as that of their husbands, but some did very well in their new positions of authority while others struggled. Mary Ingram of Hillsboro found confidence in her increased business acumen, and Harriet Perry solicited her father-in-law's advice but acted confidently on her own in many important decisions. On the other hand, Lizzie Neblett of Anderson, Texas, complained midway through the war, "I am so sick of trying to do a man's business when I am nothing but a poor contemptible piece of multiplying human flesh tied to the house by a crying young one, looked upon as belonging to a race of inferior beings."[12]

Not only were women taking on their husbands' work in addition to their own, they were doing so in the midst of a war that affected every decision— from what to plant, when to sell, and even which currency to use. Women on farms and plantations especially had to carry on the families' livelihoods in the midst of very uncertain futures. Cotton might bring the most profit, but transporting it overland to Brownsville and through Mexico in order to avoid the Union blockade was expensive and risky. Of course, growing enough food, especially corn, to feed the family and any slaves was the priority, but even estimating the amount to plant became challenging in wartime. The Confederate government enacted a tax-in-kind on corn, which subjected up to 10 percent of a corn crop to confiscation. Droughts in 1862 and 1864 exacerbated the difficulty of ensuring enough food. As the Confederate government printed more and more paper money, the value of the currency rapidly decreased, thereby making bartering, bargaining, and transacting business all the more complicated when women did grow excess corn or cotton to sell.[13]

Many women's decisions had to be predicated on available labor as well. Women of slaveholding families had the benefit of having a work force to plant and harvest the crops. During the war, however, the management of slaves became ever more problematic. Because slaves did not have control over or directly benefit from the fruits of their labor, they worked primarily out of fear of punishment. Before the war, when husbands left wives in charge of plantations for short periods, they knew that slaves would continue to work because, although women rarely punished slaves themselves, the entire antebellum culture and community supported the control of slaves, and women could find men to assist in keeping slaves in line. The overall shortage of men during the war made it difficult for women to find male overseers to instill fear into their slaves, and the remaining male neighbors and friends were stretched so thin that the threat of punishment was significantly diminished. Slaves, of course, recognized this and also heard rumors about the Emancipation Proclamation and Union armies that were fighting to free them. Although fewer slaves ran away to Union lines in Texas than elsewhere in the South (mainly because the lines were farther away than elsewhere), the slaves who remained did not work as hard. Slowdowns and work stoppages were common. As Lizzie Neblett lamented to her husband, "The negros are doing nothing. But ours are not doing that job alone. Nearly all the negroes around here are at it, some of them are getting so high in anticipation of their glorious freedom by the Yankees I suppose, that they resist a whipping."[14]

Plantation mistresses found it frustrating trying to force slaves to work, but even non-slaveholding women found themselves frightened. They were surrounded in the community by people being held in bondage but no longer afraid of punishment. Women throughout the South, including Texas, participated in letter-writing campaigns to keep white men in communities not only for their skills but for general protection.[15]

Women in yeoman families with few or no slaves probably envied the difficulties of plantation mistresses. With husbands away, yeomen's wives had to continue farming, very often performing backbreaking work in the fields. Young sons could assist with the plowing, planting, and harvesting of corn, raising hogs, and collecting syrup for molasses to feed the family. By 1864, however, the conscription age was lowered to sixteen, taking more of these young men. When women with family labor shortages barely raised enough to feed themselves and families, they were very resentful of Confederate impressment agents who collected up to 10 percent of their corn and were especially active in parts of North Texas.[16]

As a result, many women with husbands in the army could no longer support themselves or their families. From East Texas to San Antonio to Austin, associations were formed, often by women with more means, to raise money for families of Confederate soldiers who had left "hungry and half clad little ones." These voluntary associations asked for donations and hosted benefits but were unable to meet the needs even early in the war. County governments began relief efforts across the state, and on January 1, 1862, the Texas state legislature enacted a bill allowing counties to collect a tax specifically for war purposes. Both the military and state government continued to attempt to meet the problem by chartering mutual aid societies, selling cloth manufactured at the state penitentiary to needy families, and distributing medicine. Inflation, shortages, and increasing numbers of families in need, however, meant that the aid provided was never enough. Throughout the war, the suffering of families threatened the morale of soldiers and led to violence by women and children, as they organized several seizing parties or bread riots. In 1864, for instance, 125 women and children rode into Sherman in Grayson County armed with guns, axes, sledgehammers, and clubs to demand the coffee, tea, and sugar that was rumored to be stored there.[17]

Women faced difficulties when taking over their husbands' duties of agriculture, food production, and other business during the war, and they also found that their traditional duties of providing food and clothing were much more difficult in wartime. Cloth became nearly impossible to buy and exorbitant in price when available.[18] Women had to clothe and feed their families in the absence of their husbands and also had to provide for the soldiers, and not just those from their own families. Military aid societies constantly asked them to sew and knit extra clothing for soldiers whose families could not provide for them. Women rushed to make extra shirts, jackets, trousers, socks, and underwear for their husbands, fathers, and sons when they joined the army, and then they worked continually to replace those items, which wore out rapidly due to the harshness of army life. Officers' wives particularly labored to clothe their husbands, who were not issued uniforms by the military. Harriet Perry, an elite woman in a much better financial situation than most, wrote her husband: "You must take as good care as you can of your shirts—it is difficult to get cloth at any price—I do not know when I shall get more."[19]

The difficulty of providing clothing derived not just from the shortage of time to devote to making it, although that was a factor. Many women who had become accustomed to purchasing cloth before the war gladly brought the looms and spinning wheels out of the attic to supply their families' needs through homespun. Very often, wealthy women called upon older slave women with home production skills to teach them and other slaves. Home production, however, would prove to be insufficient in keeping up with private, much less public, needs for cloth during the war. Cotton and wool both had been plentiful in antebellum Texas, but the price of cotton in particular soared during the war.[20] Many planters chose not to grow cotton, leading to a shortage that drove up the prices. Those who did grow cotton quickly discovered that, despite the dangers, it was much more profitable to take it to the Mexican border rather than sell it locally—cotton valued at seven cents in Matagorda County would sell for sixty cents in Brownsville. More significantly, however, Texas suffered from a lack of cotton cards, the handheld wooden brushes with metal teeth used to comb the cotton threads before spinning. Few of these combs were manufactured in southern states. Recognizing this shortage, the Texas State Military Board purchased forty thousand cards and distributed them to county governments throughout Texas, but, even so, they remained scarce and expensive.[21]

Without the ability to comb cotton, women could not make the thread and cloth that they needed, and because of the blockade, they could not purchase it. One civilian noted, "People in this country are complaining mightily, and indeed some of them are really frightened at the thought of approaching nakedness."[22] Authorities turned the prison at Huntsville into a cloth factory, and other apparel-manufacturing depots opened, providing jobs for women in some areas. Even so, almost all the cloth was reserved for the clothes, tents, and blankets needed by the army or distributed at low cost to destitute soldiers' families. Those who could afford to meet the rapidly increasing costs of cotton cards, however, could make the purchase pay off. Harriet Perry's extended family (and their slaves) spun and wove as much as fifteen yards of cloth a day, selling it to the army and paying down debts.[23]

Women continued to produce as much cloth and as many other items at home as possible during the war, both for their family at home and to send to male family members in the army. The Union blockade, however, caused shortages of everything, even some basic agricultural products that had been plentiful before the war. Because farmers had used seed potatoes from the North, 1861 was the last crop; sweet potatoes served as a replacement for the duration. Texas was more fortunate than most other southern states in producing some sugar, but there was not nearly enough to provide for the demand, and women turned to harvesting sorghum and honey for sweeteners. Women tried replacing coffee beans with sweet potatoes, corn, beans, okra, and varieties of seeds, none of which made beverages that tasted very good. In the state that would come to be renowned for its cattle, leather was almost impossible to find by 1863, leading to a severe shortage of shoes.[24]

Texas women dealt with shortages and extra work as best they could and with varying degrees of success, based mostly upon financial situation but also upon temperament. However, they also had to worry about the war coming to them and disrupting their homes. In July 1861, the Union war steamer *South Carolina* arrived off the coast of Galveston and began a blockade of that town. The minutes of the First Baptist Church of Galveston reflected that this prompted many families to flee inland, including the pastor of the church, causing the church to close for the rest of the war. Many other families chose to remain even after Union forces took and occupied the island in October 1862. In January 1863, the "booming of cannon" disturbed a quiet morning as Confederates began an assault that would regain the island. Teenager Cecilia Labadie recorded in her diary the scene, with "women and children flying every which way."[25] Corpus Christi resident Maria von Blücher described the hardships when battles were fought nearby. When Union ships prepared to bombard the city, residents packed up and migrated in haste: "For 4–5 miles along the wayside, one saw one household after another loaded up." Her home was not damaged by the bombardment, but the danger was very real, as she reported to her parents: "In our yard the children found a shell 13 inches long, a similar one 10 inches long weighing 26 pounds, and one of 24 pounds, 9 inches long, all of them unexploded."[26] Indianola, on Matagorda Bay, was one of the few towns in Texas occupied by Union troops, and Eudora Moore, who was a child during the war, later remembered soldiers searching her home: "I heard them coming up the stairs and had the fright of my life." Although the family escaped any violence, the presence of the army led to sporadic harassment, such as raids on chicken houses. Moore's mother, like other women in occupied areas, had extra work when Union soldiers became boarders in her home during the occupation.[27]

Unlike the women of coastal Texas and unlike the women of other southern states, the vast majority of Texas women did not have invading armies in their midst or attacking navies nearby. However, they did not know whether they would be spared that calamity, and the fear of battles and occupation worried them. After a thunderstorm, Lizzie Neblett wrote to her husband, "Last night . . . I found myself sitting bolt upright in bed, listening with terror to what I thought at the moment was the noise and roar of cannon."[28]

In addition to all the other decisions that women had to make without their husbands' input, women had to plan for what to do should Union armies invade. The dangers of invading armies were not just imaginary. Most women had relatives or friends in southeastern states that did come within Union lines, and thus they heard stories of southerners fleeing their homes in advance of Union troops and moving slaves to prevent their emancipation. They heard about those who stayed in areas occupied by Union or Confederate armies and the constant drain on resources. East Texas served as a haven for many slaveholders fleeing Union armies as they occupied states to the east. Newspapers and mail also brought repeated rumors of invasions; Perry heard that there was "a fleet of Gunboats at the mouth of the Red river, some say 40 some 20—no one seems to doubt it." What to do should Union troops arrive remained a constant worry for these Texas women. Perry's mother-in-law responded to rumors of invasion by "talking strongly of packing up and moving off to a place of safety," but Perry worried, "I know not where we will find that. I wish there was such a place."[29]

Figure 4.1. Ambrotype of Anderson County resident Josie Scott holding a portrait of husband, Lieutenant John G. Scott, CSA. Early forms of photography became very popular during the Civil War as families craved likenesses of missing family members. Courtesy of DeGolyer Library, Southern Methodist University, Dallas.

Above all, however, the greatest burden for most Texas women during the war was the separation from loved ones in the army and constant worry about their safety. As Perry wrote to her husband, "This separation from you is almost insupportable, but should you never come, oh what will become of me."[30] Reports of casualties made their way back to Texas via mail and newspapers, although they were often incomplete or erroneous. Women were thus relieved at the receipt of every letter from soldier family members, especially their husbands—evidence that they were still alive, and wives chastised their spouses for long periods without letters. Men usually found time in the boredom and drudgery of camp to write home regularly (even though the delivery of mail was irregular). On the other hand, women often found themselves very short of time to write husbands, with the result that it was soldiers who often begged for longer and more frequent letters from home.[31]

While many couples attempted to continue to maintain their emotional attachment with letters, the medium was far from satisfactory for even the most loving of couples. Perry especially craved her husband's presence during her pregnancy: "I have looked and wished for you till I am worn out and heart-sick."[32] Though her husband could not get a furlough from the army to be home when she delivered the baby, like most soldiers he did occasionally gain permission to return home. As a result, women continued to get pregnant and worried about getting pregnant while their husbands were at war. For women like Lizzie Neblett, who struggled with the difficulties of being a mother even before her husband enlisted, this led couples to openly discuss methods of family limitation and birth control. Yet even Harriet Perry, a woman who relished being a mother, was relieved when she found after a husband's furlough that she was not facing another pregnancy and childbirth without her husband's presence.[33]

Separation and anxiety strained many marriages, even happy ones. Relationships that were not strong from the beginning faced even more difficult times. Henry F. C. Johnson confessed in an early letter to his wife Delilah that "I think often of you but we have talked so often about separating that I think provadance has provided a way for our separating." Two years later, the marriage did not appear stronger, as he wrote to her, "It don't appear like I have any friend to advise you or that you have any judgement when you are left to govern business. . . . I never want . . . you to write to me any more if you cant give me more satisfaction than you have. I am left to consider that I am broke up. You have rendered me vary unhappy."[34]

While Delilah and Henry Johnson's marriage barely survived to the end of the war, many relationships did not. At the onset of the war, many young women, fearing lives as spinsters, rushed into hasty marriages with young soldiers before they marched to war. For most, building a marriage via letters and the occasional furlough proved to be more difficult than maintaining an existing marriage. The absence of spouses and the tensions of wartime drove some women to find solace in the arms of other men. In fact, for some women, the absence of their husbands proved to be such a welcome relief that they would not welcome them home at the end of the war. Despite the fact that many district courts closed during the war, filings of divorce petitions did not slow.[35]

The war challenged nearly every expectation of southern white women. Their husbands and other men were often absent and unable to provide protection, they had to act often as heads of households in agriculture and other business, and they were deprived of husbands' love and affection.

Slave Women

The four years of war altered slave women's lives as much as those of free women. As a whole, the conflict disrupted the system of slavery less in Texas than in other southern states. Because the battles and occupation generally did not come very close to the state, fewer slaves found the opportunity to run to Union lines, although many did so or escaped to Mexico. Slave rebelliousness exhibited itself in different forms, primarily in work slowdowns and refusal to obey orders. With the shortage of white men on farms and plantations as well as in the communities, the rules and discipline of the antebellum era were impossible to enforce, as noted above. Even with the slight loosening of strict slave codes of conduct, most slave women worked just as hard through the war under more strenuous circumstances.

Three-quarters of the white men who fought in the Confederate army volunteered to do so, making the decision—often with the support and encouragement of their female family members—to disrupt their families and endure separations. The war also distressed slave families but rarely voluntarily. An elite man often would take a slave with him into the army as a personal servant. The wives and loved ones of men taken to war in this manner worried just as much about their safety as those with loved ones who had volunteered. Slave couples, however, could very rarely correspond with each other through the war because most slaves had not been allowed to learn how to read and write. Their contact with each other came primarily through the correspondence of their white masters and mistresses. One of the incredibly rare letters written by a slave woman to her husband expresses the same amount of fear and sorrow at their separation as expressed in the letters of free women. Fannie wrote to her husband, Norflet, "My love is just as great as it was the first night I married you, and I hope it will be so with you. . . . If I never see you again, I hope to meet you in heaven. There is no time night or day but what I am studying about you."[36]

Other slave men were separated from their families when the Confederate government began impressing some slaves in August 1863 to work on fortifications and perform other manual labor for the army, to free up more soldiers to fight. By early December 1863, the Confederate army issued orders making all able-bodied male slaves, except one per master, subject to impressment. Masters and mistresses usually fought impressment as much as they could, because of the extreme danger to the slaves. These slaves were pressed into service anyway and sent to other parts of the state for lengths of time, leaving behind family members. Sometimes they never saw their families again. Philles Thomas from Brazoria County told an interviewer, "I can't 'member my daddy, but mammy told me him am sent to de 'Federate Army and am kilt in Galveston. She say dey puttin' up breastworks and de Yanks am shootin' from de ships. Well, daddy am watchin' de balls comin' from dem guns, fallin' round dere, and a car come down de track loaded with rocks and hit him. Dat car kilt him."[37]

As in the antebellum period, the most dangerous period in the life of a slave family was at the death of their master. Probate courts divided the property of a decedent among the heirs, based upon value. In other words, the courts were more interested in making sure each recipient received an equal portion of the estate than in keeping slave families together. As a result, members of slave families often found themselves assigned to heirs of their deceased master who lived great distances from one another. During the war, the death rate of slave owners multiplied as they fought in the army, leading to more frequent redistributions of slave family members. Julia Francis Daniels remembered the uncertainty and fear at such an occasion: "Old Man Denman's boy gits kilt and two my sisters he property and they don't know what to do, 'cause they has be somebody's property and they ain't no one to 'heritance 'em. They has to go to the auction." Widows who inherited slaves often chose not to run the farms or plantations in the uncertainty of the war and "hired out"—or leased—their slaves to others instead. So a slave couple lucky enough to remain the property of the widow could still find themselves living in separate locations after being hired out to different farmers. [38]

The decrease in the number of slave men during the war left more work for the slave women to do. The gendered division of labor among slaves became even more blurred, as slave women not only had to do more work but also had to take up much of the men's work, such as plowing the fields. Those slave women who had skills spinning, weaving, or sewing, however, probably worked the hardest and longest of their lives during the war. The slaves in the Perry household spun from early in the morning until late into the night and produced yards and yards of cloth for the white family to use and sell to the army. Harriet Perry was quite proud that she made one of her slaves, Mary Ann, begin spinning every day immediately after waking before dawn. As a result, Mary Ann got as much spinning done as any other woman on the place and Perry was "determined she shall not get less."[39]

Extra labor that men left behind and the extra chores of cloth production were added to slave women's responsibilities as mothers. In the frequent absence of husbands, slave women had the exclusive care of their children, and, also like free white women, black women continued to give birth and care for infants during the war. The care of the family became more difficult, not only because of the extra work and lack of time, but also because of shortages due to the war. While Texans endured fewer major food shortages than southerners in other states, shortages of any kind affected slaves the most. The choicest foods were saved for soldiers, if possible, but otherwise the best food went to the white family. When there was a shortage, such as resulted from the droughts of 1862 and 1864, crop impressment, or poor planning, slaves were the first to have their rations cut. Further, the extra work that slave women took up during the war made it more difficult for them to cultivate their own gardens. Thus slave women had to stretch less food farther.

While Texas slave women had their lives significantly disrupted by the war, another group of slaves arrived in Texas. Refugees from other southern states often relocated to Texas, especially for the purpose of bringing their slaves to keep them from escaping to Union lines or from being freed when Union armies occupied their areas. The slave women who relocated faced the enormous burdens of packing and traveling long distances in a very short period. Upon arrival, masters bought or leased land and put the slaves to work;

women and men alike had to perform the labor necessary to start a new farm or plantation. Ella Washington remembered the difficulty of moving from Louisiana to Calvert, Texas, during the war, "Time dey ready for freedom in Louisiana, dey refugees us to Texas, in de wagons. Us travel all day and half de night and sleep on de ground. It ain't take us so long to git to Calvert, out dere in de bottom of Texas, and dey puts us on de Barton plantation." These slave women also endured separations from loved ones. Husbands and wives on different plantations faced the real possibility of never seeing one another when one master moved to Texas and the other did not. Women were torn from their extended networks and communities, sometimes losing touch with parents, siblings, and even children.[40]

Figure 4.2. Counties that voted against secession were located mainly in Central and North Texas.

Other Texans

The majority of the state's residents in 1861 lived in East Texas, which had adopted the antebellum southern culture. This majority and region had led the way to secession and experienced the Civil War much like southerners in other states. However, Texas was geographically different from other states. A border with a foreign country (Mexico), a very strong contingent of Native Americans and Tejanos, and a large colony of Germans created areas that experienced the Civil War in unique ways.

Germans in East Texas generally adopted and fit well into southern antebellum culture, but the large communities of Germans to the west in Central Texas, between American settlements and Native Americans, were more likely to maintain their German ideas and customs. Many Germans supported secession but more objected because they valued the protection of Union troops, and others were pro-Union out of conviction. Ten counties in Central Texas where Germans were the majority or significant portion of the population voted against secession in 1861. When Germans in the Hill Country organized the Union Loyal League to provide the protection missing because of the withdrawal of Union troops, Confederate forces moved to disband them. Sixty-one members of the Union Loyal League refused to disperse and tried to flee to Mexico to join the Union army, but they were captured and killed near the Nueces River.[41]

German women, therefore, had to endure many of the same hardships as the Confederate white women in East Texas: scarcity, fear, and additional hard work with husbands absent in the war or killed. However, because many German men joined the Union army, getting word or mail from them was even more difficult. Mathilda Wagner's uncle was jailed for his pro-Union opinions, and when he escaped from prison to Mexico, his wife did not hear from him or know whether she would ever see him again. While he was gone, his wife "had to take care of all the children and herself all alone." Whether family members joined the Union or not, women fought harassment by Confederate civilians and officials alike. Wagner later remembered that "the people who sympathized with the North during the Civil War had to hide out and sleep in the bushes at night to prevent being killed." With the passage of Confederate conscription, many more German men left or hid to avoid being drafted into the Confederate army. Women who protected these men lived in constant fear of attacks by Confederates and had to perform extra work, not only to make up for their absence but also to find ways of getting food and supplies to their men in hiding. One man, who had sneaked back to take water to his pregnant wife every morning, was murdered by Confederate guerrillas who had learned of his habits and met him at the spring.[42]

Of course, Germans were not the only ones to have Unionist loyalties. A handful of North Texas counties located near the frontier had also opposed secession, and families there faced the same harassment and suspicions. Fear of the growing power of a "Peace Party" in Cooke County led to hundreds of arrests and the vigilante hangings of forty-two men suspected of having Union sympathies, the largest incident of vigilante justice in US history. No women were put to death, but they suffered mightily during the hysteria and executions. An extralegal "Citizens Court" was convened in Gainesville to determine who should be hanged, and Confederate women were offended and frightened when it uncovered that a shoemaker named Henry S. Field had applauded Major General Benjamin F. Butler's order to treat as prostitutes any Confederate women in New Orleans publicly demonstrating contempt for Union soldiers. Women related to men accused of Union sympathies, however, had much more to fear. On the day of arrests in Gainesville, "screaming women and children" streamed into town, and at least two men escaped arrest by fleeing to Arkansas, leaving their wives behind to face a distrustful community alone. Widow Elizabeth Woolsey successfully pleaded for and received the release of two of her sons after pointing out that she had two others serving in the Confederate army. Other women were not so lucky, and many of the men marked for death made out their wills. Jacob Dye wrote out his last will and testament leaving everything to wife Mary Ann and his three children.[43] After initial executions, "an order passed that women should not be permitted to be present at the hanging. The women were not noisy, but the signs of deep despair was manifested by the heaving breast, the falling tears, the heavy groans as though the heart was breaking, and all the vitals of life were giving way." Thomas Barrett, who was a member of the Citizens Court but who protested the hangings, wrote a memoir in which he lamented that the first fourteen killed "were the heads of families. The sun set that night on fourteen widowed families, and thirteen families of orphans, for if I recollect right, all these men had children but one."[44]

Both the North Texas and Central Texas counties with strong pro-Union sympathies were frontier areas with more to fear from Native Americans than from Union armies. When Texas seceded, state military forces took over forts and other federal property, driving the Union forces out. Once the war began, however, Confederate military forces concentrated on defeating the Union, thus leaving small, often ineffective armies to defend the forts along the frontier of West Texas. Comanches, who had been pushed westward due to white encroachment on their lands, saw an opportunity to strike back and assaulted white families on farms and ranches. Small raids and the threat of attacks kept the people on the frontier terrified. In December 1863, three hundred Comanches raided and killed a dozen people in Montague and Cooke Counties, stealing horses, burning houses, and capturing several women. In October 1864, five hundred Comanches and Kiowas attacked homes, farms, and ranches along Elm Creek in Young County, taking seven more women and children.[45]

Not only were military forces insufficient to repel such attacks, according to one memoir, "We had no rangers or soldiers on the frontier as there was an acute shortage of manpower in the Confederacy in the last years of the War." The men from these families located at great distances from one another were often serving in the armies. The distance and isolation increased as settlers abandoned their homes to move east to safety. Sarah Hall of San Saba County later remembered that "our dear old neighbor became very much dissatisfied with the depredating Indians and moved to Bell County. Oh, such grief it gave us to see them depart. That left one neighbor five miles above us and one five miles below, and Father so poorly." After the attack at Elm Creek, many women and children on the frontier left their homes for extended periods, moving east or moving into fortified stockades with other families—"forting up."[46]

Women in South Texas and along the Mexican border also missed the protection of Union troops when Confederate troops were too thin to protect them from threats there. In addition to the fear of Native Americans, warring across the border that had begun between Texans and Mexicans before the Civil War continued. The profitability of transporting cotton through South Texas and over the border also led to increased violence as freighters competed with each other and outlaws tried to avoid Confederate regulations and impressments.

Although Anglos had been successful at wresting control of much of the land in South Texas, the majority there were Mexican or Tejano. Like the Anglo women, Tejanas had to fend for themselves and provide for their families when their husbands, fathers, sons, and brothers were absent, and during the course of the war there were many reasons for Tejano men to be away. Most Tejanos and Mexicans preferred to stay out of the fight between the warring Americans, but roughly 3,400 did join one side or the other; 958 were said to have been recruited into the Union army, while approximately 2,500 from the Rio Grande Valley, the Nueces Valley, and San Antonio enlisted in the Confederate army. Many men voluntarily joined up to protect their families in the isolated portions of frontier South Texas.[47] After the Confederate conscription act was passed, the Texas government sanctioned a vigorous campaign to draft Tejanos "into the army and in some instances treated [them] more like animals than soldiers of the Southland." Many Tejanos fled across the Mexican border in order to escape; guards even surrounded the town of Brownsville to keep eligible men from fleeing. Those who did escape often had to move quickly, leaving families in Texas to follow them south or fend for themselves. Many Tejanos also saw the war as an opportunity to participate in the freighting of cotton through Texas and into Mexico. Border and coastal towns experienced a booming economy because of the trade, and many men took advantage of labor opportunities to make money.[48]

For all these reasons, women and children often found themselves alone or with few men on isolated ranches and farms. Bandits, thieves, and outlaws took advantage of these situations, often terrifying the civilians in an area. Juan Cortina, a Mexican who had carried on a private war against the Texans in the valley, continued to be a problem and threat at the beginning of the war. By 1864, Cortina had been appointed a general in the Mexican army and primarily harassed Confederate forces, but the raiding and feuding across the border still led to sporadic violence against civilians. Large ranches, such as the Santa Anita, often faced the problem by hiring private protection forces, including a private magistrate to enforce laws.[49] The border violence became so prevalent that many who could leave Texas did so. Most sought safety in Mexico, but some who could afford it went elsewhere. The merchant John McAllen stayed in Brownsville, but he moved his wife Salomé and their children to a home she owned in Brooklyn, New York.[50]

The cotton trade in South Texas provided merchants and others with astounding economic opportunities. The demand for war supplies enabled more Tejanos to get higher-paying jobs in towns than before the war and to make more money freighting goods to and from Mexico, but there were fewer employment and economic opportunities for women. The economic boom led to soaring inflation, and poor people, including women and children without male providers, suffered the worst. In San Antonio a mutual aid society was founded in 1863 to help provide food to the poor at a low cost by purchasing it directly from merchants in Mexico.[51]

The ambivalence of most Tejanos toward the war, the widespread dislike of slavery by Mexicans before the war, the presence of Mexico as a haven for runaway slaves, and the attacks on Confederate forces by Mexican soldiers and civilians all combined to increase Confederate suspicions of all those of Mexican descent in the state. As a result, Tejanas feared the same kind of attacks and harassments by Confederate guerrillas that German women encountered in Central Texas. Additionally, however, they faced severe racism that had grown during the antebellum period and was fueled by the war. In the middle of the Civil War, a Tejana in San Patricio County became the victim of violence not by bandits or guerrillas but by the state. Chipita Rodriguez became the only woman hanged in Texas history after being convicted in 1863 of murdering a white man, despite the fact that most people in the area were certain of her innocence. (In fact, a man confessed to the murder on his deathbed twenty-five years later.)[52]

Ursuline sisters in Galveston and San Antonio had no interest in taking sides in the war and worried primarily about their safety and sustenance. Sister St. Marie Trouard of San Antonio even considered flying a French flag over the convent since most of the sisters were French. During the fighting in Galveston in January 1863, the Ursuline sisters nursed the wounded of both sides. They dealt with the horrors and bloodshed of the fighting directly, and the floors of their convent became stained with blood. The convent even came under fire until a yellow flag could be found to indicate it was a hospital and not a building used for military purposes.[53]

Women's experiences of the Civil War varied across the state, based upon race, ethnicity, and location. While some women faced increased violence and fear of personal safety, nearly all faced the probability of losing someone they loved as a result of the war. These losses, both in war and in the violence of the home front, fostered situations where more women than ever before had to take on the duties that had previously been considered appropriate only to men.

Reconstruction

At the conclusion of the war, some Confederate women were embittered and urged their men to continue fighting despite the defeat of the armies. However, most women were merely exhausted. Between the disruptions of war and the extra work that women had needed to do in men's absence, most women who had husbands and sons to welcome home usually did so gladly. The fact that women had been able to run households, farms, and businesses without the assistance of men during the war did not immediately lead to changes in attitudes about women's proper place. Instead, most white women tried to help white men reinstitute as much of the prewar social order as possible in the face of the most important change the war had wrought: freedom for the slaves. Slave women, on the other hand, anxiously worked to change the postwar social order to claim a place of equality, perhaps not with men but definitely with white women.

A white woman's place in society before the war had depended in large part upon her family's class position, but within the household she was supposed to be submissive to her husband and defer to him in matters of business and politics. In return, she was to receive his protection and affection. During the war, with so many men far away, women learned to protect themselves as well as make business decisions. Women had not participated directly in governance, but the press and society had welcomed a much greater role for women in the political process. During the period when the rebellious state governments were being "reconstructed" politically and brought back into the Union, some people in Texas believed that women's political role should be increased. In 1868, the state elected delegates to a convention to draw up a constitution that would be acceptable to the US Congress, thus allowing Texas to be reinstated to the Union (reconstructed). Besides recognizing the end of slavery, this constitution had to redefine voting rights without reference to race. One delegate to the convention, however, believed that not only should men of all races be allowed to vote but that women should have that right as well. On July 8, 1868, Titus H. Mundine of Burleson County proposed an amendment stating that "every person, without distinction of sex . . . shall be entitled to vote at any election created by this constitution." The convention eventually rejected the amendment by a margin of fifty-two to thirteen. However, that thirteen male delegates supported women's right to vote signified changes wrought by the war.[54]

It does not appear that any women openly supported or encouraged this amendment in 1868, and only one Texas woman wrote a petition in support of suffrage during the 1875 constitutional convention that marked the end of Reconstruction. While the Civil War may have demonstrated that women had appropriate abilities to participate in their own governance, most women, it seemed, were not interested in expanding their rights and duties at that time.[55]

Four years were not enough to cause a sea change in attitudes about women's rights and roles in society. White women who had gained prestige and power by virtue of being free in a slave society also had to deal with the effect of the emancipation of slaves on their status and their lives. Like their husbands and fathers, they hoped to reinstitute the old social structure as much as possible, which would keep former slaves at the bottom of society and themselves above them. Additionally, women were exhausted by four years of war, and most of those who had men return from the war were glad to turn over that significant portion of the work. Married women in Reconstruction were much less likely to act independently in business matters than they had during the war, and the courts were not willing to recognize the legality of those who did.[56]

Some women did have trouble coping with men who returned. Whether the men were changed by the war emotionally and physically or women had grown more confident and less willing to submit to bad marriages, separations and divorce rates climbed slightly after the war. In addition to the small number of women ending marriages, thousands of women were widowed as a result of the war. In many ways, the role of the widow did not change because of the war; women simply took on independent roles only because there were no longer men in their lives to whom to be submissive. The large number of these women in Reconstruction did create the basis for potential change. For instance, the number of women with jobs outside the family farm grew. The shortage of male teachers during the war had increased the need for women to take those positions, and women continued to engage in this profession after the war. Women also took jobs as milliners, ran hotels and boardinghouses, and even managed stores in much greater numbers. And widows, as before the war, continued running farms and plantations after their husbands died.[57]

Running plantations in the absence of their husbands—and even running households—changed dramatically during Reconstruction. Of all the changes wrought by the Civil War, the most permanent and enduring was the legal emancipation of slaves. For elite white women, especially, this required tremendous adjustments. Within the household, it became very difficult to find servants who were willing to do the amount of work for the small amount of pay that families were willing to provide. Ellen Lacy's difficulty in adjusting to the servant shortage was so significant that the details found their way into her divorce petition. According to this elite woman in Columbus, "the negro servant hitherto on the place having left," Lacy had to cook breakfast and "neither accustomed, nor used to it, was forced to servile labor." Her husband was not impressed with her attempts but "came into the kitchen very drunk, and commenced cursing and abusing said Ellen Lacy . . . and ridiculed her effort at cooking." Like Lacy, many white women found themselves performing unaccustomed "servile labor" such as cooking, cleaning, and tending to their own children.[58]

Many elite white women took up servile toil, and all white women lost their superior social status as a result of the ending of slavery. For these reasons, white women were as eager as white men to reestablish the prior social order that kept African Americans in the lowest and most subservient positions. Justifying this, however, did mean that women had to accept the ideas about natural places in society, including female submissiveness to men. African American women's lives, however, were the most altered during Reconstruction, and they worked to challenge ideas about black inferiority so that they could truly partake of their freedom.

Black Women and Freedom

The Emancipation Proclamation had been issued in 1863, and this presidential decree had promised that all slaves in areas in rebellion against the Union government would be "henceforth and forever free." It required Union armies occupying and taking over those rebellious areas to enforce the proclamation. With only a few coastal towns in Union control, very few slaves in Texas found their freedom during the war. After the surrender of Confederate forces, Union troops occupied the state, and General Gordon Granger read General Order Number 3, declaring over 240,000 slaves in Texas free on June 19, 1865, a day that came to be celebrated as Juneteenth. Some slaveholders refused to accept the decree and continued to hold people for months (sometimes for years) as virtual hostages by force or by keeping their emancipation secret from them. Millie Ann Smith of Rusk County did not know she was free until, "Mos' onto four year after the war, three men comes to Massa George and makes him call us up and turn us loose. I heered 'em say its close onto four year we's been free, but that's the first we knowed 'bout it."[59] While some former slaves interviewed by the Works Progress Administration writers during the Great Depression remembered the news of freedom as a moment of confusion and uncertainty, for others it was a moment of rejoicing. When a man rode up to Aunt Pinkie Kelly's farm in Brazoria and informed her master "You can't work these people, without no pay, 'cause they's as free as you is," she remembered, "Law, we sho' shout, young folks and old folks too."[60]

Nearly all formerly enslaved women began their lives of freedom with nothing at all—any property they might have accumulated during slavery belonged to the master, and very few masters gave their former slaves anything. Freedom, however, did give them the right to make decisions, and women began doing that nearly immediately. Upon emancipation, some of the bitterest whites drove all former slaves from their property, but most former masters often offered wages to the freedpeople who were willing to stay. Many women did indeed remain and work for their former owners. Some stayed for a time—until the end of the year or even through the next year— because they did not know what other options might be out there. As Aunt

Figure 4.3. Aunt Nan, a former slave in Tarrant County, remained with her former mistress, Mrs. Benjamin Franklin Barkley, after emancipation, serving as a cook. Courtesy of Tarrant County College District Archives, Fort Worth, Texas.

Pinkie Kelly said, "But we stay there, no place to go, so we jes' stay, but we gits a little pay." Some stayed with their former masters for years because they had been treated well by the family, because they had grown up on that farm or plantation and in that area, and because they believed it was their home as well.[61]

Other freedwomen chose to leave. In some cases they knew where they could get better treatment or better wages. In many cases, even if their former masters had treated them well, they knew they would never feel truly free working for those who had once held them as property. And many, of course, quickly left mean and cruel families. Many chose not to work for their former masters—or for anyone else—because to them freedom meant the choice of working exclusively for their own family, as most white women did. Given that plantations no longer provided collective care for children and the elderly, individual families had to care for their own and make their own clothes and produce food; women were needed at home to a greater extent than they had been during the days of slave quarters. Women with husbands who were earning wages, therefore, could and did make this choice. Freedpeople also wished to exercise their freedom by sending their children to school rather than to the fields, and mothers might sacrifice significantly to make that possible.[62]

The large number of formerly enslaved women and children who no longer worked in the fields caused a labor shortage in Texas and much consternation among whites. Editorials in newspapers suggested encouraging European immigration, especially German, to make up for the deficiency. Most whites, however, were determined to drive black women and children back to the fields, for both economic and social reasons—southern whites could not accept blacks as equals and were determined to keep African Americans as the lowest social caste even in freedom. The Texas legislature passed a series of "black codes" aimed at preventing freedpeople from exercising equal rights, including a vagrancy statute. This statute allowed officials to arrest as a vagrant any person who refused to sign or fulfill his or her labor contract. Local governments, including cities and counties, passed further ordinances allowing for the arrest of vagrants and then forcing them to work to pay for jail time and fines. This made it impossible for black women who dedicated their work to their families to leave their homes or else they would be arrested and fined; authorities never applied the statute to white women.[63]

Partially due to the black codes of Texas and other southern states, the US Congress insisted that state governments be restructured and that blacks be granted equal rights. As Texas Reconstruction governments removed the discriminatory laws, disenfranchised whites turned to extralegal means and violence to keep blacks from gaining economic and social power. Individual vigilantes and organizations such as the Ku Klux Klan terrorized, beat, and killed whites who sold land to blacks as well as those who bought the land. Citizens attacked black women on the streets who seemed to be acting like white women (for instance, by wearing sunbonnets or walking in town in the middle of the day instead of working in the fields). Freedmen's schools became frequent targets of organized violence as whites tried to shut them down and force children back to work. Clarissa Scales described one such attempt: "Dere was a school after freedom. Old Man Tilden was de teacher. One time a bunch of men day calls de Klu Klux come in de room and say, 'You git out of here and git 'way from dem niggers. Don' let us cotch you here when we comes back.'" Local authorities did little to stop this violence, and even Union troops and the Freedmen's Bureau (the congressionally in-stituted organization to help blacks and whites adapt to emancipation) toler-ated violence against black women. Women reported hundreds of incidents to the Bureau, but officials often failed to follow up and punish those who perpetrated acts against black women such as rapes, assaults, and, most com-monly, whippings.[64]

The threat of violence, as well as economic necessity, drove women (and children) back to work in large numbers. Yet women, especially, resisted the old plantation regime where they had worked in gangs under the watch of a white supervisor or master. Of all the violence directed at blacks during Reconstruction, the violence directed against women was most often sexu-alized. Rape presented an opportunity to force women to accept an inferior status, but it also showed the men in her family how impotent and inferior they were because they could not stop it. Being forced to answer to an over-seer put women in sexually vulnerable positions. Their reluctance to work in gangs, the propensity of overseers to continue using the whip to increase the work, and the inability of whites to pay wages during the economically ravaged period after the war all resulted in the rise of sharecropping. In these labor contracts, a family agreed to work a parcel of land and split the cotton raised on the land with the owner (the value of the split varied according to the quantity of tools and supplies the sharecroppers brought). The male head of household signed the contract on behalf of the entire family and directed the labor in the production of the crop; only when there was no husband would a woman sign the contract on behalf of her family.[65]

Sharecropping allowed families to allocate their labor throughout the year without the interference of white overseers. As a result, more women and children worked in the fields (much to the relief of whites worried about the economy), but they could choose to do so just in peak times while otherwise taking care of household matters or attending school. Sharecropping led to other significant problems, however, as many freedpeople were cheated out of their wages, families had to borrow money for food and supplies (often from the landowners at inflated prices) until the crop came in, and cotton prices declined because of overproduction. As a result, sharecroppers often ended the year owing more than their cotton was worth and were forced to sign another year's contract with the same landowner.[66]

Many women, married or not, did choose to work as household servants rather than in the fields. Women generally received better pay for skilled household labor such as cooking, cleaning, making clothes, and laundering. However, the old habits of slavery died hard, and white families often expected live-in servants, on call twenty-four hours a day, who could be directed to any type of labor at all. Freedwomen, on the other hand, most often insisted on set hours, set tasks, and leaving at the end of the day to live with and take care of their own families. The benefits of freedom became obvious when women left abusive employers or those who simply required them to perform more than they believed they should. While most searched for better domestic employment situations, a few women entered professions, becoming teachers, nurses, dressmakers, and businesswomen.[67]

Despite economic difficulties and widespread violence, freedom did give former slaves another opportunity that they joyfully and quickly embraced—the opportunity to make and keep their families together. It took the Texas legislature nearly four years after emancipation to finally recognize the marriages formed during slavery and grant African Americans the right to marry on the same basis as whites. Freedpeople were not nearly as slow as the government to recognize and reunite their families. Husbands and wives who had lived on separate plantations as slaves could now live in one household and gather their children together with them.[68]

Some of the prominent aspects of slavery, however, created difficulties in reuniting families. One reason that some freedwomen had left their residences immediately upon emancipation had been to go in search of family members, especially children, from whom they had been separated by sale or relocation. The Freedmen's Bureau fielded constant requests for assistance in finding family members. Women particularly worked hard to find lost children and often beseeched the bureau to assist in the return of children detained by former masters. Children such as Lou Turner, who did not know her mother because she had been kept by the white family, did not want to leave even when authorities intervened. "After de trouble my mammy have gettin' me 'way from there when freedome time come, she gits me after all. Old missy have seven li'l nigger chillen what belong to her slaves, but dey mammies and daddys come git 'em. I didn't own my own mammy. I own my old missy and call her 'mama.' Us cry and cry when us have to go with us mammy."[69]

Within the slave communities, when husbands and wives had been separated by sale, it had been acceptable for the parties to remarry. Upon emancipation, some men sought out and found their wives, only to find they had remarried. Women then faced difficult decisions on which of their marriages to recognize. Regardless of the difficulties, during Reconstruction the vast majority of women did marry and live with their husbands in nuclear family units—a freedom often denied to them in slavery.[70]

Violence, terror, and discriminatory laws and practices continued to subjugate African American women in Texas during Reconstruction. Freedom, however, finally provided opportunities for women to make decisions for themselves or in conjunction with their husbands for the benefit of their families.

Conclusion

Texas women of all classes, races, and ethnicities faced tremendous changes during the four years of the American Civil War. Fear of violence, economic hardship, separation from family, and the shortage of men all forced them into new roles and responsibilities. Elite white women found it difficult to maintain the wealth and households that had given them elevated social status, while other white women struggled to clothe and feed themselves and their families. Some black women, still held in slavery during the war, sensed impending freedom and participated in work slowdowns and other insubordination. Other black women, however, had to work harder than ever to compensate for the absence of men and the presence of economic problems while suffering increased separations from husbands and families.

While white women in East Texas struggled to preserve their prewar southern society, women in the rest of the state suffered more direct threats to their homes and lives. Frontier households in North, Central, and South Texas confronted many forms of violence and threats, from Native Americans to vigilantes to warring factions along the border to Confederate forces who questioned their loyalties. Many Tejanas and German women coped with their men being drafted into a war that they did not support while facing hostile communities.

After the war, white women of East Texas worked to reestablish their southern society despite the havoc caused to the economy and despite the elimination of slavery, which had guaranteed their superior social status before the war. African American women embraced emancipation in myriad ways, working to reunite their families and find means to support their families while maintaining autonomy that would give their freedom meaning.

Chapter 5

Making West Texas

Nowhere has the mythic narrative of the lone man fighting valiantly against foes and taming the frontier taken stronger root than in nineteenth-century West and South Texas. Both Americans and Texans have celebrated the iconic cowboy riding the range, driving cattle, and defending himself against animals, outlaws, and Native Americans. Yet at no point did that cowboy inhabit the area alone. The number of Native American women equaled the number of Native American men. US Army soldiers stationed throughout Texas to protect the Anglo settlements that were encroaching on Indian lands brought wives and children. Men moving onto the West and South Texas land to start farms and ranches most often brought their families. While it is true that the number of men exceeded the number of women in nineteenth-century West Texas, at no point was there a complete absence of them.

Instead women bravely faced the challenges, excitement, and opportunities of a landscape far different from that of the Eastern Seaboard or even of East Texas. Native American women enabled the growth of the buffalo hide trade and continued to uphold social practices that valued women's status despite the changes that horses caused. Army wives at their outposts created communities quite different from their eastern homes but reminiscent of them. They created entertainment, celebrated holidays, practiced religion, and cared for their families in adverse conditions while maintaining ideas of rank and class that mirrored army ranks and evoked ideas of social status. Women on ranches worked around the clock to raise children while preparing food for their families and ranch hands; hauling water long distances; making, mending, and washing clothing; and fighting the elements and prevalent violence. In South Texas, Tejanas also preserved their cultural ideals and practices, creating a multicultural society as Anglo men and women seized land and political institutions around them.

In the nineteenth and early twentieth centuries, the West tested the mettle of men and women alike. The courage and determination of Tejana and Anglo women enabled the growth and the settlement of West and South Texas, changing the lives of Native American women by pushing them out of the state forever.

Native Americans

By the time Anglo immigration to Texas under Mexican rule began legally in 1821, the power, political structures, and society of Native Americans had already transformed due to the presence of Europeans—Spanish, English, and French. Droughts, European diseases, and warfare with the Apaches, who raided southern peoples to acquire horses and goods, caused the decline of some Native American societies. By the eighteenth century, the Apaches or the Spanish had absorbed most Jumanos and Coahuiltecans. Even the Caddos, the most powerful Indian nation in East Texas, faced numerous pressures in the eighteenth and early nineteenth centuries; Osage attacks from the north pushed the Caddos south, while Choctaws, Chickasaws, Cherokees, Alabama-Coushattas (Creeks), Delawares, Shawnees, Kickapoos, Pottawatomies, and Quapaws, whom the Spanish had invited to settle in Texas and Louisiana (as buffers against the English), all invaded the remaining Caddo territory. This inevitably led to deadly conflicts. Contacts with the English were even more devastating to the Caddos, as the English traded them whiskey, which led to problems that further weakened their society.[1]

Large-scale Anglo immigration significantly sped the demise of Native peoples. The first Anglo colony under Stephen F. Austin pushed the eastern Karankawas west, where the food supply was not enough for them to survive. When Karankawas began raids in order to subsist, the Anglos waged a war to eradicate them. The remnants of the community finally moved to the Rio Grande, where Tejano ranchers attacked and killed the last of them in 1858. The significantly weakened Caddos fought Anglo encroachments on their land, but after the Texans successfully mounted a revolution against Mexico, the Caddo participation in the short-lived Kickapoo War in October 1838 led to their removal from Texas altogether. After the Cherokee War in 1839, Republic of Texas president Mirabeau Lamar fulfilled the fondest wish of most Anglos by driving out all the newly arrived Indians from East Texas as well, granting land and permission to remain only to the Alabama-Coushattas. With East Texas virtually free of original claimants to the land, southern society developed uncontested.[2]

In West, Central, and South Texas, however, Native Americans remained powerful for much longer. Before the Civil War, Plains Indians controlled the area. Apaches had expanded their control over most of central and western Texas during the sixteenth and seventeenth centuries. In the eighteenth century, however, Comanches from the north had begun migrating into Texas, cornering the buffalo trade and forcing out other peoples, such as the Wichitas. Comanches pushed the Apaches much farther south and into central Texas, causing them to come into conflict with Europeans in Texas.[3]

By the nineteenth century, the horses that Europeans had introduced to the continent had changed the way of life for Plains Indians. These Native Americans held most property communally, but horses were considered men's private property, enabling some to gain greater power and respect. A horse made it possible for a man to travel farther, hunt better, and raid with more speed and deadliness, all attributes that further increased one's honor within his band. This created class distinctions, but it also decreased women's power and the respect accorded to them because they could not own and benefit from their society's most prized possession. Men with horses also killed more buffalo and traded their hides for more material goods. Women, however, turned the buffalo into valuable commodities, spending most of their lives skinning and tanning buffalo hides, preparing them for sale, and making them into robes, moccasins, blankets, and tipis. They also prepared the buffalo meat and produced other materials necessary for survival, such as utensils for cooking and cleaning the buffalo.[4]

The number of buffalo that one man on a horse could slaughter was often more than one woman could process, and that led to an increase in polygyny. Previously, taking multiple wives had been the privilege of only the elite in the Plains Indian society, but, with horses and prowess, common men came to need more women workers in their households. With more wives came more goods and higher status. Plains Indians continued to uphold many of the age-old traditions of female power, tracing the family matrilineally and observing special rites of passage for girls and women. Society continued to highly value women's work, especially tanning hides and caring for the family, and in many ways wives and daughters had status equal to men. The workload increased when a man had horses, due to more buffalo to process. But women, who were responsible for building and carrying tipis on frequent moves, appreciated horses' ability to carry heavy loads. Women, like men, became experts in riding and caring for horses. One traveler, German geologist Ferdinand von Roemer, noted that the "women also sit astride the horses like the men, and ride almost equally as gracefully." Because men obtained and owned the horses, however, women increasingly became dependent upon the ability of their husbands to determine the status of their households.[5]

Men gained honor and prestige by leading and participating in successful raids and by acquiring horses through raids on Europeans and other Indians. In addition to horses, raiders stole other valuable goods, including cloth, guns, and humans. Taking captives was an ancient practice. Captives could be ransomed back to their people or adopted into a band that needed to replenish its population due to deaths from disease or warfare. Comanches lost people in their numerous raids but also endured five epidemics of smallpox or cholera between 1816 and 1862 and so needed to rebuild their population. The buffalo hide trade also required more women to tan hides and more boys to watch their large herds of horses, often numbering in the thousands. As a result, the Plains Indians in the nineteenth century ransomed many captives for goods, but they also wanted new people for their bands. Comanches were more likely to treat adult women as slaves to be bought and sold or ransomed, although an adult woman who spent years with a Comanche family might come to be treated as a junior wife. Child captives, male and female, were usually adopted into families and tribes as full members.[6]

A raid by Comanches on Fort Parker in 1836 led to two of the most famous Anglo captives in Texas history. An adult woman, Rachel Plummer, was one of five people taken in the raid, and upon her ransom almost two years later she published the first captivity narrative in Texas. As with most Anglo captivity narratives, the point was to convey how she suffered from "the continued barbarous treatment of the Indians." Separated from her family, including her infant son, she was beaten, forced to march long distances, made to tan hides during the day and watch horses at night, mistreated by her mistress, and compelled to witness the murder of the newborn to whom she gave birth while in captivity.[7]

Comanches captured her eight-year-old cousin Cynthia Ann Parker at the same time, but due to her age and the length of time she remained there, Parker had a very different experience. By the time she was "rescued" in 1860 during a skirmish between Texans and Comanches on the Pease River, Parker had thoroughly become a member of the Comanches, having forgotten white customs and how to speak English. She had married a warrior and raised a son who became a famous Comanche chief, Quanah Parker. Returning to white society tore her again from the only family she knew and loved, and she faced readjustment to a society that was much more restrictive of women than the Comanches were. After her uncle identified her and took her home, the Texas legislature granted her an annuity and a league of land, but she never became part of white society and several times tried to flee back to the Comanches before her death.[8]

Cynthia Ann Parker's experience as a child adopted into the community was similar to an account by Bianca Babb. Captured in 1866 and separated from her brother, Babb was kindly treated, perhaps even considered a foster daughter by her captor's sister. Children came to play with her and "everyday seemed like a holiday," she later recalled. Although the Comanches clearly planned to adopt Babb into their family and society, Babb's family persistently pursued her and ransomed her seven months after her capture.[9]

Although the Plains Indians suffered some setbacks, and some groups of Wichitas and Apaches had, before the Civil War, agreed to move to Indian Territory (land set aside by the US government for relocated Native Americans), the Comanches still controlled the northwestern portion of Texas, the Llano Estacado (Staked Plains), late into the nineteenth century. They saw the Civil War and the removal of Union troops as an opportunity to push the white settlers back and regain some of their lost land. After the Civil War, new white settlers began to move rapidly into one of the last frontiers in the United States, and the Comanches were determined to stop them. Raids, violence, and the taking of captives escalated until 1875 when federal troops amassed and forced the last of the Plains Indians, including the Comanche chief Quanah Parker, to surrender. Comanches reluctantly left Texas to take up land in the Indian Territory. For a few years after, a band of seventy-five Apaches from New Mexico conducted a bloody war on the settlements in West Texas, but they too were finally trapped and slaughtered in 1881. The few Texas Indians that remained were contained on reservations in Indian Territory (current-day Oklahoma) or on two tiny reservations in Texas (Tiguas in El Paso and Alabama-Coushattas in East Texas).

White Women in the West

From the independence of Texas through the end of the nineteenth century, settlers of European descent came into conflict with Indians who claimed the land. Apaches of South Texas and Plains Indians of West Texas defended their territory, their trade networks, and their way of life against the incursions of the white settlers and raided European settlements for horses necessary to maintain their dominance. As a result, the settlements on the frontier closest to the Plains Indians were frequent targets of raids. Historian David La Vere estimates that "from the mid-1830s to 1881 just about every Texas community west of Waco experienced some sort of negative interaction with Indians." The Plains Indians raided Texas homes and settlements hundreds or possibly thousands of times. To protect those families and break the dominance of Native Americans in the West, the United States stationed troops

Figure 5.1. Key forts, counties, and settlements in early West Texas.

in a line of some twenty forts in the West and along the Mexican border. The state also authorized a state police force known as the Texas Rangers to prevent raids and punish the Indians who perpetrated them.[10]

Wives of US Army soldiers and officers stationed at these western forts were some of the first white women in the area. Accustomed to more refined society in the East, army wives struggled to cope with rough frontier conditions. Officers' wives usually came from middle-class homes in the East and found the housing at the forts inadequate. They had difficulty turning crude barracks into the domestic havens they had learned homes should be. All goods were expensive at these outposts, and basic furnishings were difficult to obtain. Even if it were possible to purchase the more expensive furniture and drapes such as they had in the East, the probability of sudden relocation made such purchases unwise. Teresa Griffin Viele, stationed with her husband at Fort Brown along the Rio Grande before the Civil War, aptly described the sparseness of furnishings: "Cane furniture, matting, and the indispensable mosquito bar, are the only articles in general use; anything more elegant seldom reaches here, and is not required."[11]

The army provided soldiers and their families with basics such as coffee, flour, sugar, rice, and pork, but what women might consider essential staples, such as milk, vegetables, and eggs, were hard to find at any price. Even the goods provided often left much to be desired. At the Ringgold Barracks, Viele complained of the "mouldy flour and rancid pork, two luxuries that are not generally very highly appreciated, even by the unfastidious," and she wrote that "the food was flavored with red ants, which were so thick that it was impossible to eat without devouring them by scores."[12]

The officers' wives, at least, could afford to hire servants to help transform their primitive lodgings into homes and prepare meals. However, it was difficult to keep good help. Viele availed herself of slave labor, but after emancipation, the low wages and desolate conditions in these remote locations could not induce free people to stay. Many women tried to import servant women from the East, but they quickly found that none would remain long. They either returned home out of boredom or found a husband among the many eligible single enlisted men.[13]

The women who accompanied their husbands did so because they had a vested interest in the success of their spouses, and so they were preoccupied with their husbands' achievements and failures. In fact, they often considered themselves as much members of the military as the men. "No recruit ever entered the service with more enthusiasm than I did, or felt more eager to prove himself a soldier," Viele wrote at the beginning of her reminiscences of her time in Texas. Soldiers encouraged entire families to feel this way; when a child died at Fort Concho, the regiment provided a military funeral, and she was "buried like a soldier girl."[14]

Officers' wives particularly paid attention to the details regarding personnel and personality conflicts. They also found themselves as leaders of the women in the community, and other wives might ask them to intervene with their officer husbands on behalf of their own spouses on military matters. While she was visiting her home in Illinois, the colonel's wife, Alice Kirk Grierson, was called upon for help back at Fort Concho. Rachel Beck's husband had been court-martialed and sentenced to one year's dismissal without pay, and Beck asked Grierson to intercede with Colonel Grierson, for clemency. In this case, Grierson declined to get involved, not because of any qualms about interfering in military matters but because she agreed with the sentence.[15]

Officers' wives also played leadership roles organizing women to provide entertainment for the soldiers and families to keep up morale. Grierson planned dinners, encouraged excursions of hunting, fishing, and camping, and assisted her husband as he led the army band in performances. Holidays were excuses for celebrations. Christmas called for elaborate preparations, but even lesser holidays such as Valentine's Day and St. Patrick's Day provided occasions for "hops." Parlor games provided entertainment for families, while men participated in baseball and football. Weddings were particularly festive events celebrated by the entire post.[16]

Fewer Texas Rangers brought wives with them to the frontier because the Rangers generally did not even have the sparse accommodations the US Army forts had. Luvenia Roberts, however, "much in love with my gallant captain and willing to share his fate wherever and whatever it might be," left her home in East Texas in 1875 to join her new husband in West Texas. While Captain Daniel Webster Roberts intended for her to stay in Mason, near where he was stationed, an outbreak of violence in that frontier town convinced her to join him in the "Ranger Camp" near Menard. The Rangers built the newlyweds housing by converting a portion of a camp house into a kitchen and building "a room of logs with walls three feet high, on top of which they put a tent" for the bedroom. The couple did not get to enjoy the makeshift housing long, as Rangers frequently moved camps. After sojourning at some other locations, Roberts was delighted at her new accommodations at Camp San Saba, where they received a second tent. This camp was close enough to the army fort that she could visit with other army wives and share pastimes.[17]

No matter how uncomfortable the lives of women who were married to Rangers, officers, or enlisted soldiers, their greatest concern remained the safety of their husbands. Whether their husbands were guarding against and chasing Indian raiders or hunting and capturing outlaws, their jobs put them in constant jeopardy, greater than that of the women. Because the wives shared these fears, they stuck together when calamity befell them. After a company of Rangers set out in search of hostile Indians and then got lost in the unforgiving terrain of the Llano Estacado, wives learned that the men were missing. One of the women almost fainted, Alice Grierson wrote, "and felt so upset, that she was not willing to stay alone." Other soldiers' family members stayed with her until her husband was found.[18]

Pioneer Women in West Texas

Even before the army secured the frontier and made it safer for settlers, new families began streaming into West Texas. At the conclusion of the Civil War, this stream turned into a virtual flood as adventurers sought new opportunities and inexpensive (or free) land.

Many came initially to hunt buffalo, most to ranch, and others to try to turn the inhospitable environment into farms. Although most of the adventurers were men, women accompanied them almost from the beginning. In only a few counties did women make up less than one-third of the population. These counties in the Panhandle on the Llano Estacado represented one of the last frontiers in the United States with land available for homesteading into the twentieth century. However, even as early as 1880, 32 percent of the 5,388 people in these fifty counties were women.[19]

Although the percentage of women might have been higher than depicted in popular culture in the subsequent century, women who moved into West Texas suffered extreme isolation. Ella Bird's husband resigned from the Texas Rangers two months after their marriage, and the couple set out for the "wilds of the Texas Panhandle" to hunt buffalo. Fortunately they set up a camp with another family (and later added another) so that Bird had other women with whom to share her days and nights when the men were out hunting for days and sometimes weeks. Homesteaders, however, less frequently had close neighbors. Whether on a small ranch or farm, a woman might often find herself not only the sole woman but also the only other adult besides her husband. Once buffalo had been overhunted, Bird's husband took a job on a ranch. Although there were four men, Bird later remembered, "It was rather lonely for me. The men all left early in the morning, each on his line, and did not return until late in the afternoon."[20]

Like Bird's husband, other ranchmen spent much time away from home for hunting, riding the line to keep the cattle together, performing other duties such as repairing fences, traveling back to settlements for supplies, or conducting business such as filing homestead papers. These women, therefore, spent a lot of time alone, enduring agonizing isolation from human society. Historian James Fenton describes how "to lift her loneliness, one woman actually sought the company of cattle. She would go to their water places and talk to them about themselves, discussing various matters of mutual concern."[21]

At a time when women were raised to rely heavily on other women for physical and emotional support, the lack of specifically female companionship contributed to their loneliness. Some frontier women did not see another woman for over a year. Spread out long distances on isolated homesteads, women yearned for any social occasion that might bring them into contact

Figure 5.2. A pioneer West Texas picnic party, Misses Mary, Annie and Lelia Smith, and George Mayes eating watermelon which washed down the Blanco Canyon during a flood in 1899. Courtesy of University of Texas at Arlington.

with others. While men and women both sought opportunities to socialize, the amount of work necessary on these isolated homesteads made it difficult to find the time to do so.[22]

The stark nature of the landscape also made the isolation tangible. Iowa resident Nellie Perry, who visited her brother in the Panhandle in 1888, wrote, "The last 10 miles, when the Ochiltree windmill came in view, were the longest miles I ever traveled." The flat desolate plains made it possible to see great distances that contained no signs of human beings, but the poor roads made it difficult to travel quickly—requiring, for example, four hours to drive sixteen miles in a wagon.[23] Dorothy Scarborough's 1925 novel *The Wind* fictionalized a well-worn belief that the starkness of the West Texas environment—the wind, the sand, and the immense flatness—could drive a woman insane. There were definitely some women who broke down and many others who left, but many stayed successfully by adapting to the environment.[24]

Women could cope in myriad ways without completely abandoning their social ideals brought with them from the East. Housing options, for instance, were completely different from anything they had before encountered. Shortage of timber on the plains and lack of transportation to import timber made the construction of wood frame houses rare and far in the future for most pioneer families. The first homes on the prairies were usually tents or the wagons they had traveled in. No matter how primitive the abode, though, women attempted to make them comfortable. Ella Bird described her first dwelling in the Panhandle as a tent made of buffalo hides (and carpeted by the same), "and a more clean and comfortable little home you could not find in any of the Eastern cities."[25]

After a tent, the next family residence was usually a dugout carved into the side of a hill. Settlers finished dugouts with materials that could be found in the area, so most roofs were made of beargrass and sod. Perry was shocked at her first glimpse of her brother's house: "What a queer lookin' place it was," with "strips of carpet taking the place of doors and windows" making the "outlook still more desolate."[26] Upon arrival, Perry spent her first day cleaning her brother's sod house, "but though I raised a great dust and stirred things up generally, after two or three hours of hard work no great change was visible." On the other hand, dugouts could be made clean and comfortable, and most women attempted to do so. Perry visited some of her brother's neighbors, a family whose dugout was partially carpeted, clean, and "the sitting room furnished comfortably, bookcases, etc. sunk into the thick sod walls and as much as possible made of the available space. I was surprised to find that a sod house could be made so pleasant and home-like."[27]

Dugouts could be made comfortable, but their drawbacks were many. Edith Pitts had prepared a special meal for her husband and several friends when a steer walking across the sod roof broke through. Its leg dangling down through the ceiling and dirt pouring into the house ruined the dinner. During a thunderstorm, water rained into the kitchen and bedroom of Perry's expanded dugout, leaving "much sand and dirt on kitchen walls." Bird's first home after giving up her buffalo tent was a dugout with walls that "were too sandy and inclined to cave in." Additionally, sitting below ground level invited assorted other living things to join the family, including snakes, mice, lizards, scorpions, terrapins, bedbugs, fleas, and every imaginable insect. On her second night, Perry heard "a peculiar scratching and sniffing on the floor [that] convinced me that other nocturnal visitors had arrived." She woke her brother who finally shooed a "pole-cat" out the door and later related that he was "much disgusted at the 'row' that I had made over so small a matter."[28]

West Texas was full of dangers for frontier women. Snakes and spiders lurked not only in homes but also in woodpiles and near windmills and other watering spots. Sudden storms led to flash floods and scrambles for shelter. Men and women on prairies risked danger of lightning strikes during thunderstorms.[29]

As dangerous as the natural environment continued to be, the human element was even more so. Until the 1880s, Comanches, Apaches, and other Plains Indians threatened men, women, and children with death and captivity. Fear of Indians haunted Sarah Hall's childhood, and she later remembered "sitting up at night listening to the whistle of the Comanches all around and shivering with fear and trembling." Even visitors from nearby reservations who showed up at the doorstep with completely benign intentions were frightening. When seven Comanches pushed their way into the Birds' home to trade clothes for groceries while the men were away hunting, Ella Bird and the other two women were certain "they were planning to kill us." Instead the unwanted visitors waited for the men to return to trade goods with them. Non-Indian outlaws who roamed the sparsely settled areas in West Texas and South Texas also terrorized frontier societies, creating havoc among travelers and sometimes attacking and robbing homes as well. Living outside the law, these bandits did not value life very highly and might murder someone, as they did Hall's brother, to keep him from bringing them to justice, or "without any cause that any one knew of."[30]

The dangers, the isolation, the chronic shortage of water and abundance of dirt and sand, and the constant work necessary to eke out a living and raise children in the unforgiving terrain all led to the oft-repeated sentiment that Texas was hell on women and horses. After visiting twice, Nellie Perry disagreed with part of that sentiment, writing that "horses don't seem to have a hard time," but she consistently described the women as "careworn," "tired," or "used-up."[31] Ella Bird's reminiscences of her life in West Texas did not dispel the myth of hard work for women, but she did note one advantage: "Women were scarce in this country at that time. They were more appreciated, I think, than in later years, when there were more."[32]

A very few women—like Sally Scull, who ran cattle during the Civil War in a southwestern county along the Rio Grande—abandoned nearly all gendered ideals in order to flourish. Even though she wore a sunbonnet instead of a hat, Scull rode horses, herded cattle, and carried a six-shooter that she used to threaten and even kill men, including, as legend records, a husband. Men did not need or want women who fit the traditional images of fragility and dependence, and so they were very likely to encourage their wives and daughters to develop their abilities and sense of independence. Almost immediately after their marriage, Ella Bird's husband taught her how to shoot since she would be alone so much and would need to be able to defend herself. That she would also use the gun to shoot birds and other wild animals for food was a beneficial by-product. Because men were often not around to make decisions, women learned to rely upon their own judgments. And women often helped out with ranching or farming duties because of the shortage of hired hands.[33]

Most western women, however, did not venture so far from nineteenth-century ideals about women's proper place and role, instead adapting the ideals to fit their new realities. They could, like Bird, shoot a gun, stand up to Indians, and stay alone for days but still take pride in the cleanliness of their tipis. Women may have been living in dugouts, but they cleaned and furnished them as neatly as possible. They may have developed independence, but they still believed that they should be submissive to their husbands. Women who could not adapt their ideals to the environment suffered the most and sometimes went insane, as did the main character in Scarborough's *The Wind.* But those women who survived the frontier and learned to adapt and even thrive did so in a world that granted women a little more power and independence. Thus, Perry, who noted how tired and old most women looked also observed others who were happy, such as the old deaf woman who nevertheless was "very cheerful and naturally philosophical, as a woman living in this country needs to be."[34]

West Texas Ranches

After the Civil War, the demand for beef in the East rose sharply while wild cattle were abundant in Texas. As a result, the brief but amazing era of the cattle drives began, and ranching became a much more promising venture. Most of the settlers in West Texas engaged in ranching, while South Texas ranching along the Rio Grande expanded and moved north and westward. West Texans adopted many of the techniques perfected by the Mexicans and Tejanos who had been ranching for generations. West Texas ranches, however, were newer, appealed to adventurers looking for opportunities after the Civil War, and remained in a pioneer-like state well into the twentieth century.

As the ranches and farms of West Texas became more settled and transportation improved, so did the housing. Shipments of timber by rail enabled the building of small frame houses (still small because of the cost of shipping lumber), and these became more common by the end of the nineteenth century. Frame houses, which were built off the ground instead of on foundations dug into it, decreased the number of unwelcome animal and insect visitors in ranchers' homes. Some women still preferred dugout homes because they provided better protection from the high winds of the area, and these dwellings became larger and more elaborate. Nellie Perry, who had visited the region in 1888 and described the dugouts as small one-room abodes, made a second trip in 1900 and visited a family whose house was "built into the side of a hill in a beautiful spot" and who were building a one-room addition to their house, which already had at least two rooms. Ranch owners who built frame houses continued to maintain dugout homes for their hands that lived on the ranch.[35] Nicer homes with more furniture led to more work keeping them clean. Women swept and scrubbed floors, cleaned carpets, washed and aired bedding daily (to decrease fleas and bedbugs), and, as one ranch woman remembered, washed dishes "1095 times a year."[36]

Housecleaning was only one of the many arduous tasks of a woman on a ranch. By the late nineteenth century, better technology led to inexpensive consumer products that eased the amount of work that women in the United

States had to do, but the ranches remained largely pre-industrial enterprises where people made nearly everything they needed. Stores were too distant to purchase fresh produce, so women raised gardens, growing potatoes, onions, corn, and many other vegetables. Women then had to preserve these products, just as they did the meat from cattle or goats (or both), wild game, and any other foods that they could gather, including wild plums, grapes, and berries. Glass jars made canning fruits and vegetables much easier, but those women who could not afford or acquire them found other means. Mary Jane Alexander collected old beer bottles from behind the saloons in the town of Mobeetie. She would tie a kerosene-soaked string around a bottle and light it, causing the bottle to break smoothly. She then used paraffin and paper to seal the bottles. Beef was preserved by drying, by layering steaks with buttermilk, or by sprinkling the meat with cayenne and black peppers to keep flies away. Most commonly, however, families took turns butchering steers and sharing with other families to stretch the meat as far as possible. Women also raised chickens and turkeys for both their eggs and meat. They were often responsible for milking the cows and used hand churns to make butter.[37]

Besides growing and preserving food, women prepared meals constantly for their families and usually for the ranch hands. Kitchens were an important part of ranch homes, even the smallest dugouts. Each kitchen had a wood-burning stove on which were made meals of baked beans and bacon (often kept for days afterward and eaten cold), stewed chicken and dumplings, beef stew, dried beef, and rudimentary breads, biscuits, and cakes. Into the monotonous diet of beef, beans, and bread were interspersed fried chicken and dishes made out of the produce from women's gardens, such as boiled peas, potato salad, cooked squash, fruit pies, and canned pickled beets, pickled eggs, peas, fruits, and jams. Women always made plenty of extra food to be eaten cold in order to save time in cooking and also so that the men could pack food when they left for days to inspect the land and herds.[38]

On most ranches, there was always abundant food, if not in great variety, but the shortage of wood made cooking difficult. Women turned to any available source of heat, including mesquite roots, dwarf oak, corncobs, and even bones. While few were willing to use it for cooking, "surface coal"— better known as cow chips—was often burned to heat water for laundry or for heating the home. The other shortage that defined women's lives was that of water. Men usually transported water over long distances by barrels on horse-drawn carts, and then every bit of water used for cooking, cleaning, bathing, or drinking in the house had to be carried in by women. Even when ranchers installed windmills to pump water to the surface, increasing the availability of water for the home and cattle, water still had to be transported. Every drop thus preciously acquired was cherished and used wisely, meaning that bathing was infrequent.[39]

Water was necessary for women's most dreaded work, laundry, which was laborious and even dangerous. Clothes were nearly always washed outside, where wind could blow a woman's skirts into the open fire, causing great harm and even death. Women hauled water to fill large kettles, which they then heated over a fire. They added lye soap, which they had made themselves, and then agitated the water. By the late nineteenth century, manufacturers marketed washing devices, and the "hand-driven washing machine" or "wringing and drying machine" helped the process considerably. Fortunately, once clothes were washed, they dried very quickly in the arid West Texas heat, although wind might coat the clothes with dust as speedily as it dried them.[40]

Women played a crucial role in making West Texas ranches as self-sufficient as they were, but by the late nineteenth century, even self-sufficient households purchased cloth. Most families where the women continued spinning and sewing did so out of economic necessity. The vast majority of women by the 1870s and 1880s had set aside spinning wheels and looms to concentrate on sewing clothes out of prefabricated cloth instead. Sewing still took significant skill and time, but the proliferation of the sewing machine also sped up that process. Women who owned one, such as Ella Bird, could earn money making clothes—even buckskins—for the many single male cowboys. Most women used their machines for their own families, and those who did not own one could sometimes borrow time on a neighbor's. In addition to making clothing, women made, by hand or machine, many other cloth items for the home, from rugs to feather beds and pillows.[41]

Women worked hard on ranches while also bearing and raising children. The average number of living children per family was four or five, but continuing high mortality rates meant that most women endured more pregnancies than that. In order to raise children while taking care of all the other needs on the ranches, women had to be inventive. Some women had cradleboards that they hung from the ceiling to keep animals away from sleeping babies. From a very young age, children worked in order to learn the jobs that would be theirs as adults, to help with the enormous amount of work to be done, and to keep them out of mischief. Children often had to be responsible for watching and tending their siblings as well.[42]

Married ranch women served in many additional roles in the course of their lives. Most of the nursing duties fell to women, and, because doctors were so few and far between, they often enlarged this role to serve as doctor, midwife, and even mortician. Their homes also served as inns for travelers, with visitors dropping in unannounced for food and overnight shelter on their long treks across the prairies.[43]

Most women who moved to West Texas continued to uphold their ideals of separate roles for men and women, and there was so much "women's work" to do that they did not have idle time. However, even from the early nineteenth century and well into the twentieth, ranch women assisted with what would have been considered men's work. Needing protection, they learned to shoot guns and often became renowned for shooting proficiency. Frequently, women handled the business matters of ranches. Wives even sometimes served as additional hands, riding horses and roping cattle. Even women who did not regularly help out with ranch duties became adept at riding. Women in the nineteenth century were expected to ride sidesaddle, and most ranch women did so. As one later remembered, "We rode sideways then because we didn't have better sense." Women accustomed to riding frequently, however, could accomplish a lot at great speeds, even in the specially designed saddles: "We stuck to those sidesaddles like leeches." By the end of the nineteenth century, many women decided that sidesaddles were cumbersome and did not give the rider enough control, and so they began riding astride. Ranch women, unlike southern farmwives, also traveled on horseback or in horse-drawn conveyances, sometimes great distances, without chaperones.[44]

Of all the masculine endeavors in both fact and the glorified fiction of the West, driving cattle was the most dangerous, the most romantic, and the least female-influenced. However, from the beginning of the cattle drives, when cattle were driven from one ranch or pasture to another for better grazing, to the long cattle drives to markets in California or train depots in Arkansas and Kansas, a few remarkable women participated. In 1868, a seven-wagon train with men, women, and children drove 1,800 cattle and 150 horses from Hays County, Texas, to Los Angeles, California, with the women and children enduring the difficulties and dangers of the trail along with the men. Most women on the cattle drive accompanied their husbands, but

Margaret Borland in 1873 drove her own herd of horses up the Chisholm Trail from Victoria, Texas, to Wichita, Kansas, with the help of her children and grandchildren (the latter aged sixteen, fourteen, nine, and six) and several hired hands. Most drives hired a male cook, but some women went along to prepare meals for the cowboys, and they were then required to drive wagons loaded with supplies and water. Viola P. Anderson later remembered being sent ahead on the trail alone to prepare dinner for the cowboys when the cattle that her husband and hands were driving slowed.[45]

For women in West Texas there were few opportunities for support outside of a family ranch. Some women took jobs as postmasters, ran stores, or operated hotels in the small towns. However, the vast majority of women became integral parts of ranching enterprises. Because they were partners with their husbands and familiar with daily operations and business, many wives eventually ran the ranches after their spouses died, a common occurrence due to accidents and disease. A remarkable number of these widows chose never to remarry. Sometimes it was difficult, and they had to rely on the help of others, but their spirit of independence, bred in the ranch environment, reduced the number of rash remarriages. A small but significant number of single women also applied for and received homesteads, which they successfully ranched. A total of 1,481 women heads of families and single women claimed homesteads in Texas between the years of 1845 and 1898, most of these after the Civil War and in West Texas. The success rate of single women who persisted in fulfilling the requirements of settling, living on the land, and "improving" it in order to obtain a deed actually exceeded the success rate of men. These ranches were both short-term and long-term successes. The Land Heritage Program of the Texas Department of Agriculture in 1984 enumerated approximately 1,700 ranches that had been maintained by the same family for a century or more, and fifty of those were founded by single women (husbands and wives together founded over half of the total).[46]

South Texas Ranches

As a result of the booming cattle industry, better roads and railroads, and increased Anglo appropriation of lands along the Mexican border and in the southern counties, the centuries-old ranching culture of South Texas underwent significant changes. The Tejanos who owned land and who worked as vaqueros (cowboys) in this area, however, held on to many of the old social traditions and work styles, and the Anglos who increasingly bought or started ranches adapted to the Mexican and Tejano culture.

Ranching culture and tradition had begun in Mexico during a time of peonage, and South Texas ranches carried on a significant part of that culture. Workers were accustomed to deferring to the landed proprietor in nearly every matter. As historian Jovita González describes it, "The master exercised complete control of the *peon*, economically and socially as well as in religious matters."[47] Workers felt tied to the ranch by tradition and sometimes legally, and families for generations would remain and work the same land. When Anglos started ranching in South Texas and along the Rio Grande valley, they mostly adopted prevalent styles. Richard King, one of the most famous of the Anglo ranchers in South Texas, began by buying all the cattle in a drought-stricken Mexican village and then offering the entire community work and homes on his ranch. More than one hundred men, women, and children accepted the offer and brought their families to work on the King Ranch. These vaqueros remained loyal to the Kings for generations and became known as Los Kineños.[48] No matter what the background of the ranch owner, then, vaquero families of South Texas built a blended culture based on Mexican tradition but adopting some American customs. By the end of the

Figure 5.3. Example of a *jacal* near Laredo, Texas. MSS9717–0263, Houston Public Library, Houston Metropolitan Research Center.

century, this was certainly a Tejano culture, as most of those who preserved these longstanding traditions brought from Mexico had been born in the United States.[49]

The vaqueros and their families lived in *jacales*, thatched-roof huts made of stakes and mud, built in small villages on the ranches apart from the main house, which was typically constructed of logs or wood. Each *jacal* was usually one room with a thatched roof and a dirt floor, which women swept and sprinkled with water to make as hard as possible. Furniture was rudimentary and made by hand, and "the bed consisted of four poles dug into the dirt floor with boards across it, no springs, and a grass mattress." Each family had its own *jacal*, while the bachelors would often share one.[50]

Women were responsible for preparing the food, most of which was distributed by the ranch owner, and sometimes they would be the ones to receive the rations. The kinds and amounts varied by ranch but usually included meat and flour. On the King Ranch, former vaquero children later remembered items such as milk, rice, potatoes, lard, beans, and baking powder. What owners did not provide as rations could be bought from a commissary. In addition, women also kept chickens and perhaps a goat, a cow, or a pig. They also sometimes planted small gardens of corn, beans, pumpkins, squash, or other vegetables to add variety to the families' diets. Women not only prepared the daily meals, they also grew, raised, and preserved much of the food comprising these meals. They canned vegetables and dried meat in a very warm climate without refrigeration. In addition to preserving and cooking beef and goat meat that came from ranch stock, the women also prepared wild animals such as rabbits, armadillos, ducks, turkeys, deer, and quail that their husbands and sons hunted.[51]

The "kitchen" was usually an exterior oven or chimney about ten to twelve feet from the house, occasionally with walls made of corn stalks or grass to serve as windbreaks, but almost never with a roof, so the women were exposed to the elements while cooking. Women used *ollas* (black cast-iron pots), *parillas* (grills), and *comales* (large griddles) to make the mainstay of the Tejano diet, tortillas. The corn was soaked in water for hours with lime to help remove the husks. Then women beat it, turning it into dough (*masa*), and then divided it in preparation for cooking on the griddle. To heat the griddle and pots, the oven was fed with firewood, the chopping of which was also one of women's many tasks, although mothers often delegated this chore to their children. Girls were expected to begin work at an early age, learning the tasks they would need to know. Manuela Mayorga later remembered, "I started working at seven years old. I helped wash. I helped Mom fix breakfast by 5:00 in the morning. I made beds and made the fire. I chopped wood for it."[52]

Women also cooked the many traditional Mexican dishes in this outside oven, well into the twentieth century before wood-burning stoves appeared. She boiled beans all night for the frijoles or meat for the *carne guisada, caldillo con carne seca* (jerky stew), or *picadillo* (hash). As she cooked the tortillas, she would rearrange the coals from the firewood to boil rice, meat, and beans. Although the food might be lacking in variety, vaqueros' wives made sure there was plenty of it.[53]

The Tejanas of land-owning families cooked much the same kinds of foods and performed many of the same duties. They, however, could avail themselves of help. Families of any rank expected daughters to work and to learn from their mothers. Ranch-owning families, however, also sometimes hired the wives of their vaqueros to assist seasonally or temporarily, such as when the produce from the gardens needed to be preserved, or permanently as cooks, maids, or gardeners. Women of the landed class could also call upon the vaqueros to assist with manual labor, such as filling water tanks, plowing the ground for the garden, or chopping wood. On the South Texas ranch that Mary Jaques visited, "One 'hand' was told off to cut and collect wood to supply the cooking-stove; the oven being in use the greater part of the day, the demand for fuel was considerable."[54]

The manual labor that women of the landed class performed might have been less than that done by wives of the vaqueros, but women of the landed class had many other responsibilities. Petra Vela, the Tejana wife of the Anglo Mifflin Kenedy, often found herself in charge of their enormous ranch while he was away on business. Even when her husband was there to manage the ranch and vaqueros and to work with the stock, Vela's work entailed managing the domestic staff and their families, directing labor to care for gardens, slaughter animals and preserve their meat (to provide to all the vaquero families), be constantly ready to receive visitors, and prepare food for her family, the families of the domestics, and probably the bachelor vaqueros. She also ordered supplies that could not be produced on the ranch and supervised repairs on the house and its surroundings. Women like Vela saw themselves as responsible for the vaqueros and their families. Vela employed a schoolmaster for the younger children and provided medical care to all, making and administering medicines from native plants and herbs she had learned to use as a child.[55]

No matter to which class they belonged, Tejanos, like Anglos, had strong gender ideals and expectations of women. Women were chaste before marriage and faithful after, while men celebrated their sexual escapades outside of marriage. Women stayed at home unless chaperoned, and they did not mingle with men outside their families. Even at dances where young women had the opportunity to meet potential spouses, they dared not speak to their dancing partners. A woman who enjoyed two dances in a row with the same partner was scandalous. Those children from families wealthy enough to attend private schools had these ideals ingrained through the use of moral lessons that differed depending on whether one was a girl or a boy. Girls were instructed that women "should be content with the company of their own sex" and told to "be modest in all your actions, never crossing your limbs or leaning heavily on the back of your chair. See that the dress descends to the floor, covering your feet and let modesty be reflected in your eyes. It is improper to look daringly at any one and it is very perverse to try to catch the eye of men. This is the certain sign of an immoral woman."[56]

While women were not supposed to leave their homes and were to defer to the authority and protection of men, they had complete control of management of the home, from the food eaten to decorations, and from education provided in the home to religious observances. Tejanos were very religious, but men ceded authority over religion in the home to women. Women maintained altars dedicated to Our Lady of Guadalupe, decorating them with paper or natural flowers. The oldest woman in the household led readings of the Bible and prayers every night and conducted religious ceremonies to honor saints. The observances consisted of readings, prayers, and singing, and these were often female-only affairs, with men showing little interest. Ofelia M. Longória would remember, "I did the rosary every day. The rosary takes about an hour and forty-five minutes. My grandmother's altar had a cross with Christ on it, the Virgin Mary statue, the Sacred Heart of Jesus, and candles." Men made it a priority to marry devout Catholic wives but believed that religion was the responsibility of women and children. The hierarchy of the Catholic Church itself remained exclusively male, of course, but women's attention and devotion to the church enabled it to thrive. Women formed organizations, served the church in many auxiliary capacities, and donated as much money as their circumstances allowed. Petra Vela bestowed gifts to her church over and over, and once she participated with the women of the church in organizing a four-day fair to raise money for an ornate ceiling.[57]

Despite the strict gender conventions that encouraged Tejanas to be sub-missive to men and dependent on them, the reality did not always live up to the ideal. Many women exerted significant independence, whether by choice or necessity. As smaller landowners were squeezed out of their land, they, along with immigrants and workers, found it increasingly necessary for wom-en to work. By 1900 the percentage of Tejanas working outside the home for wages was nearly four times that in 1850. Women took jobs as field hands, shepherds, cooks, domestics, and gardeners. *Vaqueras* carried out work for their families and others even before the Civil War. In the 1860s, while wash-ing his clothes, William Brewer encountered "two women, one young and quite pretty who were assisting vaqueros. . . . The wife and daughter of the ranchero came out to assist in getting in the cattle. Well mounted, they man-aged their horses superbly, and just as I was up to my elbows in soapsuds, along they came, with a herd of several hundred cattle, back from the hills."[58]

Like Anglo women in West Texas, South Texas Tejanas continued to run successful ranches after their husbands died. The widow Salomé Balli carried on her ranch and the process of acquiring land that had previously belonged to her family. After Richard King's death, Henrietta Chamberlain King ran the famous King Ranch for forty years, digging the enterprise out of its heavy debt, nearly doubling the land size, and increasing the number of cattle to ninety-four thousand. The widow Doña Eulalia was one of the few early ranch owners to hold onto her property near La Atravesada after Mifflin Kenedy began buying up tracts to form his enormous enterprise. Even after her sons had sold their portions and Kenedy had completely fenced in her land, she continued to hold out and left the ranch to her daughters. Many women in South Texas inherited ranches from other family members, not just husbands, but some women founded ranches or farms. Between 1870 and 1898, forty Spanish-surnamed women took up homesteads in Atascosa, Bexar, Duval, Webb, and other South Texas counties where ranching was prevalent.[59]

Conclusion

By the early twentieth century, Native American women had lost their homes in Texas, paving the way for increased settlement by Americans. In-expensive land, better transportation, and the booming cattle industry beck-oned many adventurers looking for opportunity. Despite the mythic male cowboy figure of West Texas, however, most men went with families, taking women who were crucial to survival in the harsh environments and forming successful ranches and farms. Women carved out homes, fed and clothed families, and re-created societies in some of the most barren land in the country. Their work helped create legacies for their children, instill cultural values, and integrate West Texas and South Texas into the state's increasingly Anglo-dominated social, economic, and political structures.

Chapter 6

Women's Activism, 1870s–1920s

Following the American Civil War, women expanded their accepted roles and duties to include activities outside the home. They did not shed the ideal of domesticity or the idea that the primary focus of women's lives should be home and children. They did, however, stretch the boundaries of what should be considered domestic. Taking and creating increasingly more significant roles in churches enlarged their influence in their communities. Beyond churches, women laid claim to other forms of activism. In the late nineteenth century, rural women participated in the Farmers' Alliance and populist movement, which aimed at improving conditions for farmers. Urban women began forming study clubs dedicated to self-improvement and activist clubs dedicated to community improvement. With the rise of the ideology of "progressivism," reformers believed that government could and should make positive changes in society, especially to combat the problems caused by urbanization and industrialization. Clubwomen embraced these progressive ideas and began claiming the right to enter politics in order to demand that local governments and the state government fix problems that might touch upon their homes and domestic duties. They campaigned for government solutions, including regulations insuring clean milk and sewage disposal, and for protections for women and children, including maximum work hours for women and child labor laws. Although Texas women were slower than women in the Northeast to embrace the fight for suffrage, by the early twentieth century activist women saw the vote as essential to carrying out their perceived duties as women.

A hard-fought suffrage campaign produced greater results in Texas than in other southern states, and women set about using their vote to improve the state. Even while they sought to change politics and society to allow greater participation by women, few white women actively challenged racism or questioned its legitimacy. As a result, churches, clubs, political organizations, and nearly all sites of women's organizing remained segregated, with black women and Tejanas participating in the movements but winning fewer rewards than white women for themselves and their communities.

Religion and Women's Activities

During the Civil War, "ladies' aid societies" had for the first time brought many white women into public discussions. Using their domestic abilities to contribute physically to the needs of men in the armies, they indirectly expressed political support as well. However, this political effort was short-lived and ended with the war, after which white women and men actively sought to reestablish their prescribed gender, race, and class roles that had been threatened by the conflict.

Within these proscribed roles, church societies provided an avenue for white and black women to participate in ventures outside the family. Women drew upon their domestic abilities to form sewing circles to produce items for charity and to sponsor fund-raising activities on behalf of their churches, deflecting any complaints about their activism by drawing on women's perceived greater piety to claim this work as wholly appropriate. This acceptance of women's religious activities laid the foundations for many more women to take active roles in an increasingly larger number of religious activities, giving women opportunities to participate directly in society.

An extreme manifestation of women's claims that spiritual authority trumped male authority in their lives was the formation of a highly unusual group of women in Belton, known as the Sanctificationists. A Methodist woman, Martha McWhirter, experienced a spiritual revelation in 1866 that led her to believe that she was "sanctified" and called to share this revelation with others. Other women were open to this message, McWhirter's group grew, and she and others began to seek greater control of their lives—first refusing to sleep with their husbands and then refusing to take money from them because their husbands, they said, were not sanctified. These middle-class women instead began working as servants for other families and selling domestic products such as milk, eggs, and butter. By the 1880s, due to strains in the women's marriages and the need to have more control over their enterprises, many of the women and their children began living together in a commune they called the Woman's Commonwealth. In 1886, the fifty or so members pooled their resources to build the Central Hotel in Belton. While meeting extreme hostility from the community at first, the evident popularity of the hotel with locals and visitors alike indicates the extent to which the people of the town learned to accept this unconventional group of women. This commonwealth was one of the most successful and long-lasting of the many utopian communities throughout the United States in the nineteenth century and was the only urban commune of any size. By the end of the nineteenth century, twenty-five members of the Woman's Commonwealth sold the hotel and moved to Washington, DC, in order to enjoy their prosperity and escape the provincialism of Central Texas.[1]

The Sanctificationists were unusual in many ways but especially in their complete rejection of the religious and social ideal that women should be submissive to men. Their appeal to moral and spiritual authority to criticize the actions of their husbands specifically and the activities of men generally became widespread in the late nineteenth century, thus paving the way for greater activism. From the beginning, one of the chief topics of Sanctificationists' meetings was their husbands' drinking, and the commune had given women one way to insulate themselves from the consequences of drunkenness (including physical abuse and the loss of income). The growing concern over alcohol, however, was not isolated to Belton, and women throughout the nation were integral both to raising awareness of the ills of drinking and to combating those ills.[2]

Even before the Civil War, industrialization and urbanization in the North had led to two conditions that mobilized women's activism regarding alcohol: increased awareness of the problems caused by drunken husbands (as families became more dependent on their wage-earning capabilities) and increasing levels of women's engagement in many other social concerns. The postbellum industrial boom in the nation generated a rising number of saloons and alcohol sales. Seen as a crisis by some, this led to the formation of the Woman's Christian Temperance Union (WCTU) in Ohio in 1874 and the elevation of one woman, Frances Willard, to near-legendary status in her campaigns against alcohol.

Texas and other southern states, which remained relatively rural and un-industrialized, lacked the conditions spawning the temperance movement in the North, so southern organizations discouraging drinking originated more often from religious sentiment and included only men or mixed groups dominated by men. After the war, the WCTU brought the northern concept of women organizing for reform to the South as Willard toured southern states, including Texas, to advocate outlawing the manufacture and sale of alcohol. As the WCTU founded local chapters, or "unions," throughout the state, its leaders recruited women of all races and classes, although African American women were organized into separate, segregated unions. Hundreds of women in Texas joined the WCTU and actively worked to enact Prohibition, thus creating one of the largest networks of activist women in the state's history to that time.[3]

While Texans were receptive to Willard's ideas, they were uncomfortable with a woman speaking publicly and with women's leadership in these public matters. As a result, men, mostly from evangelical religious denominations, took control of the late-nineteenth-century political campaigns to prohibit alcohol. They distanced themselves from Frances Willard and insisted that women play supportive, auxiliary roles in the battle, not public, political ones. As one editorial in the *Texas Baptist* warned, "Take a woman out of her sphere and you dethrone a queen; place her before the public as a politician or an advocate from the rostrum, even of social reform or religion, and you rob her of her God-given retiring modesty and weaken her influence over man."[4]

At the first statewide prohibition convention, held in Waco in 1887, only one woman spoke publicly, and her speech was listed as part of the evening "entertainment." No women were elected or appointed to positions of authority. In the ensuing campaign for an amendment to the Texas Constitution banning alcohol, men exercised leadership even at the local levels. Despite being denied most leadership roles, women throughout the state continued to work in their communities to support the constitutional amendment by organizing local clubs, making prohibition literature available, and even lecturing on the topic. Unable to vote, women in the WCTU set up booths and held picnics for the voters, providing tea, lemonade, and food. Despite the efforts of the women, clergy, and their business allies, the amendment went down to a resounding defeat in the general election.[5]

After the defeat of the statewide effort, prohibition forces set about using "local option" laws to try to curtail access to alcohol, gaining some success, especially in North Texas. However, the loss of the amendment fight depleted enthusiasm for the WCTU. Then, in 1888, the WCTU endorsed "woman suffrage"—a highly controversial move in southern states. Texas membership dropped almost overnight from 1,500 to 539. As a result, evangelical clergy were the best organized to lead assaults on alcohol at the local level and then again at the state level, which they did in 1908 and 1911 (both failed). In these campaigns women continued to play important auxiliary but largely invisible roles. Eventually, however, progressives welcomed women's activism in the temperance campaign, and women played an even more visible role in the state's ratification of the federal prohibition amendment, the Eighteenth Amendment, in 1918 and a state prohibition amendment in 1919.[6]

Women discovered the same contradictions inherent in the prohibition movement in other activities that attracted them in the late nineteenth century. Their supposedly greater piety, moral authority, and devotion to the church allowed them more opportunities to organize with one another to achieve mutually desirable ends, but disapproval by clergy limited their abilities to exert much public leadership. As women worked tirelessly and sacrificed for the benefit of their churches, clergy and male members rewarded them with honor but not with positions of authority in the church. Deaconship and membership in vestries continued to be reserved for men.[7]

The lack of official positions, however, did not make women any less powerful in the churches. Women volunteered by the scores to teach Sunday schools. Originally intended just to promote literacy, these schools grew in such importance that many classes became as important or even more significant than the male clergy-led service. The new emphasis on Bible study and worship in Sunday schools enabled women to use them as "outreach" or "mission" programs as well, essentially laying the foundations for future congregations. These activities allowed them to exercise and model leadership for others. Christia Adair, later a civil rights activist, would remember that her first leadership role, at the age of sixteen, had transpired because "I had been active in my Sunday School and things like that." When a Miss Beulah, who oversaw all the Sunday school instruction at Adair's church, fell ill, on her deathbed she asked Adair, "Will you promise me that you'll be the Sunday School Superintendent?"[8]

Women particularly saw missionary work—whether near home or abroad—as crucial to the values of the church and supported it through committee work and money. "Ladies' aid societies" took over many of the basic functions of the church, such as overseeing the cleaning of church buildings, providing food for church suppers, and raising money for operational needs. In addition to baking for bazaars and making domestic products for sale at fairs and teas, women raised money in multiple ways, including asking for donations. The societies also dedicated time and effort to sewing for hospitals or for poor people. These last activities led church-women into more active roles in the community, beginning and operating benevolent institutions. In Galveston, for instance, before 1900, women had established orphans' homes, "women's homes," institutions to assist home-less children, and kindergartens. Although church-affiliated, these were very often not only started by women but also run by women.[9]

Such work made women all the more essential to the function of their churches, but it also made the churches more responsive to women's needs and values. As programs expanded due to women's participation, women made the churches more homelike. In addition to halls for worship, churches became complexes with nurseries, libraries, and Sunday school classrooms. Through fund-raising, women not only demanded these additions but also helped to fund them. Women governed the physical interiors of church buildings through donating their expertise, money, and volunteer hours to decorate.[10]

Women also learned organizational and leadership skills through this work in churches. They learned to work within all-female networks, took supervisory roles, made decisions about finances and expenditures, and even learned political maneuvering in female committees on which they served or when supplicating male or mixed membership committees.[11] The develop-ment and use of these skills in the church would make it easier for women to organize effectively later outside the church as well.

Populism

Women used their perceived greater piety to participate in religious activi-ties outside the home, some even venturing into political matters through the Woman's Christian Temperance Union. However, few Texas women re-mained members after the WCTU became associated with the controversial issue of woman suffrage. The Farmers' Alliance that evolved into the move-ment known as Populism, however, gave a much larger number of women opportunities to work with men on political action.

The Southern Farmers' Alliance formed in the 1870s in Lampasas County, and by 1891 it included members in thirty-two states. Through education and cooperation members hoped to improve farmers' deteriorating financial situation. After the Civil War, farmers throughout the nation, but especially in the South, found themselves mired in debt and held hostage by crop-lien systems and decreasing prices for their produce. Farmers and Alliance members, much like industrial workers in the rest of the country during the Gilded Age, resented big businesses that grew rich while producers labored ever harder but fell farther and farther behind. Particularly, farmers identified two categories of businessmen who robbed them of the just fruits of their labor: railroad owners, who held monopolies allowing them to charge farmers exorbitant prices, and "middlemen," whom farmers believed made the real profit in the buying and selling of farm goods. The Farmers' Alliance espoused cooperative ventures to pool resources and extend credit to members, hoping to combat the effects of national economic forces, but members also demanded that their governments make laws to protect farmers. This led to the formation of a new political party in 1891, the People's Party, also known as the Populists. This farmers' party called for legislation favorable to farmers, including laws to help decrease the cost of land, decrease the cost of shipping, and increase the amount of currency in the economy (in order to help farmers pay back debts).[12]

Farming in Texas had always been a family endeavor, with all members working in the fields, gardens, or home production to achieve self-sufficiency but also, if lucky, a profit. Although women's work was recognized and valued, American tradition long held that men represented the farm and family in the public sphere of law and politics. For this reason, some Farmers' Alliance branches in other states discouraged women from joining, holding their meetings in public places such as courthouses, where women would be uncomfortable. Most Alliance members in Texas, however, encouraged women to become members. They did not especially endorse women's participation in politics, but, much like farms themselves, the Alliance needed women's work and support. As one woman wrote to the *Southern Mercury*, "Our moralizing influence is such that no good Alliance man ever wants to meet unless the sisters are there." Because women joined the Farmers' Alliance most often with their husbands and other male family members—and practically needed the assistance of their men to have the time and transportation to do so—the Alliance was often seen as just an extension of the family project to protect the family farm.[13]

Women participated in the Farmers' Alliance and then the Populist Party in many ways. Nearly one-quarter of the members of the Alliance were women, and their presence was thought to elevate the character of meetings, which contributed to one of the main goals of the organization, the moral elevation of the country's financial and political systems. Women's membership and participation encouraged other men in their families to join, and many women gave speeches and were even appointed as lecturers to recruit other women. Through oratory and writing for the Populist newspapers, including the official organ of the Alliance, the Dallas-based *Southern Mercury*, women served the role of booster, keeping up morale, encouraging men to political action, and enhancing farmers' self-respect.[14] Women performed organizational work to support the local sub-alliances, serving on committees, especially those regarding membership, sewing banners, and planning social events. Women probably devoted more time to providing ice cream socials and picnics than any other endeavor, but a few women also served as local officers, especially in the roles of secretary and treasurer. They also encouraged each other's efforts at combating indebtedness by sharing ideas on cost-cutting and frugality and discouraging the purchase and wearing of expensive fashions.[15]

The Farmers' Alliance and the larger Populist movement of the late nineteenth century were unique in that they welcomed both blacks and whites as members. African American women formed auxiliaries, and approximately twenty-five thousand became full members of the Colored Farmers' Alliance of Texas.[16]

The women in the Alliance benefited in several significant ways. Although the social events they spent so much of their time organizing might seem trivial, the occasions were crucial in the growth of the Alliance and in women's lives. Being isolated on distant farms with crushing amounts of work afforded women few opportunities to socialize. The Alliance gatherings sometimes lasted for days and gave men and women chances to visit with others and to see that they shared their plights and struggles. Between social events and communication through papers such as the *Southern Mercury*, farm women came to experience solidarity among themselves not just as farmers but also as women. Working on committees, women learned leadership and organizational skills that boosted their self-confidence. Alliance meetings and publications provided women with advanced education on economic and political matters. Women, with the approbation of their families, could express political opinions in meetings and in print, reflecting their understanding and awareness of national as well as personal issues. Other women read and heard this with pride. As one woman wrote to the *Southern Mercury* in response to an essay, "Usury and Mortgages," by Lula Wade: "She is certainly a deep thinker. I see other interesting letters from ladies too numerous to mention. I am proud to see so much intellect among farmer's wives and daughters. I believe, according to our opportunities, we do equally as well as the men."[17]

Participation in the Alliance radicalized some women and allowed others to openly advocate for greater rights and roles. Bettie Gay of Columbus wrote to the *Southern Mercury* pointing to the many other women published in its pages: "Nature has endowed women with brains. Why should she not think . . . why not act?" Gay and some other Populist women began to argue that women should not just support men in their political efforts but also engage in action themselves by voting. In the 1880s, contributors to the *Southern Mercury* debated the subject of woman suffrage, with slightly more of the letters by women supporting suffrage than opposing it. Suffrage supporters Bettie Gay and Ellen Lawson Dabbs were elected from Texas to attend the national convention to form the new political party, the People's Party. Although Dabbs endorsed a proposed plank for woman suffrage, the new party rejected it in order to encourage support from southern states where the idea of women voting was unpopular. To support the new party in 1892, Dabbs, the first woman to speak at a Texas political convention, endorsed the party's platform even with its absence of a woman suffrage plank. With the defeat of the Populist candidate for president in 1896, the party fizzled, and the Farmers' Alliance waned in the years to come. While this reduced the possibility for women to gain experience and power through work in this group that had readily accepted women members, many of the women continued with their activism in other ways.[18]

White Women's Club Movement

The most remarkable phenomenon to sweep Texas and transform women's lives and expectations was the seemingly innocuous women's club movement. What became a national movement started locally and small in northern states before the Civil War but blossomed after the war. An increasing number of immigrants from other states to Texas, relatives living in other states, and national magazines and newspapers that began to regularly print stories about club activities elsewhere all provided inspiration for Texas women to follow suit. For instance, the Ladies' Reading Club of Houston organized in 1885 drew its structure and inspiration specifically from the Ladies Literary Club of Grand Rapids, Michigan.[19]

By 1890 Texas could already boast of clubs such as the Galveston Ladies Musical Club, Galveston Girls' Musical Club, Dallas Shakespeare Club, Dallas Standard Club, Tyler Quid Nunc Club, Dallas Pierian Club, and Clarendon Shakespeare Literary Club. Writing in a Dallas newspaper in

1903, clubwoman Mary Terrell recalled that the state had had at least twenty such clubs in the 1880s.[20] Then, in the 1890s, the enthusiasm for women's clubs exploded. Texas women who attended the Chicago World's Fair in 1893 brought home with them the excitement about organizing, speaking, and learning, especially moved by the World's Congress of Representative Women, which had sponsored around-the-clock speeches by and about women during the event. The women returned home and set up a similar event at the Texas State Fair in Dallas that fall: the Texas Woman's Congress. Lectures such as ones titled "The Evolution of Woman" and "Professional Women from a Physician's Standpoint" addressed such issues as dress reform and the cultural construction of women as frail.[21]

The success of the Texas congress at the state fair inspired women to aspire to raise money for a permanent building on the fairgrounds, and to do so they solicited the existing women's clubs. Although the Texas Woman's Congress was unsuccessful at raising money for a building in the struggling economy of the 1890s, it was successful at inspiring interest in women's clubs

Figure 6.1. Local chapter of the Texas Federation of Women's Clubs, Mineral Wells, Texas, early twentieth century. Courtesy of Texas Woman's University, TWU Libraries, Woman's Collection.

and making the clubs aware of each other. By 1897 clubwomen had formed a statewide organization, the Texas Federation of Women's Clubs (TFWC), soon thereafter affiliating with a recently formed national organization, the General Federation of Women's Clubs (GFWC).[22]

Increased urbanization had made it possible for more women to participate in group activities such as clubs without neglecting their duties at home. Although the state remained overwhelmingly rural in the late nineteenth century (84 percent of the population lived in rural areas in 1890), the expansion of railroads after the Civil War spurred rapid urban growth. Between 1870 and 1890, the number of Texas towns or cities over twenty-five hundred in population grew from nine to forty-two. Unlike rural areas, where women had to find transportation (and, to some extent, male chaperones) to see or visit other women, cities provided women with easier opportunities to congregate. Although most elite women in these urban areas had some education that promoted cultural appreciation, very few Texas women had yet had the opportunities to pursue an advanced education or professional career. As late as 1900, only 2.8 percent of young women in the nation attended college, and the number in the South was even smaller; few universities in the South admitted women before 1912. The University of Texas, one of the few schools in the South that allowed both men and women from its founding (in 1883) presented opportunities to some, but most adult women in Texas at the end of the nineteenth century did not even have high school educations.[23]

Elite women in urban areas with more education began to identify new activities for their privileged place in life: arts education and the promotion and appreciation of art, culture, and refinement. Usually the wives and mothers of elite men engaged in these pursuits in their leisure time with their family's money, although some women turned to these full-time. Ima Hogg, the daughter of a Texas governor and a member of a prominent family made even wealthier by the discovery of oil, shared with her family a belief in using such good fortune for the benefit of others. She never married but spent her time, effort, and money in enriching the people of Houston. In 1913 she formed the Houston Symphony Orchestra, served as president of its board of directors for twelve terms, and dedicated fifty years of her life to making it a premiere institution. In the 1920s she began collecting one of the world's finest assemblies of antiques at her River Oaks Mansion, Bayou Bend, a collection she would later donate to Museum of Fine Arts so that the public could enjoy it. Throughout her life she contributed money to the welfare of her city and state, promoting the arts at every turn. While her wealth and dedication were unique, her view that it was entirely appropriate for women to use their gifts for the greater good was part of the culture that would engage many elite and middle-class women in the club movement.[24]

Although the clubs met with some resistance and skepticism from husbands of club members and society in general, elite women defended their pursuits. They now identified art, drama, music, literature, and all cultural pursuits as the proper domain for women, and they argued then that intellectual attainment was consistent with their roles as wives and mothers and even necessary for them. "The clubwoman will be thoughtful and cheerful, and when the tired husband returns home to her she will have subjects of interest about which to intelligently converse, rather than a tirade on household cares."[25]

So women throughout the state formed music clubs, literary clubs (over half of which were dedicated to studying Shakespeare), history clubs, and general self-education clubs. Most members considered a club meeting "a cherished event and a sacred duty." The clubs were highly organized, with constitutions, by-laws, and officers. Each club determined how and what the members would study, most often setting a schedule a year in advance. Women learned planning, organization, parliamentary procedure, and even campaigning for office. Clubs also offered the first opportunity for many women to research, write, and present publicly, as a club often called on each member to present something at a meeting. Despite the overwhelmingly supportive environment of clubs, this was still a terrifying moment for many women.[26]

Clubs borrowed ideas from other clubs and from the General Federation of Women's Clubs, which also provided materials to its member organizations. The topics ranged from a particular Shakespearean play to explorations of jealousy, ambition, and even the morality of dress. No matter the club's larger focus, the most common subject of study was "Woman," as these women collectively attempted to understand and perform their roles in society. In the course of studying "Woman," many clubs concluded that good wives and mothers had to concern themselves with more than their immediate households.[27]

Clubwomen's first civic engagement often emerged directly from their clubs' specific purpose: for instance, musical clubs organized, planned, or encouraged concerts; a subcommittee of a culture club called for members to provide art for schools and town assembly areas. Literary clubs were some of the first to take the most obvious steps into the public sphere as they established free libraries and then insisted on public support to keep them running; 85 percent of the public libraries in Texas were founded by women's clubs. Other clubs also appealed to local and state governments to begin kindergartens (or continue the ones clubwomen started), implement training centers in public schools, set aside money and effort for city beautification, and support public parks and playgrounds.[28]

By the early twentieth century, the GFWC had adopted a progressive agenda and directed member clubs to form subcommittees for the study of specific topics related to reforming society. As Texas women began researching social problems, they were moved to campaign for government solutions. For instance, in 1898 the GFWC adopted resolutions regarding child labor and directed its clubs to investigate the working conditions of women and children locally. When the Dallas Federation of Women's Clubs learned that there were no child labor laws, no factory inspectors, and not even any statistics on the number of children working, they moved from investigation into action. Clubwomen stood outside the gate of factories in the cotton mill district and counted the number of children going to work every day. They reported their findings at the state convention of the TFWC in 1902, and that body endorsed state legislation to set the minimum age for mill labor at twelve. During the legislative session that followed, while organized labor groups lobbied the legislators for the bill, clubwomen organized campaigns to raise awareness, printing and mailing the proposed law to every club in the state and coordinating letter-writing campaigns to legislators. It took nine years, but during the 1911 legislative session, the state federation prodded the Texas commissioner of labor to draft a bill, secured legislative sponsors, and successfully lobbied to raise the minimum working age in factories to fifteen.[29]

Clubwomen, like progressive women throughout the nation, initially justified their forays into politics as a continuation of their womanly sphere. As mothers, they wanted to protect children and thus had a vested interest in child labor laws. They also wanted more funding for schools, teacher training programs, kindergartens, and home economics programs. As urbanization led families increasingly to purchase food, clubwomen pressed for pure food and milk ordinances to decrease the illnesses and deaths of children due to contamination. Dallas clubwomen advocated for a juvenile court system, police matrons, a garbage tax, and a pure water supply. Even though more middle-class women joined the club movement in the first decades of the nineteenth century, the preponderance of upper-class women helped the clubs achieve many of their objectives because these were women with husbands who could enact ordinances or sponsor child labor legislation.[30]

The public and political roles assumed by respectable club members helped gain acceptance for other women and inspired more women to undertake public activism, especially on domestic issues. Galveston clubwomen helped form a Women's Health Protective Association to oversee and enforce sanitary practices in the wake of the 1900 hurricane that destroyed the city. Other women in the state formed chapters of the Young Women's Christian Association and lent their support to home extension clubs. Children remained the most important focus of most women, whether in homes or clubs, and the clubs' study of the effects of society on children led in 1909 to the founding of the Texas Congress of Mothers (later the Parent-Teacher Association), which grew rapidly. This grassroots network of associations worked locally to raise money and supplies for schools and support greater funding for them. Clubwomen also advocated for clean milk and water supplies as well as a host of other public welfare initiatives to protect school-age children.[31]

The GFWC and Texas Congress of Mothers also embarked on a campaign to guarantee married women more control over property, beginning by researching existing state legislation and distributing the summary of these laws, the "Legal Status of Married Women," written by Hortense Ward, for study at club meetings. After years of agitation on the subject, stressing that increased power in the homes and over property was not the same as voting rights, the legislature passed a married women's property law in 1913 that gave women control over their separate property.[32]

The GFWC was instrumental in moving Texas clubwomen to consider social and legal issues that impacted the lives of women and children, and Texas women became leaders both in progressivism and the clubwomen's movement. Clubwoman Isadore Miner Callaway's pseudonym, Pauline Periwinkle, became a household name in Dallas and the rest of the state after she began writing a column for the *Dallas Morning News* in 1896, a column that would continue for two decades. Newspapers usually relegated the very few female journalists of the day to the "society" pages, but Periwinkle wrote about much more than fashion and gossip, reporting on the work of women's clubs and prodding those clubs to become involved in reform efforts. Periwinkle not only encouraged women's activism, she also helped popularize the justifications for that activism in the state: "I am a firm believer that good accrues from woman's familiarizing herself with affairs that affect her immediate community first, her state next, and her country ultimately—good both to the woman and the object of her inquiry."[33]

Anna Pennybacker became the third president of the TFWC in 1901, leading the state organization in efforts to support education, including lobbying the legislature to build a women's dormitory at the University of Texas and soliciting individual clubwomen to donate money for an endowment to provide scholarships to women studying at colleges in the state. At the biennial conference of the GFWC in 1912, Pennybacker won a heated campaign for president of the national organization, "the highest office a woman can hold in America," as one journalist noted. Pennybacker's goals as president were to reconcile the North and South, to grow the membership, and to support the education of women. She supported progressive causes, particularly those related to education, such as the improvement of school facilities, the formation of libraries, and higher education for women, and encouraged local clubs to do so. However, she wanted to steer clear of electoral politics, opposing the GFWC's endorsement of woman suffrage in her first campaign and administration. When re-elected to a second term in 1914, she supported only a lukewarm endorsement of suffrage by the national organization, and the TWFC refused to allow the issue even to be raised at the state convention. Suffrage supporters were angered, but Pennybacker's avowed intent was to grow the organization, thus preparing more women for voting rights when they did arrive. Whether or not she was successful at preparing women for citizenship, the GFWC grew to more than two million members in six hundred clubs by the end of her second term.[34]

Pennybacker succeeded in her bid for the presidency of the GFWC and in growing its membership because a growing population of clubwomen in the South accepted her. Many more southern women than northern women opposed the campaign for women's right to vote, due both to a more conservative outlook and a fear that a federal amendment on woman suffrage might tamper with the recent disenfranchisement of African Americans. Pennybacker's views on race also garnered her the support of her southern sisters. Elite white women had created the clubs during the late nineteenth century, but by the beginning of the twentieth century club membership had swelled to include women of the middle class. In some northern states, these numbers also included black women. The potential admission of black women's clubs to the GFWC thus became a major source of contention, as southern clubwomen refused to consider the possibility of attending a national meeting alongside black women. In a biennial convention before her election, Pennybacker made a name for herself through a speech on education and more especially through her parliamentary tactics that contributed to the adoption of a compromise plan on race. State federations could choose to admit black women's clubs to their federations, but a newly formed GFWC membership committee would consider each club's eligibility for membership in the national organization. With Pennybacker and other southern women taking turns serving as chair of the membership committee, the GFWC and its Texas affiliate would remain segregated for decades.[35]

African American Club Women

Segregation in the Progressive Era extended far more widely than private women's clubs, of course. Although African Americans made up a much smaller percentage of Texas's population than they did other southern states, Texas continued to have a very southern outlook and followed the pervasive legal trend of enforcing segregation between whites and blacks. In the late nineteenth century and early twentieth century, Texas laws required segregation in all public places, such as theaters, train stations, and public transportation as well as schools. In *Plessy v. Ferguson*, the US Supreme Court ruled in 1896 that such separation was constitutional if the facilities provided for blacks were equal to those for whites, but in practice they seldom were, and black schools in Texas received about one-third the funding of white schools. Although African Americans had emerged from the Civil War with no property, an economic system tilted heavily against them, limited access to education, and oppressive laws, a middle class had emerged in the black community by the late nineteenth century. The women of this class formed secret organizations for mutual support, including the Court of Calanthe, Heroines of Jericho, Sisters of the Mysterious Ten, and the Order of the Eastern Star. Like their white counterparts, this smaller number of women also started study clubs in the late 1890s, and by 1905, excluded from participation in the all-white clubs, had established the Texas Association of Colored Women's Clubs, joining with the National Association of Colored Women's Clubs (NACW).[36]

Through church organizations, mutual aid societies, associations, and clubs, black women participated in an elaborate network of institutions dedicated to assisting and protecting their communities in the segregated South. Unlike white women's clubs, which evolved gradually into community work,

NACW members made activism a priority from the beginning, particularly focused on elevating the entire African American community. As Christia Adair, who joined the NACW-affiliated 1906 Art, Literary and Charity Club of Houston, described it, "This organization is a group that has never had any barriers. Our motto is 'Lifting As We Climb,' which means that we have not tried to major [focus?] on the woman who has already reached her zenith, who has had all kinds of opportunities and advantages, but the woman who needs us, the woman who hasn't had advantages, the woman who is down and needs to be lifted."[37]

Most of the black clubwomen were educated and in slightly better economic conditions than other black women in the state, but, unlike most white clubwomen, most black clubwomen worked, usually pursuing professional careers. Only a very few black women, married to prominent men in their communities, had the wealth and status to devote themselves to full-time charitable work. In 1902 Melissa Price and Mary Crawford formed the Married Ladies Social Art & Charity Club in Houston, which focused on personal improvement as well as addressing broader issues in the African American community. One elite woman who devoted herself to social work was Jennie Covington, who attended Guadalupe College and married Benjamin Covington, the cofounder of Union Hospital in Houston. She supported her husband's career by forming women's auxiliaries to aid the hospital, but she also engaged in activism through her club activities and church organizations. She cofounded the Bethlehem Settlement, which provided programs including day care, directed the first branch of the YWCA in Houston specifically for African American girls, headed the Houston Commission on Interracial Cooperation, and chaired the Negro Women's Division of the Texas Commission on Interracial Cooperation.[38]

Many other women involved in the NACW were teachers who identified education as the key to improving the lives of African Americans. They particularly pushed the clubs to start kindergartens and raise money for the underfunded black schools. In Houston, the city with the largest black population in the state, black clubwomen participated in organizations that founded mothers' clubs at local schools and worked to provide services that the underfunded school budgets could not, ranging from landscaping to playground equipment to school supplies, such as art supplies and sewing machines. They also stepped in to provide students with nutritious lunches and looked for any other ways they could help students achieve better educations.[39] Women with any financial means saw it as their responsibility to actively assist in supporting and improving the community. They started and ran orphanages and homes for the elderly and formed hospital aid societies. Activist African American women lamented their lack of political power at many levels and began clubs dedicated to woman suffrage. The statewide suffrage movement, however, led by southern white women accustomed to racial segregation, excluded them from membership and participation.[40]

The importance of their economic contributions to their families had traditionally allowed for strong roles for African American women. Those who joined these clubs, however, faced criticism from some men for their vigorous community activism. One pastor opposed the formation of a women's organization in his church, inducing the women to operate the Willing Workers Charity Club as a secular group rather than give up their idea of charity work. Most of the women who joined the clubs and organizations that participated in community work stressed their activism as part of their female duties, attempting to emphasize rather than blur the gender expectations. Women's "nature" and "duties" were to take care of family and children, and therefore these charitable enterprises were within their sphere. These middle-class women wove gendered expectations into their goals and activism. They encouraged working women to learn and practice better homemaking skills and to raise their daughters to have ideals of middle-class femininity, including strict codes of morality. The clubwomen expected nothing less from themselves, cultivating the idea that respectability would elevate themselves and the race.[41]

Tejana Organizations

Like other women in the state, Mexican-origin women increased their activism in the late nineteenth century and early twentieth century. Despite large populations in the cities of Laredo, Brownsville, and San Antonio, Tejanas were much less likely than their white and black peers to live in urban environments conducive to study clubs and progressive organizational efforts. Cultural restrictions against women acting in public arenas were even tighter for Tejanas, with traditions of female subservience in the community working against women taking leadership roles. Although Tejanas were very active in their churches, this outlet did not lead to outside activism. Most Tejanas were Catholic and played devoted and crucial roles in supporting their churches, but Catholic clergy opposed women acting without male control and insisted upon careful supervision, leading to limited independent agency for women.[42]

In the early twentieth century, the Mexican American community in Texas did not have a large middle class with multitudes of educated women who had extra time to devote to civic and cultural activities. Most Tejanas married young, seldom had access to much education, and were barred by strong cultural expectations from public events without their husbands or fathers. As a result, Tejanas created far fewer women's clubs and at a significantly later period than other groups of women. Beginning in the late nineteenth century, women became increasingly active in mutual aid societies. These *mutualistas* were formed to support their communities by providing burial and illness benefits, legal aid, emergency loans, and employment assistance. Their members established newspapers, libraries, and private schools and held dances, celebrations, lectures, and theatrical and musical performances.[43]

Women at first joined *mutualistas* with their husbands or fathers and performed mostly auxiliary work rather than serving as leaders of groups. Before the turn of the century, many women began organizing *mutualistas* of their own. For instance, women formed four such groups in Laredo before 1900. Women's associations such as these, and women working within mixed-gender *mutualistas*, took the responsibility for planning community-wide events, from dances to heritage celebrations. In 1895 Laredo women marched in parades and gave speeches at the celebration of Mexican independence; they also planned the overwhelmingly popular Cinco de Mayo celebration, where at least fourteen women participated in oration, poetry reading, and musical performance.[44]

Planning celebrations and parties was deemed suitable to women's position, while male societies continued what was regarded as the more significant decision-making work of the communities. Yet women learned leadership and organization skills through their *mutualistas*. The celebrations were also much more than just entertainment; they were important ways in which people honored and retained their traditions and heritage. By choosing which events would be organized and how to celebrate them, the women exerted their influence. The Cinco de Mayo festivities planned by women's mutual aid societies, unlike previous purely secular celebrations, included religious activities. In 1906, the Sociedad Josefa Ortíz de Domínguez participated in celebrating the first anniversary of a labor union, Unión Obrera Federada, thus calling attention to and endorsing workers' efforts to organize. Through their activities, the women's mutual aid societies also raised substantial funds with which to support their own and others' activities.[45]

By the 1920s, nine of the nineteen mutual aid societies in San Antonio (the city with the largest Hispanic population in the United States at the time) included women, who assumed leadership positions in these mixed-gender groups. In 1920 Tejanas founded the Cruz Azul Mexicana (Mexican Blue Cross). With branches in large and small towns throughout Texas, Cruz Azul encouraged countless women to engage in activism and charitable work. The Cruz Azul chapter in San Antonio raised $4,000 to begin a free public clinic. Chapters also established libraries, assisted in educational projects, and helped plan community celebrations.[46]

Some Tejanas formed some study clubs similar to those of white and black women, although their presence and activities are hard to trace because they did not have a state or national organization that affiliated the clubs. Excluded from white women's organizations such as Parent-Teacher Associations, they formed Spanish-speaking PTA organizations. Other Tejanas took up the pen to write about improving their communities, and one columnist even wrote about women's rights. María Luisa Garza served as one of the editors of a San Antonio newspaper, *La Epoca*, and, writing under the pen name "Loreley," reported on such events as the 1922 Pan-American Conference of Women, held in Baltimore.[47]

Events in Mexico after the turn of the century would affect women's lives in Texas. The disruptions of rebellion, war, and fear of retaliation led thousands of Mexicans to make Texas their new home. While many planned to stay temporarily, many more became permanent residents, swelling the population of existing Tejano communities near the border and in South Texas and Central Texas. Thousands of women thus helped families cope with having left old lives behind and helped build new ones. Many women played even more active roles, ministering to soldiers on both sides of the border or engaging in political and intellectual activism in opposition to Mexican president Porfirio Díaz. More than thirty newspapers were started by political exiles, while existing newspapers also took active positions on the war, and many of these papers were established or written by women. Sara Estela Ramírez's paper, *La Corregidora* (the Mayor's Wife), in Laredo, advocated for the revolutionary party, the Partido Liberal Mexicano (PLM). Isidra T. de Cárdenas's *La Voz de la Mujer* (Woman's Voice) in El Paso reprinted excerpts from the PLM's call to revolution and pleaded with President Roosevelt to exert his power on behalf of one of the revolutionaries in prison. Andrea and

Figure 6.2. Leonor Villegas de Magnón and Aracelito García, around 1914, with flag of La Cruz Blanca, a volunteer organization to assist the wounded during the Mexican Revolution. Reprinted with permission from University of Houston Libraries, Special Collection by Arte Público Press.

Teresa Villarreal established and ran two periodicals in San Antonio support-ing the revolution. For her father's newspaper and then for several papers in South Texas, Jovita Idar wrote in favor of the revolution across the border, but she also criticized the discrimination practiced against Mexicans in Texas. Journalists such as these, as well as other activists and writers, such as Leonor Villegas de Magnón, not only opposed the Mexican dictator but also carved out a place for women's political and intellectual activism.[48]

Hereditary Societies

Seeing it as their duty to pass on their heritage to future generations, and inspired and encouraged by the growing women's club movement of the late nineteenth century, some women began founding and actively participat-ing in heritage societies such as the Daughters of the American Revolution

(DAR), the United Daughters of the Confederacy (UDC), and the Daughters of the Republic of Texas. Most members sought to preserve traditions, ideals, and heritage through celebrations and commemorations of the past. Because they restricted their membership to women who could prove lineage to a defender in a war, only white women and a few Tejanas became members. The organizations thus served to protect not only the memories of their family members and ancestors but also past ideals of class and race.[49]

The DAR had established local chapters in the 1890s, and a state society with five local chapters was organized in 1900. The women in the organization engaged in patriotic and commemorative activities such as collecting memorabilia, providing US flags to local schools, and preserving relics. In 1920 the DAR supported the state legislature's surveying and marking the historic Old San Antonio Road, providing 120 granite markers for the six-hundred-mile trail.[50]

The United Daughters of the Confederacy held its first state convention in Texas in 1896, affiliating five existing local clubs and encouraging the formation of new ones. Although the South had lost the Civil War, the UDC members believed that the cause and sacrifice of the soldiers had been noble and just and should be commemorated. At the convention, the UDC state president call for members to build monuments as tangible reminders of their past, a call that UDC chapters fulfilled by raising the funds to construct more than fifty large public monuments to the Confederacy throughout Texas. UDC chapters also cared for aging veterans and their families and insisted that schools teach the "true" history of southern glory, introducing nothing into the curriculum that would criticize the Old South. Although the UDC commemorated and celebrated the men who fought in the war, the members' attempt to uphold what they perceived to be old southern values of obedience, self-sacrifice, and benevolence was also an attempt to feminize society by encouraging men and women to embrace these values that by the early twentieth century were considered feminine.[51]

In 1891 the Daughters of the Republic of Texas (DRT) created a state society with local chapters to reclaim and restore the last resting places of the heroes of the Texas Revolution. They sought to enlarge women's private role of caring for family gravesites into a public duty. Members of the DRT looked for, marked, and restored graves, took steps to promote Texas history in schools, lobbied to name or rename schools for Texas sites and heroes, and sought to restore and preserve sites associated with Texas history, especially the Alamo. Adina de Zavala developed plans with her local DRT chapter to acquire and preserve the missions near San Antonio, including the Alamo, most portions of which were in private ownership by 1892. The process of trying to raise funds for the DRT to purchase the mission attracted a wealthy socialite, Clara Driscoll, who finally fronted the money after the fund-raising fell short, the legislature refused to assist, and plans were being made to raze the mission and build a private hotel. The legislature finally purchased the Alamo from the DRT and Clara Driscoll in 1906, but the fight over the preservation continued, pitting de Zavala against Driscoll in a very public debate. Despite the difficulties, the DRT was successful in exerting custodianship and preserving the important piece of Texas history. [52]

The hereditary associations were conservative in nature, wishing to preserve past racial, class, and gender hierarchies through controlling the narrative of history. At the same time, they claimed a new authority and power for this group of women. One of the founders of the DRT counseled her members, "Let us leave the future of Texas to our brothers, and claim as our province the guarding of her holy past." By eschewing claims to public policy, women expected to control how the past was presented. Thus, when Governor Oscar B. Colquitt opposed the plans of the Driscoll-led DRT, they were angry because his plans did not fit their visions of how to domesticate the space and because men were interfering in one of the few public provinces these women controlled. The leadership of the DAR, UDC, and DRT preferred to preserve traditions and ideals that celebrated heroic male acts and female domestic accomplishments. They successfully controlled the narrative through the histories that they wrote and the ways in which they encouraged the histories to be taught in schools. In the end, these women derived their significance from the success of their ability to celebrate past male accomplishments.[53]

Suffrage

While some women used the past to promote traditional ideas about women's roles and place, other Progressive Era women began using history to examine and advocate for greater rights. The greatest expansion of women's rights came as a result of the campaign for suffrage. Some women had supported "woman suffrage" even before the Civil War, and at least one bravely petitioned the legislature during the period of Reconstruction. The Woman's Christian Temperance Union was the first women's organization to endorse suffrage, in the late 1880s, but it allowed local unions the option to support or oppose the issue and always placed prohibition first and foremost. The national woman suffrage movement had split after the Civil War, and their division increased the difficulty of organizing women in Texas. Individuals like Mariana Thompson Folsom, nonetheless, crisscrossed the state giving speeches, raising the topic, and finding women and men who were sympathetic even if they were afraid for social and political reasons to admit so. Others also circulated petitions, gave speeches, organized public debates, and distributed information, such as copies of the *Woman's Journal*.[54]

After the two national suffrage associations combined in 1890 to form the National American Woman Suffrage Association (NAWSA), the individual activists and the national organization saw Texas as one of the most promising southern states in gaining the right to vote. In 1893 some forty-eight women organized the Texas Equal Rights Association (TERA). By the next year, eight local chapters operated in Denison, Taylor, Granger, Dallas, Fort Worth, Belton, San Antonio, and Beaumont. TERA formed during the initial period of women's public activities enabled by church groups, the Farmers' Alliance, and women's clubs. As a result, the members of the state organization reflected a wide range of new women activists, and their diversity would cause difficulties. Urban clubwomen clashed with rural activists, and traditionalist women, who wished to win the vote to infuse society with more female values, clashed with women who hoped to enlarge and change women's roles. Instead of growing, the executive committee split over ideological issues, and TERA ceased to exist by 1896.[55]

Another short-lived suffrage organization, the Texas Woman Suffrage Association, began in 1903 when Annette Finnigan and two of her sisters held meetings in their Galveston home. Finnigan had grown up in Galveston although she had lived in the North for years and thus had connections to suffrage societies elsewhere. Finnigan worked to build a statewide organization and began traveling to organize women elsewhere. Although she located some interested women in Beaumont, San Antonio, and Austin, she wrote that they were "too timid to organize." The activists finally held a state convention in 1904, with delegates from three suffrage leagues, all based in southeastern Texas. The next year, frustrated by the lack of progress and by the lack of assistance from the national association, Finnigan moved to New York. For the next several years, the Texas Woman Suffrage Association existed in name only and its president lived out of state.[56]

Texas had been a vital piece to the national suffrage puzzle, according to NAWSA's plan in the late nineteenth century. As part of the state-by-state strategy, NAWSA leaders believed southern support for women's votes could be gained by using racial prejudice. Southern suffragists argued that women should have the right to vote, in essence, because they were better educated and more trustworthy than black men, who already had the right. The strategy was a failure in budging a single southern state legislature, and when literacy tests, poll taxes, and "grandfather clauses" restricted the black vote, the strategy ceased to exist by the early twentieth century. NAWSA for many years gave up on the South completely and funneled its resources elsewhere. By the time NAWSA renewed its interest and belief in the promise of Texas, there had been two failed statewide organizations, and the executive committee chose to wait for the right person to attempt building a third one that would not fail. The Austin Woman Suffrage Association, organized in 1908, did not produce such a leader. Although the Austin Woman Suffrage Association paid the state's dues in the national organization, the official state president, Finnigan still lived in New York. When San Antonio organized a suffrage society in 1910, Eleanor Brackenridge emerged as the leader NAWSA had wanted. She was a respected member of an elite family, and her state and national leadership in the women's club movement garnered her respect and name recognition throughout Texas. Brackenridge worked with NAWSA to organize a conference in 1913, and there she was elected president of what would shortly be renamed the Texas Equal Suffrage Association (TESA).[57]

By 1915 TESA had twenty-five hundred members and twenty-one local organizations. The time was finally ripe for a successful suffrage movement, primarily because of the foundation laid by increased women's activism in voluntary associations. Brackenridge's prestige, built through the club movement, had enabled her to gain a following and support for suffrage. Others had also honed their leadership skills in women's organizations such as the Texas Congress of Mothers and the WCTU. As clubs and activist women had expanded their fields of interest to protecting their families in the rapidly industrializing and growing cities, women had asked governments to provide greater assistance to schools, to regulate the milk supply, to provide sanitary sewage disposal, to regulate working conditions for women and children, and to support thousands of other progressive agenda items whereby governments would improve the urbanizing and industrializing society. While progressive men in positions of power often agreed with the clubwomen who lobbied for change, they were few in number in Texas, and the laws they passed often disappointed women.[58]

Increasingly, politically active women began to argue that they needed to have more than influence in order to protect society; they needed the power of the vote. The newly elected TESA president, Minnie Fisher Cunningham, would later explain that she had "floated into the suffrage movement on a sea of bad milk." Women like Cunningham who entered politics in the 1910s argued that they should have the right to vote because they would act in the best interests of children and families and "clean up" society with their vote. By the time the Texas Federation of Women's Clubs officially endorsed suffrage in 1915, support for the vote was socially acceptable and even trendy, and organizers found more interested and less timid women.[59]

With a growing movement of women dedicated to earning the right to vote, and a new, energetic TESA president with superior organizing skills, the organization set out to lobby the state legislature and support candidates for office. By 1916, in order to make the limited voting rights of African Americans irrelevant, Texas had, like most southern states, become a one-party state, and whoever won the Democratic primary would win the general election. The Democrats, however, were split into conservative and progressive factions. In the governor's race, TESA opposed the conservative James E. (Jim) Ferguson, who had come out against woman suffrage, but he won the race. When, shortly after his election, Ferguson was impeached and removed from office, women aided in that effort. Despite his impeachment, Ferguson mounted a re-election campaign, and TESA promised to back his successor in office, William Hobby, if he would support the right of women to vote in the primary. Organized by Minnie Fisher Cunningham and Jane Y. McCallum, women from all over Texas engaged in lobbying, writing, and visiting legislators. Although Governor Hobby did not publicly endorse the bill, the legislature passed it on March 26, 1918, and Hobby signed the act into law that allowed the women of Texas the right to vote in primary elections. This essentially granted white women the right to participate in choosing most elected officials in their state. Poll taxes and other forms of discrimination continued to prevent black women from exercising the right of suffrage.[60]

The suffragists set about making a difference with their first opportunity to vote. They had just sixteen days before voter registration for the primary closed, and during that time 386,000 women were registered to vote. Upholding their promise, the TESA formed Hobby Clubs to campaign for Governor Hobby. To further encourage women to vote, they solicited a highly qualified woman, Annie Webb Blanton, to run for the state office of superintendent of public instruction. TESA printed mock ballots to instruct newly registered women how to vote. By all accounts, women were successful during their first election in Texas: a large, unknown, portion of the registered women voted, Hobby was re-elected, and Blanton became the first woman elected to a state-wide office in Texas.[61]

The progressive faction of the Texas Democratic Party was so impressed with the support of female voters that it added a platform plank to grant full suffrage. The legislature even passed an amendment to the Texas Constitution and scheduled a statewide referendum on the issue, ironically against the wishes of the suffragists. Neither TESA nor NAWSA leaders believed that the state constitutional amendment would win popular support in Texas, and they were afraid that a defeat would stall momentum just as it appeared a national amendment would be sent soon to the states. True to their predictions, the referendum failed in May 1919.[62]

Despite having their energies diluted by work on the state referendum, Texas suffragists lobbied their US senators to support a federal amendment, using telegrams, letter-writing campaigns, and personal visits from influential Texans. Their efforts were so relentless—and successful—that the NAWSA president, Carrie Chapman Catt, referred to them as the "heavy artillery down in Texas." With the two Texas senators' votes, the federal amendment was submitted to the states for approval. After another very hard-fought campaign, in which suffragists had to overcome the defeat of the state referendum a month earlier, the Texas house of representatives and senate finally agreed to approve to the Nineteenth Amendment, the first southern state to do so.[63]

Cunningham, still the TESA president, then turned her considerable experience to the national scene, helping NAWSA organize campaigns to approve the federal amendment in other states. Tennessee became the thirty-sixth state to ratify the amendment on August 18, 1920, thus giving the amendment the necessary three-quarters of the states to ratify the Constitution's Nineteenth Amendment. Texas women finally had their right to vote guaranteed, and they could proceed to use it—after registering and paying a poll tax.[64]

Post-Suffrage Movement Activism

The fight for suffrage in Texas had brought thousands of women together united for one cause. Those thousands of women, however, wanted the right to vote for thousands of different reasons. After winning suffrage, the overarching issue that had brought so many together no longer existed, and women set about using their newfound power in politics and society, splintering into many different factions to address a myriad of concerns. Many of the women who had campaigned so vigorously for suffrage turned their political activism into lifelong careers, whether paid or unpaid.

As described above, suffragist Annie Webb Blanton was the first woman elected to state office, achieving this in the first election where women were allowed to vote (a Democratic primary). In 1922 Edith Eunice Therrel Wilmans was the first woman elected to the Texas legislature, and other women gained local offices in the 1920s, most often on school boards but also on city councils.[65]

In 1924, in one of the most ironic twists in Texas history, Miriam A. Ferguson, the wife of Governor Jim Ferguson, became the first woman governor. Woman suffragists had supported the impeachment of Jim Ferguson because he had opposed suffrage and prohibition and because his administration was corrupt. Throwing their support to his opponent had been a crucial political step in gaining the right to vote. Unable to run again for office as part of his conviction, "Pa" Ferguson entered his wife into the gubernatorial race instead. Most Texans assumed that "Ma" Ferguson was merely a stand-in for Jim and thus did not consider a vote for her to be an empowering vote for women. Progressive-minded women split in the election. Although progressives opposed the Fergusons, Ma Ferguson came out vociferously against the Ku Klux Klan, which in the 1920s was in resurgence. The racist organization had targeted African Americans for violence during Reconstruction, but the new Klan also targeted immigrants, Catholics, Jews, labor unions, and other so-called foreign elements, including progressive ideas. The Klan had an active women's auxiliary in Texas, but most progressive-minded women found the Klan and their use of violence and fraud to gain political power antithetical to their goals. Miriam Ferguson's election was a repudiation of the Klan as much as it was a vindication of her disgraced husband. Although the corruption of Ma's first term would cause her to lose her reelection campaign, she would go on to run for and win another term of office in 1932.[66]

Minnie Fisher Cunningham had a long and influential career in politics, although she never won a state office. She served as a lobbyist at the national level for suffrage and for other important issues to women, including the Sheppard-Towner Act, federal legislation to extend public health programs to rural areas and improve prenatal and maternal care. She took a national role in the building and formation of the League of Women Voters (the organization formed after NAWSA met its primary mission of suffrage). After women gained the vote, she worked within Texas politics to support progressive policies and candidates but found that turning suffrage into actual political empowerment and recognition would be as hard a fight. Women, divided by their interests and party loyalties just as men were, did not vote in a bloc and, in fact, voted less frequently than men, leading male political leaders to pay less and less attention to them. Annie Webb Blanton ran for US Congress in 1922 and failed to unite women or anyone else behind her campaign. Cunningham's campaign for the US Senate in 1928 also ended in failure. Nevertheless, Cunningham and other women continued to vote, organize, and lobby throughout the rest of their lives, making politics more responsive to women.[67]

Jessie Daniel Ames, former TESA president and the first president of the Texas League of Women Voters, became horrified by the rise of the Klan. Its resurgence heightened her long-held belief that racial oppression was one of the great political and social wrongs. By the end of the decade, Ames took the paid position as director of woman's work for the Commission on Interracial Cooperation. Ames identified the connection between racial and gender injustice in southern white society's justification for lynching. White men falsely claimed that they lynched black men in order to protect the "virtue" of white women, and as a result white women were oppressed and made to feel weak, while black men and women were terrorized and forcibly kept in inferior positions. In 1930 Ames would found the Association of Southern Women for the Prevention of Lynching, and she would devote her life to the eradication of lynching in the South.[68]

Thousands more women continued to work to improve their communities and state through voluntary groups. In the 1920s many of these organizations—the Texas Federation of Women's Clubs, Texas Congress of Mothers and Parent-Teacher Associations, Texas League of Women Voters, Federation of Business and Professional Women's Clubs, Woman's Christian Temperance Union, and Texas Graduate Nurses Association—formed a powerful coalition, the Women's Joint Legislative Council (WJLC), derisively called "the Petticoat Lobby" by some representatives.[69]

The WJLC supported legislation specifically related to women, such as repealing discriminatory laws that interfered with women's rights after marriage. A married woman still could not control her own property, much less the joint property of the marriage, and did not have equal guardianship rights to her own children. When Miriam Ferguson, as governor, signed a transfer of property in 1926, the state attorney general's office was forced to research legal issues and make a ruling that her signature alone was sufficient (because it was state property and not her own, it was legal). After nearly a decade of agitation, lobbying, and working with representatives, in 1929 the Texas legislature approved a new law giving married women significantly more property rights.[70]

The WJLC agenda included a wide array of progressive reforms, such as enforcement of prohibition, better education for children, and aid to mothers and infants.[71] For instance, women's groups and the WJLC took up the cause of prison reform, envisioning more humane, educational institutions that would rehabilitate prisoners, rather than the forced convict-labor system the state employed. Women formed a state chapter of the Committee on Prisons and Prison Labor in 1920, with a board made up of former suffragists and WJLC members such as Jessie Daniel Ames and Jane Y. McCallum.[72]

One of the most resounding victories for WJLC was the passage of state legislation to provide matching funds for the implementation of the federal Sheppard-Towner Act that would provide prenatal and infant care. Unfortunately the act expired in 1929, and the state did not renew its commitment to funding programs to aid mothers and children in reducing infant mortality.[73] Overall, the WJLC wielded enormous influence early in the decade, passing all six of their proposed bills in 1923. Of course, no political group of any kind could sustain that level of success, but, throughout the 1920s and beyond, women continued to influence lawmakers to remake the state in their image, with many successes and failures along the way.[74]

The former woman suffragists in the 1920s did not merely return home to celebrate the winning of the vote. They continued lobbying for changes in laws and attempted to turn their votes into real political power. They mentored protégés and encouraged education and activism among younger women. They fought for places of power within the Democratic Party, and they ran for political office. The Democratic Party, however, conceded only symbolic positions to women, not equal participation. Women candidates faced the uphill battle of convincing men and women that women could do more than vote and could actually lead. A few women did achieve positions within the party, and a few won or were appointed to political office. This fell far short of women's dream of equal power, but it was revolutionary since more women held these positions in the 1920s than had held them in the entire previous history of Texas.[75]

The New Woman and the Flapper

At the turn of the century, Americans heralded the "New Woman." Educated, activist, middle-class, and increasingly urban, she might still celebrate domesticity, but her vision of the proper role of women expanded beyond that of her home. "New" women were more empowered than the women who came before them, and they worked hard for thousands of causes now claimed as part of women's responsibilities. Their new pursuits also demanded new clothing: high-necked shirtwaist blouses and ankle-length A-line skirts that allowed more freedom of movement.[76]

By the 1920s society and consumer culture had co-opted this image of the new woman. Short bobbed hair and straight dresses and skirts came to epitomize not just more physical freedom for women to pursue their political and career ambitions but also to symbolize sexual freedom and a desire for frivolity and fun. A graphic illustrator from Cleburne, Texas, had no small part in this transformation of the icon. Moving to New York in 1915, Gordon Conway created illustrations for numerous advertisers and more than twenty publications, including *Vanity Fair* and *Vogue*. Her line drawings of the New Woman glamorized the slim, straight figure and agility, popularizing the look for thousands of young girls who emulated it in the 1920s.[77]

Young Texas women adopted many of the fashions of the 1920s, much to the chagrin of their mothers, and also followed many other national trends. The oil boom of the early twentieth century generated wealth and led to increased urbanization. Young women left farms in greater numbers to take new jobs in cities. Undoubtedly there were many fewer women in Texas than in New York who lived up to the national image of the "flapper" who frequented speakeasies and danced the Charleston all night. Yet some of the most popular jazz and blues musicians of the Roaring Twenties hailed from the state (such as Scott Joplin, Eddie Durham, Blind Lemon Jefferson, and Huddie "Lead Belly" Ledbetter), so opportunities for such entertainment and style existed.[78]

Even women who remained on farms, ranches, and oil fields began to benefit from technological advances. Electricity was slow to reach rural areas, and families were slow to purchase even gas-powered tools to help with house-

Figure 6.3. Cars helped bridge the isolation women faced on farms and ranches. Unidentified man and woman in Texas. Courtesy of Texas Woman's University, TWU Libraries, Woman's Collection.

work. At the same time, though, the automobile broke the isolation for farm women. Cars facilitated easier, faster travel, and women could more often afford the time to accompany their husbands to visit friends and families or go into town. Like horses and buggies, automobiles were usually considered male domains, but many women did learn to drive, giving them greater independence from the men in their families. Better transportation also enabled young farm women to consider leaving their homes to take jobs in neighboring towns or cities.[79]

Many of the women who fought so hard for suffrage and expanded rights for women were mystified and horrified by the ways many young Texas women capitalized on personal independence and job opportunities. The successes of the activist women had paved the way for the women to make choices of which their mothers could not have dreamed.

Conclusion

Changes in late-nineteenth-century and early-twentieth-century Texas created opportunities for women and spurred more of them into action outside the home than ever before. Urbanization played a significant role in fostering women's regular interactions with each other and the founding of religious and secular organizations of women. However, urbanization alone cannot account for the explosion of women becoming more involved in the world outside their home. Whether participating in a farmers' rebellion, coping with segregation, or responding to political and social unrest spurred by war and revolution south of the border, women of all classes and regions of Texas actively engaged in the social concerns and political issues of their day. Expanding their ideas of domesticity into the public sphere and working for the good of society as a whole, not just their individual families, eventually led to their demand for the right to vote and the power to make necessary changes. Women may not have challenged the essential ideas about women's duties, but they expanded the arena in which they fulfilled their roles.

Chapter 7

Women's Work, 1890s–1920s

Women continued to engage in labor valuable to their households and the Texas economy throughout the nineteenth and early twentieth centuries. Much of this labor went unchanged as women continued working on farms and ranches. Access to education expanded, however, and many more women began careers as teachers, nurses, secretaries, and even politicians. Although the number of professions that were considered appropriate for women remained very small, in the early twentieth century changing attitudes toward women's abilities and aptitudes along with urbanization began to offer some greater career and personal opportunities.

Cotton Farming

Texas remained overwhelmingly rural in the early twentieth century, with 83 percent of the population in 1900 living in counties mostly engaged in farming. At the beginning of the twentieth century, most Texas women were still performing the same kind of labor in almost exactly the same way as they had done during the antebellum period. If anything, the amount of work had grown longer and harder with land tenancy and sharecropping.

Tenant farming and sharecropping had existed on a limited scale before the Civil War, but the arrangements became dominant afterward, when thousands of freed slaves without land sought a living and cash-strapped landowners looked for a way to cultivate large holdings without the use of slaves.

In tenant farming, a landowner leased a farm or portion to a family who grew crops. Tenant farmers, who used their own animals, seed, and equipment, generally surrendered about one-quarter to one-third of the crops to the landowner, while sharecroppers leased those items along with the land and owed the owner half or more of the crops. Tenants and sharecroppers did not receive any profits or money until the end of the year, and thus they purchased supplies and necessities for the family on credit, giving as collateral the crops they had not yet harvested. As a result of the risk involved in offering credit on a crop not yet planted, suppliers of goods outside the state charged high interest rates, and the storekeepers (who were often the landowners themselves) imposed even higher prices on the tenants and sharecroppers, who had no choice but to accept them. Both landowners and creditors demanded that tenants and sharecroppers grow the profitable commodity cotton, leading to overproduction throughout Texas and the South, thus decreasing the price of cotton and therefore the amount of money individual families would make. Tenants frequently ended the year owing more than they did at the beginning. Sharecroppers almost always ended in debt, forcing them to continue working the same land in virtual debt peonage that was reinforced by state laws.

While sharecropping and tenancy after the Civil War were ways to accommodate landless African Americans, the system quickly entangled white farmers as well. The majority of landowners in the state before the war had small farms on which they produced food and everything else they needed, with small crops of cotton to pay the extra bills. Bad crop years or desire for store-bought goods drew these small owners into the crop-lien system, with high-interest loans they often could not repay, resulting in loss of land. Additionally, thousands of people migrated to the state in the late nineteenth century to take advantage of West Texas acreage recently connected to markets by railroads and from which Native Americans had been forcefully removed. The number of "improved" acres of land increased from around three million in 1870 to almost twenty-one million in 1890. Many of the new arrivals did not have the money to buy property or quickly lost the land they purchased and settled into tenancy. The percentage of farmers who were tenants or sharecroppers reached 42 percent by 1890 and 50 percent by 1900, and it continued to increase until World War II.[1]

Whether in the old cotton country of East Texas or in the new western cotton belts of the Hill Country (in Central Texas), most women lived on homesteads that produced cotton. All men, women, and children on a cotton farm were expected to work on the main cash crop. Not only did the family's survival depend upon this labor in the fields, landlords made decisions about how many acres to rent to families based upon the number of children and whether the wife "worked like a man." Antebellum proscriptions against women working in the fields had long since fallen away, and women's fieldwork, especially at cotton-picking time, was necessary. Over half of the white women and nearly all black women on cotton farms labored at least some in the field.[2]

While many women working in the fields only did so at cotton-picking time, the most labor intensive time of the year, others did so year-round. Margaret Hunt Carroll remembered many years later that growing up on her family's cotton farm near Belton, "I was the oldest 'boy,' I had to [help out]! I started driving a team when I was eleven whenever I started helping my daddy. He'd do the plowing and then I'd come along with the planter and a mule." When Carroll grew older, she had to take over the plowing as well. Teenaged girls handling plows and engaged in heavy farm labor regularly proved that farm women were far from delicate creatures in need of protection. As difficult as the work was, however, Carroll was proud of her efforts and liked her assignment of plowing, planting, and picking. Her sisters did not work year-round in the fields as Carroll did, and thus they had more domestic chores that Carroll preferred to avoid: "I would rather do anything than wash dishes."[3]

Among girls and women, however, Carroll was lucky to have been assigned just male work. Most girls and women were expected to pull double duty in the field and the house. Eva Mae Glover near Columbus remembered, that as a child, "I was the boy and the girl both at home. I could cook, I could plow, would go to the fields and I would plow."[4] Margaret Bert Wilhite Bounds of Bell County remembered that her mother would pick as many rows as her father, then leave a little earlier than the family so that she could "have beans and cornbread and fried potatoes and onions and all that good stuff ready when we got there." While women often performed all kinds of work, men rarely crossed gender lines to help with domestic work. After dinner, Bound's father "would lay down and take him about a five-minute nap. And she'd be in there washing dishes!" One study of farm families found that fathers and sons only helped with household chores a few hours a week and spent even less time taking care of young children.[5]

Planning and providing inexpensive and nourishing meals occupied most of the time that women spent outside of fieldwork. As in the nineteenth century, the three staples of the diet remained pork, cornmeal, and molasses. Women assisted, but men bore the primary responsibility for raising and killing hogs, raising the corn and having it ground, and gathering the sap to make syrup. Women, however, preserved and prepared these foods. At hog-killing time, women stayed busy, scraping and cleaning intestines as well as grinding and seasoning pork to make the sausage that would last the year. The lack of refrigeration and electricity made long-term storage one of the more significant challenges. To preserve the pork women salted it for curing in smokehouses and rendered lard for use throughout the year. These tasks were similar in most rural households that had access to hogs—either their own or thanks to the generosity of neighbors. Tejanas used additional ways of cooking and preserving pork, cutting it into chunks and frying it as well as making tamales out of the hogs' heads.[6]

Families preserved corn in several ways. Men would take much of the corn to be ground at commercial mills, and cornmeal could keep for months. White and black women alike turned the cornmeal into fried patties or cornbread in skillets over hot stoves, a miserable job in the summer months. Tejanas used the ground corn to make tortillas. Women also dried corn that was later made edible through a painstaking process of boiling with lye, making hominy. Some families were lucky enough to have access to canning technology, and farmer Margaret Bounds remembered that "canning corn was a full day." After the children removed the husks and silk from the ears of corn, her mother would "cut the kernels off in a big dishpan, scald the cans, put the corn in the cans and salt them, then she would put them in the cooker and cook them."[7]

Although the three staples served as the basis for most meals, these could not provide enough vitamins for families, so the women who could do so raised extra food by tending gardens, orchards, poultry, and milk cows. The produce of these then had to be dried or otherwise preserved. As Bounds remembered, "my mother canned just about everything that she could get her hands on—out of the garden or out of the orchard, either one." Canning required hours in a small hot kitchen over a wood stove, constantly feeding it fuel and emptying the ashes, while cutting, peeling, preparing, and cooking the fruits and vegetables to be canned. Because the produce had to be processed immediately upon harvest, women canned nearly every day during the hottest months of the year. Kitty Clyde remembered, "Oh that was a terrible thing. You wore as little as you could. I wore loose clothing so that it wouldn't stick to me. But the perspiration would just pour down my face." In addition to canning, some of the produce was dried. Dried beans especially played a critical role in the diet year-round.[8]

Women's other time-consuming tasks revolved around keeping the family clothed. By the end of the nineteenth century, the spinning wheel was a relic of the past, and women no longer spun and wove at home. Despite the expense, buying manufactured cloth was the more cost-effective use of women's time. Women often obtained fabric from peddlers by trading eggs, butter, and produce from their gardens or by paying for it with money made from selling such goods. Local general stores also sold cloth, but women's work in the household did not allow much time for travel, and thus the stores remained male domains. Wives would send instructions with their husbands concerning the type, color, and quantity of fabric to purchase. Bernice Weir of McLennan County remembered giving her husband specific directives on the material she needed, but he came home with a different pattern, claiming the store did not have what she wanted. Weir recalled, "I just cried and cried. . . . And I don't know whether they was without or whether he just went in and saw that check and said, 'I want some of that.'" Additional sources of cloth were feed and flour sacks, used particularly to make underwear and bedding. In the 1920s, flour companies began printing their sacks with designs to capitalize on this widespread use. Farmwives would trade them with each other to get matching material and make clothing of all kind, including dresses.[9]

Once they had acquired fabric, women sewed clothing for their large and constantly growing families—rural Texas families still averaged more members than urban families. Women transformed sacks and bolts of cloth alike into every necessary piece of attire for the family. They also sewed and stuffed their own mattresses and pillows as well as sheets and curtains. For winter, they made quilts and other bedding. Women also constantly mended clothing and recycled worn-out articles by making them into other items. The economic contribution of homemade clothing and bedding was so immense that it often was sensible for farm families to purchase a sewing machine. Traveling peddlers sold sewing machines, and many women saved their egg and butter money to buy the labor-saving devices, though husbands and wives together usually made the decision to buy one. Those who could not afford the purchase borrowed one from others or pooled their resources with other families and shared one. Treadle machines were a great improvement over hand stitching, even though almost no rural women had electric sewing machines until mid-century. Only those closest to cities had electricity before the 1930s.[10]

Clothing also had to be washed, and this remained the most dreaded task and the first household chore to be hired out to poorer women when a family could afford to do so. Making the lye soap for laundry required saving wood ashes, mixing them with water, and allowing them to settle to make the lye, then cooking the lye with lard in an iron pot over a fire. The wealthiest families could buy soap, but store-bought soap was usually a luxury reserved for washing bodies, not clothing.[11]

The next and most difficult ingredient for washday was water. Very few rural families had indoor plumbing until the 1930s, and even by 1940 less than a quarter had it. The few lucky enough to live close to creeks or other clear surface water would carry the laundry and soap to the water. Some families, having no nearby creeks or wells of their own, had to haul water from other farms. Most, however, did have a well or cistern, but these were located, on average, over 250 feet from the house. Children helped carry some of the nearly two hundred gallons of water a family used each day, but on days that required heavy water usage, women had to carry most of it—and to wash clothes for the week required about fifty gallons. The stress of hauling water took its toll on women: "You see how round-shouldered I am? Well, that from hauling the water," reported a Hill Country farmwife.[12]

Once they hauled the water to the house, the washing began. The water was heated over a fire (with firewood often gathered for this purpose). "Then we washed on a rub board. We'd rub and rub and rub them," Gladys Merle Keener Chastain of Coryell County remembered. After the clothes were washed, laundry was transferred to another holding of water and rinsed, and then families would use whatever they could to hang them to dry. Chastain's family hung the clothes on a barbed wire fence, "then the wind would blow them off, and you'd go along on the ground and pick them up." In the summer, the job was torturously hot, but in the winter clothes often piled up because women had to wait for a sunny day. Only a few rural women had the help of washing machines even after World War I when they became more readily available, and even then had to carry the water to the machine. After the day of washing came the day of ironing, which started with heating a six- or seven-pound piece of iron on a wood stove, then using a rag or cloth to hold it while pressing on the clothes. Mary Cox

Figure 7.1. Women in rural areas were responsible for raising chickens well into the twentieth century. The eggs and meat were used to supplement the household income. Courtesy of Texas Woman's University, TWU Libraries, Woman's Collection.

remembered, "Washing was hard work, but ironing was the worst. Nothing could ever be as hard as ironing."[13]

Profit margins were so slim on cotton farms in the early twentieth century that careful home production of clothing and food could mark the difference between a profit and debt and could even keep a family from losing its land. Unfortunately, women in the families of sharecroppers and itinerant workers (those who traveled around, especially at cotton-picking season) were the least able to spare time away from the fields to grow and make food that was inexpensive yet nourishing. Ernest Allen Cole was lucky that his family "had a big garden. Some reason, the sharecroppers didn't do this. That's the reason they're sharecroppers, I guess. How'd they got enough to live, I don't know."[14] Those who could not or did not grow their own food relied upon expensive prepared foods bought on credit, or they went without. Malnourishment led to more sick days and less time for family members to work in the field. Likewise, women who made clothing, kept it clean, mended, and reused it saved the family from buying clothes on credit. Women's skills in home production along with their butter and egg money might enable a farming family to owe less than they did the year before. For tenant farmers and sharecroppers this could mean the possibility of moving to better land and better homes. For landowners, this meant that they could continue to own their land and improve their holdings.

Other Rural Occupations

Women living on cotton farms, whether as tenants or owners, made up the majority of rural women and indeed the majority of women in Texas. However, many other women also lived in rural areas, engaging in work besides cotton farming.

The politics of progressivism in the early twentieth century led to increased institutional support for agricultural extension programming intended to share scientific methods to improve farming in the South and in Texas. In 1914 Congress officially created the Agricultural Extension Service. By 1920 those who wished to improve the lives and production of farmers recognized the desirability of applying scientific methods also to "women's work," and many women found employment working as home demonstration agents. Both male and female agents worked tirelessly, traveling to different communities, but they found families resistant to change. To combat that resistance, they focused on demonstrations in which farmers could see positive results. They also found that girls and boys were more open to new ideas than their parents, and they formed girls' "Tomato Clubs" whose participants could see the benefits of better canning and share the techniques with families and friends. Home agents could then encourage women to plant large gardens, share poultry-raising ideas, demonstrate new canning techniques, and establish community canning clubs and centers.[15]

Because African Americans made up a large portion of the cotton-growing population, the Extension Service also employed black extension agents, including women home demonstrators. The USDA directed them to concentrate more on home improvement than on canning and ordered that the black groups not be called canning clubs like the white groups, suggesting instead "Home Making Clubs." Prairie View A&M University graduate Mary Evelyn V. Hunter, the first African American woman agent, however, focused on the same main areas as white agents—food preservation, gardening, and poultry-raising—techniques that would help families become less dependent on landlords and store-bought goods.[16]

Agents also encouraged women to spend their extra money on home improvements, such as a can of paint for a room in the house or labor-saving devices such as a washing machine or gasoline iron. In some areas they organized sewing clubs and home economics clubs in the schools. World War I escalated their work, as home production became more important in order to funnel resources to war needs. Dallas County hired two black agents who held ninety-eight meetings in six towns, reaching 1,518 people, demonstrating canning and drying. Throughout the 1920s, canning centers became more central and important to communities and more profitable. The greater profitability attracted more government attention, and by the end of the decade men were being hired to manage the plants instead of (or in addition to) women. Women agents then increasingly turned to other community projects, such as mattress-making.[17]

Working for the Extension Service was grueling, involving a great amount of travel and responsibility. It was, however, one of the professions open to the growing number of educated women in the state, and one of the few to include African American women. Gender and racial discrimination, however, greatly affected the employment of agents. Blacks received far less pay than whites, and women far less pay than men for approximately the same amount and type of work. There were far fewer positions available to women. When counties set up Extension Service offices, they raised the money and committed to hiring a male agent first. They hired women when there was extra money, and their work, therefore, was often temporary.[18]

The Extension Service targeted cotton farmers, with preferences toward those who owned their own land. Many rural women throughout the state lived in families who neither owned farms nor sharecropped. In order to survive, all members of the household had to work for wages in someone else's fields, and this decreased the time women could spend caring for their families, procuring and preparing foods, and otherwise saving expenses. The majority of women agricultural laborers working for wages in Texas were African Americans in the cotton-growing regions of the state. They and their families sometimes traveled great distances to find work and took whatever they could find, being busiest at cotton-picking time. These poorest women also offered their services in domestic tasks, especially washing clothing, a job that farmwives often wanted to hire out.[19]

The number of Mexican immigrants to the state increased significantly in the early twentieth century due to political and economic disruption in Mexico. The estimated population of immigrants rose from almost 72,000 in

1900 to nearly 252,000 in 1920. Some immigrant families secured places as tenant farmers, but widespread discrimination led many cotton landowners to prefer American tenants, white or black. As a result, most Mexican agricultural workers participated in a migratory pattern of labor. Families would follow the crops, harvesting spinach in the valley in the winter and early spring, tending onions through the spring, then moving to Central Texas in the summer and fall to provide labor during the cotton-picking season. Women worked alongside their husbands and children in the fields. The frequent moving meant that women could not grow gardens for household use, generally preserve food for the future, or even spend any time making comfortable homes. Housing in any location was uncertain at best, and families camped anywhere they could: smokehouses, shacks, or overcrowded tents. In such conditions one hot meal a day was the most women could provide for their families. They used rocks and hot coals to make the necessary tortillas and open fires to cook whatever meat could be acquired.[20]

Meanwhile, ranching continued to occupy some rural women. Farms spread throughout the state, overtaking more territory and pushing ranching farther to the south and west. Raising cattle still continued to be profitable, and women made important contributions throughout the twentieth century, even owning a small but notable percentage of ranches themselves. Women on the ranches worked hard at tasks similar to those of their farm sisters: raising gardens and chickens, preserving food, preparing meals, making and caring for clothing, milking cows. Of course, on cattle ranches, beef replaced pork as the main meat for the family. Much of the work with the cattle was considered more appropriate for men, but women of all ethnicities on ranches did what was best for their families despite gendered expectations. Hallie Crawford Stillwell, an Anglo woman, learned how to ride on her father's ranch near Alpine, chasing off bandits and fixing fences. After marriage, she assisted her own family on a ranch near Big Bend, finding scattered cattle over miles of rough terrain, gathering them into a pen, and throwing and tying them for branding. Gertrude Ross Rydolph, an African American woman, served as secretary, bookkeeper, and horsewoman on the ranch she and her husband started together near Bloomington. Women on ranches also arranged provisions for the men of their family on overnight campouts while rounding up cattle, and they often accompanied the men on these roundups. Women with sons could expect to work less as the sons matured and took over the duties. In addition to women in families that owned the ranch were the wives and daughters of ranch hands who worked for wages. These women often also worked for wages, washing laundry or assisting with food preparation.[21]

The great oil strike at Spindletop in southeastern Texas in 1901 opened petroleum production in the region and created a different experience for many women in the state. In the next decades, families moved to extremely isolated rural areas in order for men to take jobs in newly opened oil fields, usually remaining in each location less than a year before new fields opened. When oil was struck near a town, the influx of workers and their families quickly overran the accommodations, and so they had to improvise housing, making shelters from crates and boxes or metal cans. The most common form of shelter was the "boarded tent" with four-foot walls, covered by canvas roofs. In their tents and shanties, women attempted to provide domestic comforts with limited furniture and appliances. With no running water, women had to haul water from barrels of delivered water to clean homes and clothes often coated with dust, grime, and soot spewed from manufacturers nearby. The omnipresent dirt as well as abundant insects

Figure 7.2. Woman in Orangefield, oil field, 1920s. Courtesy of Heritage House Museum, Orange, Texas.

made houses difficult to keep clean and traditional meals hard to prepare, but women improvised. Clell Read later remembered that "we had many, many meals with our heads under a sheet" to protect the food from dust and bugs. Unlike sharecroppers, who also dealt with primitive living conditions, oil field families often earned good money. Demand in oil field areas outstripped supply, however, and so women constantly scrounged to get basic necessities. Nonetheless, to improve their living conditions women invested in amenities such as linoleum, carpets, and even radios or wind-up Victrolas, while keeping in mind the need to move frequently.[22]

Urban Work

Although Texas remained predominantly rural before 1940, cities grew at increasing rates in the state, creating both new opportunities and new problems for women. The oil boom encouraged new industries and businesses and increased migration to Texas cities, which facilitated other types of manufacturing. These industries employed many men—unskilled, skilled, and professional—and the presence of the industries demanded support services. Men at the bottom of the pay scale often could not afford to make ends meet, and their wives and sometimes children were forced to find paid employment. Young single women took advantage of the urban opportunities to find work until they were married. Many educated, professional women were also able to develop and use their skills effectively in towns and cities.

Women did not need to engage in as much home production of goods when family members were earning wages, but early twentieth-century urban homes still relied on their crucial economic work in conditions nearly as primitive as those in rural areas. Many families continued to keep horses and use their yards to raise gardens, chickens, hogs, and even cows to provide milk. Sewer lines, paved streets, gas, and electricity were available only in parts of towns and were prohibitively expensive for most. Women thus continued to churn butter, preserve fruits, vegetables, and meats, and otherwise produce as much as 80 percent of what the family ate.[23]

Although their work at food production remained similar to that of rural women, urban women's work otherwise differed. Wages earned by men, women, and sometimes children in towns and cities allowed families to purchase more of the goods that they needed, especially cloth and clothing. Women spent less time producing and much more time cleaning and performing continual maintenance chores, such as sweeping, mopping, laundering, ironing, mending, and making meals. The expected level of cleanliness was greater in cities, and women fought the dirt brought in by the wind and muddy boots, wielding brooms, buckets, mops, and brushes. Houses were heated with coal, kitchen stoves fueled by wood, and rooms lighted by oil lamps, and thus walls had to be constantly scrubbed to remove the grime deposited by the flames. Women dreaded laundry day just as much in the cities because few people had running water, and thus water still had to be carried from wells to washtubs.[24]

For obvious reasons, then, the wealthiest families hired domestic help whenever possible. The less wealthy struggled to perform these tasks with the labor of wives and children alone. Many women could not afford to devote all their time to their families and had to earn wages. They were the ones who took the domestic jobs as well as the many other jobs that began to open to women in the urban areas. In 1900 more than 26 percent of women in Dallas were employed; and by 1920 more than 36 percent were. A higher percentage of single than married women worked, but significant numbers of both groups either provided for or contributed to their household incomes by earning wages.[25]

Many of the occupations that women entered in urban areas were related to domestic duties as maids and cooks in private homes. Although ready-made clothing decreased the need for dressmakers, the number of women employed in clothing factories and textile mills increased. The demand for women with sewing skills also increased in other industries, such as mattress and awning factories. Shops and department stores also needed women with sewing expertise to provide tailoring services. The demand for lodging was higher in the cities, and women used their domestic abilities to run or work in hotels and boardinghouses. Some women began their own businesses in personal services such as hairdressing and cosmetics. Department stores and the variety of services that they offered in the early twentieth century contributed to the fastest-growing new occupations. Women took jobs as hairdressers, shampooers, candy makers, nurses, teachers, and clerical helpers. Overwhelmingly, however, women found new jobs in these stores as sales clerks, particularly for women's items. By 1920, 17,667 women held 29 percent of all retail sales positions, a percentage that would continue to climb for the rest of the century. As the term "salesgirl" implied, many of these employees were young single women who intended to marry eventually, although some married women kept their positions until having children. White women predominated in these sales positions. African American and

Figure 7.3. Women switchboard operators, Cumberland Telephone Company, Port Arthur, Texas, 1914. *Left to right*: Daisy Neal, unidentified woman, Lillian Frost, and Flora Tucker. *Rear*: "Mrs. Stanley" (*at desk*) and "Mr. Toples." Courtesy of Museum of the Gulf Coast, Port Arthur, Texas.

Mexican American women, however, were hired in stores that catered to their ethnic populations.[26]

Clerical occupations were the fastest-growing ones for women in the cities, and by the 1920s these jobs had become feminized despite having little connection to traditional women's domestic expectations. Nearly fourteen thousand Texas women held 87 percent of the jobs as secretaries and typists in 1920. Their numbers were also growing in bookkeeping, making up 38 percent of the people employed in this occupation. Women also laid claim to one of the newest jobs, with nearly sixty-four hundred women comprising 92 percent of the telephone operators in the state.[27]

Although few clerical and sales positions were open to African American women in the early twentieth century, black women increasingly comprised a significant part of the working population in cities. World War I sparked a migration of African Americans from the rural South to the North and to southern cities, a migration that increased gradually until it boomed during World War II. African American families took advantage of the expanding number of jobs in growing urban areas to leave the endless cycle of poverty involved in tenant farming. Beginning with little and relegated to the lowest-paid positions, these families needed any and all possible income, and, just as they did on the farms, women and children as well as men worked, but in the cities they worked for wages. A much higher percentage of black women than white women therefore worked for wages, contributing vital labor for the development of these urban areas. In 1920 women made up 38 percent of the African Americans working in Houston.[28]

The African American women who had to earn wages to contribute to their families were almost always relegated to the lowest-paid jobs. They worked as maids, cooks, and cleaners in private homes. They served as washerwomen, traveling to homes to do laundry or "taking in" laundry and washing it at their own homes. Long-held southern traditions associated black women with this type of backbreaking manual labor, and thus, in East Texas, black women were usually preferred as domestic help. Because black women needed jobs and there were few other opportunities open to them, black women took these positions with the very low wages attached. In 1920 black women made up 81 percent of the women in domestic labor in Texas. African American women in much smaller numbers also worked as "seamstresses," cleaned cotton at warehouses, ran lodging houses, operated as beauticians, and engaged in some manufacturing. A much smaller percentage of black women than white women were able to earn an education and use it in professional positions.[29]

In Texas's southern and western cities such as San Antonio, El Paso, and Houston, the number of Tejanas and Mexican women earning wages as domestics began to rival or exceed the number of African Americans. In El Paso in 1920, over 1,700 Hispanic women worked as servants and another 710 as launderers. The number working as domestics also rose in East Texas. Women found jobs as unskilled laborers in industrial laundries and garment factories and worked at cigar manufacturing and pecan shelling. Very few Tejanas worked at skilled jobs or pursued careers in professions requiring education. One contributing factor to this was the strong cultural proscription against married women working. Although single and widowed women found it necessary to contribute wages to their families, married women with working husbands were expected to stay at home to take care of the house. According to a sampling from the 1900 El Paso census, 17.1 percent of Hispanic households contained a woman working outside the home, but not a single household included a working married woman with an employable husband. The large number of unskilled women workers in cities drove the wages down to poverty levels. Poor conditions and low wages led women, mostly Tejanas, working in El Paso laundries to try to unionize and then strike in 1919. Although women exerted strong leadership and walked off their jobs, the male officials of the Central Labor Union took over the management of the strike and the negotiations. Unfortunately, the proximity of Mexican workers willing to cross the border and replace the strikers led to the end of the strike within a few months.[30]

Teaching as an Occupation

In the late nineteenth century, Texans wanted to provide basic education more extensively and as a result more teachers were needed. In 1879 the state legislature established the Sam Houston Normal Institute in Huntsville to train white teachers and funded training at Prairie View Institute for black teachers. The founding of these schools coincided with women's greater interest in advanced education as well as a desire for professions in which to respectably use their educations. In the early twentieth century the need for teachers increased, leading to the need for more opportunities for formal training. Between 1901 and 1925 another seven normal schools were established throughout the state. As a result, more and more women chose to pursue that profession, one that offered them independence—at least until marriage.[31]

During and following the Civil War, teaching became an acceptable occupation for women, easily perceived as an extension of women's duties of taking care of children. Thus teaching became both the most respected profession for a woman and the most acceptable justification for further education. Gladys Peterson Meyers, who grew up in Kerrville later recounted that her "father didn't think of a female as a good investment education-wise. His real reason was, I think, that he didn't have the money because there were three of us." She ended up taking out a loan in 1925, cosigned by her uncle.[32] Elizabeth Stroud Shelton began teaching in Medina County in 1922 and later remembered, "It was all right for a woman to get a college education as long as she was planning to be a teacher. But if it were any other profession, it wasn't. They'd say, 'Why was it necessary?' A woman needs to stay home and learn to cook, wash and iron, and get married and have children."[33]

The overall number of Texas teachers grew from 1,621 in 1870 to 14,681 in 1900. The percentage of those teachers who were women also increased dramatically, with women making up 49.5 percent of the teachers in Texas in 1890 but 81 percent in 1920.[34] For many women, teaching represented the only respectable occupation. Knowles Witcher Teel, who began teaching in Lake Victor in 1924, later recalled, "Teaching was about the only decent thing when I was growing up for a girl to be."[35] Some women were able to forego marriage altogether because teaching provided both an income and continued respectability. Most teachers, however, taught only until they married, and most school districts until World War II would not allow married women to teach.[36]

A degree was not required to teach, and rural school districts often hired girls or young women with only high school educations. In these situations, small communities often viewed the teachers as not quite adults, thus justifying strict regulations of their actions. Teachers could not drink, have boyfriends, or go to parties. They were required to attend church and could not live alone, so they frequently boarded with a local family. This arrangement worked well for some young teachers who were treated as members of the family where they stayed. For others, living in someone else's household could have serious disadvantages, including lack of privacy, lack of respect, and expectations of additional duties such as caring for children or manual labor around the home. Nineteen-year-old Knowles Witcher Teel had to solicit help from her mother to find a different and more suitable lodging situation after she found herself expected to sleep in the baby's room in the school principal's house.[37]

Teachers in the ubiquitous one-room schoolhouses of rural Texas taught in difficult conditions with few supplies, roofs that leaked, and doors that would not stay shut against the wind. To operate the schools they engaged in many difficult chores, such as chopping wood, hauling water, and scrubbing floors. They also mended clothes and made meals for children whose families could not provide them. Through this all, they taught children of every grade level in the same room. Ethyl Scott remembered that in Evergreen, "I had most of the grades. I had all the elementary grades, one boy in junior high school and two girls in high school." And teachers did all this while educating children who wandered in and out during the short academic year, depending on the seasonal demands of helping their families on farms.[38]

For those who stayed in the profession for any length of time, they hoped for one of the better jobs in a town or city. These positions not only paid more but also had the benefits of sharing the work with other teachers and professionals in larger schools. Urban schools also tended to require greater academic preparation than rural ones, either in terms of experience or advanced training. The numbers of women attending college were gradually increasing, but the new state teachers' college and numerous private normal schools attracted hundreds more women every year, giving women the opportunity for advanced learning without compromising their social position. The proliferation of normal schools also required that a smaller group of women enter another occupation: normal school faculty. Because these teachers' colleges paid their faculty poorly, many jobs opened to women in training teachers. Annie Webb Blanton, who would become the first woman elected to statewide office, began her career in a one-room school house in Pine Springs, moved to a more desirable urban school in Austin, and then, after receiving an advanced degree, taught at the North Texas Normal Institute.[39]

A growing African American middle class encouraged daughters to get an education, but black women were even more limited than white women in their opportunities to use that education. Teaching was one of the few professional avenues for African American women. Both of Itasco Wilson's parents and many of her relatives were teachers: "That's the professions there were back then. You could take piano, be a teacher, or be a nurse. That's all we knew about then." In 1920 teachers made up 71 percent of the black women professionals. Undoubtedly they comprised an even greater percentage of professionals in rural areas. Like her parents, Wilson became a teacher in rural Kerrville.[40]

Other Professional Women

Propriety, or expectations of women's proper place, constricted the professional choices for many women. At least one other occupation merged ideals about womanhood with the ability to earn a living and pursue a career: nursing. Catholic orders of women had been at the forefront of nursing in Texas, caring for soldiers during the Civil War and nursing the sick during outbreaks of yellow fever before and after the war. Three experienced nurse members of the Sisters of Charity of the Incarnate Word traveled to Galveston in 1866 to establish the Charity Hospital (later St. Mary's Infirmary), and, after recruiting new members, established Santa Rosa Hospital in San Antonio in 1869. Following the war, secular women began pursuing the profession as an acceptable way of serving others while earning income, because caring for the physical and emotional needs of human beings was seen as women's work within the family. More schools began providing professional training: John Sealy Hospital in Galveston started a school for nurses in 1890, and Sisters of Charity of the Incarnate Word trained nurses at St. Joseph's Hospital in Fort Worth beginning in 1906. By 1923 eighty-five nurses' training schools were accredited by the state. In 1920 3,265 women made up 96 percent of the nurses in the state. While Texans clearly saw nursing as a woman's occupation, nursing did not carry the same social acceptability that teaching did. It was not considered ladylike to dress the wounds of strangers or perform the manual labor that nursing care required. Because low wages and low respectability deterred some white women from entering the field, it opened the doors for many African American and Mexican American women.[41]

One special type of medical care, midwifery, had always been the purview of women, and it continued to offer a career path for many women. Midwives attended over half of the state's births as late as 1900, and midwives continued to practice through the early twentieth century despite the professionalization of medicine and doctors who disdained these childbirth attendants, deeming them untrained. As a result, women turned more and more often to male physicians for childbirth, especially in urban areas. Galveston boasted nine midwives in 1900, but the percentage of the births that midwives attended decreased every year, and by 1919 the Galveston directory had ceased listing midwives, even though many women continued to act as childbirth attendants. In rural areas, however, midwives continued to play an important role in the health and safety of mothers and infants, with about four thousand midwives still practicing in 1924.[42]

Despite their success in nursing and midwifery, few women were able to obtain advanced medical training. In the late nineteenth century, the few women who became physicians had to do so by training outside the South. Margaret Holland, who practiced in Harris County, graduated in 1873 from Northwestern in Illinois, while Grace Danforth of Austin and Frances (Fanny) Leak of Dallas both got their training in Chicago. Ellen Lawson Dabbs earned her medical degree from the College for Physicians and Surgeons in Keokuk, Iowa, in 1890. The first African American woman to practice as a physician in Texas, Mary Susan Smith Moore, earned a medical degree from Meharry Medical College in Nashville and opened Hubbard Sanitarium in Galveston as a hospital for African Americans. Sofie D. Herzog opened her practice in Brazoria after earning her degree in Austria and practicing in New Jersey. Not until 1897 did a woman receive her medical degree in Texas: Marie

DeLalondre Dietzel graduated that year from the University of Texas Medical Branch in Galveston. Even then, few women were admitted to the school. When Claudia Potter graduated in 1904, she was only the sixth woman to have done so. In 1920, according to the decennial census, 133 women made up 2 percent of state's physicians.[43]

Like women who eschewed gender expectations and constrictions in the late nineteenth century to become physicians, others stepped beyond their gender roles to take occupations more commonly associated with men. The sculptor Elisabeth Ney left her birthplace in Westphalia (now part of Germany) in 1871, and, after a couple of quiet decades, opened a sculpting studio in Austin in 1892. Ney's work successfully impressed powerful men, and men were the subjects of most of her sculptures and paintings, such as numerous busts and statues of Sam Houston and Stephen F. Austin (still housed at the state capitol). Ney benefited primarily from the support of women, however. Women of the Texas World's Fair Association provided her first opportunity to complete a large project. Subsequently, prominent women as individuals and groups lobbied for commissions for Ney.[44]

Few women made names for themselves in the early twentieth century through sculpting, but some took up other arts, such as music and drama. A few African American women found success singing and recording a new style of music, the blues. For instance, Beaulah "Sippie" Wallace and Victoria Spivey both had success in the state and beyond, entering the music business and recording hits.[45] The Mendoza family, particularly Lydia Mendoza, who made her first recording playing the mandolin at the age of twelve, would become stars in Tejano music.[46] Rosita Fernández likewise began singing and touring with her family but went on to become "San Antonio's Rose" in city promotions.[47] Many Tejanas also entered professional careers in the theater. While large touring companies constituted most of the Anglo American theatre, Mexican American communities supported local theatre companies in which women such as Magdalena Solórzano, Margarita Fernández, and Concepción Hernández found careers and even acclaim, as long as they played parts in dramas suitable for the whole family.[48]

The creative endeavor that attracted the greatest number of women, however, was literature. Upper- and middle-class American women had been combining writing careers with ideals of domesticity since before the Civil War. Only a few women in Texas could support themselves with their writing, although a few in the late nineteenth and early twentieth centuries gained some critical acclaim. In 1899 Mollie E. Moore Davis published

The Wire Cutters, based on the time she had spent on her brother's ranch near Comanche; this was the first novel to seriously portray western life and the cowboy.[49] Karle Wilson Baker, who taught at Stephen F. Austin State Teachers College, received more honors than any other Texas woman poet in the twentieth century. She also wrote novels and children's books including a history of Texas.[50] The widely acclaimed author Katherine Anne Porter received her inspiration growing up in Kyle and several other Texas towns, although she left the state to make good as a writer.[51] In the 1920s, several Texas women met success writing fiction, including Ruth Cross, who depicted tenant farmers; Dorothy Scarborough, who described the barren West Texas plains; and Winifred Sanford, who explored the social effects of the oil boom in Wichita Falls.[52]

As difficult as it was for white women to achieve critical or economic success as writers in the early twentieth century, doing so proved nearly impossible for black women. While living in Fort Worth, Lillian Jones Horace became the first African American in the country to publish a utopian novel, *Five Generations Hence*, which appeared in 1916. The work depicted a back-to-Africa movement before Marcus Garvey began lobbying for such in the 1920s. As an African American author in Texas, however, Horace could not find a publishing house willing to take a risk on the novel, and she had to pay for it to be published.[53] Josie Briggs Hall of Mexia published a nonfiction book in 1905 that posited a solution to the race problem by advocating increased education and more financial security for African Americans. Maud Cuney Hare of Galveston, who would later gain success writing about music and theater, published a biography of her father in 1913. Like Katherine Anne Porter, at least some African American women left the state to become writers. Gwendolyn Bennett, for one, left Giddings and joined hundreds of African Americans in New York to contribute to the flowering of the Harlem Renaissance.[54]

Tejanas and Mexican women also picked up the pen in the early twentieth century. The emergence of the Spanish-language press in Texas engaged several women in these literary endeavors as editors and writers (as noted in chapter 6). Some who used their newspapers as forms of activism also became well known for more literary endeavors, as did poet Sara Estela Ramírez. Leonor Villegas de Magnón wrote an autobiographical account of the Mexican Revolution, *La rebelde*. Josefina María Niggli published her first book of poetry in 1928, when she was only eighteen. Maria Elena Zamora O'Shea in 1935 wrote a novel highlighting the Tejano contributions to the state, this at a time when official Texas centennial celebrations were ignoring their presence.[55]

Few other professions welcomed women. Social and family pressures kept some women from pursuing their dreams and entering male occupations. Attending school in the rural Hill Country in the 1920s, Elizabeth Shelton wanted to be a lawyer, but her father would not allow it, and she yielded to his demands and social pressures to become a teacher.[56] Legal restrictions and traditions often prevented women from getting hired in other fields. Minnie Fisher Cunningham earned her pharmacy degree but in Huntsville could only get hired as a clerk at half the pay of the male pharmacist, who did not even have a degree.[57] In 1910 Hortense Ward became the first woman licensed to practice law in the state, and she had been forced to earn her education through correspondence courses. In addition to sharing a thriving law practice with her husband, Ward led efforts for married women's property rights, prohibition, and woman's suffrage, becoming the first woman to vote in Harris County. As in the rest of the country, the percentage of women lawyers was small; the census of 1920 showed 52 women made up 1 percent of the profession in Texas. Many of these women probably were still not licensed to practice law despite having the education and performing legal work in law offices. Ward and two other attorneys, however, did have the chance to make history when a case came before the Texas Supreme Court in 1925 concerning the Woodmen of the World fraternal society. All the Supreme Court justices and virtually all lawyers in the state were members of the Woodmen and thus had conflicts in hearing the case. Governor Pat Neff granted a temporary commission to Ward to act as chief justice of the Supreme Court and commissions to Ruth Virginia Brazzil and Hattie L. Henenberg to act as associate justices to decide the case *Johnson* v. *Darr*.[58]

Other occupations may have seemed even more out of reach than law and medicine, but a few women followed their dreams anyway. Katherine Stinson, who in 1912 was the fourth American woman to earn her pilot's license, and her younger sister Marjorie Stinson, who in 1914 was the ninth American woman and the youngest woman in the world to do so, moved from Arkansas to San Antonio and opened the Stinson Aviation Company. The sisters traveled the air show circuit, dazzling crowds with their daring stunts. After World War I broke out, Marjorie trained pilots for the British Royal Flying Corps and US Army Air Corps, becoming the first woman member of the US Aviation Reserve Corps, while Katherine flew from Buffalo, New

York, to Washington, DC, to raise money for the Red Cross. In 1921, Bessie Coleman, who had to travel to France because no American schools would train her, became the first woman from Texas and the first black person in the world to obtain her pilot's license. After she perished during a plane stunt in 1930, an organization founded in her honor, the Bessie Coleman Aero Club, sponsored the first black air show the following year.[59]

On the ground, other women chose to turn domestic skills into paying enterprises, running boardinghouses, opening dressmaking or millinery shops, and operating beauty parlors. These commercial ventures thrived in cities, along with other new entrepreneurial endeavors, such as grocery stores, dry good stores, and bakeries. María Luna used her baking skills to open Luna's Tortilla Factory in Dallas, while Faustina Porras used her cooking ability to open a restaurant that would later in the century become a major chain restaurant in the Dallas area, El Fenix. Women also continued the businesses of husbands and fathers, opened companies with other men, and more and more often in the early twentieth century became sole proprietors of a wide variety of enterprises unrelated to domestic pursuits, including publishing, manufacturing, and even a circus. In 1920 the Dallas city directory listed almost one thousand women as proprietors. In order to support themselves and their families, many women began businesses or continued ones started by husbands, but many married women pursued these avenues out of desire for personal and financial satisfaction. One of the most successful Texas businesswomen, Carrie Marcus Neiman, used her skills and talents as a top salesperson and buyer to found, with her husband and brother, the high-end department store Neiman Marcus. The Texas legislature responded to the influx of married women into commercial ventures with a statute in 1911 allowing married women who ran businesses and gained their husband's written permission to act as independent financial agents and to have the same legal and financial rights as single women.[60]

Cities fostered the development of another entrepreneurial field, that of the madam or proprietor of a brothel. Prostitution thrived in cities after the Civil War, and in the late nineteenth and early twentieth centuries, municipalities exhibited varying degrees of toleration. Some cities had ordinances forbidding prostitution but did not enforce them. Others enforced them with an aim to raise money from fines, and still others, such as Dallas and Waco, legalized and regulated prostitution. In the 1880s more than a hundred prostitutes plied their trade in each of the state's largest cities, such as

Galveston and Dallas, and by 1910 that number had tripled. In 1890, El Paso had at least six hundred. Prostitutes could work on the streets or in single rooms, but red-light districts in each city, with distinctive names such as Hell's Half Acre (Fort Worth), Utah Street Reservation (El Paso), and Skiddy Street (Denison), led to the predominance of the brothel, run almost exclusively by women. Some madams, mostly former prostitutes themselves, became legendary and were able to capitalize on their business skills and other attributes to accumulate significant wealth and independence. Pauline Lester owned and ran both a brothel and a saloon in Denison for nearly two decades. Mollie Adams's career in Waco also spanned decades, winning her notoriety but also enough wealth to travel to places like New York and to have her formal portrait painted. Most madams had much more limited success, running their businesses for only a few years and never expanding in size or wealth.[61]

Rarely did any of the hundreds of prostitutes become madams. Mostly young women in their late teens to mid-twenties, few continued in the profession in one town for over five years. Women turned to prostitution for a wide variety of reasons, including seduction or rape, economic circumstances, abandonment by husbands or lovers, alcoholism, and abuse. Few entered the profession as a conscious career choice, although some did indeed recognize that selling sexual favors brought more income than many other occupations open to uneducated women. With the exceptions of those who stayed to become house proprietors, most prostitutes moved frequently to different houses, cities, or states. Others eventually married or found other forms of employment, and some committed suicide.[62]

Progressives at the beginning of the century, often led by women, clamored against vice districts, advocating laws prohibiting prostitution along with alcohol. They were most successful during World War I as thousands of soldiers were stationed in Texas and were seen as being in need of protection against such vices. Suffragist Minnie Fisher Cunningham led sixteen organizations to form the Texas Women's Anti-Vice Committee to put pressure on the War Department to protect soldiers from venereal disease by shutting down the red-light districts. As with the prohibition of liquor, one of the unintended consequences of the criminalization of prostitution was a rise in the rate of organized crime, increasing the likelihood that prostitutes and brothels came under the control of men, such as crime bosses and pimps.[63]

Conclusion

Daily work for most Texas women in the early twentieth century remained similar to that of the nineteenth century: farm labor with few technological conveniences. However, as Texas entered the oil boom years, the state attracted more industries, and urban areas began to grow. Women gained opportunities to obtain conveniences to improve their working conditions at home as well as opportunities for employment outside the home. Changing attitudes about women's work, as a result of urbanization and the agitation for suffrage, also opened a few avenues for professional life, especially teaching and nursing. The small but increasing number of women who sought careers outside the home was a harbinger of changes to come.

Chapter 8

Depression and War

Women's activism, urbanization, and economic changes in Texas at the beginning of the twentieth century created new opportunities for women in their private and public lives, including new career options. But as women were developing new ideas about themselves, the Great Depression that followed the 1929 stock market crash challenged these new gender constructions. The profound economic stresses affected women of all classes and ethnicities, sparking a national conversation about women's roles. Despite opposition to women taking jobs, more women worked outside the home during the Depression than ever before. The work, however, did not represent the freedom and independence envisioned by the generation of women who had been fighting for women's rights. More women worked harder, took on more responsibilities, and took any job that would help supplement the family's income.

The US entry into World War II would bring the Texas—and the nation—out of the Depression and cause the largest cultural and economic shifts ever, affecting every aspect of women's lives. In order to win the war, gender constructions were yet again altered to encourage women not only to work outside the home but also to engage in previously masculine employment, including skilled and manual labor. Texas women rose to the patriotic challenge by taking jobs in industry, by working at home production and conservation, and by joining the military. By the end of the war, despite the push then for women to quit the workforce, women's new expectations were hard to quell.

Great Depression

The stock market crash of 1929 led to a decade of depression in the nation and the world, with severe consequences for women in Texas. Despite increasing oil production since the gushing of Spindletop in 1901, the state's economy was still heavily dependent on cotton production. Cotton prices had begun falling after World War I, and the stock market crash exacerbated the plight of cotton growers and devastated financial companies and retailers that relied upon cotton farmers for their business.

Women of landowning and sharecropping families alike found themselves working harder than ever before, continuing to cut corners and minimize expenses as much as possible. Wilma Earl Colvin Edwards of Boaz recalled how her ninety-eight-pound mother would "stand over that hot stove all day long . . . pregnant with my brother" and prepare "hundreds of cans of beef and everything in the year of 1931 and '32, all kinds of vegetables, and preserved all kinds of fruits." Her mother told her father "that she would can everything she possibly could, and they wouldn't have to buy groceries."[1] In addition to the extra work in the household, women had to spend more time working in the cotton fields. As cotton prices dropped from thirty cents a pound in 1923 to five cents a pound in 1932, farmers grew more cotton to bring in more income, and this required women to contribute more labor in the fields. Natural disasters such as the boll weevil infestation, floods, and droughts reduced many families to poverty and starvation.[2] Lillie Freis of Colorado County described the Depression years as "the hardest times. . . . That's the time when we always had to depend on our cotton crop to make some money, and that's the time we lost our cotton crop. The river got it. And then we didn't have no kind of money, no way, 'cept things to sell, and you couldn't get no job nowhere—there was no job to get. No way to make money."[3]

Unable to support their families on their farms, some men left to find employment elsewhere, relegating women to take care of the farms themselves. Charles Trefny's father left Osage "seeking work because it was just not enough money to be made on the farm to make a living at it." His father was fortunate to find a job and send money home to the family, but meanwhile his mother "took care of the farming operation and took care of the field hands when the cotton needed chopping and plowing and things like that."[4] Marital separations such as this, and even desertions, were common during the Depression. Most married couples remained together, but the number of marriages dropped during the 1930s as single men and women put off marriage and starting new families in financially difficult times.[5]

The need to limit the number of children after marriage propelled the development of a birth control movement in the state. Women who had been advocating for greater access to contraceptives as a way to have more autonomy found receptive allies during the difficult financial times. A coalition of elite women, prominent physicians, wealthy businessmen, and clergy argued for the funding, availability, and respectability of contraception, asserting that the pressures of the Depression demanded the distribution of safe and effective contraceptives as an alternative to abortion. Despite much antagonism from some members of the public, including lawmakers and non-supportive clergy, birth control clinics were established in Dallas, Houston, El Paso, Austin, Fort Worth, San Angelo, Waco, and San Antonio between 1935 and 1939. A state-level organization joined the Birth Control Federation of America, which later changed its name to Planned Parenthood to de-emphasize connections with women's rights advocates and to emphasize the need to limit reproduction of those who could not afford more children.[6]

The federal government implemented New Deal programs addressing rural poverty in the South by targeting the overproduction of cotton and livestock that had contributed to falling prices. The Agricultural Adjustment Administration rewarded farmers for limiting the size of their cotton crops and bought and destroyed cattle to decrease the supply. Most landowners decided to grow their allotment of cotton instead of sharing it with tenant farmers and sharecroppers. As a result, throughout the state and the entire South, farmers were turned off land, reducing the number of tenants and sharecroppers by half in some parts of the state and increasing desperation and destitution in rural areas. These landless farmers looked for new farming situations, went on government relief, or moved to towns to look for work. Women performed whatever work they could find—in industries, by taking in washing, as house servants and maids—to supplement the family income while also struggling to make new homes in new locations and produce food and clothing for their families.[7]

As had been the case before the Depression, single women were more likely to move to cities and towns in search of better opportunities. They wanted to escape the incessant toil and debt of sharecropping by taking other employment, and they hoped towns would enable them to better find husbands too.

During the Depression, these single women in urban areas were more likely to put off marriage, but they were joined in their migration by thousands of married women with their families who had been squeezed out of farming. In the towns, as on the farms, men and women took whatever work they could, and this meant that men often traveled looking for jobs. They looked for permanent employment in the cities but usually took seasonal and temporary positions instead, which often included returning to the countryside during cotton-picking season, when demand for labor was highest. African Americans were more likely to lose their tenant or sharecropping positions, and as a result the number of African Americans living in cities grew. For instance, Houston swelled with over eighty-four hundred additional African Americans in the decade of the Depression.[8]

The crash of cotton prices and the ruin of financial institutions nationwide had severe effects on women in the cities. Single and professional women who worked outside the home at the beginning of the Depression found their livelihoods threatened. May Eckles, a clerk at a realty title office in San Antonio, was fifty-four years old, single, living with her sister, and supporting herself relatively well at the beginning of the decade. Within the first few months after the crash, Eckles and her sister both suffered significant pay cuts from their employers, which would be followed by even more in the years to come. In 1933 Eckles wrote in her diary, "We were knocked cold today when they phoned us this morning from the office we had to take another 20% cut, effective the 15th. . . . Guess we will get through some way." In addition to making less money, workers' paychecks began coming erratically, making it more and more difficult to meet financial obligations. The Eckles sisters took every step they could to make less money go farther: they rented out a room of their house, refinanced debts, cut the services and pay of the maid, searched for bargains on groceries, and took on additional work selling silk stockings.[9]

Although the Eckles sisters constantly worried about paying their mortgage, they were able to keep their home. Other women were not as lucky and had to turn to renting or crowding into houses with relatives. Single women suffered pay cuts and layoffs that forced them to economize. Middle-class married women took many of the same steps to cope with the economic changes that came when their husbands faced the same. Married women of all ethnicities tried to do as much as they could, cutting expenses by doing more of the cooking and cleaning themselves, taking in boarders, providing child care, and selling products from their homes. About 75 percent of Texas women worked at home, contributing economically on the periphery rather than as wage earners. When their husbands could not find new jobs, married women looked for employment outside the home. One of the few employment sectors to grow in the 1930s was clerical work, and those jobs, along with other traditional jobs for women, enabled more middle-class women than ever to earn wages. Nearly half a million Texas women were employed during the decade, representing a significantly increased percentage of women who worked outside the home.[10]

The presence of married women in the workforce became a focal point of public concern and comment. With so many Texas men unable to find employment, many feared that married women were selfishly taking their positions, even though most women performed jobs that men would not or could not take, such as those in the growing clerical and secretarial sector. Nevertheless, in response to public sentiment that married women should not work if their husbands were employed, in 1932 Congress prohibited both a husband and a wife from employment in the federal government at the same time. Because men usually made more money than women, this forced some women out of their jobs. The Texas legislature considered banning the employment by the state government of any person whose spouse was employed, even in the private sector. The Texas Federation of Business and Professional Women's Clubs (BPW) lobbied vigorously against such restrictions, and the legislation eventually only prohibited spouses from working for the state government at the same time. Widespread antipathy toward professional women continued, however. When, in 1935, Governor James Allred nominated Sarah T. Hughes for the Fourteenth District Court judgeship, many men agreed with state senator Claud Westerfield, who opined that "Mrs. Hughes is a married woman and should be at home washing dishes or something else." The BPW encouraged its members in sixty cities to write letters to their senators and successfully overcame the opposition: Hughes became Texas's first woman judge.[11]

Local governments followed Congress and the state legislature and particularly targeted teachers. By 1932 approximately 31 percent of school districts formally barred married women from teaching and had dismissed all married women from their positions. As many as 62 percent of the schools informally discriminated against married women, telling applicants "they weren't hiring married teachers there" and making it clear that "married teachers were second choice." Gladys Peterson Meyers could not find a teaching job during the Depression and was told, "You have a husband. You don't need the position as much as somebody who has little children to be supported." Even in school districts that did not forbid employing married women, some women teachers were still fearful. Rachael Luna remembered that she "was scared to death" when she married "and didn't make a big splash about it," afraid that she would lose her job. Others kept their marriages secret or delayed their weddings.[12]

Married or single, teachers faced other obstacles as many school districts tried to save money by cutting teaching positions, wages, and supplies. Teachers lucky enough to have and keep jobs found their workload increased and themselves struggling financially. Districts such as those in San Antonio began paying their teachers in "scrip," paper money issued by the schools and supposedly redeemable at local stores. Payment in scrip was why Sibyl Sutherland "constantly had a note in the bank. With the interest on the note, I was really getting less than seventy-five dollars a month, when you get down to it."[13]

New Deal programs (federal initiatives to create jobs and improve the economy) reflected the public sentiment that married women should not seek employment and, in fact, discouraged women from working at all. Single women and married women with husbands who could work (even if the men could not find jobs) were denied employment by the Federal Emergency Relief Administration and the Works Progress Administration (WPA). Women who were heads of household had preference in hiring, but, even so, the jobs offered to women paid far less than the jobs offered to men. Nevertheless, educated women sometimes found positions as librarians, editors, writers, musicians, or artists through the WPA and other agencies, such as the Public Works of Art Project, which sponsored the painting of ninety-seven murals in Texas post offices. The government programs reserved almost all of the positions in Texas for white women, and only a few African American artists were able to support themselves in this period. For instance, Naomi Howard Polk received welfare and sold cosmetics to survive the Depression, and her family did not discover her paintings until 1984.[14]

Most women entering or remaining in the workforce during the Depression did not have the education to aspire to jobs as writers or teachers. Thousands of women with little education or few skills had to earn wages to support families, whether as heads of households, spouses supplementing insufficient income of their husbands, or young single women working to assist their parents and siblings. More than half a million women in Texas worked for wages during the Depression: one-quarter of white women and over half of black women in urban areas. Many more women would have taken jobs if they could have obtained them.[15]

This was particularly true for African American women, whose unemployment rate was the highest of any group of women and higher than African American men in cities like Houston, where 46 percent of women workers were jobless. Discrimination, segregation, and low wages paid to African American men had required a significant number of women to work before the Depression. During the Depression, as even more women entered the market, New Deal programs discriminated and employers preferred giving jobs to white women, leaving few options besides domestic toil; 69 percent of employed African American women worked in such occupations during the 1930s. However, as middle-class families cut back on expenses, they laid off their maids, laundresses, and cooks or drastically cut their wages. Those retaining jobs had no choice except to take the pay cuts, often working sixty to seventy hours a week for as little as $3.50, far less than they needed to get by.[16]

African American women did benefit from some of the relief programs, but the emphasis in these programs kept them segregated and in subservient positions. Training schools for domestics emphasized the skills needed to be "happy and contented workers doing superior jobs for satisfied employers," skills such as table service, etiquette, cooking, household management, child care, and proper employer-employee relationships. The Works Project Administration in Texas filled only 3 percent of its 4,493 positions with African American women, and over half of those carried out sewing projects. Other women did get some better positions as library assistants, adult educators, and extension agents, but all of these were at lower pay than white women received.[17]

Government programs to ease the difficulties for Texans during the Depression did not target the plight of Tejanas. Instead, the US Immigration Service aimed to deport as many Mexican Americans as possible, with little regard for whether they were legally within the United States. Women were caught up in these deportation sweeps, both as immigrants and as dependent spouses of men who had been born in Mexico (because women lost their legal citizenship when they married noncitizens). Between these sweeps and the economic and social pressures, some 250,000 Mexicans and Mexican Americans left Texas for Mexico during the 1930s.[18]

With little help from government programs, extremely low wages in the work that Tejanos could get, and chronic unemployment, more Tejanas had to enter the job market. A few entrepreneurs became successful businesswomen, such as Adelaida Cuellar, who turned her talent for making tamales into a small vending operation and then, with her sons, opened a café in Kaufman County, the precursor of a string of restaurants named El Chico. Some Tejanas found jobs as store clerks, while others competed for domestic positions. Most continued to congregate in industries such as garment-making, cigar-rolling, and pecan-shelling, where they saw their wages cut and conditions deteriorate. Large numbers of married women who needed money during the Depression drove wages even lower, as manufacturers distributed piecework to women who would take home bundles of unfinished garments and sew them at home, averaging about five cents an hour for their labor.[19] The women employed at garment factories did not fare much better, earning between $1.10 and $3.30 per week, while those shelling pecans made only about $2.65 per week. (Anglo women shelling pecans made $4.15 per week.) A family of four working in a shelling factory at those wages would earn about one-fifth of the estimated annual cost of living at the time, $1,374. [20]

Figure 8.1. Tejana pecan shellers at work, union plant, San Antonio, Texas. Courtesy of Farm Security Administration—Office of War Information Photograph Collection (Library of Congress).

The National Recovery Administration (NRA) was one of the few New Deal programs that offered much relief to Tejanas, with measures to raise the wages and conditions of industrial workers. (Such laws specifically did not apply to agricultural and domestic employment, leaving out significant numbers of Tejanas and almost all African American women.) Texas manufacturers, however, evaded the laws through loopholes such as paying apprenticeship wages even to seasoned personnel and requiring employees to clock out after forty hours but continue working. NRA regulations, however, galvanized women by raising their awareness of the unfairness of their wages and conditions as well as by guaranteeing them the right to unionize. Between 1933 and 1935, Tejanas staged three strikes of Finck Cigar Company in San Antonio. The strike leaders, Mrs. W. H. "Refugio" Ernst, Adela Hernández, Modesta Herrera, and Mrs. E. J. Padilla, organized striking workers, raised funds for them, and lobbied city and national leaders to recognize their plight of low wages and unhealthy work conditions. Although the Cigarmakers' International Union finally sent organizers after the walkout had begun, local Tejanas led the massive strike. They won temporary concessions from the owner, but the strike eventually failed after violence on the picket lines, police brutality, and the hiring of non-union workers.[21]

Sixteen-year-old Emma Tenayuca, who walked the picket line during the cigar strikes, would use her experience to become a champion of workers' rights in San Antonio and Texas. In 1938, pecan shellers in San Antonio asked Tenayuca to lead them in a walkout and strike after a wage cut. Despite being teargassed and jailed, Tenayuca remained an eloquent spokesperson and committed to the cause. When Tenayuca's Communist Party ties became a means by which to discredit her and the strike, she voluntarily stepped down from the organizing committee. The strikers won a temporary victory when industry leaders agreed to reinstate the previous pay and to renegotiate higher pay later. Employees were hired back at their original wages, but manufacturers soon began replacing the workers with machinery.[22]

While San Antonio served as the hotbed of Tejana union organizing, both Tejana and Anglo women in other parts of the state also unionized and struck for better wages and working conditions. Employees in some Dallas garment factories walked out over poor conditions and dehumanizing rules; organizer Charlotte Graham was spurred to action when a coworker who was not allowed to go to the restroom urinated in her seat. The pro-industry newspaper coverage in the city made it difficult for the workers to get sympathy and support, and the strike ended when the union ran out of funds without any concessions from the employers. Other garment worker strikes in Houston and San Antonio, however, were more successful, with official recognition of their unions and small wage increases.[23]

Between the thousands of Texans who were working for wages insufficient to support their families and the thousands more who could find no jobs at all, the Depression led to privation that job programs and direct government relief could barely begin to alleviate. As they had before the Depression, women banded together wherever they could to help their communities. Tejanas participated in mutual aid societies such as Cruz Azul and the Comisión Honorifica to help repatriated families and to financially assist unemployed people. In 1931 alone Cruz Azul raised money to aid fifteen hundred individuals in Houston.[24] African American women worked through their churches to provide direct relief to the needy. The Texas Association of Colored Women's Clubs continued to fight against lynching and racial injustices but during the Depression shifted its efforts to home and family life, recognizing that economic and social advancement of the community could only come with the improvement of women's earning potential. To advance this, club members founded and raised money for nursery schools, homes for aged women, community centers, training centers, youth organizations, and colleges.[25] White women also continued their club work and voluntary associations, with many of these forming charity committees. The Junior League sponsored free health clinics and opened soup kitchens, while the Young Women's Christian Association provided shelter for homeless women.[26]

The decade of the Depression was probably the most difficult in history for Texas women. This period, however, set in motion substantial changes in the state that would affect women's lives for decades: the beginning of the breakup of sharecropping and tenant farming, migration to the cities, entry of more women into the workforce, unionization and women's activism, and growth of the clerical employment sector, among many others. The Depression also left a lasting impact on the psyche of those who survived it.

World War II

The Japanese bombing of Pearl Harbor in December 1941 brought the United States into World War II with immense consequences for women in Texas. Even before entry into the war American industries had been increasing manufacturing, and this had eased many of the symptoms of the

Depression by pumping money into the economy. After Pearl Harbor the United States moved from a depressed economy without enough jobs for its workers to an economy stretched to its limits, one without enough workers for its jobs.

Texas men answered the nation's call for soldiers at a greater percentage than any other state. While Texas made up 5 percent of the country's population, 750,000 of its residents made up 7 percent of the armed forces. Delay of marriage and temporary and permanent separations had been common during the Depression, but the improving economy and the rush of men to war increased the marriage rate. Women on the Texas home front, many of them recently married and with small children, faced a new set of challenges created by the war. They worried about the safety of loved ones in the armed forces and, as events transpired, thousands grieved the loss of husbands, fathers, and sons. These feelings permeated daily life. Henrietta Rivas remembered that in her neighborhood "there was not one young man left, and many of them [had been] killed. It was a horrible time for us. You could hear . . . the women crying for their sons."[27] The absence of so many men required many married women to take charge and care for their families and many single women to support themselves and their extended families. This created hardships that exhausted many women but also provided new opportunities and rewards.

As part of the military effort, the US government awarded contracts to companies throughout the country, and Texas cities received their fair share. As men left for the war or took jobs at home in defense industries, and as money flowed into the state, the number of traditional women's jobs increased, as did pay for those jobs, leading to better opportunities for women, married and single. Often these jobs were in urban areas, and women and men moved to towns and cities in record numbers. In the 1940s half a million Texans moved from rural to urban areas, joined there by thousands of migrants from other states. By the end of the war, for the first time in its history, more people lived in urban areas of the state than lived in rural areas. Young women left farms to take advantage of the opportunities of city life and to escape the drudgery of farm work, in the process asserting independence from their families.

Even with the massive migration to the cities, the defense industries experienced a shortage of workers. As in the rest of the country, Texas industries gradually turned to hiring women, not just for every conceivable support and clerical role but also for heavy manufacturing jobs. Eleven National Youth

Administration centers operated in the state, and they sponsored schools that trained women in welding, sheet-metal work, machine-tool operation, woodwork, and drafting. Defense industries located in large and small cities recruited women to positions never open to women before. In Houston women worked as airplane mechanics at the army training facility at Ellington Field and as welders, burners, and eventually every position at the

Figure 8.2. Three women working on aircraft wing, May 9, 1942. Courtesy of Lockheed Martin Aeronautics Company, Fort Worth.

city's shipyards, where they comprised up to 12 percent of employees. They sewed parachutes, handled explosives, processed meat, made synthetic rubber, manufactured machine tools and ordnance, and performed hundreds of other occupations, making up 18.2 percent of the total employees in Houston defense industries.[28] In Angelina County women took jobs welding and in machine shops: "Lufkin Foundry and Machine Company employed so many women to work on the Sherman tank gears that the company nicknamed the department the 'boogie woogie shop.'"[29] In Waco, black women and white women filled the expanded number of job openings at garment factories but also worked in heavy defense industries, including producing, packing, cleaning, and shipping bombs and operating heavy machinery such as forklifts at the Bluebonnet Ordnance Plant. They also served as mechanics, painters, engine installers, and in the machine shop at the Waco Army Flying School and Blackland Army Air Field.[30] In Humble, women took positions at the Baytown Oil Refinery in the testing, instrument, engineering, and machinist departments. There they performed a wide variety of jobs, from surface grinder operator and radial drill operator to engineering and drafting positions.[31] In San Antonio women welded bombs at the Friedrich Refrigeration Company and balanced airplane propellers and manufactured parts at Kelly Field.[32] These industrial jobs were physically demanding and often dangerous, requiring significant adaptation by women in their ideas about their abilities and even the clothes they wore. Juana Portales Esquivel later remembered her acceptance of the dangers in her welding job but also about being struck by the change of clothing: "We had to wear coveralls because [of] the sparks. We had to cover up. I still have spots [points to scars on her neck]. We wore shields and a cap and gloves and heavy shoes. Pants. I used to buy coveralls."[33]

Despite the dangers, women took these jobs for a variety of reasons. To some degree or another, most worked in defense industries out of a sense of patriotism and saw it as a way of helping the country and bringing men home from war. Edwina Walker Barclay, who operated a drill press at the Lufkin Foundry, would remember, "It was exciting to think you were helping the war. Everyone had a real patriotic feeling at the time."[34] Also at the foundry, Cletis Wells Fuller and Orpha Norton McCall could see and touch the results of their labor: "We worked on the big guns, and these big gears. We were just all working for the war effort, and that was mostly the attitude and feeling."[35] Even women in the garment industries in Waco felt this way. "My machine is a weapon . . . of war," one declared.[36]

With husbands and other family members gone due to the war, many women had no choice but to earn wages to support themselves and families, and defense work paid better than any jobs they had ever had. Fuller and McCall might have toiled out of patriotism, but they were also happy to receive better pay (thirty-five to fifty cents an hour) than they had at their retail jobs (a dollar a day).[37] After a year Anne Baker earned $2,260 annually at the Waco Army Flying School as a junior machinist. While the men hired at the same time had been promoted faster and made more, she was thankful to earn more than she could in a traditional woman's job. A friend of hers who was a teacher only made $1,000 a year.[38]

In addition to being attracted by good pay and motivated by patriotism, women often found jobs in the factories more exciting and challenging. Violet Holmes constructed and installed conduit lines in the wings of planes at the North American Aviation plant. It was dangerous, difficult work, but, she later said, "I was happy because it was *not* the farm!"[39] Rachel Bates found immense pride in her work in the gear shop at the Lufkin Foundry: "I went into it with the intention of doing the job, and that's what I did."[40] Delfina Cooremans Baladez proudly recalled that balancing propellers properly would prevent vibrations that would cause a plane to go off-course or even crash.[41]

Women often faced antagonism as well as physical dangers at the work place. Boilermakers in the Baytown refinery worried about being forced to have a "Rosie" working with them, leading women to laughingly refer to "how hard it is on men to put up with a bunch of gals."[42] Male coworkers were not always confident in women's abilities. At the Waco Army Flying School, the men would only allow Anne Baker to perform light work in the machine shop: "As a matter of being a woman and not having the sense to operate with a brain, they watched you really close and put you on things that they figured you could do."[43] Wilhelmina Cooremans Vasquez remembered that men treated the women as nuisances: "The men were more resistant because it was something so new it'd never happened before."[44] The women faced other types of harassment in an environment of men not accustomed to working with women. Florence Neil was sexually harassed at the Bluebonnet Ordnance Plant in Waco: "One old guy down there tried to make a play on me and he was ugly." Fortunately Neil's supervisor witnessed some of the behavior and intervened on her behalf. Others, of course, were not so lucky and had to handle such harassment on their own. And men were not the only ones having trouble adapting to the changes. One woman later remembered carpooling with one of her male coworkers until his jealous wife assaulted her.[45]

Time usually changed the minds of male coworkers and bosses about women's abilities, and many women, especially those who worked in smaller plants or communities, would later remember a supportive atmosphere at their jobs. Ginnie Rector recalled that her boss at a box factory recognized women's skills and said that "any job a woman was capable of doing she could do better. They were quicker and more careful to detail, and better with their hands."[46]

Despite the drawbacks, women did want to take these jobs, and the airwaves and print media were full of messages from the industries themselves and the War Department convincing women that it was their duty to take them. The War Manpower Commission established a Women's Advisory Committee in August 1942 and began a campaign to break down legal and social barriers to women's work, including increasing the visibility of women taking on war industry jobs, thus increasing their respectability. Ads imploring "National Defense Needs Your Help Now!" appeared in Waco newspapers in early 1942, with information about training available in office work and the availability of positions at new military bases. By late 1942, Texas media encouraged women to take on even more industrial jobs. Radio stations throughout the state broadcast a Womanpower Spots Series featuring one-minute pleas to women. In one, Edna Bly urged "housewives" like herself to get jobs outside the home, explaining, "I got an eight hour a day job, and manage to run my home besides. . . . I feel I'm really helping to make the war end sooner . . . and maybe saving the life of just one boy from home."[47] Local and national newspapers and magazines tried to demystify war-related jobs by featuring stories about women workers. In August 1942 Houston papers ran pictures of repair crews composed solely of women who were dressed in coveralls and working on huge machines.[48]

In hindsight it is easy to see the barrage of Rosie the Riveter messages on radio, at movies, and in print as wartime propaganda, but women did not necessarily identify it as such. At least some women in Lufkin later remembered that these messages and images simply made them aware that such positions were open to them, and they did not feel they had been persuaded to take those positions. Clearly the advertising campaign worked, making women aware of the positions and reducing social stigmas against women taking them, in large part by running pictures of stylish women and ads for attractive "work clothes."[49]

While advertising aimed at getting women to take defense jobs had tremendous success, women received mixed messages from the press and society. The

Baytown refinery newsletter, the *Humble Bee*, simultaneously praised women's good work while treating them as novelties and not capable of the same work as men and needing the protection of men.[50] The same newspapers and magazines that ran stories encouraging women to take defense jobs also featured stories about the dangers to society of working women. The *Houston Post* reported in July 1943 that the rate of juvenile delinquency had skyrocketed, and papers throughout the state printed sensationalistic stories about out-of-control youth left unsupervised by working mothers.[51] The California Child Welfare Services director, Herbert E. Chamberlain, visited Houston in 1942, and the *Houston Chronicle* reported that he claimed "anxiety and emotional disturbances, insecurity, overexertion, malnutrition and many other factors [were] contributing to the undermining of child security in wartime" and that these were attributable to mothers who left their children in the care of others.[52]

Child care was indeed one of the chief concerns for mothers who needed or wanted to work. As often as possible, women tried to leave their children with family members, commonly known then as "foster-family day care."[53] Not only did this prove to be the least expensive option but also the more socially acceptable one. Women who left their children with those outside the family were stigmatized, as such actions were associated with poverty. Working Tejanas with children most often lived with other family members who cared for them. Nonetheless, the sheer numbers of women entering the workforce, and the many more who were needed, forced national and local government agencies to act in order to insure child care. The Federal Works Agency disbursed money to help fund local day-care operations run by churches, charities, and schools. School districts in Texas also began expanding kindergarten programs and extending care for schoolchildren before and after school. The stigmas remained, however, and, even before the war ended, members of the Houston Independent School District board objected to funding day care, arguing that it "tends to break down the family unit."[54]

More women took the opportunity to earn higher pay than ever before, but the majority of women in the state did not take defense industry jobs. Some were excluded. Although in need of workers, industrial employers still segregated African American women and refused to hire them for the best positions. Vocational-technical schools and services provided by national and local agencies to put women to work were more available to white women than black women. The races remained segregated during the war, preventing African American women from taking advantage of the majority of extended school and day-care opportunities. When defense industries hired black women, they worked in separate facilities, often in the less-desirable positions, such as manufacturing and packing ordnance or as cooks and cleaners. In a Lufkin factory that did hire African American women, they worked side by side with white women but were forced to use a separate bathroom and separate lunchroom and even stand in a separate line at the post office. While few African American women secured the best defense industry jobs, they often took work vacated when white women took higher-paying positions. For instance, the number of black women hired in the garment industries rose significantly during the war, allowing many women to leave the lowest-paying service work as maids and cooks.[55]

Tejanas also made up a small percentage of women working in defense industries: less than 10 percent of the Tejana workforce landed these higher-paying positions. Official policies of segregation and discrimination against Mexican Americans were fewer than against African Americans, as Mexican Americans were still considered by law to be white. However, long-standing prejudices that had become particularly virulent during the Depression contributed to fewer defense employers offering jobs to Tejanas. Those who were able to obtain such work, however, experienced major changes in their opportunities and attitudes. Henrietta López Rivas quit her job as a housekeeper to work as an interpreter and then took a job repairing airplane instruments at Kelly Field in San Antonio. "I was getting $90 a month for that. That was a heck of a lot of money. . . . From $1.50 a week [as] a domestic to $90 a month!" In addition to the increased pay and standard of living, she also gained confidence as a woman and as a Mexican American: "I think it made me feel like I was equal. [It made me feel] more intelligent because what I did, very few Anglos could do."[56] Many other Tejanas made similar gains, working in other high-paying occupations, such as nursing, teaching, clerical, and administration. Aurora González Castro took dictation at the State Department of Public Welfare for $100 per month.[57]

Middle-class white women generally preferred not to take jobs outside of the house or were enabled by their husbands' income, but they still wanted to do something to help the war effort. The Texas Federation of Women's Clubs involved their clubwomen in education efforts about nutrition and conservation. The TFWC and national agencies encouraged women to plant "victory gardens," use substitutions for scarce items in cooking, and save and reuse everything possible in order to conserve resources for the soldiers at war. "Rationing at home 'keeps 'em flying' on the battle front," *Parents'*

Magazine encouraged its readers in 1943.[58] Texas Extension Service agents stepped up their efforts to encourage canning and teach women how to do so properly. As a result, the agency's 1943 report recorded that Texas families had prepared nearly two hundred million cans of vegetables, meats, and fruits and cured over fifty million pounds of meat.[59] The collective efforts of homemakers to do all they could to save, ration, and produce their own goods promoted the idea of shared sacrifice and almost certainly stemmed some of the drain on resources that instead were used for war.

Other women joined efforts to keep up the morale of troops and assist soldiers directly. For example, the Bluebonnet Brigade, a group of over one thousand Abilene women, provided companionship and support to those stationed at Camp Barkeley there. The women hosted discussion groups, provided music, encouraged hobbies, and hosted and attended parties, giving soldiers dance partners.[60] A group of students at the University of Texas formed a troupe that performed traditional Mexican dances and visited the United Service Organizations at Camp Swift in Bastrop.[61] The respectable leaders of communities in Texas that had military bases promoted such organized entertainment, where girls in the community could interact with the soldiers in chaperoned environments. The presence of many young men, usually single, suddenly located nearby did provide some women the opportunity to engage in sexual encounters outside of those deemed acceptable before the war. With military bases also came the increased presence of prostitution. Local leaders wanted to curtail prostitution to protect the local communities' girls, and the armed forces needed to stop the spread of venereal disease that threatened the strength of the fighting forces. Congress passed laws making prostitution near military bases a federal offense, and the newly created Division of Social Protection of the federal Office of Defense and Welfare Service joined forces with the army and navy to put pressure on towns to bolster the fight against prostitution. Austin, Beaumont, Corpus Christi, El Paso, Galveston, and San Antonio all increased arrests and stings to shut down houses of ill repute. However, even in those towns, the commitment to eradicating prostitution ebbed and flowed during the war. In Galveston particularly, lavish houses of prostitution continued to operate with the knowledge of authorities.[62]

The lives of rural women also changed during the war. The increased need for agricultural products, the migration of workers to cities, and the departure of men to serve in the war increased the workload for Texas farm women, many of whom were left running farms alone. Women on ranches felt these strains even more acutely, since meat, wool, and leather supplies were low at the beginning of the war due to the drought and depression, and the demand for these products quickly escalated to an all-time high. At the same time, many ranchers left to join the army, and industries in the cities drew workers away. One ranch in Hood County went from employing thirty cowboys to only being able to hire six by the end of the war. With the high demands for products and decreasing labor supplies, ranch women, most of whom had learned from an early age how to handle horses, cattle, and business for those situations when men were away, found themselves pressed into service more often as ranch hands. Nesseye Mae Proffitt Roach's husband joined the navy, and she stayed on a ranch with her father, the two of them working the cattle, sheep, and goats.[63]

Women in the Service

Women at home, on farms, and on ranches worked extra hard during the war to earn better incomes but also—and most important for many—out of patriotism and a desire to help the war effort. Many women wanted to take a much more active role in service to their country than allowed on the home front, but women could only serve as nurses in the army at the onset of the war. Nursing had been one of the few professions open to women before the war, and the war increased opportunities for nurses. The Army Nurse Corps, an official division of the Army Medical Department, had been established at the beginning of the twentieth century, and women had served ably in the corps during World War I. Even more nurses were called for during World War II, many to work overseas. Texas women volunteered in large numbers for this traditional job that they performed in very nontraditional ways and settings. Marion Kennedy remembered setting up a primitive hospital in the South Pacific in bamboo buildings: "There was a limited amount of electricity, so it went to the operating room. . . . We used Kerosene lanterns for light. . . . Also, we didn't have running water."[64] Rafaela Muñiz Esquivel's family took an enormous risk by taking out a loan to send her to nursing school. The risk paid off when she joined the Red Cross and later enlisted in the Army Nurse Corps. The Nurse Corps did not segregate Mexican Americans, and Esquivel completed the same hectic, dangerous shifts alongside Anglos in Texas and Europe.[65] Working as an army nurse put one at great risk. In the Pacific Theater, the Japanese army took sixty-six US nurses prisoner in 1941, ten of whom were from Texas.[66]

Not all women could be or wanted to be nurses, of course. The home front's immersion in the war and the mobilization of women for everything from gardening to war industry led to thousands of women sending inquiries to the War Department asking what more they could do. Early in 1941, the War Department's public relations office created a Woman's Interest Section and named Texan Oveta Culp Hobby the director. Hobby had been the quintessential "new woman," having come of age during the 1920s when women were taking advantage of the right to vote and expanded education. Her social class made it possible for her to go to school and pursue a career as a journalist, and eventually she married a prominent leader in the state, former governor William Hobby. Her background and education made her the perfect public relations liaison for the War Department, but her understanding of women's untapped abilities led her to recognize that women could contribute much more than gardens. Just a few weeks after the US entry into the war, Hobby appeared before the US House of Representatives Committee on Military Affairs to support the establishment of a Women's Army Auxiliary Corps (WAAC). When the WAAC bill passed Congress, Hobby was the top choice for director of the new division. Hobby's leadership was so effective that the next year the WAAC was converted to the Women's Army Corps (WAC), becoming fully part of the army.[67]

Other branches of the service began establishing their own women's units: the US Navy's Women Accepted for Voluntary Emergency Service (WAVES), the Coast Guard Women's Reserve (SPARS), the US Marine Corps Women's Reserve, and the US Air Force's division of civilian women aviators, the Women Airforce Service Pilots (WASP). In the course of the war, twelve thousand Texas women joined these branches in total. Women who served in these were never intended to engage in battle but instead to serve in roles that would free more men to fight. Military officials reasoned that every woman who could type up paperwork could free a man to engage in combat. At first women primarily performed jobs deemed suitable to women in the civilian world—working as stenographers, typists, switchboard operators, and launderers—but by the end of the war women performed nearly every duty except fighting.[68]

Women joined these forces for a variety of reasons, but primarily out of patriotism. Mary Ellen Ancelin Guay, only sixteen at the time, later remembered that when she heard that Japan had bombed Pearl Harbor, "my brother and I looked at each other and said, 'Well, we've got to sign up.'" Guay finished high school and some college before she was old enough to join the

Figure 8.3. Women's Army Corps members on parade in Abilene, Texas. Courtesy of 12th Armored Division Memorial Museum, Abilene.

WAVES, and she finished basic training in time to complete paperwork for the thousands of discharges at the end of the war. Janie "Tex" Sheppard from Midlothian quit a much higher-paying position to enter the Marine Corps Women's Reserve: "I just felt like I had to join the service and do my part."[69]

Although many women, such as Guay and Sheppard, saw service as natural because they came from military families, women who joined the military were very aware that their gender made that an unusual choice. McWilliams Barry, known as Mac, was one of the first Texas women to join the WACs. "We were told the 'eyes of the world' would be on us," she later remembered, "so we should set an example by our military demeanor." While many people celebrated the women's dedication and devotion, there was still much opposition to women in uniform. Some soldiers resented women because they increased the men's likelihood of being sent to battle. Other soldiers and civilians alike believed it altered "natural" gender roles. Others felt women could not and should not be subject to military discipline. Rumors about the incompetency and promiscuity of the WACs abounded on bases and in the media. During an uprising of sorts by some men who resented the WACs, according to Barry, "We were forbidden to go out on the streets alone, and never at night, for days until it was stopped."[70]

As in the Nursing Corps, Mexican Americans served alongside Anglos and saw service to their country as both patriotic and an opportunity for eco-

nomic advancement, independence, and travel. Concepción Alvarado Esc-
obedo joined the WACs after attending a military rally encouraging women's
service: "I felt if I could play some small part in the war, I would want to do
it."[71]

No matter the reasons or level of patriotism, the women's services that
allowed African American women to serve remained segregated. In the WACs,
African American women lived and worked in separate facilities and were
more likely than white women to carry out cleaning and cooking duties than
clerical jobs. Ten graduates of Prairie View A&M University were part of
the initial 400 WACs nationwide, some of whom continued military careers
after the war. Texas women were also among the 343 African Americans who
served in the Army Nurse Corps. The WAVES and SPARS did not admit
black women until too late in the war to serve significant roles, while the
Marines and the WASP did not admit them at all.[72]

Women in the military acquitted themselves well, performing nearly
every role except battle, and served overseas, even in dangerous positions.
Lois C. Jones, a WAC enlistee whose group was stationed in England, later
remembered, "The night before we left they showed us a film about a con-
voy of American ships attacked by submarines. They did this because we
would be traveling across the Atlantic unaccompanied. That was quite a
picture to see before getting on board a ship to sail across the Atlantic."[73]

The women's branches of the military engaged in significant recruitment
campaigns to encourage women to enlist, but the Women's Army Corps was
unable to fill all of its twelve thousand positions. The Women Airforce Service Pilots, however, filled its openings through individual invitations and
word of mouth. Nearly twenty-five thousand applied for the two thousand
positions open to women as noncombat pilots. Florene Miller Watson of
Odessa was the twelfth woman to fly military airplanes when she joined the
Women's Auxiliary Ferrying Squadron that would later become WASP, and
in the two short years of the program she flew bomber, fighter, training, and
cargo airplanes. Although women pilots were not allowed to fly combat missions or even overseas, their jobs were dangerous, and thirty-eight members
of WASP were killed in duty. Not only did Texas women join WASP, its
main training base was in Texas, first Houston and then Avenger Field in
Sweetwater. Although Sweetwater had welcomed the base when men trained
there, the residents were skeptical of the women at first. Many local women
wanted to assist the war effort by entertaining male soldiers, not women, and
businesses were convinced women would not spend as much money. When

a group of prostitutes began calling themselves WASPs, casting aspersions on the women training there, it confirmed the suspicions of many that members of WASP were essentially immoral women. Director Jacqueline Cochran tried to woo the town, inviting all to the next graduation to witness the high caliber of the program and encouraged the trainees to join local churches. The campaign for respectability had many positive results but did not eliminate the distrust of all in the community.[74]

Women's Expectations in the Postwar Period

The government's wartime spending had fueled a booming economy, but economists predicted that the end of the war would lead to a drastic cut in industry and that thousands of returning soldiers would have trouble finding work. In order to open as many jobs as possible for soldiers, as the war entered its final throes government policies and propaganda shifted to sending new messages to women. No longer was it women's patriotic duty to work in industries or serve in the armed forces to support men. Postwar patriotism required that women give up industrial jobs so that returning soldiers could have employment—after all, they reminded women, men had risked their lives for the country. The new patriotism required that women get married, have many children, and stay home full time to take care of those children.

Even the military based policies on this new message. The Women's Airforce Service Pilot program was eliminated in late 1944, and the military refused to award veteran status to its members. The messages from government and society to women changed. While some women had risked their lives to fly airplanes for the country, now they were seen as unpatriotic for attempting to continue their service beyond the duration of the war. Similar to the demobilization of male soldiers, most women left the other armed forces near or after the end of the war. Recognizing the impact that the Women's Army Corps made during the war, the military requested that the division be made a permanent part of the army. Even this appeal, however, met with serious opposition in Congress, delaying its approval until 1948.[75]

Despite the need for increased production in its final push to end the war, early in 1944 prominent figures such as First Lady Eleanor Roosevelt and anthropologist Margaret Mead, as well as the Office of War Information and women's magazines, engaged in a campaign to convince women to leave jobs and "return home." "Rosies" interviewed for propaganda films proclaimed that they had been happy to work in industries while their men needed them but they would be happier to go home so that men could have the jobs they deserved. Emphasizing that soldiers deserved jobs and that women preferred domesticity, the *Lufkin Daily News* reported that "when Johnny comes marching home to Texas chances are bright that he'll have a job waiting for him. . . . Many women are becoming housewives again and glad of it."[76]

Indeed, many women in the war industries were happy to quit when the war ended. The Houston Chamber of Commerce conducted a survey that found that six thousand of the fifteen thousand Houston women working in 1945 did not expect to continue working in 1946. The United States Employment Service in 1944 estimated that in Dallas County thirty thousand women expected to quit their jobs after the war. Many of these women had delayed marriage due to the Depression or war and were ready to start families. Francis Janelle Beaugh Milner was proud to work in the machine shop in a Humble refinery until the fall of 1946, when her "husband returned from overseas and I was anxious to start a family."[77] Others absorbed the ubiquitous messages that true patriotism required them to stay at home and out of the workforce. From magazines to local Rotary Club presentations they were reminded that "women are needed for production in war, but in practice their place must be in the home if our nation is to maintain its progress. . . . Our future depends on our homes. Women are happier in the homes, and after the war we will find the home life of the nation rebuilt."[78]

Although many were ready to quit their high-paying industrial jobs and stay at home to raise families, most working women wanted to keep their jobs. National surveys conducted by the Women's Bureau of the National War Labor Board indicated 75 percent of women working in industries wanted to retain their positions. While surveys in Houston and Dallas showed that thousands planned to leave their jobs, 60 to 70 percent intended to continue working. In Houston, this meant that six thousand, or twice as many women as had worked in 1940, wanted to continue working outside the home, and in Dallas the number of women who worked in 1940, sixty thousand, rose to nearly seventy-two thousand who wanted to continue working after the war.[79] A few prominent Texas women expanded upon their wartime service and served as models for those who wanted to continue to work and pursue careers. Most notable was Oveta Culp Hobby, who had been instrumental in establishing the Women's Army Corps. After returning to Houston, she guided one of the city's two major newspapers, the *Houston Post*, as executive vice president and served as director of KPRC radio and KPRC-TV. In 1953 President Dwight D. Eisenhower appointed her to the newly created cabinet position of secretary of health, education, and welfare.[80]

Despite prominent women with careers and the desire of many to stay in the workforce, the pressure for women to quit the jobs they loved came from all sides: national leaders, government propaganda, women's magazines, newspapers, family, society, and, not least, the employers themselves. As factories converted their facilities for peacetime production, they laid off their women employees and did not rehire them when they reopened. In 1945 the Houston newspapers reported layoffs of "mostly women" and reassured their readers with statistics showing that by September of that year 11 percent of the city's women workers had lost their jobs, but only 5 percent of the men had.[81] In August 1945, Lufkin Foundry laid off all its women employees.[82]

The public at large welcomed the actions of industries. Whereas women had been more than capable in heavy industries during the war, officials argued that peacetime production was no place for a woman. As Anne L. Baker remembered, even if she had been able to retain her machinist's job in Waco, "I don't think I would have lasted because there was too much dissention," with men implicitly or explicitly asking her what she was doing there: "You are taking a man's job." As a single woman she supported herself after the war with a series of menial jobs but never found a career that provided her the same high pay and sense of pride that her job as a machinist did.[83]

Surveys during the war had indicated that many women, like Baker, wanted or needed to continue earning a paycheck. While not as high as during the war years, the number of Texas women working in 1950 was 38 percent more than the number in 1940. The percentage of women in Texas who worked outside the home rose from 22.9 percent in 1940 to 26.8 percent in 1950; in raw numbers the increase was from 542,385 to 750,384 women.[84] The type of employment women could get, however, changed after the war. No longer eligible for high-paying heavy industrial jobs that suddenly "only men could do," women who earned wages in factories most often worked for the garment industries. Florence Neil, who had worked for Bluebonnet Ordnance, took a job sewing jeans, paid on a quota system that made it difficult to earn much money.[85]

As Texas consumer spending after the war ballooned, retail sales grew rapidly, and women took 39 percent of the positions in that sector, mostly at department stores selling clothing and cosmetics. The number of telephones in homes increased, and the rapidly expanding occupation of telephone operator included 17,267 women who made up 96 percent of those employed in the position. Ninety-four percent of the secretary and typist positions went to women (63,680 of them), while another 45,171 women took similar clerical positions as bookkeepers, cashiers, or file clerks. A few of the professional fields remained dominated by women: 90 percent of librarians and elementary teachers were women, as were 97 percent of nurses.[86]

Strong social pressure and legal restrictions actively discouraged women from pursuing professional careers. For instance, in the early 1940s Hermine Dalkowitz (later Tobolowsky) was called to a meeting of first-year women law students at the University of Texas where the assistant dean advised, "Girls, there is no need for you to study law. I know that you are here just to find husbands, so I'm giving you a list of all of the eligible men right now. We don't want you to waste your time here."[87] By 1950, women made up only 3 percent of the state's lawyers and judges, 5 percent of the physicians, 1 percent of the engineers, and 15 percent of the accountants.[88]

During the first half of the twentieth century, women had proved that they could perform and succeed in a wide range of occupations. Yet in the postwar period, their opportunities for personal and professional growth dwindled.

Conclusion

During a decade of depression in the 1930s, men and women struggled to survive. Economic and personal realities drove more women to work for wages than before at the same time that social condemnation of women working outside the home escalated. World War II, however, brought an economic boom and a public embrace of women's potential to contribute to society in thousands of new ways. Women joined the military, worked in factories, earned high wages, and became local leaders, proving that they were capable of much more than the long-held gender roles allowed them to do. At the end of the war, those gendered ideals, however, resurfaced, denying that women had the right to pursue meaningful and remunerative employment.

Chapter 9

Accepting and Rejecting Conformity in the Postwar Decades

A strong cultural impulse to return to normalcy after the Depression and four intense years of war created a desire among many to reestablish rigid gender roles. Although women might be capable of any work, the prevailing narrative after the war was that they were naturally suited for certain work in the home and therefore should leave the major jobs and breadwinning to men. This ideology paved the way to insure work for returning soldiers, encouraged family formation and childbearing, and became foundational in the Cold War era's philosophical fight against America's new enemy, communism. Many Texas women participated in the promotion and protection of American ideals against the seemingly encroaching threat by embracing the new paradigm, reinforcing the ideals in their daily lives, and sometimes participating in political actions and statements against potential subversion.

Other Americans, however, identified the hypocrisy of the country's claims of freedom and equality while whole segments of the population, including African Americans and Mexican Americans, were discriminated against and denied their rights. Texas women played significant roles in sparking and continuing major civil rights movements during the 1950s and 1960s, serving as leaders, bridging local communities with national movements, organizing, boycotting, developing ideas, and demanding political change. Women participating in these and other national movements for change began identifying the sexism in supposedly egalitarian enterprises. As a result, a new energy emerged in the struggle for women's rights.

Embracing Conformity

Despite the increase in the number of women working for wages in the postwar years, the predominant Anglo culture promoted the ideal that women should be happily and exclusively housewives. Part of the campaign to persuade women to give up their jobs for returning soldiers had been to convince women that they wanted to stay home to raise families. Magazines, popular culture in general, and some women themselves glorified the role of woman in the home.[1] The homes to which women were said to be returning, however, were changing significantly. Several factors contributed to a shift in women's lives, including increased consumer spending, the growth of urban and suburban areas, and the glorification of the role of the housewife.

Due to rationing during the war and experience from the Depression, Americans had saved money and, with signs of continuing economic stability, were willing to spend it in the postwar decades. As the Cold War emerged between the United States and its former ally, the Soviet Union, the threat of attack with nuclear weapons escalated, and the military made the strategic move to disperse military facilities. Texas became the recipient of much military spending, which further stimulated the economy. Finally, the increased prevalence of air conditioning made Texas a more attractive place for businesses to locate. All of these factors led to more state revenues, the creation of more high-paying jobs, and more Texans eager to spend their money on consumer goods.

Families purchased many of these consumer goods for use by women in the home. Labor-saving devices such as vacuums, washing machines, refrigerators, and stoves were heavily advertised and increased significantly in sales. As had frequently happened in the past, however, these devices did not decrease the work of housewives—the expected level of cleanliness increased while the practice of paying for maids or other helpers in the house decreased. Women's magazines, whose subscription numbers increased, supported these expectations. The magazines also promoted increasingly complicated and time-consuming meals for families.[2]

Affordable automobiles, the construction of interstates and better roads, and a desire by the many new families formed after the war to purchase their own homes led to new neighborhoods of affordable houses constructed farther from the center of the cities. Established, crowded cities throughout the country found increased out-migration to these new suburbs. Likewise, Texas experienced the rapid rise of suburbs populated not only by former residents of cities but by new residents in the state and others who were leaving rural regions to take advantage of the opportunities that cities offered. By the 1950 US Census, more Texans lived in urban areas than in rural areas for the first time in the state's history. Cities in the southern and western United States coped with suburbanization better than older, established northern cities because of the southern cities' ability to annex suburbs. Dallas, San Antonio, and Houston all annexed surrounding suburbs to grow five to seven times in size between 1930 and 1970.[3]

The growth of the suburbs had a profound effect on a certain class of women. When a new suburb was constructed, most homes were bought by young couples of roughly the same age, just starting their families, with husbands who had urban jobs that enabled them to afford new homes. These families were also almost exclusively white. Deed restrictions, segregation, and the practice of redlining effectively prohibited nonwhite families from owning homes in these suburbs. Ann Richards, who would become governor of Texas, later remembered that, like most white couples in the 1950s, "we got married; we had babies." They moved to a suburb of Dallas where she "would cook dinner, iron shirts, look after the children," raising them, like most couples across the nation, based on the advice in the popular guide by Benjamin Spock, *The Common Sense Book of Baby and Child Care* (1946).[4]

High expectations of starched shirts, spotless homes, and perfectly raised children kept these middle-class women very busy (and thus supposedly out of the workforce), but it also caused at least some of them to feel frequently "frantic and overwhelmed" and to wonder, as Richards often did, "Can I get everything done?" The repetitiveness could also feel oppressive: "It started to dawn on me that this is what life was going to be like for a long time."[5] Betty Friedan, in her 1963 exposé of the suburban phenomenon, *The Feminine Mystique*, suggested that many women in that stultifying environment felt like failures because the duties of wife and mother alone were not fulfilling to them, yet they were afraid to express this view because no one around them seemed to share it.[6]

Those women who did not share the ideals of these homogenous suburbs found it difficult to express differing values, whether about the roles of women or other issues such as race relations, in part because many women found great comfort in sharing similar dreams with their neighbors. The ongoing Cold War contributed to the need for conformity, as any expression of unfamiliar or contradictory values was seen as undermining American ideals and thus aiding the enemy. US Senator Joseph McCarthy became the primary symbol of this national mood with his aggressive use of congressional hearings to hunt down and punish anyone insufficiently "American" as communist, potential communist, or communist sympathizer. Some Texas women played very active roles in reinforcing the McCarthy values (which defined Americanism as supporting a wide range of ideas from capitalism to nuclear families with stay-at-home mothers) and used some of his bullying tactics to attack those who did not conform to their ideals of patriotism. In particular, over five hundred suburban Houston women, most from the very wealthy and established suburb of River Oaks, formed a local chapter of a national organization, the Minute Women, in 1951. The Minute Women attempted to remove all supposed supporters of communism and socialism from local and state governments and schools. Members used telephone chains to spread information and organize protests, engaged in letter-writing campaigns, produced newsletters, distributed propaganda, and campaigned for board of education candidates. Their pressure techniques led to the cancellation of many speaking engagements, and the tactics of heckling and picketing rendered others ineffective. One of their most successful campaigns resulted in the removal of the Houston school board's deputy superintendent, George Ebey, for supposedly subversive ideas.[7]

The exalted ideal of the housewife in the 1950s actively discouraged women from entering supposedly male domains, such as business or politics. The suburban landscape, however, did give women, like the Minute Women, time and proximity to organize and affect politics without taking public leadership positions. Suburban women would, in fact, form the core of support for one of the largest political shifts in the state's history as they participated in revitalizing and building a viable Republican Party, thus making Texas into a two-party state for the first time since Reconstruction. Republican men and women rejected the idea of women in leadership roles, so women followed the time-honored tradition of working together in clubs, forming the Texas Federation of Republican Women in 1955 with local clubs throughout the state. Working through their organizations, women supported candidates and served as the volunteer foot soldiers in a rapid rise of the Republican Party, gradually winning local, state, and national elections, including both houses of the state and nation by the end of the 1960s.[8] While the Republican women produced many successes in recruiting members to the party and electing candidates, some of their actions backfired. A notable example that received national attention occurred when young, wealthy, Republican women heckled, spat on, and physically accosted Lady Bird and Lyndon Johnson, the vice presidential nominee, at an appearance in Dallas. The backlash against the actions of this "mink coat mob" helped ensure that John F. Kennedy carried Texas in the 1960 presidential election.[9]

Asian Women

Although the idealization of the white, middle-class suburban lifestyle permeated postwar culture, the same period witnessed an increase in nonwhite minorities establishing counter images to that homogeneous and imaginary standard. In particular, during World War II and the Cold War that followed, Asian women moved to Texas, increasing their population and presence from almost none to becoming part of significantly growing communities and families.

Before World War II, very few Asian women called Texas home. The first Asians in Texas were Chinese who arrived as fieldworkers and laborers on the railroads in the late nineteenth century. Due to the Chinese Exclusion Act and the type of work in which they were engaged, almost all were men. Those who stayed, as well as many of the small number of Japanese immigrants, intermarried with Mexican women, Tejanas, and sometimes African American women but rarely white women. El Paso and San Antonio contained small communities of Asian and Mexican families. By 1940 there were fewer than fifteen hundred Asians recorded in the entire state, and men significantly outnumbered women.[10]

In the postwar period, the male-to-female ratio evened out, as thousands of Asian women came to Texas. Some came as a result of changes in immigration policies regarding Chinese, allowing men to bring wives and families from China. Some Japanese, mostly from South America, who had been interned at the harsh wartime Immigration and Naturalization Service camps at Kenedy, Seagoville, and Crystal City, chose to remain in Texas after their release. The largest influx of Asians in this period came after the 1945 War Brides Act that allowed military men stationed overseas who married foreigners to return to the United States with their wives. During World War II, over a hundred thousand Japanese and Filipino women married American servicemen, and in the postwar period, as US troops were stationed in Asia fighting communist governments, even more did so, as did thousands of Korean and Chinese women. When the servicemen finished their tours of duty, because of its several large military bases, Texas became home to thousands of these women, especially in Killeen, El Paso, and San Antonio.[11]

Unfortunately, only sparse research has been published on the lives of these war brides. It is clear that most faced language and other cultural barriers in their new homes and that many suffered from isolation. Even Japanese women who married Japanese American men suffered loneliness as they adjusted to a new culture to which their husbands were already accustomed. Most war brides, however, including the Japanese, married white servicemen. Their isolation and sense of difference was multiplied, and some women even felt alienated from their own English-speaking children. The stress on the marriages sometimes broke them, leading to divorce.[12]

Many other women took steps to overcome the stressors of their new environments, creating support groups to help each other in their communities and in their marriages. In El Paso, Japanese war brides created clubs for socializing as well as their own Buddhist group in order to share their spiritual practices. Military wife Candice Apuan founded the Filipino-American Association of El Paso, which facilitated social events and opportunities to share culture and speak their language. In Killeen, Japanese women gathered at each other's homes; Korean women did likewise. Being isolated from the rest of the society in Killeen, these social groups of women were very important. But as one member of the Korean community of women remembered, merely getting together to play cards gave the wives very little purpose, and they would start petty arguments with each other. Forming the Japanese Wives Association and the Korean Wives Association gave the wives something more productive in which to participate and helped them adjust to their new culture.[13]

Despite marital stresses, many war brides had long, happy marriages and eventually settled into their new state and communities, bringing with them new perspectives and culture. With their arrival, the number of Asians in Texas increased to over twenty-one thousand by the 1970 census, and the gender ratio had evened out, laying the groundwork for larger, more cohesive, communities of Asian groups, who did not look like the white, suburban communities.[14]

African American Women and Civil Rights

Equating white suburban ideals with American ideals left out Asian women and also many other of the state's citizens. African Americans, Tejanas, and other minorities were excluded from this image as well as from the rights and opportunities the vision celebrated. World War II had changed the outlook and circumstances for many of these Texans who resisted their continued exclusion from society, and women who faced the double burden of race and gender discrimination participated in this resistance.

World War II had led to unprecedented opportunities for African Americans in the country. Many Texans left the state, its segregation, and its discrimination when jobs became available in the North and the West. Even more simply fled the grinding poverty of sharecropping and tenant farming to take jobs in Texas's cities, joined by African Americans escaping from other southern states. Between 1940 and 1950, the percentage of African Americans living in the rural farming areas of Texas decreased by 47 percent (from 354,485 to 186,751), while the percentage in the state's urban areas increased nearly as much (46 percent). During the war, African American women had found some work in heavy wartime industries, but they assumed even more work in the garment factories, domestic service, and other positions that white women had left for better jobs.

After the war, however, due to highly discriminatory hiring policies, African American women were again relegated primarily to domestic service and unemployment. African American men who had served as soldiers during the war returned home to discrimination in employment and segregation in society. While African Americans in Texas had been attempting to fight segregation and unjust laws throughout the twentieth century, the concentration of population in urban areas (made more segregated due to white flight to the suburbs), the heightened awareness of rights and opportunities during the war, and the emerging civil rights movement throughout the South all contributed to a significant increase in activism.

In this new crusade for equal rights in Texas, African American women played major roles as supporters, role models, and leaders. Lulu B. White became the first full-time executive secretary of a branch of the National Association for the Advancement of Colored People (NAACP) in the South when she took the position in Houston in 1943. From there, she worked to engage the community in activism, mobilizing blacks to take advantage of the Supreme Court's *Smith v. Allwright* ruling that the state's all-white

Democratic primary was unconstitutional. She effectively recruited vol-
unteers to challenge discrimination of all types throughout the state. She
identified people to apply to work as Southwestern Bell operators in 1948,
mainly to highlight that company's policy against hiring African Americans.
She convinced Hattie M. White to run for the Houston Independent School
Board in 1957, and the run was successful: Hattie White became the first
African American to be elected to office in Houston since Reconstruction.
Lulu White enlisted an African American man, Heman Sweatt, to apply to
the University of Texas School of Law and organized financial, legal, and
community support for his case when he was denied admission. In order to
thwart the lawsuit and avoid admitting Sweatt to the all-white university,
Texas founded a law school for African Americans at Texas Southern University. The US Supreme Court decision *Sweatt v. Painter* (1950), however,

Figure 9.1. Thurgood Marshall pins orchid on Lulu White, director of
branches for the Texas State Conference of NAACP branches, at Freedom
Fund Dinner, Sheraton-Palace Hotel, San Francisco, June 28, 1956, during
47th annual NAACP convention. Courtesy of Library of Congress.

ruled that Texas had to admit Sweatt to the University of Texas law school, implying that "separate but equal" facilities were unconstitutional. The case foreshadowed the Supreme Court case *Brown v. Board of Education* (1954), in which separate was ruled to be inherently unequal.[15]

Another woman crucial to the civil rights movement in Texas, Christia V. Adair, served as executive secretary of the Houston chapter of NAACP from 1949 to 1957, pushing for the integration of public facilities, including Houston's public airport, golf courses, and the city hall cafeteria. She personally, and on behalf of the organization, withstood an assault by the state's attorney general who tried to close down the NAACP in Texas by filing suit against it. Adair was questioned in the case for seventeen days yet refused to divulge any membership information.[16] Juanita Craft of Dallas became state organizer for the NAACP in 1946 and by 1958 had organized 128 new chapters. Also serving as the youth advisor, Craft saw education and involvement of young people as the key to long-term changes in society. Craft took young people to state and national conferences and got them involved in direct action, organizing pickets of Negro Appreciation Day at the Texas State Fair, to protest segregation there, and organizing sit-ins at lunch counters in downtown Dallas in 1961.[17]

In addition to these three major leaders in the civil rights movement in Texas, hundreds of other women made up the backbone of the movement, organizing, protesting, raising money to defray legal costs, boycotting department stores, and forming other organizations to fight for civil and political rights. The Mother Action Committee picketed the Ice Palace in Dallas for a year until the skating rink desegregated. Future congresswoman Eddie Bernice Johnson, who had moved to Dallas where she experienced "the most blatant, overt racism that I ever experienced in my life," helped to organize a group that boycotted Dallas department stores where African American women were not allowed to try on clothes. As Johnson remembered, "People tried them on for you, or they would measure your foot and guess your size."[18] Women also supported college students with money, legal assistance, and advice as they protested and conducted sit-ins in cities such as Austin and small towns such as Marshall.[19]

Women were among the Texas Southern University students (inspired by the sit-ins at Greensboro, North Carolina) who began the first sit-ins west of the Mississippi as they targeted segregated lunch counters near the university in March 1960.[20] At the Houston sit-ins, and in others throughout the state, students were sometimes arrested. Most often, lunch counters would just be closed in order to avoid confrontation. Althea Simmons remembered her being ignored during a Dallas sit-in as "the most dehumanizing incident of my life. . . .[We] sat at the lunch counter at the bus station downtown. Nobody shouted at us, nobody said anything to us, nobody wiped the counter where we were. They just ignored us. We sat there for about five or six hours. Nobody made any kind of gesture that could be perceived as being hostile. We just didn't exist."[21]

In addition to forming local groups, Texas women participated in the national movement by founding new chapters of the NAACP and local chapters of the Southern Christian Leadership Conference, originally established in Georgia by Martin Luther King, Jr., Eva McMillan, known as Mama Mac, founded a chapter of the Student Nonviolent Coordinating Committee (SNCC) in Dallas.[22] As elsewhere in the South, women were particularly adept at serving as "bridge leaders," connecting organizations with communities.[23]

Desegregation of public facilities in Texas was slow, halting, and purchased by the time, energy, perseverance, and willingness to risk jail by hundreds of black and white activists across the state. When it did occur, it generally happened peacefully without the violence seen in other southern states, mostly due to businesses and police wanting to avoid confrontations.[24]

School boards across Texas resisted implementing the 1954 *Brown v. Board of Education* Supreme Court decision, which explicitly stated what had only been implicit in *Sweatt v. Painter*, that separate is inherently unequal. While many schools in West Texas and South Texas integrated peacefully and voluntarily, school board officials and white community members opposed action in East Texas. Following the lead of other southern states, Texas formed a White Citizens' Council that opposed the implementation of the Supreme Court ruling. In Mansfield, mobs prevented a school from being desegregated, and the state refused to enforce the law. Despite multiple lawsuits won by the NAACP, the largest school districts in the state, including Dallas and Houston, had not desegregated by 1960. Women such as Hattie White used her newly won position on the Houston Independent School District (HISD) board to fight for integration, while Yvonne Ewell fought from within the ranks in Dallas Independent School District (DISD) as a school principal.[25] The HISD in 1960 finally allowed a few black students to transfer to white schools, while the DISD adopted a "stair-step plan" to integrate very slowly. By 1964, fewer than eighteen thousand—or less than 6 percent—of African American children in the state attended school with whites. After the passage of the 1964 Civil Rights Act, school districts began finally desegregating under the threat of losing federal funding for schools. By 1970, three-quarters of African American students attended Texas schools that were integrated.[26]

The 1964 Civil Rights Act not only furthered desegregation, it also outlawed discrimination in the workplace. As with education, Texans resisted complying, and African American women were among those who brought suits to ensure fair treatment. Annie Mae Carpenter sued and won a case against Stephen F. Austin State University for systematic discrimination against African Americans. These changes in law, and even culture, enabled many African Americans to pursue educational and career goals previously impossible for them. African American women, long discriminated against due to their race and gender, took advantage of the new opportunities. By the 1960s, Hattie Briscoe had become the first African American woman in Texas to receive a law degree, Vivienne Malone-Mays the first African American to earn a doctorate in mathematics, and Cora Eiland Hicks the first African American professor at the University of Texas. Physician Connie Yerwood Conner was appointed the first black director of the state's Maternal and Child Health Services, and Ida Johnson became a news anchor for a major television channel in Dallas.[27]

The Civil Rights Act of 1964 also assured African Americans the right to vote for the first time in the twentieth century, and women took advantage of the opportunity to vote and run for office. In addition to Hattie White who became a member of the Houston school board, Wilhelmina Delco was elected to the Austin Independent School District board in 1968. Further lawsuits to guarantee voting rights led to redistricting the Texas senate's seats, giving the woman who would become one of the most influential African American women in US politics, Barbara Jordan, the opportunity to win election, which she did in 1966.[28]

In addition to the notable African American women firsts, other women saw growing opportunities. In just one decade, the sixties, of all employed African American women, the percentage working in private domestic service decreased from 47 percent to 26 percent. The percentage employed as professionals (including teachers and nurses) increased from 7 percent to 10 percent. And 10 percent of all employed African American women were in clerical positions, up from 2 percent. Black women were still much more likely to work in the lowest-paying service jobs than white women, but the fight for civil rights, nonetheless, had ushered in many changes in a positive direction.[29]

Tejanas and Civil Rights

Like women of other ethnicities, Tejanas lost the better-paying positions that they had gained during World War II. Women who had had the opportunity to move away from familial restrictions and earn money of their own during the war returned to their homes, communities, and prewar social expectations, but their lives had been changed in many ways. As Aurora González Castro of San Antonio later remembered, "It did change our lives. We didn't have money [before the war]. . . . We didn't have a . . . nice house. We had an outdoor toilet. We never knew the other world. I never knew the other world. We didn't have a car. We didn't have a radio. . . . But how has it changed my life? . . . I feel like we're a middle-income family, lower middle-income. . . .We have everything we need now." Tejanas brought back to their communities confidence, skills, and often greater access to and appreciation of education.[30] They used their empowerment to take more professional positions than before and to insist on better education and lives for their children. In Houston, for instance, the number of adult women in the workforce continued to increase after the war, from 23 percent of Spanish-surnamed women over the age of fourteen in 1950 to 28 percent in 1960. By 1970, the largest employment sector for female "Mexican Origin Workers" was clerical, exceeding the previous principal occupation: household and service workers. More Tejanos were employed in middle-class occupations as well in the same period.[31]

The growing desire and ability to enjoy middle-class privileges increased the organized efforts to end discrimination against those of Mexican origin. The League of United Latin American Citizens (LULAC), founded in 1929, continued its efforts to foster assimilation into the American (Anglo) community with full equal rights. After the war, it was joined by the American GI Forum, founded in 1948, which focused on demanding rights for the Mexican Americans who had fought for their country during the war. Both organizations had "women's auxiliaries." During the 1940s and 1950s, the women in these auxiliaries labored to assist the goals of the main groups, primarily by raising money through barbecues, dances, tamale sales, and queen contests. These fund-raisers brought in crucial seed money for their organizations and kept dues low so that they could appeal to more mem- bers. The Ladies LULAC council also continued the spirit of old mutual aid societies by implementing a milk fund for needy families, an eyeglasses fund, a Christmas toy fund, and a baby garments fund. Members of the council worked with local agencies to raise money and provide a variety of services to those in need, ranging from cancer patients and polio sufferers to victims of natural disasters.[32]

Women of both LULAC and the American GI Forum agreed with men that educational disadvantage was one of the many factors preventing Tejanos from gaining the benefits of expanding opportunities in the postwar society. In the 1950 census, Anglo adults in Texas had received an average of 10.3 years of school, while Spanish-surnamed adults had received an average of 3.5 years. Poverty and migrant farm labor prevented many children from attending school regularly, but the discrepancy also arose from policies of school districts providing separate, inferior schools for Tejanos, segregating them into separate classrooms when there were not separate schools, failing students repeatedly in early grades so that they dropped out in frustration, and not allowing them to transfer to Anglo secondary schools even when they did pass. In 1948 LULAC and the American GI Forum won a district court decision (*Delgado v. Bastrop ISD*) finding that separating the children was illegal.[33]

Unfortunately, most school districts in Texas continued to ignore that de- cision and the multitude of decisions that followed, claiming that poor lan- guage skills justified separating all Mexican and Mexican American children in the first grade, where the majority of those children would not pass. While not conceding the justice of the segregation, activist Felix Tijerina proposed the idea that children be taught important English words before entering the first grade. Women, such as Isabel Verver, who organized the first class of Spanish-speaking preschoolers, and Elizabeth Burrus, who developed the first list of four hundred words, designed and taught the Little Schools of the 400. The success of their pupils in first grade warranted the spread of the concept, and Tijerina successfully lobbied the state legislature to provide funding for a statewide program in 1958. Funding cuts limited full implementation, but later the federal government's Head Start program would be modeled after the Little Schools.[34]

In addition to improving education, Tejanas assisted in a myriad of other demands for equal and just treatment. Sara Moreno, the president of a Tejana social club, asked for assistance from the American GI Forum president,

Hector P. Garcia, to overturn a Mathis skating rink's discriminatory policy after her club was refused the right to skate there. After the GI Forum's success in having the policy reversed, Moreno recommended that her sister contact the organization to help with another egregious example of discrimination. When Beatrice Moreno Longoria had taken a bus to the funeral home in Three Rivers to arrange for the funeral of her husband Félix, who had been killed in service, she was told, "I'm sorry, but the whites would object . . . because Mexicans are not served here." Garcia raised such publicity about the wife of a war hero being refused services that the funeral director relented, but by then Senator Lyndon B. Johnson had arranged for the burial of Félix's body in Arlington National Cemetery.[35] Moreno remembered, "Right after the funeral, I got more involved in the Ladies Auxiliary of the G. I. Forum because I realized that so much work needed to be done. And, I joined along with other members, in going all over Texas to organize new chapters of the G. I. Forum. And, I also participated in going and urging people to buy their voters registration."[36] Many other women in LULAC and the American GI Forum auxiliaries also continued systematic efforts to combat racism and improve the status of their community through raising money to pay poll taxes and participating in efforts to integrate public places throughout the state. Dominga Coronado, for instance, often spearheaded dangerous efforts to desegregate restaurants and theaters in New Braunfels.[37]

While conducted on behalf of all people of Mexican descent in Texas, the efforts to desegregate public schools and facilities were led by the liberal-minded upper- and middle-class Tejano leadership of LULAC and the GI Forum. Women in these movements had opportunities to participate actively, but their roles were often tied to traditional ideas of women's place, as mothers, teachers, widows, and organizers of social events such as dances and tamale sales. In the 1960s, a more radical movement began which included a much wider swath of the Tejana population and also made room for women to demand, if not always receive, more powerful leadership roles. The Chicano movement—or *movimiento*—attracted those who worked for far-reaching changes, including economic and social reforms or downright revolution. Because the ideology of the movement included a rethinking and remolding of society, activist women found space to argue for new roles for women, including leadership positions.

Women participated in all aspects of the movement, from organizing and farm workers' strikes to running for political office. Virginia Múzquiz played an active role in electing an all-Mexican city council in Crystal City in 1963 (the only one in Texas) and the next year ran unsuccessfully for state representative, possibly the first Texas Chicana ever to run for that office. The takeover of the Crystal City government, even though short-lived, proved to be a spark for political organizing, for which women were the heart. They became the leaders of the grassroots group, Ciudadanos Unidos (United Citizens), ran for office and won, and were appointed to city agencies. Women took up this highly public mantle because they were capable of doing so, because they could identify their cause with that of building and supporting local communities, and because some men encouraged them to do so. In the midst of this profound change, many of the women of Crystal City who took on leadership roles could be more politically outspoken because they were homemakers who could not be threatened with the loss of their jobs. Crystal City continued to be a hotbed of activism throughout the 1960s. In 1969 Chicana activist students Diana Serna, Severita Lara, and others teamed with local Chicano activist José Ángel Gutiérrez to lead a boycott of the public schools for their racist policies, while women such as Virginia Múzquiz, Juanita Santos, Luz Gutiérrez, and Elena Díaz organized hundreds of local women to support the students during the walkout. After federal intervention, the school board agreed to the students' demands, including bilingual instruction, more accurate testing and placement, and more cultural celebrations.[38]

The Crystal City activism sparked organizing for justice throughout the southwestern United States. The Mexican American Youth Organization (MAYO), founded in 1967 in Crystal City, organized youth throughout Texas to work together to combat discrimination and police brutality and to advocate for political representation and equal education. Tejanas took leadership roles in the organization and learned leadership skills to propel them into community activities. For instance, MAYO member María Jiménez served as vice president and president of the University of Houston Student Association, as the president of other student groups, and then as a candidate for the state legislature in 1974.[39]

After the successful boycott of public schools in Crystal City in 1969, Chicano activists formed La Raza Unida Party (RUP), whose power spread through Texas and the Southwest. From the beginning of RUP, women played active roles. Luz Gutiérrez served as the first RUP county chair, Virginia Múzquiz went on to become the national chair of the party from 1972 to 1974, and María Elena Martínez served as the last Texas chair. Evey Chapa helped write the party platform, which gave a predominant place to women, celebrating motherhood and family, guaranteeing a state executive commit-teewoman, and supporting equal rights for women. In a 1974 essay, Chapa proudly pointed out that "La Raza Unida Party was the only major party that included in its platform a section devoted to *la mujer*." She went on to sum-marize that platform: "The Raza Unida Party declares the belief in the family structure as the basis of development, but also clearly states that it must be a *total* development of the family—men, women, and children."[40]

The RUP resolved "that the participation of women, to include the de-cision making positions of the Raza Unida Party, be actively continued through political education and recruitment of women," but not all men in the party or in the Chicano movement more broadly were as welcoming of women's leadership as the party's resolution envisioned.[41] Martha Cotera, one of the first activists to move to Crystal City specifically to participate in the revolution happening there, would remember, "We came across bad attitudes on giving women credit and sharing the glory and all that stuff." As the Chicano movement widened regionally and nationally, women con-tinued to face overt hostility. As Cotera recalled, to the women "it was im-portant to include female bodies presenting [the female] agenda, so that others in the community would see that activism and leadership could come from both genders." After insisting that women be allowed to present at a conference in Houston, one of the audience members yelled, "Why don't you go home and do the dishes where you belong?" Cotera realized that these men were "acting out of ignorance. . . . They are cultural nationalists, but these people don't know that part of our culture is the participation of women." Just as the Chicano movement had proudly turned to their history to celebrate Chicano heritage, Cotera began researching and writing a his-tory of Mexican women, *Diosa y Hembra*, the first of its kind. Between the history and her frequent other writings on women, RUP, and the Chicano movement, Cotera became one of the leading intellectuals of the Chicano and feminist movements nationwide.[42]

The resistance of some men of the Chicano movement inspired women to begin "caucusing" at RUP conventions and meetings to identify issues of di-rect impact and interest to women. In 1971 a Houston branch of the Young Women's Christian Association (YWCA) hosted the Conferencia de Mujeres por la Raza, probably the first national conference of its kind. Hundreds of delegates arrived and set out an agenda addressing the unique issues that con-fronted Chicanas and criticizing the machismo and sexism of the Chicano movement as well as the Anglocentrism of the feminist movement (discussed in the next chapter). Although the conference participants passed what many Chicanas considered to be radical resolutions, calling for free legal abortion, birth control, and breaking with the Catholic Church because of its oppression of women, a large number of Chicana activists boycotted the convention due to its threat to divide the Chicano movement.[43] A later state convention of Chicanas held in conjunction with the RUP convention in San Antonio in 1973 led to the formation of Mujeres por la Raza, a group whose primary purpose was to train and support women's active participation in all aspects of society, especially politics. Mujeres por la Raza would be instrumental in keeping women's issues in the foreground of the Chicano movement and inserting Chicanas' concerns and views into the feminist movement.[44]

Decade of Unrest

The Chicano movement in the 1960s was not alone in embracing what, at the time, were considered radical positions. Many Americans in this decade—especially youth—rebelled against the conformity of the postwar generation. They became frustrated with the slow progress of liberal movements, such as the civil rights movements, that sought to change laws to lessen discrimination. Instead they increasingly engaged in efforts to completely overhaul society. Chicanos protested, boycotted, and eventually rejected the established political system and formed an alternative political party. The African American civil rights movement engaged in direct action, spurred by young people who founded the Student Nonviolent Coordinating Committee (SNCC). Young people in this organization risked their lives by sponsoring and participating in Freedom Rides (riding buses into the South to protest continued segregation in interstate transportation) and voter registration drives in the South. By the end of the decade, many African Americans embraced the Black Power movement that reconsidered the previous strategies of nonviolence and advocated a more forceful self-determination. Inspired in part by the Chicano and African American civil rights movements, other groups burgeoned, especially among college students, advocating a more just and inclusive society. These groups gained momentum in large part due to protests over the country's increased participation in the war in Vietnam. The rise of a New Left challenged the country on many levels.

As in the rest of the country, much activity in Texas centered in the state's colleges and universities, and the state's flagship, the University of Texas in Austin, became one of the sites of the greatest activism. As the university began its slow integration process, women like Linda Lewis, who was one of six African Americans in a dorm of two hundred, found it overwhelming to be the representative of "an unknown class and gender in a laboratory setting—coed dormitory living." She found herself "doubly exhausted" by the demands of being a freshman student and being "constantly barraged with questions about any and every detail of our lives and thoughts." As a small minority, she and other women and men worked hard to sustain black organizations on and off campus.[45]

The bravery of Chicanas and African American women in civil rights movements inspired some white students to protest the racism inherent in the conforming Cold War society. A young Casey Hayden found her commitment to combat racism strengthened by living in an integrated community near the Austin campus and participating in integrated meetings of the YWCA. Growing up in Waco and raised like most southern white women, this was her first opportunity to learn how black students felt about segregation. Hayden then convinced the National Student Association (NSA) at its Minnesota meeting to endorse the sit-in movement and later formed Students for Direct Action on the UT campus, which engaged in sit-ins at lunch counters and "stand-ins" at movie theaters.[46] Hayden's activism demonstrates the ways that national movements affected Texas. She attended regional and national meetings of the YWCA, the NSA, SNCC, and Students for a Democratic Society (SDS), and from those she brought back not only determination to enact change but also ideas and tools with which to do so. However, Hayden's activism also demonstrates the important roles in the national movement that Texas women played. Due to her work in Texas as well as national meetings, she was included in a 1962 *New York Times* feature story about the national student movement. Hayden eventually left Texas to take wider leadership roles.[47]

Other women of the New Left remained in Texas and led youth in protests of the racism, war, poverty, and postwar conformity. Susan Torian Olan, who had also been a University of Texas student in the 1960s, later explained, "Why so many of the Baby Boom turned dramatically, politically, and culturally radical is this: We were born into a world of lies where everything was façade and reality was denied." She pointed specifically to the sham of the happy suburban household and the drills in which children were taught how to supposedly survive a nuclear attack. The civil rights movement—and the conservative backlash against it—highlighted that the great American way of life was neither uniform nor fair. Then the Vietnam War erupted, leading to the drafting of young men into the army who could not even vote. Young adults desperately sought ways in which to exert more control in the world. Some, like Olan joined the Communist Party at least nominally, while others engaged in direct activism through groups like SNCC and SDS.[48]

Men held most of the very public leadership roles in student organizations. Women, however, formed the backbone of the movement, doing much of the work such as typing, mimeographing, raising money, and organizing. They played significant roles in writing, publishing, and distributing the *Rag*, one of the nation's most influential underground newspapers in the 1960s published in Austin. They also participated in potentially dangerous protests, sit-ins, and other actions alongside men and sometimes alongside only other women, such as when a group of women staged a sit-in at the Austin draft office and were arrested.[49]

While much of the work was directly political, a new emerging culture became another way for many young women to express their distance from the generations before them. In other parts of the nation, the counterculture movement represented by "hippies" was distinct from the student protest movements, but at the University of Texas "the politics and counterculture merged."[50] Drugs and rock 'n' roll provided multiple avenues for young men and women to have different experiences from their parents and the older generations they distrusted. Music, not just rock, played an important part of the counterculture and protest scene. The national tradition of Gentle Thursdays began when a group of students sat on the grass on the UT campus to talk about peace, and "some folk singer joined us and played a bunch of music."[51] The vibrant Austin music scene provided a magnet to musicians and an incubator for new sounds in country and rock but particularly for folk music. Of those attracted to the city and the university for its large population of young people throwing off convention, none would become more famous than Janis Joplin. Moving from Port Arthur to attend college at the University of Texas, Joplin was much more interested in the art, music, and social scenes than in college classes. She found a crowd of supportive friends who were as anti-conformist as she and a group of people who saw music as a way of defining themselves and their lives. Kenneth Threadgill, the owner of Threadgill's Bar, recognized and encouraged her talent. After learning to perform and sharpening her skills, she left Texas for the West Coast and became a national sensation. Like many of the counterculture, Joplin never considered herself political, but her music helped define a generation of youth yearning for change.[52]

Sex, one of the keystones of the 1960s counterculture ("sex, drugs, and rock 'n' roll"), revolutionized many women's lives and became a major component of politics and culture. According to Mariann Garner-Wizard, in high school "sex was the area wherein we had the most misinformation fed to us [and] we were warned that if we gave up our virginity no decent man would ever want us."[53] Young college students who had begun to question everything about society and politics also questioned their parents' advice on sex. "Free love" expressed the desire that sexual acts should not be regulated by antiquated institutions such as marriage. Yet the sexual revolution was not as freeing for all women as it was envisioned to be. Frieda Werden remembered that "looking back on it, it wasn't much fun. . . . Where sex was assumed, courtship and foreplay became minimal." Many young women had not yet learned to seek their own pleasure in sexual encounters.[54]

Another reason the sexual revolution created problems for women was the risk of pregnancy. Although the birth control pill was introduced in 1960, university health centers and organizations like Planned Parenthood would rarely prescribe it to single women.[55] Single women who became pregnant sometimes found their lovers unwilling to support or raise a child, and even many young women who had supportive partners risked losing their livelihoods or education or both as a result of an unplanned pregnancy. Increasing numbers of these women sought abortions. Abortions, however, had been outlawed in Texas since 1854 except to save the life of the mother, and illegal abortions were difficult to obtain and dangerous. In the late 1960s, the *Rag* began to print articles about safe and unsafe methods of ending pregnancies, hoping to reduce the number of injuries and deaths caused by untrained practitioners, including from the so-called back-alley doctors who were often not doctors at all. Some Austin women began an underground referral service for women seeking abortions.[56] Even with the dangers and drawbacks of sex, however, single women were more willing to engage in it than ever before. Thus, the ancient strictures attaching sex to marriage came under assault in the 1960s, with long-term results for Texas women.

The antiestablishment, egalitarian nature of New Left movements opened up opportunities for significant participation by women. Yet, because men most often took the public leadership positions in the political movements of the 1960s, women's work was frequently obscured or later forgotten. Despite Casey Hayden being one of the founders of Students for a Democratic Society and the crucial link between it and the civil rights movement, early histories of SDS identify her primarily as the spouse of another leader, Tom

Hayden. In SDS and other organizations, men routinely excluded women from strategy discussions and decision-making. Even Casey Hayden, who had greater access to the inner circle of SDS than most members, spent her first summer at the New York headquarters typing and thus excluded from strategy discussions.[57]

Many women in the movement became frustrated when men ignored their voices in meetings, expected them to do the menial duties, dismissed their visions of the future, and treated them as objects or accessories to the men's attempts to change the world. Sharon Shelton-Colangelo recognized this inequality when she was asked to pose naked for the *Rag*. Whenever the paper's sales were down, they would print a picture of one of the women typing in the nude. When someone pointed out that it was Shelton-Colangelo's turn, she reacted without fully understanding why she objected until she suggested that perhaps one of the men should be the nude instead. Her suggestion was laughed off, but the incident caused her to understand the clear double standard through which women but not men were treated as sexual objects.[58]

Young women had already become accustomed to unequal treatment in society, such as when Garner-Wizard's first-year journalism instructor told her "that women should not expect above a B in the course, no matter how good their work, because women were not cut out to be journalists." But as more and more women experienced sexism within supposedly egalitarian organizations, such as SNCC, NSA, and SDS, they began to recognize these injustices and connect them to the other areas of their lives. Upon marrying her husband, he and Frieda Werden shared the cooking and housekeeping —until they moved in with another couple. Then she "felt pressured to do housework while the men played the 'Big Pink' album and got high."[59]

Having grown up in the 1950s, most of them were unaware of vibrant women's movements of the past and of the organizations that continued to work for women's rights. As Werden explained, "In the '50s women were robbed of our collective history and our personal ambitions. . . . Glimpses of women in '50s textbooks were more humiliating than nothing at all: scolds and 'termagants' being dunked in colonial New England; cheerleader Betsy Ross; stoic 'pioneers and their wives'. . . plodding across the plains; nurturer of men at war, Florence Nightingale."[60]

In addition to often being unaware of past and current fights for women's equality, the young women of the New Left had embraced the concept that political solutions were not enough and that a full-scale social revolution was necessary to change the world. Thus, as these women in the state and nation—brought together for the purpose of changing the world—began discussing their problems—from being objectified to being ignored to doing all the housework—they started connecting the issues into an understanding of the ways that women were treated as inferiors in public and private, leading to the defining phrase, "the personal is political." Rap groups, or "consciousness-raising" groups, sprang up in Austin and other cities and even small towns. By the end of the 1960s, the women's liberation movement had begun.

Emergence of Women's Liberation

The civil rights movement, opposition to the Vietnam War, and the rise of a New Left intent on revolutionizing social structures led young women involved in these movements to identify multiple forms of women's oppression. In 1965 Casey Hayden, who had already left Texas for New York, worked with another SNCC member, Mary King, to draft a tract, "Sex and Caste: A Kind of Memo," which they distributed widely to women in many organizations. According to "Sex and Caste," "Having learned from the movement to think radically about the personal worth and abilities of people whose role in society had gone unchallenged before, a lot of women in the movement have begun trying to apply those lessons to their own relations with men." One of the most important complaints in the tract was that inequality was not being discussed or even recognized: "Nobody is writing, or organizing or talking publicly about women, in any way that reflects the problems that various women in the movement come across." Many women in the movement ignored "Sex and Caste," and many more men dismissed it as nonsense. As late as 1968 in the Austin chapter of Students for a Democratic Society, women who called attention to sexism within the organization "were put down hard and fast."[61]

The reactions of the male leaders, however, did not halt the growing discontentment of women at being treated as inferiors. Meeting together in women-only consciousness-raising groups, they began to gain confidence in voicing their opinions and identified personal mind-sets and social attitudes that limited their choices. Throughout the nation, women began forming very loosely affiliated "women's liberation groups" that sought to bring greater awareness to sexism and thus change attitudes. The 1968 protest of the Miss America beauty pageant in New Jersey was probably the most famous attempt at garnering publicity for the cause. Pictures of protesters throwing make-up, false eyelashes, pots and pans, and bras into a trash can—discarding symbols of the ways in which women were convinced to conform to a social standard—were published throughout the country and began a national conversation.[62]

By 1969 Austin had formed its own women's liberation organization, and in 1970 the members hosted a women's liberation conference for the state.[63] Austin Women's Liberation also staged guerrilla actions, protesting a Neiman Marcus fashion show held on the university campus by dressing as beauty and feminine hygiene products to highlight the way that media enforced expectations of women in order to sell products. Others parodied sexist traditions on campus, and another group of women gathered to place a "witches' hex" on the LBJ Presidential Library when it was dedicated.[64] They communicated their frustrations with social issues, including sexist language in the *Rag*. A new magazine begun by Frieda Werden, *The Texan Woman*, insisted, among other things, on the cessation of using the term "chick" to refer to a woman: "A chick is fluffy, cute, stupid and in need of protection."[65] Students ran a women's center on campus for three years, and then other activists in Austin formed the Austin Women's Organization (AWO) and opened the Austin Women's Center in 1972. The latter operated for over two decades. According to Werden, who was one of founders of the AWO, "A lot of brilliant women attended those meetings . . . and we had great, great rap sessions ranging over personal experience, analysis, literature, and theory." Women-only spaces, such as the Austin Women's Center, provided women accustomed to deferring to men in group settings opportunities to express their opinions, practice leadership skills, and develop a sense of competence and self-worth.[66]

Fighting for Equal Rights

Although the women's liberationists of the 1960s may have been unaware of the many efforts on behalf of women's equality that preceded them, many women as individuals and groups had been working for greater rights for decades. The Federation of Business and Professional Women (BPW) was the leading group fighting for women's rights from the 1920s through the 1960s. Strong local BPW chapters provided support and opportunities for women who were a distinct minority in the professions and provided training and moral support for its members during this period of antipathy toward women with careers. One of the most prominent BPW members was lawyer and judge Sarah T. Hughes, who in 1931 was one of the first women to serve in the state legislature (only five had ever served before). As a representative, she introduced legislation to promote women's legal equality, including bills to allow women to serve on juries and to remove the requirement that women be examined separately from their husbands before selling property. The latter practice, she argued, "questions the intelligence of a married woman." Both bills failed. After Hughes was appointed to the Fourteenth District Court in Dallas, she used her position as the first woman state judge to advocate for other professional women, serving as president of the local, state, and national chapters of the BPW. Hughes would later become Texas's first federal judge in 1961 when President John F. Kennedy appointed her to the US District Court for the Northern District of Texas. In that position she gained national prominence in 1963 when she administered the oath of office of the president of the United States to Lyndon B. Johnson after Kennedy's assassination, the only woman to ever

Figure 9.2. Judge Sarah T. Hughes becomes the only woman to administer the oath of office to a US president when she swears in Lyndon B. Johnson after the assassination of John F. Kennedy.

administer that oath. In 1954, after many years of championing the cause, Hughes finally was instrumental in winning an amendment to the state's constitution allowing women to serve on juries.[67]

Hughes served as state president of the BPW when the organization endorsed an equal rights amendment to the US Constitution in the 1940s, an amendment that had been introduced in Congress every year since 1923. That effort stalled, however, and the proposed amendment never got out of committee until the 1970s. As efforts continued on the national level, another Texas BPW member, Hermine Tobolowsky, became frustrated that state laws regarding married women's property rights were among the most restrictive in the country. She began an effort in 1957 to pass an amendment to the state constitution that would address all the areas of inequality in state law: the Texas Equal Legal Rights Amendment (ELRA). The effort gained national attention, and the *Saturday Evening Post* ran a feature in January 1961, "The Revolt of Texas Women," outlining Tobolowsky's leadership in the organization's efforts. Although the amendment would be introduced in every session of the legislature, the state amendment, like the national amendment, went nowhere for years, as many legislators believed that women should be at home and dependent upon their husbands.[68]

Yet another BPW member, Dallas attorney Louise Ballerstedt Raggio, became chair of the Family Law Section of the State Bar of Texas in 1965 and examined the hundreds of laws that needed to be changed in order to remove legal impediments for women. She became convinced that the Equal Legal Rights Amendment would do little to assist women. Instead, she spent two years working with the bar association to draft a "Marital Property Act" that would remove the legal disabilities of married women in reference to nearly every aspect of business and personal life, including property ownership and control, family relationships, and rights to contract.[69]

When both the ELRA and Marital Property Act were introduced in the state legislature in 1967, Raggio and Tobolowsky fought each other as well as oppositional state legislators, each to get her bill—and only her bill—passed. Each truly believed that the strategy of the other would undermine women's rights rather than bolster them, and they testified in committee hearings against each other's legislation. In that session, many legislators who bore hostility toward the Equal Legal Rights Amendment decided to support the Marital Property Act because of Tobolowsky's opposition to it. As a result, the Marital Property Act (1967), one of the most far-reaching pieces of legislation regarding women's rights in Texas up to that point, passed that session.[70]

Tobolowsky and ELRA supporters redoubled their efforts, mobilizing grassroots support to put pressure on state legislators, who, of course, were overwhelmingly men. One of the greatest objections the State Bar of Texas had voiced against that amendment was that it would cause too much chaos in the courts because of the many laws "protecting" married women, but the provisions of the Marital Property Act had mostly eliminated that fear. Some state legislators who continued to oppose the amendment argued that it would dissolve "the protection of special rights women now enjoy," such as exemptions from jury duty for homemakers with young children and laws criminalizing rape. Many other legislators identified the ELRA with an erosion of traditional and supposedly "natural" sex roles, fearing that if women had equal legal rights, then men's role as the head of the house would be threatened. Yet the national and state discussions of women's issues and the rise of feminist movements, as well as sustained and tireless work by Tobolowsky and the BPW, finally prevailed leading to ELRA's passage in the legislature and then approval by voters in 1972. The amendment discouraged state, county, and municipal governments from passing laws and ordinances that discriminated by gender, and it gave men and women the legal basis to challenge existing and future attempts to do so.[71]

Feminism in Texas and Texas Feminists in the Nation

Between the awakened consciousness of young women who demanded liberation and the continued struggle of women working toward equality through legislation, it seemed to some as if the entire nation was suddenly reconsidering the place, status, and role of women. Many who began advocating new roles and opportunities for women embraced the term "feminism" to describe themselves and their agendas for change. Whatever they called themselves, with awakened consciousness they set about to revolutionize their state and their nation. Not only did feminism affect women in the state, women in the state played a significant role in the development and impact of feminism in the nation.

The National Organization for Women (NOW), formed in 1966 by Betty Friedan and others frustrated at the lack of progress being made by state commissions on women, established its first chapters in Texas in Houston in 1970, San Antonio in 1971, and Austin and Dallas in 1972. After creating a state chapter in 1973, the organization grew to twenty-nine local chapters. NOW combined the elements of "liberal feminism," whose adherents (such as Raggio and Tobolowsky) sought primarily to change laws discriminating against women, with those of "radical feminism," whose activists (such as the students in the New Left) were interested in changing social ideas and structures. NOW task forces formed to combat family violence and rape, eradicate sexist language in textbooks, assist displaced homemakers, lobby for legislation increasing child support enforcement and day-care options, and support lesbian civil rights.[72]

As activists lobbied the Texas legislature, the State Board of Education, and city and county governments on a wide range of women's concerns, they faced the stark reality that many of these bodies were all-male or nearly all-male institutions. Frustrated that they often could not convince these men of the importance of what were often called "women's issues," several Texas women assisted in the formation of the National Women's Political Caucus (NWPC) in 1971. This new organization, which was dedicated to recruiting, training, and electing qualified women to public office, held its first conference in Houston in 1973. Texas state representative Sissy Farenthold became the first national chair, and Texas would play a vital role in the organization. The Texas chapter (TWPC) became one of the strongest state chapters and

Figure 9.3. Gwen Cherry presents Frances "Sissy" Farenthold with the gavel of the National Women's Political Caucus after Farenthold's election as the NWPC's first chairwoman.

one of the few to hire its own director and lobbyist when it hired Cathy Bonner. The 1973 Texas legislative session included only 6 women out of the 181 members, but that was a threefold increase over the previous decade. Backed by a statewide membership of over two thousand, the TWPC pushed for a wide range of legislation regarding child care, credit discrimination, maternity leave, reproductive services, and rape. Some successes (including revising the infamous law that allowed a man to kill his wife and her lover if he found them in the act of intercourse) and some failures (including Governor Dolph Briscoe's veto of a bill that would have funded family planning services) led the organization to expand its efforts to elect more women to office and also to support male candidates for the legislature who would support their agenda.[73]

Ratification of the Equal Rights Amendment (ERA) to the US Constitution was one of the primary objectives of the NWPC, NOW, and many other groups, including a newly formed organization, ERAmerica. Women in these organizations pushed state legislatures to ratify the amendment that read simply "Equality of rights under the law shall not be denied or abridged by the United States or by any State on account of sex." After years and years of relentless lobbying, the Texas legislature had just passed the Texas Equal Legal Rights Amendment, which was then approved by the state's voters by a four-to-one margin. As a result, state legislators wasted very little time on debating the very similar national amendment, and Texas became one of the first twenty-two states to ratify—and one of only two southern states to do so.[74]

Of all the issues to arise during the feminist movement of the 1960s and 1970s, reproductive rights and control became central. Professional women's careers often suffered due to pregnancy—whether they became pregnant or employers merely assumed that they eventually would. Young women, especially, wanted to experience and enjoy their sexuality in the same ways that men did, without the fear of pregnancy. Despite changing mores, pregnancy out of marriage still carried significant social stigmatization, and there were few places where a single woman could get assistance. Thus, feminists argued for greater maternity leave policies and child-care options, as well as increased funding for family planning services and wider access to birth control. (Single women, especially, had difficulty getting the birth control pill due to the cost and many doctors' refusal to prescribe to them.) And, for those women who suffered unwanted pregnancies, they pressed for access to safe abortions.

Texas law declared abortion illegal, and, as a result, women seeking abortions who could not travel to states like New York and California where it was safe and legal, or to Juarez, Mexico, where it was safe, resorted to illegal, unlicensed, and unregulated practitioners or attempting abortion themselves. Judy Smith and Bea Durden, prominent women involved in the women's liberation movement in Austin, used the *Rag* to advise women about unsafe abortion techniques. They then proceeded to run an underground referral service that informed women about birth control measures and sexually transmitted diseases and connected women with abortionists who operated illegally but safely in Texas or Mexico. Unsure about the legality of their referral service, they asked for the assistance of a recent University of Texas law graduate, Sarah Weddington. The subject was significant for Weddington, since she had previously had an illegal abortion. As she researched the topic, Weddington and others became convinced that the laws needed to be changed so that women could have access to information and safe and legal abortion services.[75]

While others advocated changing the laws, Weddington and some others looked for a court case to overturn the law against abortion in Texas. After finding a pregnant plaintiff who could give them legal standing to challenge the law, Weddington filed the case, which, as *Roe v. Wade*, eventually came before the US Supreme Court. In 1973 the justices ruled not only that Texas's law criminalizing abortion was unconstitutional but also that women had the right to abortion, at least in the first trimester of pregnancy. Weddington, at the age of twenty-seven, not only helped make safe and legal abortion available for thousands of women, she also became the youngest person to successfully argue a case before the Supreme Court.[76]

In addition to bringing the historic case to the Supreme Court, Texas feminists achieved national prominence by hosting the nation's largest women's conference. The United Nations 1975 International Women's Year Conference charged every member nation to hold a conference to "identify the barriers that prevent women from participating fully and equally in all aspects of national life and develop recommendations for means by which such barriers can be removed."[77] In the United States, all states held preconferences at which attendees discussed issues and elected delegates to the national convention, which became known as the National Women's Conference. The Texas preconference held in Austin chose its delegates among the strong network of feminist activists across the state. By prioritizing diverse representation, it created a delegation that included poor, rural, older, and student members; nearly half were ethnic minorities.[78]

Fifty states and six territories sent their delegates to the National Women's Conference, held in Houston in 1977. The National IWY Commission chose Houston as the site due to a few persuasive factors, chief among them the "strong and wide volunteer support" offered by women in the city's many feminist activist groups and philanthropic and social women's clubs. Houston also had the only "women's advocate" position in the nation at the time, held by Nikki Van Hightower.[79] Hightower, a feminist activist with a doctorate in political science, served as the liaison between the city and the "Houston Committee" charged with preparing for the conference. She later remembered that the mix of women on the committee was crucial to its success because women in charitable organizations "were very skilled organizers," while feminist organizations contributed new ideas, "making a very positive dynamic, and we learned a lot from each other."[80] The Houston Committee, chaired by Mary Keegan, successfully planned and implemented the largest women's convention held in the United States, which two thousand delegates and twenty thousand spectators attended.

At the National Women's Conference, with thousands of observers and some fifteen hundred members of the media reporting the proceedings nationwide, delegates debated twenty-six resolutions, eventually passing twenty-five recommendations. Texas women played prominent roles in this convention and in these debates: Lady Bird Johnson addressed the convention as a former First Lady; Lady Bird's former press secretary, Liz Carpenter, and the president of the Girl Scouts of America, Gloria Scott, served as International Women's Year commissioners; Congresswoman Barbara Jordan gave the keynote address; Travis County Commissioner Ann Richards gave the seconding speech for support of the Equal Rights Amendment; and Sarah Weddington gave the seconding speech for the recommendation supporting women's right to abortion.[81] Prudence Mackintosh, writing in *Texas Monthly*, summed up their participation: "Texans didn't exactly run the National Women's Conference, but they made it work." The conference was in many ways the culmination of the feminist movement, identifying the barriers to women's equality, suggesting the means of removing those barriers, and transmitting the recommendations in a formal report to Congress and the president. As Liz Carpenter noted in her opening speech to the convention, "The president of the United States and the Congress have asked us to assess our needs, assert our worth, and set our goals for filling the legislative gaps. I thought they'd never ask!"[82] Texas women not only felt the effects of this national movement, they had also participated in shaping it at the national level.

Conclusion

The postwar generation of women in Texas participated, often reluctantly, in building a world that would protect the best of American ideals for their children. A woman's main identity was that of "housewife," women played supportive roles to husbands, families consumed and kept the capitalist economy running, and everyone fought any ideas that deviated from the perfect Anglo-American picture because those ideas might allow the communists to win the Cold War.

Women also participated, however, in challenging the façade of a perfect and free society by serving as the backbone of the African American civil rights movement, the Chicano movement, and the New Left. Children of the postwar generation grew up frustrated by the constrictions of conformity, witnessing the unrest of civil rights movements, and eventually questioning the very basis of the Cold War when the fighting turned hot in Vietnam.

These young women (accompanied by older ones) who assisted the New Left and the counterculture in identifying many problems in politics and society eventually began to identify gender constrictions as one of the many areas of American society that needed a social revolution. The emergence of the women's liberation movement gave new energy to old feminist organizations and sparked the creation of new ones. Texas women were at the forefront of these new movements both in the state and in the nation.

Chapter 10

Taking Charge
Women to the End of the Twentieth Century

The rise of feminism in the late 1960s and 1970s ushered in the era of the most substantial change for women in Texas. During the rest of the twentieth century, activists and theorists challenged nearly every aspect of the accepted social structure, envisioned new roles for women, and fought for a wide range of legal rights for women. Feminists, however, had differing ideas about how to achieve equality for women and what that equality would look like, leading to many different feminisms. The disruption to established ways of thinking also triggered a backlash and prompted some women to take leadership positions in groups attempting to preserve traditional roles for women and ideas about families. The consequences of the feminist movements and the backlash would have long-lasting impact on Texas through the century and beyond.

Divisions

The feminist movement that began in the late 1960s and early 1970s in reality consisted of many different agendas, goals, and ideologies clustered around gender and its place in society. In addition to the many adherents to liberal feminism and radical feminism, some women embraced socialist feminism (identifying capitalism as key to women's oppression) and cultural feminism (embracing and valuing women's differences from men). And, as Austin feminist activist Frieda Werden summed up, "Because the women's movement was so diverse, there were naturally . . . blowups."[1] For instance, in its early years, the Texas Women's Political Caucus nearly fractured over whether the organization, dedicated to helping women get elected, should endorse men running for office who supported its legislative goals. They did decide to endorse qualified male candidates but only financially support qualified women (until 1991 when it instead began rating men on their support of women's issues).[2]

Within the radical movements of the 1960s, increased experimentation with sexuality enabled many more lesbians to understand and express themselves. While some increasingly found acceptance in small communities that they formed through bars and groups, they found themselves marginalized in the gay movement by men who dismissed their issues as irrelevant and unimportant. Gay men of the 1960s and 1970s were often reluctant to treat women as equals both because of their greater interest in socializing with other men and because they often exhibited the same sexism inherent in mainstream society. One of the few places to gather were bars, but gay clubs in San Antonio, Dallas, and Houston excluded lesbians.[3] Apart from the social scene, conflicts arose between gays and lesbians in the new political movements organized to fight against discrimination and for greater rights. Tensions escalated in Houston, forcing the resignation of the president of the Houston Gay Political Caucus, and a debate over the name of the Dallas Gay Political Caucus turned into a bitter fight resulting in most women resigning. In neither caucus would the men allow the inclusion of the word "lesbian" in the organization's name.[4] In Austin, lesbians also complained that their lives and concerns were ignored. In a letter to the newsletter *Gay Austin*, a reader complained, "You have almost nothing about us, almost completely about men. If you consider yourselves to be a community newspaper, the fact that you print almost nothing about women makes your title 'Gay Austin' ridiculous."[5] Many lesbians began arguing that only complete separatism would allow lesbians, and in fact all women, to be able to claim their own power and voices. The separatist constituency led to divisions in gay and lesbian groups as well as feminist groups.[6] However, when the AIDS crisis hit Texas in the 1980s, thousands of lesbians put differences aside to assist gay men who were being devastated by the disease, by setting up hospices and through direct care. As gay male leaders of political groups began dying, lesbians took larger roles in political action groups, leading the fight against AIDS discrimination and demanding compassion and government assistance to fight the disease. New organization names were only one important indicator of this strengthened alliance in the 1980s and 1990s: Dallas Gay and Lesbian Alliance, Houston Gay and Lesbian Political Caucus, and the Austin Lesbian/Gay Political Caucus.[7]

While lesbians fought for power, acceptance, and roles in the gay movement, they also felt similarly ignored and excluded from the women's movement. In the 1970s, many feminists believed lesbian rights were distinct from women's rights. National Organization for Women (NOW) founder Betty Friedan even labeled lesbians "the lavender menace" for fear that support for their issues would taint the organization's fight for women's rights, and she pushed NOW to cut all ties with lesbians. NOW's bitter division, however, was mostly settled by 1971 with a resolution at the national convention recognizing lesbian rights as a true feminist concern. By the time chapters of NOW and the Texas Women's Political Caucus (TWPC) formed in Texas, a lesbian task force offered a venue by which lesbians in the organizations could assert their concerns.[8] Even with the nominal inclusion of lesbian rights within the stated goals of these groups, their dedication to the cause was often lukewarm. After the Austin Lesbian Organization (ALO) held an all-women's dance at the Austin Women's Center, the center's landlord, the Texas Federation of Women's Clubs, demanded that the center cease support of the lesbian group and association with it. The center chose to move, but it (and its member institutions, which included local chapters of TWPC and NOW) also voted to not publicly support the ALO. Mainstream feminists in Texas continued to fear that being associated with lesbians would hurt their chances of making political gains.[9] That fear subsided slowly, and the rift took even more time to heal. Nonetheless, Austin activist Janna Zumbrun pressed the Texas Women's Political Caucus to include lesbian and gay issues in its agenda, so that the TWPC lobbyist, Jody Richardson became the first to lobby the state legislature for gay and lesbian rights in 1977.[10] Throughout the 1970s and into the 1980s, lesbians in both gay rights groups and women's groups continued to be frustrated by marginalization and real or perceived discrimination.[11]

In addition to arguments over ideology, tactics, and lesbian rights, race divided feminists. By concentrating on those issues that affected all women, such as equality before the law, the feminists in groups like NOW deemphasized issues that were of even more importance to minority women, whose race often determined their status as much, or more so, than their gender. Even though the rise of feminism in the New Left had originated from within the ranks of those fighting for African American civil rights, most black women distanced themselves from the white feminist movement. They almost uniformly ignored Casey Hayden's plea to end sexism in the movement in her pamphlet, "Sex and Caste." In a state and country where race led to more hardship and discrimination than gender, African American women often believed that fighting for more power and rights for their men would do more to promote their own well-being. Linda Lewis remembered that women "worked behind the scenes so our men could deal with the Establishment. Because of the draft and the [Vietnam] war, we deferred to our brothers as leaders. Their futures were a lot more uncertain than ours, so the argument went."[12] Beyond the war, women identified threats to their families and their communities as more significant than sexism, including widespread poverty in the black community. Velma Roberts, president of the Austin Welfare Rights Organization from 1968 to 1975, saw her organization as one of the first women's groups, but recalls that "we didn't call ourselves a women's group—we understood that our problems had to do with being poor, first."[13] Although, when surveyed, African American women were more likely than any other group of women to support the aims of the feminist movement, they were less interested in actively working for the ERA or abortion rights and more interested in finding solutions to problems such as teen pregnancy, domestic violence, insufficient child care, poor diets, unemployment, and widespread poverty.[14]

Chicanas came to feminism through active participation in the Chicano movement, and in that movement they asserted their rights to equal participation. Evey Chapa, serving on the Raza Unida Party (RUP) platform committee, insured that the 1970 party platform supported equal rights for women, and by 1973 Chicanas had formed Mujeres por la Raza to train and support women for active participation in all aspects of society, especially politics (see chapter 9).[15] Yet Chicanas met resistance to feminism from within the Chicana movement and resistance to Chicana concerns from within the broader (white) feminist movement. Chicanos accused Chicana feminists of trying to assimilate white ideals and betraying the movement. White feminists rejected Chicana activism "because Chicanas seem reluctant to assimilate into the dominant culture." Chicanas did fight for a position in the feminist movement, however. In a report about the National Women's Political Caucus convention in 1973, Chapa described how sixty Chicanas from seven states worked together to propose several resolutions: support of Chicanas striking for better wages, support for concerted efforts to provide Chicanas better educational opportunities, recognition of the Raza Unida

Party, and formation of a Chicana caucus within the NWPC. The last resolution caused the most dissension, with many members of the NWPC taking the "suggestion like a slap in the face. They refused to understand why we felt this move was necessary." However, even the last resolution passed, and the NWPC allowed for local and state caucuses, as well as Chicano caucuses within each state.[16] In Texas, the Chicana caucus successfully recruited members but remained frustrated by the lack of support from white feminists. In 1973 those who belonged to the RUP resigned from the caucus, angry at what they felt was merely half-hearted support for RUP lieutenant governor candidate Alma Canales.[17]

Chicanas had the same experience with other feminist organizations. Prominent Chicana activists such as Martha Cotera openly criticized them, arguing that radical social and political change was needed to ensure equality for women and Chicanos but that members of organizations such as NOW were only interested in "anything that would benefit their careers. Anything that would give them more money and better jobs and access to credit." Chicanas, on the other hand, were focused on racial oppression and economic survival for all in their communities.[18]

Conservative Women

In the late 1960s and early 1970s, the diversity of feminism also included many conservative women. Fiscal conservatives opposed the expanding role of the federal government in the economy, labor legislation, the expanding welfare system, increased social services, and taxes for these and other federal programs. These conservatives, who increasingly found a new home in the Republican Party, also supported many feminist positions, including equal pay for equal work and the ERA. However, during the 1970s, the Republican Party in the United States and Texas shifted toward a socially conservative position that also favored government's protection of moral and religious values, leaving little room for feminist conservatives.[19]

Fiscally conservative women were crucial in building the Republican Party in Texas, a previously one-party state that Democrats had controlled since Reconstruction. The Texas Federation of Republican Women (TFRW), formed in 1955, patterned their involvement on the women's clubs of the late nineteenth and early twentieth centuries, except their focus was on electing Republican candidates. Beginning in urban and suburban areas, they built a grassroots network in the state where women recruited other women to the TFRW and supported particular candidates. These women canvassed neighborhoods identifying potential voters, raised money for advertising, and, most effectively, ran phone banks for hours and days on end. As early as 1952, after Republican women's clubs helped win Texas for Dwight D. Eisenhower, state Republican Party leaders recognized that "the ladies are powerful."[20] When Republican John Tower called upon the TFRW during the special election for the US Senate in 1961—dubbing it the "Women-power for Tower" strategy—he became the first Republican elected to the Senate from the South since Reconstruction. From that point on, Republican candidates recognized and counted on women to conduct the "shoe leather politicking" that was necessary to win races.[21]

The Republican Party in the South as a whole and in Texas, in particular, exploited the national Democrats' new support of African American civil rights legislation to win voters. Some southern Democrats moved toward the more liberal policies of their national brethren, some stayed within the party to try to stop the shift, but many others, seeing a viable Republican Party that opposed civil rights legislation, began defecting to this growing party. Because the TFRW and the Texas Republican Party needed to appeal to Democrats and former Democrats to win elections, the party emphasized inclusion. There were few liberal Republicans but a wide variety of conservative ones.

The 1967 National Federation of Republican Women (NFRW) Convention, however, accentuated an emerging divide. During a very contentious election for president of the national organization, the TFRW delegation was split between supporting the heir-apparent, Janice O'Donnell, who favored "unity" and "inclusion," over longtime social conservative political activist Phyllis Schlafly. The Texas women, along with the national conference, narrowly chose O'Donnell, and later that year the Texas conference also elected a slate of officers who favored inclusion. In 1972, when Congress passed the ERA, the TFRW and NFRW stood firmly in favor of its ratification, and the Republican Party's official platform endorsed it as well as equal pay for equal work. Four years later the party platform reminded voters that "our Party was the first national party to endorse the E.R.A. in 1940. We continue to believe its ratification is essential to insure equal rights for all Americans." In the 1972 election, the work of Republican women produced significant gains for the Republican Party as well as the election of two of their own, the first two Republican women elected to the Texas legislature: Betty Andujar of Fort Worth to the senate and Kay Bailey of Houston to the house.[22]

Phyllis Schlafly was not, however, finished. She would go on to spark the social conservative movement in her own party and the nation and lead a major movement in opposition to feminism. After the 1967 convention of Republican women she formed the Eagle Forum and encouraged Republican women to support it instead of the NFRW. When Congress passed the ERA in 1972, Schlafly articulated not only an opposition to the ERA but also a fundamental justification for opposing the feminist movement: "Of all the classes of people who ever lived, the American woman is the most privileged. We have the most rights and rewards, and the fewest duties. Our unique status is the result of a fortunate combination of circumstances." Far from helping women, she claimed, the ERA would erode respect for the family and women's right to be protected within it, would make women subject to the draft, would abolish a woman's right to child support and alimony, would make it possible for a husband to demand that his wife go to work, and would interfere with mothers' rights to their children. Thus, "the women's libbers are radicals who are waging a total assault on the family, on marriage, and on children."[23]

Schlafly saw the fight against the ERA as an opportunity to recruit new social conservative activists to the party. By charging that the ERA was an assault on the family and a feminist attempt to challenge God's design for men and women, she appealed to a group of conservative Christian women. Later Schlafly and evangelical women would also identify the 1973 Supreme Court ruling upholding a woman's right to abortion as further evidence of feminist success at thwarting Christian principles. These issues would encourage a new cadre of religiously conservative women to become more politically active and support the Republican Party.[24]

STOP ERA (Stop Taking Our Privileges), Schlafly's activist umbrella group, encouraged the formation of secular and religious organizations in all states to block the ratification of the ERA. In Texas, the Committee to Restore Women's Rights and the Happiness of Womanhood organized secular opposition to the amendment. The largest opposition group, however, was Women Who Want to Be Women (WWWW), formed by Lottie Beth Hobbs and Becky Tilotta of Fort Worth. These women were prominent members of the conservative denomination, the Church of Christ, and believed that gender roles were divinely ordained. When Hobbs read about the ERA, she feared it was just one arm of an attack against women and Christian morality: "I knew it was much bigger than just ERA . . . the feminists weren't proud to be women."[25]

In order to recruit women, WWWW produced a flyer that became known as "the pink sheet," attacking the ERA, enumerating the alleged effects of its passage, and calling it the "Loss of Rights Amendment." It alleged that women would no longer have the right to stay at home with their children supported by their husbands: women would be required to support the family financially and men could sue for divorce if women did not. Additionally, women would "be forced to put [their children] in a federal day care center"; divorced women would lose custody, child support, and alimony; and wives and children would "not be required to wear the name of husband and father."[26] The pink sheet was distributed at churches and throughout neighborhoods, printed in local newspapers, and copied throughout Texas and other states.

Because Texas had already ratified the ERA before any opposition to it was organized, the WWWW's tactic was to convince the legislature to rescind its approval (a constitutionally questionable action, even if accomplished). Bowing to pressure from ERA opponents, the Texas legislature held public hearings in 1975 and 1977. ERA and anti-ERA forces descended on the capitol, filling the halls with women. Anti-ERA women wore pink to stress their femininity and delivered homemade bread to legislators to remind them of the importance of preserving women's traditional roles. A study of the "ladies in pink" in 1975 showed that most were white, middle-class women with strong fundamentalist Christian affiliations.[27] Despite these women's best efforts, the Texas legislature chose not to vote on rescinding the state's ratification. As one legislator said at the time, "We've got enough problems without taking this one on."[28]

Galvanized by the ERA fight, groups of conservative women challenged other feminist positions. For instance, countering NOW's attempts to have the State Board of Education adopt textbooks for the public schools that included diverse and less stereotypical depictions of women, conservative women appeared before the board and blocked the adoption of many books they deemed "objectionable." While most of the conservative women involved in this fight had taken part in other political campaigns and belonged to one or more conservative political groups, they identified themselves to the board primarily as concerned wives and mothers. And also as in the ERA fight, most of the women were members of fundamentalist Christian churches.[29]

By the time of the National Women's Conference in 1977 (see chapter 9), Lottie Beth Hobbs's recruitment efforts for WWWW in Texas had built a large group and coalition that she renamed the Pro-Family Forum, and Hobbs also served as a vice president of the Eagle Forum. Conservative women attempted to gain delegates to the National Women's Conference by attending the state preconferences, but they won fewer than 20 percent, far too few to block convention resolutions that they found odious. The Pro-Family Forum instead planned an alternate rally. Hobbs booked the Astroarena, and, using the *Phyllis Schlafly Report*, they recruited thousands of women from all over the country to attend and raised thousands of dollars to defray their expenses. The "Pro-Family Rally" passed resolutions against the ERA, abortion, federal child care, and "the Teaching or glorification of Homosexuality, Lesbianism, or Prostitution." With the twelve-thousand-seat Astroarena overflowing, the Pro-Family Rally demonstrated a significant opposition to feminism and gave the social conservative movement, called the "New Right," a rallying cry of "family values."[30]

As the Republican Party nationally and in the state embraced "family values," the platform no longer supported the ERA and other feminist positions. By 1980 Republican feminist women found themselves marginalized or forced to shift their positions to fit with their political party. In Texas, as elsewhere, conservative women were significantly responsible for the resurgence of a Republican Party focused on gender issues and based upon opposition to social changes, serving as the foundation for the "Reagan Revolution" in 1980. The TFRW contributed to Reagan's win of Texas in many ways, most significantly by working over 650,000 volunteer hours. The extraordinary popularity of the Republican president that appealed to conservative Texas voters accelerated the growth in political power of the Republican Party, and by 1984 even many prominent Democratic officeholders defected, such as Democratic congressman Phil Gramm, who switched parties to win a US Senate seat as a Republican. By 1984 Republican women were well on the way to helping the Republican Party become not just a viable alternative but the dominant party in the state.[31]

Feminism and Its Impact

The 1977 National Women's Conference marked the high point of the feminist movement in Texas and the nation. Afterward, organized opposition to feminism dramatically slowed the advancement of feminist goals, especially the ERA and abortion rights. Although President Jimmy Carter sent recommendations based upon the conference's resolutions to Congress, the rise of the political power of the New Right blocked the passage of such legislation. However, feminists continued to push for and win reforms, and the effects of the movement continued to be felt in society at large for decades to come.[32]

At the National Women's Conference, staff of the six battered women's shelters in Texas decided to form the Texas Council on Family Violence (TCFV) to serve as a network for those working to address the issue, then termed "battered women." Particularly, the organization's founders wanted to work together to get stable funding for new and existing shelters, share information, educate the public, and lobby the legislature for financial support and changes in the laws to combat family violence. By 1979 the legislature was allocating $200,000 annually for domestic violence programs. After a widely viewed *60 Minutes* segment on domestic violence and shelters in Austin gave the movement national attention in 1982, the TCFV gained increased support. Over the next fifteen years the Texas legislature passed laws providing protective orders for abused women and protection from stalkers, allowing police to arrest batterers without a warrant, and requiring family violence training and education for police and judges, as well as increasing the allocation of funds for family violence services to over $9 million annually.[33]

Women also banded together to combat old, dangerous laws and social attitudes toward rape. Activists in communities such as Austin and Houston formed rape crisis centers where women who had been raped could get help and counseling from trained staff and volunteers. Representatives Sarah Weddington and Kay Bailey cosponsored legislation reforming rape statutes to protect the privacy of those who filed charges of rape and to discourage law enforcement personnel and judges from treating rape victims as if they were guilty.[34] In 1982 the Texas Association Against Sexual Assault was formed to provide education, prevention, and advocacy. That association, along with many women's groups, worked toward ending spousal exemption from rape laws—under state law, a husband could not be charged with rape because, it was reasoned, when a woman married, she gave her consent to sex. In the 1980s the legislature allowed a spouse to be prosecuted if bodily injury occurred. In 1993 Texas made rape of a spouse illegal on the same grounds as any other sexual assault, although prosecutions remained difficult.[35]

Increased attention to women's issues, feminist lobbying efforts, and an increasing number of women representatives led to other legislative changes. For instance, as early as 1973, Sarah Weddington, still stinging from having been denied credit while she supported her husband as he attended school, introduced the Equal Credit Act that allowed married women to get credit cards in their own names. Other legislation prevented school districts from firing pregnant teachers and provided for limited alimony for spouses who had not worked outside the home. Feminist groups like NOW and TWPC continued to lobby for laws to help displaced homemakers, to enforce collection of child support, and to provide options for better, more affordable day care.[36]

Feminist efforts also began to change the way that educational materials portrayed women. NOW and other groups pushed the Texas Education Agency to recommend to the State Board of Education textbooks that depicted women in jobs and roles other than homemakers (an effort that met with significant resistance from conservative women, as discussed above). As women began being portrayed in textbooks and children's readers as more active in society, the omission of women in history books at any level became more glaring. When Ann Richards took her children to an exhibit at the Institute of Texan Cultures, her daughter Ellen asked where all the women were. Richards was serving on the Texas Foundation for Women's Resources, which had been founded in 1973 to develop programs and projects to advance and improve the status of women. After the foundation published its first book in 1977, *Texas Women in Politics*, Richards pushed for a statewide effort to research and publicize women's contributions to Texas history. Mary Beth Rogers, a private consultant in Austin, took on the project, raising over $400,000 to pay for research and creating the exhibit. The most difficult task turned out to be finding information about women in the Texas past. As in the rest of the nation, the field of women's history was just beginning to emerge, and sources about women were incredibly difficult to find. The final 500-foot-long, multicultural museum exhibition, *Texas Women: A Celebration of History: 1730–1980*, spent four months at the Institute of Texan Cultures and then toured the state in 1981 and 1982. It included a printed guide, a bibliography of Texas women's history, and a book for young people. The touring exhibit sparked enormous public and academic interest in the subject, and thus Texas surged ahead of most other states in engaging in the study of women in the past.[37] Asserting that women were worthy objects of study, whether in the past or the future, contributed to a related development: the founding of women's studies departments at several universities in the state.

Feminists pushed to ensure that girls and women would have equal opportunities in education, resulting in the passage of national legislation referred to as Title IX. This portion of the Education Amendments of 1972 required that no school, public or private, receiving federal funds discriminate or exclude any person from educational programs or activities on the basis of sex. Its application revolutionized opportunities as public schools made efforts (some successful, many not) to allow and encourage girls to participate in math, science, and vocational classes such as shop and auto mechanics, to expect teachers to give girls equal opportunities to engage in classroom activities, and to otherwise protect girls' access to education. More women subsequently had opportunities to pursue higher education since college admission standards forbid sex discrimination, and by 1998 women earned over half of the bachelor's degrees in the nation (although still highly concentrated in traditionally female fields, such as education).[38]

The most public and controversial effect of Title IX, however, was on athletics. Before its implementation public schools routinely provided sports, such as football and basketball, for boys, while offering girls cheerleading only. When girls were allowed to play sports, the school often required them to buy their own equipment and uniforms and asked the girls' coaches to volunteer their time, while giving coaches of boys' sports extra pay and class release time. In the early 1970s, Waco's school district budgeted $250,000 per year for boys' teams and only $970 for girls. At that time, the lack of money and attention led to only 871 girls playing sports in the entire Dallas school district, while 8,809 boys participated. In order to comply with Title IX, schools throughout Texas began adding girls' sports, such as field and track, volleyball, and basketball. Although studies continue to show that Texas high schools are still far from equity (despite the beliefs of administrators), the results have been staggering. Nationally fewer than three hundred thousand girls made up 7 percent of high school varsity athletes in 1971. By 2001 2.8 million girls comprised 41.5 percent.[39]

Title IX faced the most opposition at the collegiate level. Only 2 percent of overall college athletic budgets went to female athletes in 1971. Texas colleges, such as the University of Texas and Texas A&M, added women's sports so that the number of teams for women equaled the number for men. But with the large rosters of football and basketball teams at most schools, as well as the huge budgets for those sports, the inequity remained glaringly obvious. In 1974 the University of Texas spent $14,911 on coaches' salaries for women's teams and $300,950 on men's; $2,200 for publicity versus $30,000; $16,000 for travel versus $155,000. Ten athletic scholarships were available for women and 216 for men. At Southern Methodist University, the women's tennis team was not allowed to practice on varsity courts reserved for men, and the women's swimming team was allowed to use the pool only when the men's team did not reserve it, allowing them to practice only from 6:00 to 6:45 p.m.[40]

When universities complained about even small concessions for women's sports, Texas US senator John Tower introduced amendments to exempt sports that generated their own revenue from being considered in equity formulations. The Association for Intercollegiate Athletics for Women (AIAW), including Donna Lopiano, the women's athletic director at the University of Texas at Austin, testified against one such amendment before the Senate Subcommittee on Education. Lopiano, despite fear of losing her job, argued that even large men's programs, such as football, were not actually self-sustaining because they were subsidized by publicly funded university budgets, and she asserted that women had a right to that money as well. While she did not go so far as to advocate equal funding, she and the other members of the AIAW insisted that the Senate not only reject the amendment but also that it direct universities to address the disparity in budgets, numbers of athletes, scholarships, and practice facilities and equipment.[41]

Lopiano continued to advance the cause of women's athletics in the nation and went on to turn the University of Texas women's athletic program into a powerhouse that attracted significant talent as well as public support and spectators. The Lady Longhorn basketball team, under the direction of coach Jody Conradt, abandoned half-court basketball, becoming one of the premier teams in the nation, raising revenue and ticket sales to cover their expenses. Other Texas university women's basketball teams followed, nurturing incredible talent such as Cheryl Swopes, sometimes called "the female Michael Jordan," who played for Texas Tech and led her Lady Raiders team to defeat the powerhouse Lady Longhorns. Reluctance, recalcitrance, and outright resistance to implementing Title IX continued, however, with many male athletes and fans believing that women's achievements came at the expense of men's sports. Others clung to the belief that sports were too masculine for real women—with the implication that women who played sports were lesbians. Sometimes this assertion became overt rather than implied: in 1993 the *Austin American-Statesman* published an article claiming that the Lady Longhorns were known as being "a bunch of dykes up there." Afterward, copies of the article were sent anonymously to every player that Conradt tried to recruit, leading many to believe that male boosters were trying to sabotage women's sports. Continued challenges to Title IX and lack of enforcement of its provisions have prevented it from fully being effective in Texas, but the increase in the number of women athletes at all levels of competition has been dramatic.[42]

After the 1970s, women's roles and position in Texas would never be the same. Feminists and antifeminist women organized, petitioned, publicized, and fought for myriad issues affecting women, families, and gender in society. The feminist movement's greatest long-term effects in the state were undoubtedly on work and politics.

Work

The subject of "women's work" was intertwined with nearly every aspect of the women's movement in the late twentieth century. The number of women employed outside the home increased markedly every decade after World War II for many reasons, including increased urbanization, technological advancements, rising numbers of women supporting themselves or their families, and women's search for economic and career fulfillment. Between 1950 and 1980, the percentage of Texas women employed nearly doubled, and in absolute numbers more than tripled.[43] Social conservatives worried that women's working outside the home would erode their elevated and "sacred place" as wives and mothers. Feminists generally applauded the trend and advocated opening more careers for women, equal pay for equal work, affordable child care, and protecting women's rights in the workplace.

Working Texas women took advantage of a national development that was never really meant to help women. Title VII of the Civil Rights Act of 1964 prohibited both public and private employers from discriminating against employees because of "race, color, religion, sex, or national origin." Drafted primarily to end discrimination on the basis of race, opponents of the act added the category of "sex" not to help even the playing field for women but instead hoping that adding gender would make the bill so outrageous that Congress would vote against it. The bill passed, and the Equal Employment Opportunity Commission (EEOC) was established and prepared to investigate claims of employment discrimination against African Americans. The commission was surprised to be inundated with grievances filed by women, but the EEOC's directors and employees continued to think of them and the provision regarding sex discrimination as a joke. NOW, however, forced the EEOC to begin taking the issue seriously. NOW organized women to picket local EEOC offices in protest of sex-segregated job advertisements in newspapers, a practice the EEOC had previously reviewed and approved. Bowing to the pressure, in 1968 the EEOC banned the "Help Wanted-Male" and "Help Wanted-Female" categories from advertising.[44]

A reluctant EEOC, growing acceptance of women choosing careers due to changing cultural and social ideals, and an increase in the number of women getting a higher education led to significant gains for women in their professions. The percentage of lawyers who were women jumped from 3 percent in 1950 to 12 percent in 1980; physicians from 5 percent to 10 percent; college professors from 26 percent to 34 percent; accountants from 15 percent to 41 percent. Women even broke into the elite corps at NASA. In 1978 Sally Ride became the first woman astronaut to go to space, followed by sixty other women, including Mae Jemison, who became the first African American woman to travel to space in 1992. Aside from astronauts, women took other professional positions at the agency; in 1984, 13 percent of the women employed there were professionals. Despite the gains, there were still many professions in which women made little progress. In 1980 women still made up only 4 percent of the engineers in Texas, 4 percent of the veterinarians, and 4 percent of the clergy. In most professions, women were far from making equal progress with men, and professional women still found themselves segregated into the lowest paid professions long associated with women's roles as mothers. In 1980 women made up 83 percent of elementary and 61 percent of secondary teachers, 94 percent of nurses, 94 percent of dieticians, 85 percent of librarians, and 63 percent of social workers.[45]

Throughout the rest of the century, these trends continued: women made gains in many professions while also making up the vast majority of those who took the lowest-paid professional positions. By 2000 nearly 40 percent of the graduates from dental and medical schools were women, and by 2013 35 percent of the physicians in Texas were women. But even within the gains in the medical profession, women still congregated in primary care, obstetrics, and pediatrics, the lesser-paid positions within the field. Nonetheless, women were taking leadership roles in the medical and other professional fields. In 1997 Texan Nancy Dickey became the first woman president of the American Medical Association.[46]

One of the most significant changes in the workforce was the growth in the number of "pink collar" jobs—jobs that did not require higher education or manual labor and were held predominately by women. Over half a million more women were employed as bookkeepers or cashiers, secretaries or typists, or in retail sales in 1980 than had been in 1950. Women comprised 90 percent, 99 percent, and 67 percent of these positions respectively. Women also made up 90 percent of bank tellers, 91 percent of telephone operators, 93 percent of teacher aides, and 87 percent of file clerks. Tejanas and African American women did not benefit from the gains in professional jobs nearly as much as white women, but the pink-collar positions did create more opportunities. Twenty-six percent of working Hispanic women held clerical positions, as did 22 percent of African American women and 35 percent of white women. [47]

The majority of women who worked, however, still had limited education and took unskilled and low-paying manual labor jobs in service occupations or manufacturing. Service occupations remained overwhelmingly female, with women making up 96 percent of household servants, 84 percent of housekeepers and waitresses, and 68 percent of launderers in 1980. In manufacturing, women made gains in a few areas between 1950 and 1980, rising from 15 percent of bakers to 52 percent and from 4 percent to 24 percent of workers in the food industry, as well as dominating the new field of electronic equipment assemblers, making up 80 percent of that workforce in 1980. However, even in manufacturing, women were congregated in the lowest-paid segments, making up 95 percent of textile manufacturing, for example.[48]

Throughout the workforce, women earned significantly less than men. In 1980 the median women's earnings were 59 percent of that of men; by 1999 that discrepancy still remained significant but had improved to 75 percent. The low rate of unionization made it difficult for women to organize for better wages, even—or especially—in industries where most women were concentrated. In 1972 the predominately female and predominately Chicano workforce at Farah Manufacturing Company in El Paso went on strike for two years, demanding the right to a union, higher wages, better working conditions, and the elimination of sexist policies and practices. The nearly four thousand women strikers endured not only financial disaster while not working but also harassment from the community and violence on the picket lines, as un-muzzled police dogs threatened them, Farah trucks hit them, and police arrested them, requiring them to post bail eight times higher than usual. The strike led to a nationwide boycott that decreased sales and to the National Labor Board ordering Farah to allow unionization and to reinstate the workers. The months of striking emboldened many women and instilled newfound confidence. One woman remembered reevaluating her life and passing new ideas on to her children: "I want my daughter to be able to do what she's gotta do . . . and not always comply to whatever her boyfriend or her husband [wants] . . . [S]he should be the person that she is." The same woman also decided that her sons should learn how to wash dishes.[49] Within a few months of the workers' return, however, Farah fired many of the strikers in violation of the National Labor Board order, and the male union representatives did not contest the pretexts given for the dismissals. Conditions in textile manufacturing actually worsened, as larger manufacturers transferred operations overseas, leaving textile workers in smaller, less-regulated sweatshops.[50]

Another new development at the end of the century was the increase of Asian women in the workforce. After World War II, the number of Asians in Texas increased to a record 21,000 in 1970. After 1970 the number rose even more dramatically. In the 2000 census, over 640,000 people, 3.1 percent of state's population, identified as Asian or mixed-race including Asian. Several factors played a role in this new surge: a national exchange program began to fill the need for certain professionals; immigration laws no longer discriminated against Asian entry into the country; and wars in Asian countries led to geographic dislocation and economic calamities.[51] In this period, the state's greatest demand was for engineers, computing professionals, and health-care professionals, which attracted mostly men from the Philippines, Korea, Vietnam, India, Pakistan, and Bangladesh. These men brought their

Figure 10.1. Farah strikers and supporters, El Paso, Texas, 1972. Photographer unknown. Courtesy of Kheel Center, Cornell University.

wives and families with them. Large numbers of Filipino and Korean professional women also immigrated, the largest group being nurses, and they settled in the Houston and Galveston area, where they filled a critical shortage
in one of the largest medical centers in the country. The wives of professional
men often also had college degrees and took a variety of jobs in their new
cities, such as teaching. Professional Asian women, despite holding full-time
jobs, struggled with the expectations that they also continue to satisfy their
culture's traditional roles of women at home. The strains of these roles hit the
Filipino community particularly hard during the oil bust of the 1980s when
many professional men in Houston lost their jobs. As men stayed home to
take care of the children, the role reversal strained marriages, leading some to
seek divorces.[52]

Most of new Asian immigrants settled in Houston and Dallas, outstrip-
ping the growth of older communities in El Paso, Killeen, Laredo, and San
Antonio, although the Asian population continued to grow in those cities
too. With the growth of these communities, many women worked in family-
owned businesses, such as groceries and restaurants, catering to their specific communities, the concentration of which led to a portion of Southwest
Houston being called Chinatown (despite a large population of non-Chinese
Asians residing there as well).[53]

One of the largest waves of immigration came between 1978 and 1980,
when over a million refugees left Vietnam to escape brutal government policies. Over thirty thousand of these "boat people" eventually made it to Texas,
where many settled along the coast and engaged in shrimping. It is unclear
what work women in Vietnamese shrimping families performed; they most
likely did not journey on the boats, but they probably helped clean, sort,
and prepare the catch. Part of a woman's role in Vietnamese culture was gardening, which they continued in Texas, selling at least some of their excess
produce to local grocers. Vietnamese women who moved to towns and cities
looked for work and found it as custodians, cashiers, and other unskilled
labor. However, word spread among the community that a cosmetology
course and license as a nail technician were relatively easy to acquire, and
with the introduction of the acrylic nail, Vietnamese women kick-started
the discount nail salon industry. Tens of thousands of Vietnamese women
so dominated the field that activist Nguyen Cao My convinced the Texas
Cosmetology Commission to offer manicurist exams in Vietnamese.[54]

Overall, during the 1970s and 1980s the number of women of all ethnicities in the workforce at all levels increased. In 1970 41 percent of women

held paid employment, but by the end of the century 60 percent did so. With over half of mothers entering the workforce, the press began covering the so-called "mommy wars" in the 1980s as mothers who stayed home accused mothers who worked of neglecting the needs of their children. Newspapers and magazines covered the increasing number of mothers who needed places for their children while they worked full-time or part-time jobs. Feminist organizations such as NOW and TWPC lobbied the state legislature to take measures to assist in assuring safe, affordable day-care options, but this was to little avail. But despite the mommy wars, the oft-voiced conservative position that women should stay home with their children, the discrepancy in pay between men and women, and continuing overt and subtle discrimination, it has become the accepted norm in Texas and the nation for women to pursue careers and work outside the home.[55]

Politics

When Texas women demanded and won suffrage in the early twentieth century, they expected to use the vote to transform Texas politics and reform the state. Winning the vote, however, did not lead to the political power that they hoped, because they remained underrepresented in the elected offices where decisions were made. Between 1919 and 1973, women did not get elected to office in numbers sufficient to make serious changes in laws or attitudes. Of the 181 members who served in the Texas legislature in each of those fifty-four years, the most women who served in any legislative session was five, and the average number of women per session was 2.6. A grand total of twenty-two women had ever served in the legislature before 1973, and only two women had been elected to any statewide office (Miriam Ferguson and Annie Webb Blanton).[56]

Barbara Jordan won a historic race in 1966 to become the first African American elected to the Texas senate since Reconstruction and the first African American woman elected to the state legislature. As the sole woman and the sole African American member during her first term, Jordan refused to allow the other legislators to define her by race or gender, recognizing that "to be effective I had to get inside the Club and not just inside the chamber." Her ability to charm and work with other senators did indeed make her effective in her two terms as state senator. Jordan went on to run for and win a seat in the US Congress, becoming the first African American woman elected from the South. There she became nationally recognized with an im-

Figure 10.2. US Representative Barbara Jordan was the first African American woman from the South elected to Congress.

passioned speech about the Constitution during the congressional hearings on the Watergate scandal that ended Richard M. Nixon's presidency.[57]

Frances "Sissy" Farenthold joined Jordan in the state legislature in 1969 after she was elected the sole female member of the Texas house of representatives. Farenthold, however, rejecting the sexism she experienced there, refused to try to enter the legislature's male "club." She suffered the fate of many women in the capitol as male members treated her as an anomaly rather than a representative. She later remembered, "I was not a token, I was a joke. There was a sort of pethood ordained for you if you accepted it." After the state's Sharpstown stock fraud scandal in 1971–72 (two dozen elected officials were indicted and many others implicated in fraud and bribery), she led a group of like-minded house members to attempt political reform. Ultimately convinced, however, that the only way to get male politicians to respect their female counterparts was to get more women elected, she helped found the National Women's Political Caucus and became its first chair.[58]

Despite these two notable women, Texas politics had long been ruled by the "good ol' boy" system, in which those in political power were only likely to share their power with friends and people like themselves—certainly not with women or minorities. Not only were women mostly excluded from this system, it was difficult for any newcomers to break through because incumbents won reelection term after term. After the Sharpstown scandal created a desire among voters to clean up politics by removing those implicated, the Texas Women's Political Caucus encouraged, endorsed, and cheered to victory many women candidates in 1972. Farenthold lost in the primary race for governor, although she came in second in a crowded field and forced a runoff. The Raza Unida Party's first statewide ticket included Alma Canales for lieutenant governor, but she also lost. In the legislature, however, women made significant progress, tripling the number of women state legislators to six, the most ever to serve at one time. Republicans Betty Andujar and Kay Bailey were elected to the senate and the house respectively. Democrats and TWPC founders Chris Miller and Sarah Weddington were elected to the house, as were Eddie Bernice Johnson and Senfronia Thompson, the first African American women to serve in that body.[59]

The number of women in the Texas legislature rose the next session to nine and to fourteen by 1977. Although it dipped back to twelve for two sessions after that, in 1982 fourteen women were elected, and Ann Richards, the first woman elected to statewide office since Miriam Ferguson, won the state treasurer's position. The year before, the first woman, Kathy Whitmire, was elected mayor of Houston, the largest city in the state and the fifth-largest in the nation, Janice Coggeshall served as mayor of Galveston, and Lila Cockrell had just stepped down after three terms as mayor of San Antonio.[60] The sudden upsurge of women in politics in what was thought to be a "macho," conservative southern state garnered national publicity as a groundbreaking and fascinating phenomenon. As early as 1977, the authors of *Texas Women in Politics* had indeed argued that "the Texas Women's Political Caucus . . . seemed more vibrant, more enthusiastic than other groups, more creative in its political involvement and more effective in reaching its goals" than other caucuses. Women activists in Texas did attract more national attention than many other states, especially southern states.[61]

Between 1975 and 1991, most of the largest cities in Texas had elected women mayors at some point: Austin, Dallas, Houston, San Antonio, Galveston, Corpus Christi, El Paso, Fort Worth, and Garland. Dallas mayor Annette Strauss jokingly welcomed so many people to "Texas: A state where the men are men and the women are mayors," that it became a popular bumper sticker. Texas had significant bragging rights when it came to mayors, electing women to mayoral offices at a higher rate than the rest of the country: thirteen of the twenty largest cities in the United States have elected a female mayor at some point, and six of those thirteen are in Texas. Some of those cities have also elected more than one female mayor; Houston is the largest city in the nation to have elected two women mayors. Laredo elected the first Latina mayor and Houston elected the first openly lesbian mayor. In addition to the large cities, women have also been successful at winning election in small cities and towns, serving as mayor in half of the state's municipalities.[62]

Minority women also made gains at all political levels. Latinas particularly made an impact at the local level. In 1991, 361 Latinas held elected office in Texas, the most of any state in the country. Mujeres por la Raza and other Latino organizations encouraged women to take leadership roles. Latinas also took active roles in the Texas Women's Political Caucus, demanded and ran their own caucus, and worked within the caucus to reach out to and train Latinas. Above all, however, most Latinas began their public service at the local level out of a desire to assist their communities. For example, María Cárdenas joined neighborhood associations in San Angelo made up of people who were trying to find solutions to the problems in their barrios. Her skills in these organizations led her to chair a state advisory board to assist other groups as they dealt with local governments and businesses. Cárdenas went on to win a seat on the city commission of San Angelo, one of the first women and the only Mexican American woman on that body.[63]

Although most successful at the local level, Latinas did have some limited success in the Texas legislature. Irma Rangel became the first Mexican American woman elected to the legislature in 1976, and she felt the pressure of her novelty: "I didn't know I was going to be the first one. I felt like I was really going to have to deliver. If I didn't succeed, they were going to say, 'All Mexican American women are failures.'"[64] Rangel did succeed and served for twenty-six years, introducing legislation from her very first session to assist her communities and guarantee equal rights for minorities, especially in education. She was the only Latina in the legislature for a decade before Lena Guerrero joined her in the house in 1985, and Judith Zaffirini from Laredo became the first Latina elected to the senate in 1987. Only one other Latina, Leticia van de Putte, has ever served in the senate, but twelve other Latinas have served in the house.[65]

The first African American women elected to the Texas house, Senfronia Thompson and Eddie Bernice Johnson became stalwarts of the state legislature. Johnson became the only African American woman other than Barbara Jordan to serve in the Texas senate. Thompson has served forty-five years in the house—longer than any other African American and long enough to be named Dean of the House in 2013. She has earned the respect of her fellow politicians, earning many nicknames but calling herself the "House Lion": "I prowl around to make sure people keep working for good." These two were joined or followed by only eight other African American women before the end of the century, and none served otherwise in statewide office in the twentieth century, although they were very successful in local elections.[66]

All women, not just minority women, struggled with winning state legislative races, but women continued a slow ascent in the legislature, with the number gradually rising each election from 12 in 1982 to 33 in 1999. However, Texas women fell behind the national trend. By 1999, women comprised 22.3 percent of state legislators nationwide, while women made up 18.2 percent of the Texas legislature. Small though their numbers may be, women have made a difference in that body. In her study of the women of the Texas legislature, Terry Gilmour found that "women both sponsored more bills and helped to enact more legislation that would promote the status of children, families and women." Additionally, the presence of more women created an atmosphere where "women's issues" came to be regarded as "people's issues," and more men wanted to introduce and enact legislation traditionally seen as being of interest to women.[67]

At all levels women faced difficulties raising funds for campaigns because of the assumption that men were more likely to win primary races. Women were less likely to be encouraged and nurtured by the "good ol' boy" system and much less likely than men to just be asked to run. And women faced more difficulties blending family obligations with politics. Voters worried that women with children would not be good legislators because they would not devote enough time to their work, while at the same time women who devoted enough time to lawmaking were deemed poor mothers. Men did not face similar criticism. In addition to the effect in the polls and elections, women elected officials faced difficult personal decisions. State Representative Libby Linebarger, elected in 1988, earned a bipartisan reputation as a hardworking, intelligent, and fair legislator with the "potential to become the first female speaker of the House." Yet, after three terms in which she was highly successful at advancing her legislative agenda and solving some of the state's stickiest issues, such as school finance reform, Linebarger chose not to run for office again after missing her daughter's tenth birthday because of her work at the capitol: "When you miss significant events in your children's lives that you can never relive, maybe it's time to rethink your priorities."[68]

Of course, the greatest symbol of women's political empowerment in Texas in the twentieth century was the election of Ann Richards as governor. Richards and her husband had entered the political scene in Austin, supporting and encouraging many candidates to run for office. Richards ran the successful legislative campaigns of Sarah Weddington and Wilhelmina Delco before running for county commissioner and winning the very male-dominated position in 1976. Richards was not only good at campaigning, she was good at governing, and so in 1982 she ran for state treasurer and became the first woman elected to statewide office since Miriam "Ma" Ferguson. After two terms of office, she embarked upon the very unlikely run for governor of Texas in 1990.

That 1990 election epitomized the struggle between old Texas "frontiersman" machismo and the new Texas modernization and urbanization, in which women also exercised power. The Republican nominee, Clayton Williams, unapologetically made sexist remarks to reporters, including jokingly equating the weather with rape, bragging about "being serviced" by prostitutes while he was in college, and, regarding Richards, promising to "head her and hoof her and drag her through the dirt." While Williams painted himself as a manly Texas cowboy, as a woman candidate Richards had to walk a fine line between projecting herself as tough enough to run the state yet still compassionate and able to fulfill social expectations of her gender. Thus, she went duck hunting and posed atop a Harley motorcycle but also promoted photos of herself at family gatherings and featured her family in campaign ads.[69]

Richards, like most women running for office, had tremendous difficulty raising money. Most traditional male donors had a difficult time believing she could win the office, and women had not yet developed the habit of financially supporting candidates. Instead of raking in large donations, her campaign prided itself on receiving thousands of small contributions, many of them from women donating to a candidate for the first time. Women also played significant roles in running her campaign; Mary Beth Rogers was her campaign manager.[70]

Although the state had moved significantly to the right, and victory by a progressive Democrat was unlikely, Richards capitalized on the celebrity that her keynote speech at the Democratic National Convention in 1988 had brought her and appealed to voters by playing the part of a tough grandmother. It was finally Williams's refusal to shake Richards's hand after a joint appearance that swung public opinion in the race. Republican women especially made a difference. While many of them embraced traditional roles for women and saw Richards as antithetical to that position, Williams could not claim to uphold traditional civility. After Williams refused to shake Richards's hand, his credibility as a gentleman was gone. Republican women did not engage as vigorously in their famous grassroots efforts to get out the vote for their party's candidate, and many Republican women voted for Richards.[71]

On election day, Richards exultantly held up a T-shirt stating "A Woman's Place is in the Dome," and on inauguration day she led a parade of thirty thousand across Austin's Congress Avenue bridge to the capitol, promising to "Let the People In."[72] As governor Richards kept her promise, appointing more women and minorities to positions in state government than any other previous governor: 48 percent of her first 650 appointments were women, 25 percent were Hispanic, and 12 percent were African American.[73] One of her most prominent appointees was that of Lena Guerrero to a vacant position on the state Railroad Commission, making Guerrero the only Latina to serve in state-wide office. Guerrero later resigned and lost her attempt to be reelected to the position after admitting that she had lied about graduating from the University of Texas at Austin.[74]

Figure 10.3. Governor Ann Richards, 1992.

Richards had significant accomplishments and setbacks as governor, but political analysts writing in 1993 predicted she would win reelection. George W. Bush, her well-funded Republican opponent in 1994, however, was the son of a president. Bush was able to avoid angering Republican women in the 1994 campaign, and the traditionally conservative state rejected the liberal Democrat Richards, choosing the conservative Republican candidate in that race as it would the governor's races for the next twenty years.[75] The women and minorities appointed by Richards, however, proved to be one of her greatest legacies, as new people with new perspectives and ideas entered Texas politics, continuing to fight for change and inclusion in her vision of a "new Texas." Additionally, Richards's nationally visible election and her fund-raising strategies proved to be significant role models for women throughout the country, paving the way for the "Year of the Woman" in 1992, when the number of women elected to public office throughout the country and to the US Congress skyrocketed.[76]

Conclusion

The last three decades of the twentieth century produced a dizzying level of change for women in Texas. Not only did Texas women change ideas about gender and women's role within the state, they were prominent leaders nationally. While the cause of this change is generally referred to as the "feminist movement," no state better than Texas demonstrates that it was actually multiple feminist movements, bred from many different concerns yet each identifying women's empowerment as critical. These movements generated significant opposition, and in many arenas, such as politics and high-paying professions, women made only small gains. However, at the end of the century, Texas women had more options than before, were more politically engaged than at any time in history, and were members of a national discussion about women's rights, roles, and responsibilities.

Conclusion

On June 25, 2013, Senator Wendy Davis from Fort Worth stood for over eleven hours on the floor of the Texas senate in pink sneakers purchased for the occasion. She was filibustering to prevent the passage of SB5, a bill that would significantly restrict women's access to abortion in the state. By the time that the filibuster was technically ended (by Texas senate rules, three points of order sustained by the lieutenant governor end a filibuster), the women of Texas had caught the attention of the nation and world once again. Even President Barack Obama had declared through social media, "Something special is happening in Austin tonight . . . #StandWithWendy."[1]

Although the filibuster was ruled finished before the mandatory midnight adjournment, other senators took up the effort to block the bill by challenging parliamentary procedure. Both male and female senators asked questions and made motions to delay the vote on the bill in an increasingly chaotic environment as the clock ticked down to midnight and the end of the session. Two more of the record-breaking eight women serving in the senate highlighted gender issues so apparent in the debate and in this historically male-dominated political institution. Senator Judith Zaffirini argued with the lieutenant governor that one point of order against Davis should be dismissed because the senate rules regarding filibusters stated that a senator "may not lean on *his* desk, *his* chair" and therefore this should not apply to *her*, Davis, who had been so accused. At 10:00 p.m. Senator Leticia van de Putte, having just rushed back to the chamber, asked for an explanation of each of the three points of order that ended the filibuster: "Since I was at my father's funeral, I ask that you please let me know, what were the three motions or the three points of order so that I may understand?" At 11:45

p.m. when all parliamentary procedures seemed to have run out, van de Putte made a motion to adjourn but was ignored, and a vote on the bill was called. Out of frustration, van de Putte asked, "At what point must a female senator raise her hand or her voice to be recognized over the male colleagues in the room?"[2]

Van de Putte's question ignited a firestorm—not among the senators, 75 percent of whom were male—but among the majority-female crowd that had been streaming into the senate gallery, the balconies, and the rotunda of the state capitol all day long as word of the filibuster spread. Shouting and applause drowned out efforts to conduct business until well after midnight, and, despite attempts to claim that the vote was taken before adjournment, the bill was declared dead that session.[3]

The filibuster and parliamentary moves prevented SB5 from becoming law on that night in June 2013, but Texas governor Rick Perry immediately called a new special session, during which thousands of women both for and against the bill rallied, protested, and testified before committees. Although the protesters outnumbered those in support, the bill passed, and two of its provisions—requiring abortion clinics to meet the same standards as hospital-style surgical centers and that doctors who perform abortions have admitting privileges at local hospitals—would have forced the closure of all but five of the forty abortion clinics in the state.[4] Legal challenges to the bill delayed the enactment of some of the provisions, but one year later the number of clinics in the state had been reduced by over half, resulting in "significant burdens for women able to obtain care." Women, especially poor women, did not have the funds or the time to travel across such a large state to one of the few providers. According to a study by the Texas Policy Evaluation Project, in the next two years over 100,000 women attempted abortions at home without medical assistance, reminiscent of the 1960s before abortion became legal.[5] Thus the state whose women had won the right to legal abortion for the whole nation struck one of the most serious blows to that right. Agreeing with opponents that the bill's intent was to limit access to abortion and not to protect women's health, in 2016 the US Supreme Court overturned two key provisions, allowing nineteen remaining clinics to continue operating.[6]

The twenty-first-century debate over abortion is a stark reminder that the history of women has not developed in a single straight line and that there is no consensus, even among women, about what constitutes progress. From the beginning, Texas's size, location, and historical development have contributed to a great diversity of people. Women's experiences, daily lives, values, and gender roles have been shaped by many factors, including race and ethnicity, class, religion, geographical location, surrounding culture, and their own individual abilities and fortitude. As a result it has been difficult to write one history of Texas women because there have been so many histories of Texas women to be told.

Even the first women in the area had vastly different experiences and gender roles depending upon whether they lived in agricultural or hunting societies, shaped primarily by the geographical location and terrain and whether they lived in matrilocal or patrilocal societies. The Spanish arrived in the Americas with very different ideas from the women who lived there. They attempted to force their ideas about women's roles into new physical environments as well as onto people of differing cultures and ideologies, with varying degrees of success, eventually developing in Texas a mixed culture. When Anglo-Americans arrived in Texas, they carried with them yet another set of gender roles and expectations that conflicted with Native Americans, Spanish, and the mixed culture that had developed. A few African Americans had arrived with the Spanish, but they were brought in larger numbers by the Anglo-Americans. As enslaved persons, their gender roles were shaped not only by their own ideology and culture and by the environment in which they lived, but also by the Anglo-Americans who were able to dictate what African American women did and when they did it. Germans arrived in large numbers a bit later, with yet another slightly different ideology of gender that they adapted to the environment and Anglo-American legal structure of the state. The confluence of these diverse cultures within the geographic boundaries of what would become the state of Texas shows how gender roles did not naturally develop but were socially constructed by ideas about nature, religion, and race. Ethnicity and the cultures and ideals that evolved in these ethnic groups continued to contribute to differences among women throughout the nineteenth and twentieth centuries, and they continue to do so today.

Geographical location has shaped the daily lives of women, and Texas has vast differences in landscape and temperature. Whether in cattle-raising West Texas or cotton-raising East Texas, the first large in-migrations of Mexican, German, Anglo-American, and African American women to the state faced a "frontier" in which an unfamiliar nature and people dominated their daily lives. Often isolated from other women and helping to establish homesteads for their families or masters, they stretched their traditional ideology of gender roles to take on work necessary for survival and success. As more migrants settled, making the establishment of communities possible, families were able to follow more traditional ideals of gender roles, and women settled into more familiar daily routines. However, the social restrictions on women and their work differed according to location. In East Texas, where raising cotton could be profitable, southern ideals took hold, including expectations that white women should be employed primarily in the home and enslaved black women employed anywhere, including in the field. In South Texas and West Texas, both Anglo and Mexican American women incorporated traditionally unacceptable activities into their ranching and farming lives, such as outdoor work, riding, marksmanship, and even riding the trails.

Into the late nineteenth and twentieth centuries, geographical location shaped women's activism and abilities. Declining farm profitability and the oppressiveness of sharecropping led to rural women's activism in the Populist movement. These women who participated in political activity with the goal of making their own and their families' lives better almost always joined the fray along with their husbands and other family members. In approximately the same period, another kind of women's activism arose in urban areas. In towns and cities, women's work differed greatly from that of women in rural areas, and, due to proximity, women could more easily congregate and work together. Urban women began forming clubs, both for personal edification and for improving their lives and those of their families. Support for woman suffrage organizations and for progressive reforms, ranging from safe milk to public libraries, came primarily from women living in towns and cities. By 1950 more Texas women lived in urban areas than in rural areas, and by the end of the century urban women were more likely to accept and even agitate for change and increased rights, while rural women were more likely to accept and adhere to traditional ideas about gendered roles.

Class or economic status has also shaped Texas women's experiences and contributed to differing values. The work of white women whose families held slaves in antebellum Texas was far less strenuous and provided more leisure time than for those in families that relied exclusively on family labor. In the mid-twentieth century, those women in wealthy or middle-class urban families were not expected to work outside the home and had less difficult work to do in the home, while thousands of other women had to find outside employment (often in the homes of the wealthy) as well as labor at home for their families. Religion has also divided and affected women's actions and ideals. Catholic women found fewer avenues for formal power within the church but perhaps wielded more informal power in shaping religion in their homes. Evangelical Protestant women favored a more restrictive interpretation of gender roles and family structure while also spending much of their energy in supporting their churches and religion. Other Protestant women, especially upper-class and upper-middle-class women, supported their churches as well, but they also used their church affiliations and organizations to work together for changes in society. They were the women most likely to join Progressive Era clubs that worked toward a myriad of improvements.

Despite the factors that divided women and shaped their lives differently, a common experience over the centuries of Texas history has been significant change in gender roles and legal rights. Spanish law influenced early Texas legislation regarding women, especially women's property, but English common law remained the predominant model under the Republic of Texas and State of Texas constitutions and legislation. As a result, Texas adopted community property law and provided for the right of married women to own property separately. These rights gave women significantly more rights to property than women in most southern states. However, women's right to control their property and thus exert any independence was minimal and increasingly curtailed as the state became more settled. Divorce was rare but available through local district courts on the grounds of abandonment, adultery, and cruelty, allowing women (and men) in the most unfortunate situations to end their marriages and be able to marry again.

Texas women, therefore, might have greater access to property and divorce than women in most southern states, but as in the rest of the nation women could not vote, serve on juries, or hold public office throughout the nineteenth century. Married women could not sue, be sued, or control or sell their own property without the permission of their husbands. The ideal of the patriarchal family, headed by a man who directed the work and commanded the obedience of his wife, children, and any servants on land he owned, guided the understanding of women's rights in law. But after the American Civil War disrupted Texas women's lives and gender ideals, women increasingly took on new roles: many earned higher levels of education, some took employment outside the household as teachers and nurses, and many others became activists, working as volunteers to improve their communities and the status of women and children. These women pushed against patriarchal ideals, claiming public roles for women, and thus changing gender ideals. Changes in women's public activism contributed to the agitation for woman suffrage. The national suffrage movement had begun in 1848 but did not draw support in Texas until the end of the century. Not until the early twentieth century did a major suffrage movement begin in the state, but then Texas was unusual among southern states, both for the amount of support for suffrage and the effectiveness at winning the vote, becoming the first southern state to do so.

Even after winning the right to participate equally in electing leaders for the state, a whole body of legislation continued to deny women equal rights. In the first half of the twentieth century, women worked diligently, if slowly, to chip away at the laws that placed obstacles to equality as well as to enact legislation to assist women, such as expanding married women's rights to control separate property, funding prenatal and infant care, and establishing women's right to serve on juries. A major push in the 1960s led to the passage of a married women's property act that allowed wives to operate almost equally to husbands in regard to their property. In 1972, Texans approved an equal legal rights amendment to the state constitution, indicating, at least in theory, that women of the state were legally equal to men in the state.

Theory was a long way from reality, however, and powerful feminist movements within the state in the 1970s agitated for more changes in law and society to allow women to achieve equality with men. They fought to end family violence and rape, to eradicate sexist language in textbooks, to assist displaced homemakers, to lobby for legislation increasing child support enforcement and day-care options, to support lesbian civil rights, and to uphold reproductive freedom, including abortion. Laws against discrimination in employment and education, including school sports, were passed and over the years expanded in scope. By the end of the twentieth century, women had gained the right to vote, hold office, and the right to employment without discrimination by gender.

Although a century seems a long time for these rights to evolve, the pace was much too rapid for some, and a backlash in the late twentieth century put a brake on what had already been slow movement toward equality. By the twenty-first century, divisions between men and women as well as among women brought the legal and social changes regarding women into statewide dispute. Some fought these changes as assaults on traditional ideas about society and women's place within it, preferring ideals in which a woman remained dependent on, if not submissive to, her husband, and in which women found their highest calling and true fulfillment in motherhood.

Thus, the bill targeting clinics that performed abortions came in the midst of what many national journalists called a "war on women." Even before

Wendy Davis's filibuster and the debate over SB5, in order to avoid funding Planned Parenthood the 2011 legislature cut family-planning funding from $111.5 million to $37.9 million, decreasing or eliminating services to low-income women. This occurred while the state's maternal mortality rate doubled between 2010 and 2012, highlighting the need for more assistance to mothers before, during, and after pregnancy. The legislature instituted an alternative women's health program (which excluded Planned Parenthood), but the new program was not as successful. According to a study, the number of women receiving regular, effective birth control decreased, and the rate of childbirth for low-income women receiving Medicaid increased. In 2016 the legislature approved another new model for funding women's health services and allocated a record $260 million to the Healthy Texas Women project and family planning (with the stipulation that no agency or health care provider receiving this money perform abortions).[7]

Women in the twenty-first century, therefore, remain divided over whether to embrace or reject the changes in women's status, but change has come. In addition to the unpaid labor performed in the home, more women than ever are employed full-time, earning wages outside the home. In 2015 women aged sixteen and over made up 45.5 percent of the workforce in the state. The number of women employed has nearly doubled since 1980, and the percentage of women who are employed has increased from 50 percent to 58 percent. As in the twentieth century, women still predominate in positions in education, nursing, and clerical work. Women comprise 80 percent of primary and secondary school teachers, 94 percent of child-care workers, 86 percent of nurses, 79 percent of librarians, and 78 percent of social workers. Clerical work is still the most sex-segregated: 95 percent of secretaries and administrative assistants are women. These and closely related occupations account for almost half of employed women in Texas (48.8 percent). Another 28 percent of women work in retail sales, food service, or custodial positions.[8]

Women have gained some ground in several professional occupations. Compared to 1980, in 2015 women comprised a larger percentage of college professors (going from 34 to 49 percent), engineers (up from 4 to 15 percent), lawyers and judges (from 12 to 35 percent), and accountants (from 41 to 63 percent). Likewise, in the medical profession women's gains have been remarkable, as 33 percent of the physicians and surgeons in the state are women (up from 10 percent in 1980). More women are also taking management positions: 43 percent of management, business, and financial occupations are held by women, although they seem to be still concentrated in lower

management and human resources positions. Only 25 percent of top execu-
tives are women. Few of those head the largest corporations: of 257 publicly
held corporations in 2005, only two had women chief executive officers.[9]

Despite gains in some areas of employment, as of 2013 women still were
making significantly less money than men: Texas women earned an average
of 78 cents for every dollar a man earned. At the current rate of change, this
wage gap will not close for another three decades. The wage gap is even more
significant for those with higher education: women with bachelor's degrees
or higher earn on average 65 percent the amount that men earn. Though
it is illegal for employers to pay women less than men for the same work, it
is often difficult to discover and prove this in court. Whether for the same
employers or not, women earn less in the same occupations (doing the same
work) as men. Affecting the gap even more is that women are still segregated
into many of the lowest-paying positions. Even within higher-paying professions, women are still the most likely to be employed in those subfields that
pay the least. For instance, women comprise 60 percent of pediatricians and
more than 51 percent of obstetricians and gynecologists but as little as 19
percent of surgeons. Despite overwhelmingly outnumbering men as teachers,
women make up only 17 percent of superintendents in the state.[10]

In politics, women have made similarly small gains. The number of women
serving in the state legislature rose only marginally from the 1990s, exceeding
20 percent of the legislators only once by 2015.[11] The only woman to serve
as US senator from the state, Kay Bailey Hutchison, stepped down in 2013
after ten years of service. In 2017, only three of the state's US representatives
were women, and only one woman held statewide office (Christi Craddick,
railroad commissioner). Women have run for statewide office in the twenty-
first century. Most notably Hutchison held an early lead in the polls for governor but lost the Republican nomination to Rick Perry in 2010, and Wendy
Davis won the Democratic nomination for governor in 2014 but lost in the
general election. Women still face difficulties navigating the political context
of Texas, which expects them to act as "ladies" while trying to win offices that
require them to demonstrate their toughness. In this environment women
have adapted different strategies and narratives about their service. Much
more than men, they must downplay personal ambition and describe their
desire for political leadership as "mothering." They often emphasize their
own roles as mothers to justify their desire to gain power in order to help
their own and others' children.[12]

The emphasis on community activism has helped women to be more successful on the local level of politics than in statewide races. The number of women in elected municipal offices continues to grow, with large and small cities both electing women to city councils and as mayors. With the election of Annise Parker in 2010, Houston became the first major city in the nation to have elected two women as mayor and the largest city to elect an openly gay mayor.

Whether they are running for office or not, women activists are still playing a major role in the state. Raising money for cultural events and venues such as opera, theatre, and ballet relies on women's organizing and efforts. Women are still agitating for changes to laws to protect women and children, advocating for tougher domestic violence laws and increased funding for domestic violence shelters, and fighting for increased oversight and funding for the foster care system. Many women are also still working to change the very social structures that underlie gender roles and inequality between men and women, challenging "rape culture" as well as advocating for greater prosecution of rape, encouraging more girls to pursue science and technological professions, and sharing domestic responsibilities, including child rearing, more equally with men.

Whatever the future holds for Texas women, for centuries they have proven their strength and ability to shape politics and culture even in the most oppressive environments. Their roles and expectations have changed significantly over the years, allowing women greater expressions of their individuality and economic independence. In their old roles as well as their new ones, women have been crucial in creating the state of Texas.

Notes

Preface

1. For an excellent discussion of the development of the field of Texas women's history, see Nancy Baker Jones, "Making Texas *Our* Texas: The Emergence of Texas Women's History, 1976–1990," *Southwestern Historical Quarterly* 120 (January 2017): 279–313.

Chapter 1

1. C. Britt Bousman, Barry W. Baker, and Anne C. Kerr, "Paleoindian Archeology in Texas," in *The Prehistory of Texas*, ed. Timothy K. Perttula (College Station: Texas A&M University Press, 2004), 85.

2. David La Vere, *Texas Indians* (College Station: Texas A&M University Press, 2004), 3–9.

3. Ibid., 9–10.

4. Ibid., 9–14.

5. Patricia M. Bass, "A Gendered Search through Some West Texas Rock Art," in *New Light on Old Art: Recent Advances in Hunter-Gatherer Rock Art Research*, ed. David S. Whitley and Lawrence L. Loendorf (Los Angeles: UCLA Institute of Archaeology Press, 1994), 67–74, http://www.ruf.rice.edu/~raar/bassdoc.pdf.

6. La Vere, *Texas Indians*, 12–13, 17–19.

7. Diane Wilson, "Division of Labor and Stress Loads at the Sanders Site (41LR2), Lamar County, Texas," *Bulletin of the Texas Archeological Society* 65 (1994): 129–60; Carol J. Loveland, "Vertebral Anomalies and Degenerative Lesions in the Caddoan Skeletal Population, Kaufman-Williams Site, Red River County, Texas" *Bulletin of the Texas Archeological Society* 65 (1994): 161–81.

8. La Vere, *Texas Indians*, 18–23.

9. Ibid., 20–22.

10. Ibid., 23; David E. Stuart, *Anasazi America: Seventeen Centuries on the Road from Center Place* (Albuquerque: University of New Mexico Press, 2000), 45.

11. La Vere, *Texas Indians*, 31–33.

12. William Joyce Griffith, *The Hasinai Indians of East Texas as Seen by Europeans, 1687–1772* (New Orleans: Tulane University Press, 1954), 53, 119.

13. Ibid., 50–52.

14. Cecile Elkins Carter, *Caddo Indians: Where We Come From* (Norman: University of Oklahoma Press, 1995), 82–83.

15. La Vere, *Texas Indians*, 31–33.

16. W. W. Newcomb, Jr., *The Indians of Texas: From Prehistoric to Modern Times* (Austin: University of Texas Press, 1961), 47.

17. La Vere, *Texas Indians*, 65–67; T. N. Campbell and T. J. Campbell, "Cabeza de Vaca among the Indians of Southern Texas," in *The Indians of Southern Texas and Northeastern Mexico: Selected Writings of Thomas Nolan Campbell*, ed. T. N. Campbell (Austin: University of Texas, 1988), 20–21.

18. Newcomb, *Indians of Texas*, 47.

19. La Vere, *Texas Indians*, 59–61; W. W. Newcomb, Jr., "Karankawa," in *Ethnology of the Texas Indians*, ed. Thomas R. Hester (New York: Garland, 1991), 145.

20. La Vere, *Texas Indians*, 69; Nancy Parrot Hickerson, *The Jumanos: Hunters and Traders of the South Plains* (Austin: University of Texas, 1994), 15.

21. La Vere, *Texas Indians*, 85–86; H. Henrietta Stockel, *Chiricahua Apache Women and Children: Safekeepers of the Heritage* (College Station: Texas A&M University Press, 2000), 15.

22. Stockel, *Chiricahua Apache Women*, 10, 16; La Vere, *Texas Indians*, 86.

23. La Vere, *Texas Indians*, 72–73.

24. Ibid., 73.

25. Carter, *Caddo Indians*, 177; Juliana Barr, *Peace Came in the Form of a Woman: Indians and Spaniards in the Texas Borderlands* (Chapel Hill: University of North Carolina Press, 2007), 5.

26. Ramona Ford, "Native American Women: Changing Statuses, Changing Interpretations," in *Writing the Range: Race, Class and Culture in the Women's West*, ed. Elizabeth Jameson and Susan Armitage (Norman: University of Oklahoma Press, 1997), 55–59; Pekka Hämäläinen, *The Comanche Empire* (New Haven: Yale University Press, 2008), 244, 247–49, 288.

27. Donald E. Chipman and Harriett Denise Joseph, *Notable Men and Women of Spanish Texas* (Austin: University of Texas Press, 1999), 50–55.

28. Salomé Hernández, "*Nueva Mexicanas* as Refugees and Reconquest Settlers, 1680–1696," in *New Mexico Women: Intercultural Perspectives*, ed. Joan M. Jensen and Darlis A. Miller (Albuquerque: University of New Mexico Press, 1986), 41–69 (quote on 54).

29. Randolph B. Campbell, *Gone to Texas: A History of the Lone Star State* (New York: Oxford University Press, 2003), 43–45.

30. Jean A. Stuntz, *Hers, His and Theirs: Community Property Law in Spain and Early Texas* (Lubbock: Texas Tech University Press, 2005), 1–14.

31. Campbell, *Gone to Texas*, 47.

32. Barr, *Peace Came in the Form of a Woman*, 33–42.

33. Ibid., 60–63.

34. Ibid., 65.

35. Ibid., 92; Donald E. Chipman, *Spanish Texas, 1519–1821* (Austin: University of Texas Press, 1992), 112.

36. Barr, *Peace Came in the Form of a Woman*, 116.

37. Ibid., 127.

38. Jesus F. De La Teja, *San Antonio de Bexar: A Community on New Spain's Northern Frontier* (Albuquerque: University of New Mexico, 1995), 23–25; Andrés Tijerina, *Tejanos and Texas under the Mexican Flag, 1821–1836* (College Station: Texas A&M University Press, 1994), 8–10.

39. David J. Weber, *The Spanish Frontier in North America* (New Haven: Yale University Press, 1992), 307; Gerald E. Poyo and Gilberto M. Hinojosa, "Spanish Texas and Borderlands Historiography in Transition: Implications for United States History," *Journal of American History*, 75 (September 1988): 395–416; Barr, *Peace Came in the Form of a Woman*, 157.

40. Jane Dysart, "Mexican Women in San Antonio, 1830–1860: The Assimilation Process," *Western Historical Quarterly* 7 (October 1976): 368.

41. Barr, *Peace Came in the Form of a Woman*, 139–44.

42. Ibid.

43. Weber, *Spanish Frontier*, 316–17.

44. Barr, *Peace Came in the Form of a Woman*, 141–57.

45. Ibid., 286.

46. Weber, *Spanish Frontier*, 316–17.

47. Kimberly Gauderman, *Women's Lives in Colonial Quito: Gender, Law, and Economy in Spanish America* (Austin: University of Texas Press, 2003), 1, 28–29; Patricia Seed, *To Love, Honor, and Obey in Colonial Mexico* (Stanford: Stanford University Press, 1988).

48. Jean Stuntz, "Spanish Laws for Texas Women: The Development of Marital Property Law to 1850," *Southwestern Historical Quarterly* (April 2001): 542–59.

49. Jack Jackson, *Los Mesteños: Spanish Ranching in Texas, 1721–1821* (College Station: Texas A&M University Press, 1986), 419.

50. Teresa Palomo Acosta and Ruthe Winegarten, *Las Tejanas: 300 Years of History* (Austin: University of Texas Press, 2003), 16–18.

51. David J. Weber, *The Mexican Frontier, 1821–1846* (Albuquerque: University of New Mexico Press, 1982), 216.

52. Rodolfo Rocha, "Early Ranching along the Rio Grande," in *At Home on the Range: Essays on the History of Western Social and Domestic Life*, ed. John R. Wunder (Westport, Conn.: Greenwood Press, 1985), 10–12.

53. Odie B. Faulk, *The Last Years of Spanish Texas, 1778–1821* (London: Mouton, 1964), 94; Acosta and Winegarten, *Las Tejanas*, 26.

54. Charles R. Cutter, *The Legal Culture of Northern New Spain, 1700–1810* (Albuquerque: University of New Mexico Press, 1995), 118–19.

55. Weber, *Mexican Frontier*, 16, 216; Stuntz, *Hers, His and Theirs*, 33.

56. Jackson, *Los Mesteños*, 544–45; Gilberto M. Hinojosa, *A Borderlands Town in Transition: Laredo, 1755–1870* (College Station: Texas A&M University Press, 1983), 34–35.

57. Acosta and Winegarten, *Las Tejanas*, 37–38.

58. Hinojosa, *Borderlands Town in Transition*, 34–36.

59. Jesus F. De La Teja, "Indians, Soldiers, and Canary Islanders: The Making of a Texas Frontier Community," *Locus* 3 (Fall 1990): 88.

60. Dysart, "Mexican Women in San Antonio," 367; Fane Downs, "Texas Women

at Work," in *Texas: A Sesquicentennial Celebration*, ed. Donald W. Whisenhunt (Austin: Eakin Press, 1984), 314–15.

61. Arnoldo De León, *The Tejano Community, 1836–1900* (Albuquerque: University of New Mexico Press, 1982), 7.

62. Tijerina, *Tejanos and Texas*, 23.

63. Mark A. Carroll, *Homesteads Ungovernable: Families, Sex, Race, and the Law in Frontier Texas, 1823–1860* (Austin: University of Texas Press, 2001), 13–20.

64. Armando C. Alonzo, *Tejano Legacy: Rancheros and Settlers in South Texas, 1734–1900* (Albuquerque: University of New Mexico Press, 1998), 130, 240; David Montejano, *Anglos and Mexicans in the Making of Texas, 1836–1986* (Austin: University of Texas Press, 1987), 36–37.

65. Dysart, "Mexican Women in San Antonio," 374.

66. Carroll, *Homesteads Ungovernable*, 4–7, 11–15; Stuntz, *Hers, His and Theirs*, 36–38.

Chapter 2

1. Anne A. Brindley, "Jane Long," *Southwestern Historical Quarterly* 56 (October 1952): 211–38.

2. Mark A. Carroll, *Homesteads Ungovernable: Families, Sex, Race, and the Law in Frontier Texas, 1823–1860* (Austin: University of Texas Press, 2001), 4.

3. Gregg Cantrell, *Stephen F. Austin: Empresario of Texas* (New Haven: Yale University Press, 1999), 176.

4. Walter Struve, *Germans and Texans: Commerce, Migration, and Culture in the Days of the Lone Star Republic* (Austin: University of Texas Press, 1996), 43–46, 81.

5. Dedra S. McDonald, "To Be Black and Female in the Spanish Southwest: Toward a History of African Women on New Spain's Far Northern Frontier," in *African American Women Confront the West, 1600–2000*, ed. Quintard Taylor and Shirley Ann Wilson Moore (Norman: University of Oklahoma Press, 2003), 46–47.

6. Randolph B. Campbell, *An Empire for Slavery: The Peculiar Institution in Texas, 1821–1865* (Baton Rouge: Louisiana State University Press, 1989), 16–34; Paul D. Lack, "Slavery and the Texas Revolution," *Southwestern Historical Quarterly* 89 (July 1985): 183–84; Andrew J. Torget, *Seeds of Empire: Cotton, Slavery, and the Transformation of the Texas Borderlands, 1800–1950* (Chapel Hill: University of North Carolina Press, 2015).

7. Cantrell, *Stephen F. Austin*, 36–37; David La Vere, *Texas Indians* (College Station: Texas A&M University Press, 2004), 182–83.

8. "Mary Crownover Rabb" and "Mary Sherwood Wightman Helm," in *Texas Tears and Texas Sunshine: Voices of Frontier Women*, ed. Jo Ella Powell Exley (College Station: Texas A&M University Press, 1985), 9–10, 26–28; Jane Clements Monday and Frances Brannen Vick, *Petra's Legacy: The South Texas Ranching Empire of Petra Vela and Mifflin Kenedy* (College Station: Texas A&M University Press, 2007), 63.

9. "Mary Crownover Rabb," in Exley, *Texas Tears and Texas Sunshine*, 18; Angela Boswell, *Her Act and Deed: Women's Lives in a Rural Southern County, 1837–1873* (College Station: Texas A&M University Press, 2001), 31, 34–35.

10. Adrienne Caughfield, *True Women and Westward Expansion* (College Station: Texas A&M University Press, 2005), 45–48 (quote on 48).

11. Crystal Sasse Ragsdale, *The Women and Children of the Alamo* (Austin, TX: State House Press, 1994).

12. Jane Hallowell Hill Narrative, Thomson Family of Texas Papers, 1832–1898, MS 288, Woodson Research Center, Fondren Library, Rice University, Houston; Dilue Rose Harris, "The Reminiscences of Mrs. Dilue Harris II," *Quarterly of the Texas State Historical Association* 4 (January 1901): 157.

13. Harris, "Reminiscences of Mrs. Dilue Harris," 163; Caughfield, *True Women and Westward Expansion*, 15.

14. Hill Narrative.

15. Caughfield, *True Women and Westward Expansion*, 84–85.

16. Joan E. Cashin, *A Family Venture: Men and Women on the Southern Frontier* (Baltimore: Johns Hopkins University Press, 1991), 32–52; Boswell, *Her Act and Deed*, 14.

17. "Mary Crownover Rabb," in Exley, *Texas Tears and Texas Sunshine*, 7; Linda S. Hudson, *Mistress of Manifest Destiny: A Biography of Jane McManus Storm Cazneau, 1807–1878* (Austin: Texas State Historical Association, 2001), 27.

18. "Mary Sherwood Wightman Helm," in Exley, *Texas Tears and Texas Sunshine*, 21.

19. "Mary Crownover Rabb," in Exley, *Texas Tears and Texas Sunshine*, 7; Cashin, *A Family Venture*, 48, 57; "Reminiscences of James Williams Holt," *Nesbitt Memorial Library Journal* 6 (September 1996): 152–54.

20. "Mary Crownover Rabb," in Exley, *Texas Tears and Texas Sunshine*, 5–18.

21. Cantrell, *Stephen F. Austin*, 109.

22. "Mary Crownover Rabb," in Exley, *Texas Tears and Texas Sunshine*, 12.

23. "Mary Crownover Rabb" and "Mary Sherwood Wightman Helm," in Exley, *Texas Tears and Texas Sunshine*, 10, 23.

24. Ibid., 12–13, 23.

25. "Ann Raney Thomas Coleman," in Exley, *Texas Tears and Texas Sunshine*, 32.

26. Noah Smithwick, *The Evolution of a State; or, Recollections of Old Texas Days* (Austin, 1900), chap. 3.

27. Boswell, *Her Act and Deed*, 12–16; Cashin, *Family Venture*, 66–69.

28. "Mary Crownover Rabb," in Exley, *Texas Tears and Texas Sunshine*, 14–15.

29. Boswell, *Her Act and Deed*, 16; Smithwick, *Evolution of a State*, chap. 3.

30. Harriette Andreadis, "True Womanhood Revisited: Women's Private Writing in Nineteenth-Century Texas," *Journal of the Southwest* 31 (Summer 1989): 179–204. See also Elizabeth Jameson, "Women as Workers, Women as Civilizers: True Womanhood in the American West," in *The Women's West*, ed. Susan Armitage and Elizabeth Jameson (Norman: University of Oklahoma Press, 1987), 150.

31. "Mary Crownover Rabb," in Exley, *Texas Tears and Texas Sunshine*, 10.

32. Campbell, *Empire for Slavery*, 16–34; Lack, "Slavery and the Texas Revolution," 183–84.

33. Campbell, *Empire for Slavery*, 33.

34. Millie Forward and Rosanna Frazier *Federal Writers' Project: Slave Narrative Project*, vol. 16, *Texas, Part 2, Easter-King* (Washington, DC: Library of Congress, 1941), https://www.loc.gov/item/mesn162/, 47, 63.

35. Cashin, *Family Venture*, 49–51; Ruthe Winegarten, *Black Texas Women: 150 Years of Trial and Triumph* (Austin: University of Texas Press, 1995), 16.

36. Angela Boswell, "Black Women during Slavery," in *Black Women in Texas History*, ed. Bruce A. Glasrud and Merline Pitre (College Station: Texas A&M University Press, 2008), 16–19.

37. Ibid.; Boswell, *Her Act and Deed*, 82–83.

38. Benjamin Lundy, *The Life, Travels, and Opinions of Benjamin Lundy, including His Journeys to Texas and Mexico* (Philadelphia: William D. Parrish, 1847), 41; Boswell, *Her Act and Deed*, 85–86.

39. Smithwick, *Evolution of a State*, chap. 17; Ann Patton Malone, *Women on the Texas Frontier: A Cross-Cultural Perspective*, Southwestern Studies, Monograph 70 (El Paso: Texas Western Press, 1983), 30–31; Harold Shoen, "The Free Negro in the Republic of Texas, I," *Southwestern Historical Quarterly* 39 (April 1936): 295–96.

40. Deborah Gray White, *Ar'n't I a Woman? Female Slaves in the Plantation South* (New York: W. W. Norton, 1985), 98; Winegarten, *Black Texas Women*, 16–17, 22–24.

41. Winegarten, *Black Texas Women*, 22–24; Boswell, "Black Women during Slavery," 20–24; Marie Jenkins Schwartz, *Born in Bondage: Growing up Enslaved in the Antebellum South* (Cambridge: Harvard University Press, 2000).

42. Rosa Kleberg, "Some of My Early Experiences in Texas," *Quarterly of the Texas State Historical Association* 1 (April 1898): 297; Ingeborg Ruberg McCoy, "Tales of the Grandmothers, II," in *Eagle in the New World: German Immigration to Texas and America*, ed. Theodore Gish and Richard Spuler (College Station: Texas Committee for the Humanities, by Texas A&M University Press, 1986), 216.

43. Struve, *Germans and Texans*, 81.

44. McCoy, "Tales of the Grandmothers," 218 (quote); Crystal Sasse Ragsdale, "The German Woman in Frontier Texas," in *German Culture in Texas: A Free Earth: Essays from the 1978 Southwest Symposium*, ed. Glen E. Lich and Dona B. Reeves (Boston: Twayne, 1980), 144–45.

45. Glen E. Lich, *The German Texans* (San Antonio: University of Texas Institute of Texan Cultures, 1981), 83.

46. Ragsdale, "German Woman in Frontier Texas," 146–47.

47. Boswell, *Her Act and Deed*, 50–51.

48. Jean A. Stuntz, *Hers, His and Theirs: Community Property Law in Spain and Early Texas* (Lubbock: Texas Tech University Press, 2005), 136–45.

49. Boswell, *Her Act and Deed*, 26–30, 34, 45, 46.

50. Ibid., 26–30.

51. Ibid., 34, 45, 46; Stuntz, *Hers, His and Theirs*, 136–45.

52. Boswell, *Her Act and Deed*, 26–30, 34, 45, 46.

53. Ibid., 46–52. See also Robin C. Sager, *Marital Cruelty in Antebellum America* (Baton Rouge: Louisiana State University Press, 2016).

Chapter 3

1. Randolph B. Campbell, *Gone to Texas: A History of the Lone Star State* (New York: Oxford University Press, 2003), 207; Light Townsend Cummins, *Emily Austin of Texas, 1795–1851* (Fort Worth: Texas Christian University Press, 2009), 102, 107–8.

2. Angela Boswell, *Her Act and Deed: Women's Lives in a Rural Southern County, 1837–1873* (College Station: Texas A&M University Press, 2001), 55–56; Cummins, *Emily Austin of Texas*, 94.

3. Carolyn Earle Billingsley, *Communities of Kinship: Antebellum Families and the Settlement of the Cotton Frontier* (Athens: University of Georgia Press, 2004); Boswell, *Her Act and Deed*, 56.

4. Barbara Welter, "The Cult of True Womanhood: 1820–1860," *American Quarterly*, 18 (Summer 1966): 151–52; Harriette Andreadis, "True Womanhood Revisited: Women's Private Writing in Nineteenth-Century Texas" *Journal of the Southwest* 31 (Summer 1989): 179–204.

5. Louisa S. McCord, "Woman and Her Needs," in *Louisa S. McCord: Political and Social Essays*, ed. Richard C. Lounsbury (Charlottesville: University Press of Virginia, 1995), 125–55.

6. Linda S. Hudson, *Mistress of Manifest Destiny: A Biography of Jane McManus Storm Cazneau, 1807–1878* (Austin: Texas State Historical Association, 2001), 39–40.

7. Hudson, *Mistress of Manifest Destiny*, 36–40.

8. Campbell, *Gone to Texas*, 209–10.

9. John Boles, *The South through Time: A History of an America Region* (Upper Saddle River, NJ: Simon & Schuster, 1999), 243; Sally G. McMillen, *Motherhood in the Old South: Pregnancy, Childbirth, and Infant Rearing* (Baton Rouge: Louisiana State University Press, 1990), 30–33.

10. Michelle Cochrane, "Educational Opportunities Available for Women in Antebellum Texas," (master's thesis, University of North Texas, 2006), 17, 21, 26, 32, 84–85; James Talmadge Moore, *Through Fire and Flood: The Catholic Church in Frontier Texas, 1836–1900* (College Station: Texas A&M University Press, 1992), 84, 98–99, 120; S. M. Johnston, *Builders by the Sea: History of the Ursuline Community of Galveston, Texas* (New York: Exposition Press, 1971).

11. Erika L. Murr, ed., *A Rebel Wife in Texas: The Diary and Letters of Elizabeth Scott Neblett, 1852–1864* (Baton Rouge: Louisiana State University Press, 2001), 3–5, 45–46.

12. Sean M. Kelley, *Los Brazos de Dios: A Plantation Society in the Texas Borderlands, 1821–1865* (Baton Rouge: Louisiana State University Press, 2010), 66–67.

13. Angela Boswell, "The Meaning of Participation: White Protestant Women in Antebellum Houston Churches," *Southwestern Historical Quarterly* 99 (July 1995): 32–33, 40–42.

14. Elizabeth York Enstam, *Women and the Creation of Urban Life: Dallas, Texas, 1843–1920* (College Station: Texas A&M University Press, 1998), 13, 49.

15. Boswell, "The Meaning of Participation," 46; Enstam, *Women and the Creation of Urban Life*, 13, 49.

16. Enstam, *Women and the Creation of Urban Life*, 49; excerpt from the diary of Fannie Darden, reprinted in *History of St. John's Episcopal Church, Columbus, Texas, April 14, 1856–April 14, 1956* (n.d., 1956?), 4.

17. Boswell, "The Meaning of Participation," 44.

18. Ibid., 35.

19. Ginny McNeill Raska and Mary Lynne Gasaway Hill, eds., *The Uncompromising*

Diary of Sallie McNeill, 1858–1867 (College Station: Texas A&M University Press, 2009), 77.

20. Enstam, *Women and the Creation of Urban Life*, 25; Raska and Hill, *Uncompromising Diary of Sallie McNeill*, 9.

21. Raska and Hill, *Uncompromising Diary of Sallie McNeill*, 9.

22. Scott Stephan, *Redeeming the Southern Family: Evangelical Women and Domestic Devotion in the Antebellum South* (Athens: University of Georgia Press, 2008), 2–5; Boswell, "Meaning of Participation," 38.

23. Murr, *Rebel Wife in Texas*, 65.

24. Amy L. Wink, ed., *Tandem Lives: The Frontier Texas Diaries of Henrietta Baker Embree and Tennessee Keys Embree, 1856–1884* (Knoxville: University of Tennessee Press, 2008), 51, 54, 55, 79.

25. Raska and Hill, *Diary of Sallie McNeill*, 35 (first quote), 63 (other quotes).

26. Fane Downs, "Texas Women at Work," in *Texas: A Sesquicentennial Celebration*, ed. Donald W. Whisenhunt (Austin: Eakin Press, 1984), 313–14.

27. Downs, "Texas Women at Work," 314–15; Paula Mitchell Marks, *Hands to the Spindle: Texas Women and Home Textile Production, 1822–1880* (College Station: Texas A&M University Press, 1996), 34–35, 44, 72.

28. Marks, *Hands to the Spindle*, 61, 72.

29. Downs, "Texas Women at Work," 314–15.

30. Boswell, *Her Act and Deed*, 59; Downs, "Women at Work," 313–14.

31. Randolph B. Campbell, *An Empire for Slavery: The Peculiar Institution in Texas, 1821–1865* (Baton Rouge: Louisiana State University Press, 1989), 55–56, 68.

32. Williamson S. Oldham and George W. White, *A Digest of the General Statute Laws of the State of Texas* (Austin: John Marshal, 1859), 26; Noah Smithwick, chap.17 in *The Evolution of a State; or, Recollections of Old Texas Days* (Austin, 1900).

33. Sarah Ford, *Federal Writers' Project: Slave Narrative Project*, vol. 16, *Texas, Part 2* (Washington, DC: Library of Congress, 1941), https://www.loc.gov/item/mesn162/, 42; Angela Boswell, "Black Women during Slavery," in *Black Women in Texas History*, ed. Bruce A. Glasrud and Merline Pitre (College Station: Texas A&M University Press, 2008), 24–25; Campbell, *Empire for Slavery*, 118.

34. Boswell, "Black Women during Slavery," 22–23; Campbell, *Empire for Slavery*, 156.

35. Irella Battle Walker, *Federal Writers' Project: Slave Narrative Project*, vol. 16, *Texas, Part 4, Sanco-Young*, 122; Boswell, "Black Women during Slavery," 24–25.

36. Emma Taylor, *Federal Writers' Project: Slave Narrative Project*, vol. 16, *Texas, Part 4*, 4; Sarah Ford, *Federal Writers' Project: Slave Narrative Project*, vol. 16, *Texas, Part 2*, 43; Boswell, "Black Women during Slavery," 24–25.

37. Boswell, "Black Women during Slavery," 24–25.

38. Campbell, *Empire for Slavery*, 176; Ruthe Winegarten, *Black Texas Women: 150 Years of Trial and Triumph* (Austin: University of Texas Press, 1995), 31.

39. Ingeborg Ruberg McCoy, "Tales of the Grandmothers, II," in *Eagle in the New World: German Immigration to Texas and America*, ed. Theodore Gish and Richard Spuler

(College Station: Texas Committee for the Humanities by Texas A&M University Press, 1986), 212.

40. Crystal Sasse Ragsdale, "The German Woman in Frontier Texas," *German Culture in Texas: A Free Earth. Essays from the 1978 Southwest Symposium*, ed. Glen E. Lich and Dona B. Reeves (Boston: Twayne, 1980), 146–52.

41. Boswell, *Her Act and Deed*, 39–42, 52–53, 57–58, 70.

42. Terry G. Jordan, *German Seed in Texas Soil: Immigrant Farmers in Nineteenth-Century Texas* (Austin: University of Texas Press, 1966), 195; Boswell, *Her Act and Deed*, 32.

43. Lauren Ann Kattner, "The Diversity of Old South White Women: The Peculiar Worlds of German American Women," in *Discovering the Women in Slavery: Emancipating Perspectives on the American Past* (Athens: University of Georgia Press, 1996), 299–311.

44. Arnoldo De León, *They Called Them Greasers: Anglo Attitudes toward Mexicans in Texas, 1821–1900* (Austin: University of Texas Press, 1983), 49–50, 75–80; Arnoldo De León, *Mexican Americans in Texas: A Brief History*, 2nd ed. (Wheeling, IL: Harlan Davidson, 1999), 38–40, 47.

45. David Montejano, *Anglos and Mexicans in the Making of Texas, 1836–1986* (Austin: University of Texas Press, 1987), 50–74; De León, *Mexican Americans in Texas*, 42–43.

46. Teresa Palomo Acosta and Ruthe Winegarten, *Las Tejanas: 300 Years of History* (Austin: University of Texas Press, 2003), 52–53; Arnoldo De León, *The Tejano Community, 1836–1900* (Albuquerque: University of New Mexico Press, 1982), 17.

47. Ana Carolina Castillo Crimm, *De León: A Tejano Family History* (Austin: University of Texas Press, 2003), 202 (first quote), 203–4, 207–8 (second quote); Amy Meschke, "Women's Lives through Women's Wills in the Spanish and Mexican Borderlands, 1750–1846 (PhD diss., Southern Methodist University, 2004), 20, 94–129.

48. Mary Margaret McAllen Amberson, James A. McAllen, and Margaret H. McAllen, *I Would Rather Sleep in Texas: A History of the Lower Rio Grande Valley and the People of the Santa Anita Land Grant* (Austin: Texas State Historical Association, 2003), 129; Armando C. Alonzo, *Tejano Legacy: Rancheros and Settlers in South Texas, 1734–1900* (Albuquerque: University of New Mexico Press, 1998), 187.

49. Acosta and Winegarten, *Las Tejanas*, 53; Jane Clements Monday and Frances Brannen Vick, *Petra's Legacy: The South Texas Ranching Empire of Petra Vela and Mifflin Kenedy* (College Station: Texas A&M University Press, 2007), 42–43, 98–100, 169.

50. Meschke, "Women's Lives through Women's Wills," 59.

51. Ibid., 3 (quote), 13–14.

52. De León, *Tejano Community*, 122, 130–31; Rodolfo Rocha, "Early Ranching along the Rio Grande," in *At Home on the Range: Essays on the History of Western Social and Domestic Life*, ed. John R. Wunder (Westport, CT: Greenwood Press, 1985), 7, 11.

53. De León, *Tejano Community*, 131.

54. Downs, "Texas Women at Work," 314–15; Gilberto M. Hinojosa, *A Borderlands Town in Transition: Laredo, 1755–1870* (College Station: Texas A&M University Press, 1983), 70.

Chapter 4

1. *Colorado Citizen* (Columbus, TX.), May 30, 1860.

2. Caroline Baldwin Darrow, "Recollections of the Twiggs Surrender," reprinted in *Texas: The Dark Corner of the Confederacy: Contemporary Accounts of the Lone Star State in the Civil War*, ed. B. P. Gallaway, 3rd ed. (Lincoln: University of Nebraska Press, 1994), 81.

3. *Galveston Weekly News*, February 2, 1861, from Vicki Betts, ed., "Public Voice of Texas Women," Scholar Works at UT Tyler, 2016, https://scholarworks.uttyler.edu/cw_newstopics/19; Vicki Betts, "'Everyone Has the War Fever': Anglo-Texan Women Prepare for Secession and War," in *Women in Civil War Texas: Diversity and Dissidence in the Trans-Mississippi*, ed. Deborah M. Liles and Angela Boswell (Denton: University of North Texas Press, 2016), 20–21.

4. Gallaway, *Texas: The Dark Corner of the Confederacy*, 77.

5. *Colorado Citizen* (Columbus, TX.), March 2, 1861.

6. *Colorado Citizen* (Columbus, TX.), September 21, 1861; Drew Gilpin Faust, *Mothers of Invention: Women of the Slaveholding South in the American Civil War* (Chapel Hill: University of North Carolina Press, 1996), 20.

7. *Texas Republican* (Marshall, TX.), April 27, 1861, from Betts, "Public Voice of Texas Women"; Betts, "Everyone Has the War Fever," 22–25.

8. Angela Boswell, *Her Act and Deed: Women's Lives in a Rural Southern County, 1837–1873* (College Station: Texas A&M University Press, 2001), 93.

9. Boswell, *Her Act and Deed*, 54–72; Vicki Adams Tongate, *Another Year Finds Me in Texas: The Civil War Diary of Lucy Pier Stevens* (Austin: University of Texas Press, 2016).

10. Theophilus Perry to Harriet Perry, February 2, 1863, in *Widows by the Thousand: The Civil War Letters of Theophilus and Harriet Perry, 1862–1864*, ed. M. Jane Johansson (Fayetteville: University of Arkansas Press, 2000), 91; "Civil War Letters of John Samuel Shropshire," *Nesbitt Memorial Library Journal* 7 (January 1997): 69.

11. Boswell, *Her Act and Deed*, 95–97.

12. Sarah Joyce Rutherford Starr, "'Yours Heart and Hand': An Analysis of the Correspondence of James and Patience Crain Black, 1861–1865 (master's thesis, Baylor University, 1990), 60; Angela Boswell, "Harriet Perry: A Woman's Life in Civil War Texas," in *Texas Women: Their Histories, Their Lives*, ed. Elizabeth Hayes Turner, Stephanie Cole, and Rebecca Sharpless (Athens: University of Georgia Press, 2015), 116–20; Erika L. Murr, ed., *A Rebel Wife in Texas: The Diary and Letters of Elizabeth Scott Neblett, 1852–1864* (Baton Rouge: Louisiana State University Press, 2001), 1.

13. Vera Lea Dugas, "A Social and Economic History of Texas in the Civil War and Reconstruction Periods" (PhD diss., University of Texas, 1963), 256.

14. Lizzie S. Neblett to William H. Neblett, August 13, 1863, in Murr, *Rebel Wife*, 134; Drew Gilpin Faust, "Trying to Do a Man's Business: Gender, Violence, and Slave Management in Civil War Texas," in *Southern Stories: Slaveholders in Peace and War* (Columbia: University of Missouri Press, 1992), 174–91.

15. George C. Rable, *Civil Wars: Women and the Crisis of Southern Nationalism* (Urbana: University of Illinois Press, 1989), 84–85.

16. Dugas, "Social and Economic History of Texas," 256–67; Laura F. Edwards, *Scarlett Doesn't Live Here Anymore: Southern Women in the Civil War Era* (Urbana: University of Illinois Press, 2000), 90–91.

17. Vicki Betts, "'A Sacred Charge upon Our Hands': Assisting the Families of Confederate Soldiers in Texas, 1861–1865," in *The Seventh Star of the Confederacy: Texas during the Civil War*, ed. Kenneth W. Howell (Denton: University of North Texas Press, 2009), 246–67 (quote on 248); Betts, "Everyone Has the War Fever," 25–27.

18. Betty J. Mills, *Calico Chronicle: Texas Women and Their Fashions, 1830–1910* (Lubbock: Texas Tech Press, 1985), 24; Paula Mitchell Marks, *Hands to the Spindle: Texas Women and Home Textile Production, 1822–1880* (College Station: Texas A&M University Press, 1996), 78–79.

19. Harriet Perry to Theophilus Perry, July 28, 1863, in Johansson, *Widows by the Thousand*, 157.

20. Marks, *Hands to the Spindle*, 79–86.

21. Ibid., 78–81; Dugas, "Social and Economic History of Texas," 263, 284–86; Jerry Bryan Lincecum, Edward Hake Phillips, and Peggy A. Redshaw, eds. *Gideon Lincecum's Sword: Civil War Letters from the Texas Home Front* (Denton: University of North Texas Press, 2001), 207–11; Faust, *Mothers of Invention*, 45–52.

22. Lincecum, Phillips, and Redshaw, *Gideon Lincecum's Sword*, 188, 195 (quote), 207.

23. Harriet Perry to Theophilus Perry, September 24, 1862, and Levin Perry to Theophilus Perry, July 20, 1863, in Johansson, *Widows by the Thousand*, 41, 154.

24. Dugas, "Social and Economic History of Texas," 284.

25. Cecilia Labadie Diary, 1863, folder 94–0004, Galveston and Texas History Center, Rosenberg Library, Galveston, Texas.

26. Maria von Blücher, *Maria von Blücher's Corpus Christi: Letters from the South Texas Frontier, 1849–1879*, ed. Bruce S. Cheeseman (College Station: Texas A & M University Press, 2002), 130.

27. "Eudora Moore," in *Texas Tears and Texas Sunshine: Voices of Frontier Women*, ed. Jo Ella Powell Exley (College Station: Texas A&M University Press, 1985), 146–47.

28. Murr, *Rebel Wife in Texas*, 96.

29. Harriet Perry to Theophilus Perry, April 5, 1863, July 20, 1863, and January 18, 1864, in Johansson, *Widows by the Thousand*, 119, 155, 197 (first quote).

30. Harriet Perry to Theophilus Perry, December 23, 1862, in Johansson, *Widows by the Thousand*, 74.

31. Faust, *Mothers of Invention*, 114–23.

32. Harriet Perry to Theophilus Perry, October 30, 1862, and December 23, 1862, in Johansson, *Widows by the Thousand*, 51, 65 (quote).

33. Faust, *Mothers of Invention*, 123–29.

34. Henry F. C. Johnson to Delilah Johnson, September 23, 1861, and April 10, 1863, MA83–19, Henry F. C. Johnson Civil War Letters, Texas/Dallas History & Archives Division, Dallas Public Library.

35. Boswell, *Her Act and Deed*, 102–5.

36. Randolph B. Campbell and Donald K. Pickens, "'My Dear Husband': A Texas Slave's Love Letter, 1862," *Journal of Negro History* 65 (Autumn 1980): 361–64 (quote on 363).

37. Philles Thomas, *Federal Writers' Project: Slave Narrative Project*, vol. 16, *Texas, Part 4, Sanco-Young* (Washington, DC: Library of Congress, 1941), https://www.loc.gov/item/mesn164, 77; Randolph B. Campbell, *An Empire for Slavery: The Peculiar Institution in Texas, 1821–1865* (Baton Rouge: Louisiana State University Press, 1989), 236–39.

38. Julia Francis Daniels, *Federal Writers' Project*, vol. 16, *Texas, Part 1*, 276; Boswell, *Her Act and Deed*, 89–91, 101–2.

39. Harriet Perry to Theophilus Perry, January 20, 1864, in Johansson, *Widows by the Thousand*, 200; Ruthe Winegarten, *Black Texas Women: 150 Years of Trial and Triumph* (Austin: University of Texas Press, 1995), 36.

40. Ella Washington, *Federal Writers' Project*, vol. 16, *Texas, Part 4*, 132–33; Campbell, *Empire for Slavery*, 243–46.

41. Judith Dykes-Hoffman, "German Texas Unionist Women on the Civil War Home Front," in Liles and Boswell, *Women in Civil War Texas*, 181–202; Ralph Wooster, *Civil War Texas: A History and a Guide* (Austin: Texas State Historical Association, 1999), 40–42.

42. "Mathilda Wagner," in Exley, *Texas Tears and Texas Sunshine*, 113–14. See also Dykes-Hoffman, "German Texas Unionist Women," 181–202.

43. Richard B. McCaslin, *Tainted Breeze: The Great Hanging at Gainesville, Texas, 1862* (Baton Rouge: Louisiana State University Press, 1994), 1, 7, 66–67 (quote), 74, 77, 83.

44. Thomas Barrett, "The Great Hanging at Gainesville, Cooke Co., Texas," program of the Texas Historical Association Sixty-Fifth Annual Meeting, Driskill Hotel, Austin, Texas, April 28 and 29, 1961, reprinted in Gallaway, *Texas: The Dark Corner of the Confederacy*, 120–21. See also Rebecca Sharpless, "'In Favor of Our Fathers' Country and Government': Unionist Women in North Texas," in Liles and Boswell, *Women in Civil War Texas*, 205–26.

45. Deborah M. Liles, "Not Your Typical Southern Belles: Women on the Western Frontier of Texas," in Liles and Boswell, *Women in Civil War Texas*, 259–81; Wooster, *Civil War Texas*, 47–48.

46. Phin W. Reynolds, "Chapters from the Frontier Life of Phin W. Reynolds," ed. J. R. Webb, *West Texas Historical Association Year Book* 21 (1945): 113–20, reprinted in Gallaway, *Texas: The Dark Corner of the Confederacy*, 230 (first quote); Sarah Harkey Hall, *Surviving on the Texas Frontier: The Journal of an Orphan Girl in San Saba County* (Austin, TX: Eakin Press, 1996), 17 (second quote); Wooster, *Civil War Texas*, 47–48.

47. Jerry D. Thompson, *Vaqueros in Blue and Gray* (Austin, TX: State House Press, 2000), xi–xii, 5–7.

48. Ibid., 6–7, 55–56 (quote); Teresa Palomo Acosta and Ruthe Winegarten, *Las Tejanas: 300 Years of History* (Austin: University of Texas Press, 2003), 57: Jerry Thompson and Elizabeth Mata, "Mexican Texan Women in the Civil War," in Liles and Boswell, *Women in Civil War Texas*, 151–79.

49. Mary Margaret McAllen Amberson, James A. McAllen, and Margaret H. McAllen, *I Would Rather Sleep in Texas: A History of the Lower Rio Grande Valley and the People of the Santa Anita Land Grant* (Austin: Texas State Historical Association, 2003), 179–80; Wooster, *Civil War Texas*, 50.

50. Miguel Gonzalez Quiroga, "Mexicanos in Texas during the Civil War," in *Mexican Americans in Texas History: Selected Essays*, eds. Emilio Zamora, Cynthia Orozco, and

Rodolfo Rocha (Austin: Texas State Historical Association, 2000), 56; Wooster, *Civil War Texas,* 50; Amberson, McAllen, and McAllen, *I Would Rather Sleep in Texas,* 231.

51. Quiroga, "Mexicanos in Texas during the Civil War," 56–61; Acosta and Winegarten, *Las Tejanas,* 57–58.

52. Thompson and Mata, "Mexican Texan Women in the Civil War," 157–58; Acosta and Winegarten, *Las Tejanas,* 58–59.

53. James Talmadge Moore, *Through Fire and Flood: The Catholic Church in Frontier Texas, 1836–1900* (College Station: Texas A&M University Press, 1992), 125, 130–37.

54. Jessica S. Brannon-Wranosky, "Southern Promise and Necessity: Texas, Regional Identity, and the National Woman Suffrage Movement, 1868–1920 (PhD diss., University of North Texas, 2010), 22–23, 24–30.

55. Ibid., 40–48.

56. Boswell, *Her Act and Deed,* 114–15.

57. Ibid., 109–11, 123–25.

58. Petition, Ellen Lacy vs. Beverly M. Lacy, September 7, 1865, Docket File No. 1813, Colorado County (Texas) District Court.

59. Millie Ann Smith, *Federal Writers' Project: Slave Narrative Project,* vol. 16, *Texas, Part 4, Sanco-Young,* 43; Campbell, *Empire for Slavery,* 244.

60. Pinkie Kelly, *Federal Writers' Project: Slave Narrative Project,* vol. 16, *Texas, Part 2,* 254.

61. Ibid.; James M. Smallwood and Barry A. Crouch, "Texas Freedwomen during Reconstruction, 1865–1874," in *Black Women in Texas History,* ed. Bruce A. Glasrud and Merline Pitre (College Station: Texas A&M University Press, 2008), 40–41; Winegarten, *Black Texas Women,* 42.

62. Winegarten, *Black Texas Women,* 43–45; Smallwood and Crouch, "Texas Freedwomen during Reconstruction," 61, 62.

63. Winegarten, *Black Texas Women,* 43–44; Linda K. Kerber, *No Constitutional Right to Be Ladies: Women and Obligations of Citizenship* (New York: Hill and Wang, 1998), 55–67.

64. Clarissa Scales, *Federal Writers' Project: Slave Narrative Project,* vol. 16, *Texas, Part 4,* 4; Smallwood and Crouch, "Texas Freedwomen during Reconstruction," 39, 43–47; Winegarten, *Black Texas Women,* 43–44; Rebecca A. Kosary, "'To Punish and Humiliate the Entire Community': White Violence Perpetrated against African-American Women in Texas, 1865–1868," in *Still the Arena of Civil War: Violence and Turmoil in Reconstruction Texas, 1865–1874,* ed. Kenneth W. Howell (Denton: University of North Texas Press, 2012), 327–51; Rebecca A. Czuchry, "In Defense of Their Families: African American Women, the Freedmen's Bureau, and Racial Violence during Reconstruction in Texas," in *Lone Star Unionism, Dissent and Resistance: Other Sides of Civil War Texas,* ed. Jesús F. de la Teja (Norman: University of Oklahoma Press, 2016).

65. Kosary, "To Punish and Humiliate the Entire Community," 337; Winegarten, *Black Texas Women,* 43–45; Boswell, *Her Act and Deed,* 112.

66. Smallwood and Crouch, "Texas Freedwomen during Reconstruction," 43–44, 48.

67. Ibid.; Winegarten, *Black Texas Women,* 42; Boswell, *Her Act and Deed,* 109.

68. Smallwood and Crouch, "Texas Freedwomen during Reconstruction," 61.

69. Smallwood and Crouch, "Texas Freedwomen during Reconstruction," 43, 47; Winegarten, *Black Texas Women*, 42.

70. Smallwood and Crouch, "Texas Freedwomen during Reconstruction," 43, 47, 61; Winegarten, *Black Texas Women*, 42.

Chapter 5

1. David La Vere, *Texas Indians* (College Station: Texas A&M University Press, 2004), 97–102, 150, 153–76.

2. Ibid., 150, 153–76, 177–80, 201.

3. Ibid., 84–92.

4. Ibid., 95–97, 181–84.

5. Paul H. Carlson, *The Plains Indians* (College Station: Texas A&M University Press, 1998), 81; La Vere, *Texas Indians*, 86, 191–93; Ferdinand Roemer, quoted in Carolyn Porter Norgaard, "Women A-horseback, Side or Astride," in *2001: A Texas Folklore Odyssey*, ed. Francis Edward Abernethy (Denton: University of North Texas Press, 2001), 176; Laura Jane Moore, "Lozen: An Apache Woman Warrior," in *Sifters: Native American Women's Lives*, ed. Theda Perdue (New York: Oxford University Press, 2001), 100–101.

6. Daniel J. Gelo and Scott Zesch, eds., "Every Day Seemed to Be a Holiday: The Captivity of Bianca Babb," *Southwestern Historical Quarterly* 117 (July 2003): 36–37; La Vere, *Texas Indians*, 182.

7. "Rachel Parker Plummer," in *Texas Tears and Texas Sunshine: Voices of Frontier Women*, ed. Jo Ella Powell Exley (College Station: Texas A&M University Press, 1985), 75–88 (quote on 80).

8. Jo Ella Powell Exley, *Frontier Blood: The Saga of the Parker Family* (College Station: Texas A&M University Press, 2001).

9. Gelo and Zesch, eds., "Every Day Seemed to Be a Holiday," 39–41, 44.

10. La Vere, *Texas Indians*, 180 (quote), 196.

11. Teresa Griffin Viele, *Following the Drum: A Glimpse of Frontier Life* (Lincoln: University of Nebraska Press, 1984), 3, 106 (quote).

12. Shirley Anne Leckie, ed. *The Colonel's Lady on the Western Frontier: The Correspondence of Alice Kirk Grierson* (Lincoln: University of Nebraska Press, 1989), 5; Viele, *Following the Drum*, 137, 140.

13. Ibid., 5, 96.

14. Viele, *Following the Drum*, 13; Leckie, *Colonel's Lady*, 119 (second quote).

15. Leckie, *Colonel's Lady*, 124.

16. Ibid., 77, 81, 85–86, 96.

17. "Luvenia Conway Roberts," in Exley, *Texas Tears and Texas Sunshine*, 193–208 (first quote, 194; second quote, 197).

18. Leckie, *Colonel's Lady*, 106.

19. Elizabeth Maret, *Women of the Range: Women's Roles in the Texas Beef Cattle Industry* (College Station: Texas A&M University Press, 1993), 31; Georgellen Burnett, *We Just Toughed It Out: Women in the Llano Estacado* (El Paso: Texas Western Press, 1990), 13.

20. "Ella Elgar Bird Dumont," in Exley, *Texas Tears and Texas Sunshine*, 210 (first quote), 214–18 (second quote on 218).

21. Ibid., 213–14, 218; James I. Fenton, "Critters, Sourdough, and Dugouts: Women and Imitation Theory on the Staked Plains, 1875–1910," in *At Home on the Range: Essays on the History of Western Social and Domestic Life*, ed. John R. Wunder (Westport, CT: Greenwood Press, 1985), 24 (quote), 27; E. W. Black, *A Pioneer Texas Family Follows Free Grazing* (New York: Carlton Press, 1967), 9. See also Sandra L. Myres, *Westering Women and the Frontier Experience, 1800–1915* (Albuquerque: University of New Mexico Press, 1982), 167–212.

22. Paula Mitchell Marks, "Trials, Tribulations, and Good Times: Westering Women in Frontier Texas, 1821–1870," in *Invisible Texans: Women and Minorities in Texas History*, ed. Donald Willett and Stephen Curley (New York: McGraw-Hill, 2005), 83; Burnett, *We Just Toughed It Out*, 15, 17; Paula Mitchell Marks, introduction to Sarah Harkey Hall, *Surviving on the Texas Frontier: The Journal of a Frontier Orphan Girl in San Saba County, 1852–1907* (Fort Worth: Eakin Press, 1996), xvii.

23. Nellie M. Perry, *Woman of the Plains: The Journals and Stories of Nellie M. Perry*, ed. Sandra Gail Teichmann (College Station: Texas A&M University Press, 2000), 17–19 (quote on 19).

24. Vera Norwood, "Crazy-Quilt Lives: Frontier Sources for Southwestern Women's Literature," in *The Desert Is No Lady: Southwestern Landscapes in Women's Writing and Art*, ed. Vera Norwood and Janice Monk (New Haven, CT: Yale University Press, 1987), 86; Burnett, *We Just Toughed It Out*, 12. See also Myres, *Westering Women and the Frontier*, 12–36.

25. "Ella Elgar Bird Dumont," in Exley, *Texas Tears and Texas Sunshine*, 212; Burnett, *We Just Toughed It Out*, 16. See also Myres, *Westering Women and the Frontier*, 141–66.

26. Perry, *Woman of the Plains*, 19.

27. Ibid., 20, 22 (first quote), 27 (second quote).

28. "Ella Elgar Bird Dumont," in Exley, *Texas Tears and Texas Sunshine*, 221 (second quote); Perry, *Woman of the Plains*, 24 (third and fourth quote), 41 (first quote); Fenton, "Critters, Sourdough, and Dugouts," 30.

29. Perry, *Woman of the Plains*, 28, 39, 40; Mary J. Jaques, *Texas Ranch Life, with Three Months through Mexico in a "Prairie Schooner"* (College Station: Texas A&M University, 1989), 79.

30. Marks, introduction to Sarah Harkey Hall, *Surviving on the Texas Frontier*, xv (first quote); "Ella Elgar Bird Dumont," in Exley, *Texas Tears and Texas Sunshine*, 216 (second quote), 213 (third quote).

31. Perry, *Woman of the Plains*, 39, 45, 46.

32. "Ella Elgar Bird Dumont," in Exley, *Texas Tears and Texas Sunshine*, 218.

33. Dan Kilgore, "Two Sixshooters and a Sunbonnet: The Story of Sally Skull," in *Legendary Ladies of Texas*, ed. Francis Edward Abernethy (Denton: University of North Texas Press, 1994); Sandra L. Myres, introduction to Mary Kidder Rak, *A Cowman's Wife* (Austin: Texas State Historical Association Press, 1993), xii; Joyce Gibson Roach, "Introduction: Cowgirls and Cattle Queens," in *Texas Women on the Cattle Trails*, ed. Sara R. Massey (College Station: Texas A&M University Press, 2006), 18; Judy E. Sneller, "Saints, Hell-Raisers, and Other 'Typical Texans': Frontier Women and the Humor of Mollie Moore Davis," *Journal of the American Studies Association of Texas* 25 (October 1994): 16.

34. Jacqueline S. Reinier, "Concepts of Domesticity on the Southern Plains Agricultural Frontier, 1870–1920," in Wunder, *At Home on the Range*, 67; Sneller, "Saints, Hell-Raisers, and Other 'Typical Texans,'" 27; Roach, "Introduction: Cowgirls and Cattle Queens," 18; Perry, *Woman of the Plains*, 43.

35. Fenton, "Critters, Sourdough, and Dugouts," 29; Perry, *Woman of the Plains*, 39.

36. Burnett, *We Just Toughed It Out*, 16.

37. Black, *Pioneer Texas Family Follows Free Grazing*, 80; "Ella Elgar Bird Dumont," in Exley, *Texas Tears and Texas Sunshine*, 220; Burnett, *We Just Toughed It Out*, 22, 60; Fenton, "Critters, Sourdough, and Dugouts," 28; Myres, introduction to Rak, *Cowman's Wife*, xvi.

38. Perry, *Woman of the Plains*, 21, 34, 39, 45.

39. Fenton, "Critters, Sourdough, and Dugouts," 28–29, 32–33.

40. Marks, introduction to Hall, *Surviving on the Texas Frontier*, xvi; Paula Mitchell Marks, *Hands to the Spindle: Texas Women and Home Textile Production, 1822–1880* (College Station: Texas A&M University Press, 1996), 92; Burnett, *We Just Toughed It Out*, 34 (first quote); Jaques, *Texas Ranch Life*, 66 (second quote).

41. Marks, *Hands to the Spindle*, 92; Burnett, *We Just Toughed It Out*, 16.

42. Burnett, *We Just Toughed It Out*, 32–33.

43. Ibid., 34, 38; Fenton, "Critters, Sourdough, and Dugouts," 31.

44. Roach, "Cowgirls and Cattle Queens," 18; Burnett, *We Just Toughed It Out*, 9; Norgaard, "Women A-horseback," 173 (second quote), 174 (first quote), 178; "Ella Elgar Bird Dumont," in Exley, *Texas Tears, Texas Sunshine*, 224.

45. Patricia A. Dunn and Sara R. Massey, "Catherine (Kate) Malone Medlin," in Massey, *Texas Women on the Cattle Trails*, 25–27; Phyllis A. McKenzie, "Margaret Heffernan Dunbar Hardy Borland," in ibid., 89; and Harriet L. Bishop and Laurie Gudzikowski, "Ellen Viola Perry Wilson Anderson," in ibid., 213–14.

46. Burnett, *We Just Toughed It Out*, 18–20; Lois E. Myers, *Letters by Lamplight: A Woman's View of Everyday Life in South Texas, 1873–1883* (Waco, TX: Baylor University Press, 1991), 172; Perry, *Woman of the Plains*, 42; Florence C. Gould and Patricia N. Pando, *Claiming Their Land: Women Homesteaders in Texas* (El Paso: Texas Western Press, 1991), iii, 8, 26–27, 36–37; Maret, *Women of the Range*, 33.

47. Jovita González, *Life along the Border: A Landmark Tejana Thesis* (College Station: Texas A&M University Press, 2006), 77.

48. Jane Clements Monday and Betty Bailey Colley, *Voices from the Wild Horse Desert: The Vaquero Families of the King and Kenedy Ranches* (Austin: University of Texas Press, 1997), xix; Jane Clements Monday and Frances Brannen Vick, *Petra's Legacy: The South Texas Ranching Empire of Petra Vela and Mifflin Kenedy* (College Station: Texas A&M University Press, 2007), 57; David Montejano, *Anglos and Mexicans in the Making of Texas, 1836–1986* (Austin: University of Texas Press, 1987), 80.

49. Arnoldo De León, *Mexican Americans in Texas: A Brief History*, second ed. (Wheeling, IL: Harlan Davidson, 1999), 45, 54.

50. González, *Life along the Border*, 78 (quote); Margaret Maud McKellar, *Life on a Mexican Ranch* (Cranbury, NJ: Associated University Presses, 1994), 41, 50.

51. Monday and Colley, *Voices from the Wild Horse Desert*, 131–33; González, *Life along the Border*, 77; McKellar, *Life on a Mexican Ranch*, 47; Jaques, *Texas Ranch Life*,

61; Andrés Sáenz, *Early Tejano Ranching: Daily Life at Ranchos San José and El Fresnillo* (College Station: Texas A&M University Press, 2001), 57.

52. Jaques, *Texas Ranch Life*, 41–42; Sáenz, *Early Tejano Ranching*, 57; Monday and Colley, *Voices from the Wild Horse Desert*, 106 (quote), 130–31; Roberto M. Villarreal, "The Mexican-American Vaqueros of the Kenedy Ranch: A Social History" (master's thesis, Texas A&M University, 1972), 53–54.

53. Monday and Colley, *Voices from the Wild Horse Desert*, 130–31; Sáenz, *Early Tejano Ranching*, 57.

54. Teresa Palomo Acosta and Ruthe Winegarten, *Las Tejanas: 300 Years of History* (Austin: University of Texas Press, 2003), 63; Jaques, *Texas Ranch Life*, 63.

55. Monday and Vick, *Petra's Legacy*, 194, 261, 268.

56. González, *Life along the Border*, 70, 80, 88–90 (quotes); De León, *Mexican Americans in Texas*, 61–62; Villarreal, "The Mexican-American Vaqueros," 55.

57. Monday and Colley, *Voices from the Wild Horse Desert*, 138 (quote); González, *Life along the Border*, 78, 85; McKellar, *Life on a Mexican Ranch*, 90–91; Rodolfo Rocha, "Early Ranching along the Rio Grande," in Wunder, *At Home on the Range*, 12; Monday and Vick, *Petra's Legacy*, 3, 161, 219; De León, *Mexican Americans in Texas*, 61–62.

58. De León, *Mexican Americans in Texas*, 62; Acosta and Winegarten, *Las Tejanas*, 63; Roach, "Cowgirls and Cattle Queens," 13–14 (quote).

59. Mary Margaret McAllen Amberson, James A. McAllen, and Margaret H. McAllen, *I Would Rather Sleep in Texas: A History of the Lower Rio Grande Valley and the People of the Santa Anita Land Grant* (Austin: Texas State Historical Association, 2003), 176; Maret, *Women of the Range*, 26; Acosta and Winegarten, *Las Tejanas*, 62; Monday and Vick, *Petra's Legacy*, 179.

Chapter 6

1. A. Harriette Andreadis, "The Woman's Commonwealth: A Study in the Coalescence of Social Forms," *Frontiers: A Journal of Women Studies* 7, no. 3 (1984): 79–86; Jayme A. Sokolow and Mary Ann Lamanna, "Women and Utopia: The Woman's Commonwealth of Belton, Texas," *Southwestern Historical Quarterly* (April 1984): 371–92; Sally L. Kitch, *This Strange Society of Women: Reading the Letters and Lives of the Woman's Commonwealth* (Columbus: Ohio State University Press, 1993).

2. Andreadis, "Woman's Commonwealth," 79–80.

3. Judith N. McArthur, *Creating the New Woman: The Rise of Southern Women's Progressive Culture in Texas, 1893–1918* (Urbana: University of Illinois Press, 1998), 16; James D. Ivy, *No Saloon in the Valley: The Southern Strategy of Texas Prohibitionists in the 1880s* (Waco, TX: Baylor University Press, 2003), 19–23.

4. *Texas Baptist* quoted in Ivy, *No Saloon in the Valley*, 21. See also ibid., 19–23, 48–51.

5. Ibid., 48–51, 103–20.

6. Ibid.; McArthur, *Creating the New Woman*, 8; Jessica Brannon-Wranosky, "Southern Promise and Necessity: Texas, Regional Identity, and the National Woman Suffrage Movement, 1868–1920 (PhD diss., University of North Texas, 2010), 81–82.

7. Elizabeth Hayes Turner, *Women, Culture, and Community: Religion and Reform in Galveston, 1880–1920* (New York: Oxford University Press, 1997), 78.

8. Linda L. Black, "Female Community Leaders in Houston, Texas: A Study of the Education of Ima Hogg and Christia Daniels Adair" (PhD diss., Texas A&M University, 2008), 161–62 (quotes); Turner, *Women, Culture, and Community*, 121–50.

9. Turner, *Women, Culture, and Community*, 82, 83, 85, 121–50.

10. Ibid., 42.

11. Ibid., 41–43.

12. Marion K. Barthelme, *Women in the Texas Populist Movement: Letters to the* Southern Mercury (College Station: Texas A&M University Press, 1997), 10; Charles Postel, *The Populist Vision* (New York: Oxford University Press, 2007).

13. Barthelme, *Women in the Texas Populist Movement*, 11 (quote); Jennifer J. Bess, "Equal Rights for All and Special Privileges for None: Women's Participation in the Farmers' Alliance of Texas" (master's thesis, University of Houston, 1998), 70.

14. Barthelme, *Women in the Texas Populist Movement*, 4, 12, 18–19; Bess, "Equal Rights for All," 32, 79–80.

15. Bess, "Equal Rights for All," 18, 32–33, 75–76, 78, 80.

16. Ruthe Winegarten, *Black Texas Women: 150 Years of Trial and Triumph* (Austin: University of Texas Press, 1995), 76.

17. Barthelme, *Women in the Texas Populist Movement*, 14 (quote), 23–24, 25–27, 35, 40, 44–48; Postel, *Populist Vision*, 69–101.

18. Barthelme, *Women in the Texas Populist Movement*, 45–59, 66 (quote on 46); Ruth Hosey Karbach, "Ellen Lawson Dabbs: Waving the Equal Rights Banner," in *Texas Women: Their Histories, Their Lives*, ed. Elizabeth Hayes Turner, Stephanie Cole, and Rebecca Sharpless (Athens: University of Georgia Press, 2015), 185; Postel, *Populist Vision*, 69–101.

19. Megan Seaholm, "Earnest Women: The White Woman's Club Movement in Progressive Era Texas, 1880–1920" (PhD diss., Rice University, 1988), 200, 208, 215.

20. Turner, *Women, Culture, and Community*, 156–158; Seaholm, "Earnest Women," 213; Stella L. Christian, ed., *The History of the Texas Federation of Women's Clubs* (Houston: Dealey-Adey-Elgin, 1919), 12.

21. McArthur, *Creating the New Woman*, 12–15.

22. Ibid.; Seaholm, "Earnest Women," 213.

23. Randolph B. Campbell, *Gone to Texas: A History of the Lone Star State* (New York: Oxford University Press, 2003), 309; Turner, *Women, Culture, and Community*, 151–53.

24. Virginia Bernhard, *Ima Hogg: The Governor's Daughter* (Austin: Texas Monthly Press, 1984); Kate Sayen Kirkland, *The Hogg Family and Houston: Philanthropy and the Civic Ideal* (Austin: University of Texas Press, 2009); Turner, *Women, Culture, and Community*, 153.

25. Mrs. Frank Tompkins, "Is the Club Woman a Better Mother and Homemaker?" *Club Monthly* 1, no. 8 (1898): 32, quoted in Seaholm, "Earnest Women," 219. See also Seaholm, "Earnest Women," 24, 209, 215, 218, 230–31; McArthur, *Creating the New Woman*, 31–53; Turner, *Women, Culture, and Community*, 153.

26. Seaholm, "Earnest Women," 217–42 (quote on 226).

27. McArthur, *Creating the New Woman*, 76–96; Seaholm, "Earnest Women," 217, 244.

28. McArthur, *Creating the New Woman*, 54–55, 58, 76–78; Turner, *Women, Culture, and Community*, 160.

29. McArthur, *Creating the New Woman*, 18–20.

30. Turner, *Women, Culture, and Community*, 153, 187–227; McArthur, *Creating the New Woman*, 14, 33, 42, 45–52; Jacquelyn Masur McElhaney, *Pauline Periwinkle and Progressive Reform in Dallas* (College Station: Texas A&M University Press, 1998), xvi.

31. Turner, *Women, Culture, and Community*, 198; McArthur, *Creating the New Woman*, 33, 45–52, 61–64.

32. McArthur, *Creating the New Woman*, 101–4.

33. McElhaney, *Pauline Periwinkle and Progressive Reform*, xv–xvi.

34. Kelley M. King, *Call Her a Citizen: Progressive-Era Activist and Educator Anna Pennybacker* (College Station: Texas A&M University Press, 2010), 71–126; McArthur, *Creating the New Woman*, 21–30 (quote on 28).

35. King, *Call Her a Citizen*, 87–95.

36. Alwyn Barr, *Black Texans: A History of African Americans in Texas, 1528–1995*, 2nd ed. (Norman: University of Oklahoma Press, 1996), 167; Bernadette Pruitt, *The Other Great Migration: The Movement of Rural African Americans to Houston, 1900–1941* (College Station: Texas A&M University Press, 2013), 102–5; Winegarten, *Black Texas Women*, 187–93; Turner, *Women, Culture, and Community*, 153; McArthur, *Creating the New Woman*, 16–17.

37. Black, "Female Community Leaders in Houston, Texas," 168.

38. Audrey Crawford, "'To protect, to feed, and to give momentum to every effort': African American Clubwomen in Houston, 1880–1910," *Houston Review* 1 (Fall 2003): 15–16; Pruitt, *Other Great Migration*, 108; McArthur, *Creating the New Woman*, 17–18; Turner, *Women, Culture, and Community*, 256.

39. Crawford, "To protect, to feed," 21; McArthur, *Creating the New Woman*, 89–90.

40. Turner, *Women, Culture, and Community*, 252–56; Pruitt, *Other Great Migration*, 101–10.

41. Pruitt, *Other Great Migration*, 101–10; Rebecca Sharpless, "'Us Has Ever Lived De Useful Life': African American Women in Texas, 1874–1900," in *Black Women in Texas History*, ed. Bruce A. Glasrud and Merline Pitre (College Station: Texas A&M University Press, 2008), 89–92; Turner, *Women, Culture, and Community*, 255–56.

42. Clara Lomas, *The Rebel: Leonor Villegas de Magnón* (Houston: Arte Público Press, 1994), xiii; Cynthia E. Orozco, "Beyond Machismo: La Familia, and Ladies Auxiliaries," *Renato Rosaldo Lecture Series* 10 (1994), 39.

43. Roberto R. Calderón, "Unión, Paz y Trabajo: Laredo's Mexican Mutual Aid Societies, 1890s," in *Mexican Americans in Texas History: Selected Essays*, ed. Emilio Zamora, Cynthia Orozco, and Rodolfo Rocha (Austin: Texas State Historical Association, 2000), 66.

44. Calderón, "Unión, Paz y Trabajo," 72–73; Teresa Palomo Acosta and Ruthe Winegarten, *Las Tejanas: 300 Years of History* (Austin: University of Texas Press, 2003), 209–13.

45. Calderón, "Unión, Paz y Trabajo," 72–73; Acosta and Winegarten, *Las Tejanas*, 209–11.

46. Acosta and Winegarten, *Las Tejanas*, 211–13; Orozco, "Beyond Machismo," 39, 50.

47. Julie Leininger Pycior, "Tejanas Navigating the 1920s," in *Tejano Epic: Essays in Honor of Félix D. Almaráz, Jr.,* ed. Arnoldo De León (Austin: Texas State Historical Association, 2005), 80–81.

48. Lomas, *Rebel,* xiii–xvii; Gabriela González, "Jovita Idar: The Ideological Origins of a Transnational Advocate for *la Raza,*" in Turner, Cole, and Sharpless, *Texas Women: Their Histories, Their Lives,* 225–48.

49. Turner, *Women, Culture, and Community,* 165–66.

50. Ibid., 168–69.

51. Kelly McMichael Stott, "From Lost Cause to Female Empowerment: The Texas Division of the United Daughters of the Confederacy, 1896–1966 " (PhD diss., University of North Texas, 2001), 201.

52. Turner, *Women, Culture, and Community,* 169–74; L. Robert Ables, "The Second Battle for the Alamo," *Southwestern Historical Quarterly* 70 (January 1967): 372–413.

53. Turner, *Women, Culture, and Community,* 165–84; Gregg Cantrell, "The Bones of Stephen F. Austin: History and Memory in Progressive Era Texas," in *Lone Star Pasts: Memory and History in Texas,* ed. Gregg Cantrell and Elizabeth Hayes Turner (College Station: Texas A&M University Press, 2007), 56–65; Kelly McMichael, "'Memories Are Short but Monuments Lengthen Remembrances': The United Daughters of the Confederacy and the Power of Civil War Memory," in Cantrell and Turner, *Lone Star Pasts,* 95–118.

54. Nancy Baker Jones, "Making Texas *Our* Texas: The Emergence of Texas Women's History, 1976–1990," *Southwestern Historical Quarterly* 120 (January 2017): 286–87; Brannon-Wranosky, "Southern Promise and Necessity," 49, 57, 62–64, 75–76, 80, 83.

55. Brannon-Wranosky, "Southern Promise and Necessity," 90, 99–100, 108, 121, 133–34; McArthur, *Creating the New Woman,* 98; A. Elizabeth Taylor, "The Woman Suffrage Movement in Texas," *Journal of Southern History* 17 (May 1951): 201.

56. Brannon-Wranosky, "Southern Promise and Necessity," 140–44, 166 (quote); Taylor, "Woman Suffrage Movement in Texas," 202.

57. Brannon-Wranosky, "Southern Promise and Necessity," 145–76.

58. Elizabeth Hayes Turner, "'White-Gloved Ladies' and 'New Women' in the Texas Woman Suffrage Movement," in *Southern Women: Histories and Identities,* ed. Virginia Bernhard, Betty Brandon, Elizabeth Fox-Genovese, and Theda Perdue (Columbia: University of Missouri Press, 1992), 129–56; Judith N. McArthur and Harold L. Smith, *Minnie Fisher Cunningham: A Suffragist's Life in Politics* (New York: Oxford University Press, 2003), 30, 37–39; McArthur, *Creating the New Woman,* 91–109; Brannon-Wranosky, "Southern Promise and Necessity," 157, 164.

59. Quoted in McArthur and Smith, *Minnie Fisher Cunningham,* 30; McArthur, *Creating the New Woman,* 105–7; Brannon-Wranosky, "Southern Promise and Necessity," 157, 164.

60. Judith N. McArthur, "Minnie Fisher Cunningham's Back Door Lobby in Texas: Political Maneuvering in a One-Party State," in *One Woman, One Vote: Rediscovering the Woman Suffrage Movement,* ed. Marjorie Spruill Wheeler (Troutdale, OR: NewSage Press, 1995), 315–31; Jessica Brannon-Wranosky and Bruce A. Glassrud, eds., *Impeached: The Removal of Texas Governor James E. Ferguson* (College Station: Texas A&M University

Press, 2017); McArthur, *Creating the New Woman*, 137–40; Brannon-Wranosky, "Southern Promise and Necessity," 196–206.

61. McArthur and Smith, *Minnie Fisher Cunningham*, 64–65; Brannon-Wranosky, "Southern Promise and Necessity," 206–11; Taylor, "Woman Suffrage Movement in Texas," 211.

62. McArthur and Smith, *Minnie Fisher Cunningham*, 74–83; Brannon-Wranosky, "Southern Promise and Necessity," 226–27, 230.

63. Brannon-Wranosky, "Southern Promise and Necessity," 233 (quote); Taylor, "Woman Suffrage Movement in Texas," 214–15; McArthur and Smith, *Minnie Fisher Cunningham*, 83–84.

64. McArthur and Smith, *Minnie Fisher Cunningham*, 68–88.

65. Cary D. Wintz, "Women in Texas," in *The Texas Heritage*, ed. Ben Procter and Archie P. McDonald (Wheeling, IL: Harlan Davidson, 1998), 202; Debbie Mauldin Cottrell, *Pioneer Woman Educator: The Progressive Spirit of Annie Webb Blanton* (College Station: Texas A&M University Press, 1993), 42–63; Nancy Baker Jones and Ruthe Winegarten, *Capitol Women: Texas Female Legislators, 1923–1999* (Austin: University of Texas Press, 2000), 77.

66. McArthur and Smith, *Minnie Fisher Cunningham*; Shelley Sallee, "'The Woman of It': Governor Miriam Ferguson's 1924 Election," *Southwestern Historical Quarterly* 100 (July 1996): 1–16; Carol O'Keefe Wilson, *In the Governor's Shadow: The True Story of Ma and Pa Ferguson* (Denton: University of North Texas Press, 2014).

67. McArthur and Smith, *Minnie Fisher Cunningham*; Cottrell, *Pioneer Woman Educator*, 42–63.

68. Jacquelyn Dowd Hall, *Revolt against Chivalry: Jessie Daniel Ames and the Women's Campaign against Lynching* (New York: Columbia University Press, 1993); McArthur and Smith, *Minnie Fisher Cunningham*; Sallee, "The Woman of It," 1–16.

69. Hall, *Revolt against Chivalry*; Norman D. Brown, *Hood, Bonnet, and Little Brown Jug: Texas Politics, 1921–1928* (College Station: Texas A&M University Press, 1984), 157.

70. Emma Louise Moyer Jackson, "Petticoat Politics: Political Activism among Texas Women in the 1920s" (PhD diss., University of Texas, 1980), 233–34, 517–22.

71. Ibid.

72. Paul M. Lucko, "The 'Next "Big Job"': Women Prison Reformers in Texas, 1918–1930," in *Women and Texas History: Selected Essays*, ed. Fane Downs and Nancy Baker Jones (Austin: Texas State Historical Association, 1993), 72–87.

73. Judith N. McArthur, "Maternity Wars: Gender, Race, and the Sheppard-Towner Act in Texas," in Turner, Cole, and Sharpless, *Texas Women*, 249–76; Judith N. McArthur and Harold L. Smith, *Texas through Women's Eyes: The Twentieth-Century Experience* (Austin: University of Texas Press, 2010), 70–71.

74. Jackson, "Petticoat Politics," 1–20.

75. McArthur and Smith, *Texas through Women's Eyes*, 69; Jackson, "Petticoat Politics," 598–601.

76. McArthur and Smith, *Texas through Women's Eyes*, 1–2.

77. Raye Virginia Allen, "An Image-Maker from Texas: Gordon Conway and a New Look for a New Woman," *Southwestern Historical Quarterly* 101 (July 1997): 17–57.

78. Jesús F. de la Teja, Paula Marks, and Ron Tyler, *Texas: Crossroads of North America* (Boston: Houghton Mifflin, 2004), 351–52; Pycior, "Tejanas Navigating the 1920s," 81.

79. Rebecca Sharpless, *Fertile Ground, Narrow Choices: Women on Texas Cotton Farms, 1900–1940* (Chapel Hill: University of North Carolina Press, 1999), 221–23.

Chapter 7

1. Randolph B. Campbell, *Gone to Texas: A History of the Lone Star State* (New York: Oxford University Press, 2003), 311–12, 348–49.

2. Neil Foley, *The White Scourge: Mexicans, Blacks, and Poor Whites in Texas Cotton Culture* (Berkeley: University of California Press, 1997), 145 (quote); Rebecca Sharpless, *Fertile Ground, Narrow Choices: Women on Texas Cotton Farms, 1900–1940* (Chapel Hill: University of North Carolina Press, 1999), 2.

3. Margaret Hunt Caroll in *Harder than Hardscrabble: Oral Recollections of the Farming Life from the Edge of the Texas Hill Country*, ed. Thad Sitton, (Austin: University of Texas Press, 2003), 76–77, brackets in original; Sharpless, *Fertile Ground*, 70.

4. Quoted in Patsy Cravens, *Leavin' a Testimony: Portraits from Rural Texas* (Austin: University of Texas Press, 2006), 19.

5. Margaret Bert Wilhite Bounds, in Sitton, *Harder than Hardscrabble*, 78–79; Foley, *White Scourge*, 143–44.

6. Sharpless, *Fertile Ground*, 112–19.

7. Sharpless, *Fertile Ground*, 87–89, 113–16, 121; Teresa Palomo Acosta and Ruthe Winegarten, *Las Tejanas: 300 Years of History* (Austin: University of Texas Press, 2003), 95–96; Bounds, in Sitton, *Harder than Hardscrabble*, 38.

8. Sharpless, *Fertile Ground*, 87–89, 113–16, 121; Bounds, in Sitton, *Harder than Hardscrabble*, 38–39 (first quote); Clyde quoted in Robert A. Caro, *The Years of Lyndon Johnson: The Path to Power* (New York: Alfred A. Knopf, 1982), 507–8.

9. Bernice Weir quoted in Sharpless, *Fertile Ground*, 96; Elizabeth York Enstam, *Women and the Creation of Urban Life, Dallas, Texas, 1843–1920* (College Station: Texas A&M University Press, 1998), 91–92. See also Sharpless, *Fertile Ground*, 97–99.

10. Sharpless, *Fertile Ground*, 80–81, 88–89, 96–101.

11. Sharpless, *Fertile Ground*, 95, 102–6; Enstam, *Women and the Creation of Urban Life*, 93.

12. Sharpless, *Fertile Ground*, 90–95; 102–3; Caro, *Years of Lyndon Johnson*, 504–05.

13. Sharpless, *Fertile Ground*, 90–95, 102–6; Gladys Merle Keener Chastain in Sitton, *Harder than Hardscrabble*, 34; Mary Cox, in Caro, *Years of Lyndon Johnson*, 510.

14. Ernest Allen Cole, in Sitton, *Harder than Hardscrabble*, 39.

15. Sharpless, *Fertile Ground*, 128; Judith N. McArthur and Harold L. Smith, *Texas through Women's Eyes: The Twentieth-Century Experience* (Austin: University of Texas Press, 2010), 64–65; Debra A. Reid, *Reaping a Greater Harvest: African Americans, the Extension Service, and Rural Reform in Jim Crow Texas* (College Station: Texas A&M University Press, 2007), xxiv, 18.

16. Reid, *Reaping a Greater Harvest*, 18, 22, 23, 31.

17. Ibid., 41, 66–67, 75, 137.

18. Ibid., 33, 47, 108–9.

19. Ruthe Winegarten, *Black Texas Women: 150 Years of Trial and Triumph* (Austin: University of Texas Press, 1995), 156.

20. Campbell, *Gone to Texas*, 328; Acosta and Winegarten, *Las Tejanas*, 97–99; Sharpless, *Fertile Ground*, 76–77, 88, 155; David Montejano, *Anglos and Mexicans in the Making of Texas, 1836–1986* (Austin: University of Texas Press, 1987), 175–77.

21. Elizabeth Maret, *Women of the Range: Women's Roles in the Texas Beef Cattle Industry* (College Station: Texas A&M University Press, 1993), 27–31; Acosta and Winegarten, *Las Tejanas*, 97; Ruthe Winegarten, *From Ranchers to Reformers: South Texas Women in Texas History*, South Texas Studies (Victoria, TX: Victoria College Press, 1998), 79.

22. Diana Davids Olien, "Domesticity and the Texas Oil Fields: Dimensions of Women's Experience, 1920–1950," in *Women and Texas History: Selected Essays*, ed. Fane Downs and Nancy Baker Jones (Austin: Texas State Historical Association, 1993), 116–26 (first quote on 120; second quote on 122); Bobby D. Weaver, *Oilfield Trash: Life and Labor in the Oil Patch* (College Station: Texas A&M University Press, 2010), 87.

23. Enstam, *Women and the Creation of Urban Life*, 91–92.

24. Ibid., 90–95.

25. Ibid., 75–76; Fane Downs, "Texas Women at Work," in *Texas: A Sesquicentennial Celebration*, ed. Donald W. Whisenhunt (Austin, TX: Eakin Press, 1984), 318–19.

26. Enstam, *Women and the Creation of Urban Life*, 75–78; Downs, "Texas Women at Work," 321.

27. Downs, "Texas Women at Work," 321; Enstam, *Women and the Creation of Urban Life*, 84.

28. Bernadette Pruitt, "'For the Advancement of the Race': The Great Migrations to Houston, Texas, 1914–1941," *Journal of Urban History* 31 (May 2005): 458; Bernadette Pruitt, *The Other Great Migration: The Movement of Rural African Americans to Houston, 1900–1941* (College Station: Texas A&M University Press, 2013), 213–39.

29. Pruitt, "For the Advancement of the Race," 457–59; Enstam, *Women and the Creation of Urban Life*, 80.

30. Mario T. García, *Desert Immigrants: The Mexicans of El Paso, 1880–1920* (New Haven: Yale University Press, 1982), 75–79; Pruitt, "For the Advancement of the Race," 457; Irene Ledesma, "Unlikely Strikers: Mexican-American Women in Strike Activity in Texas, 1919–1974" (PhD diss., Ohio State University, 1992), 33–40, 60–63, 68, 83–84, 86, 91.

31. Alan W. Garrett, "Teacher Education," *Handbook of Texas Online,* http://www.tshaonline.org/handbook/online/articles/kdtsj.

32. Gladys Peterson Meyers, in Diane Manning, *Hill Country Teacher: Oral Histories from the One-Room School and Beyond* (Boston: Twayne, 1990), 73.

33. Elizabeth Stroud Shelton, in Manning, *Hill Country Teacher*, 90.

34. US Census, 1900; Downs, "Texas Women at Work," 320.

35. Debbie Mauldin Cottrell, *Pioneer Woman Educator: The Progressive Spirit of Annie Webb Blanton* (College Station: Texas A&M University Press, 1993), 12; Knowles Witcher Teel in Manning, *Hill Country Teacher*, 35.

36. Manning, *Hill Country Teacher*, 5, 133.

37. Ibid., 36.

38. Ibid., xviii–xix.

39. Cottrell, *Pioneer Woman Educator*, 12–13, 18–22.

40. Pruitt, "For the Advancement of the Race," 459.

41. Downs, "Texas Women at Work," 320–21; James Talmadge Moore, *Through Fire and Flood: The Catholic Church in Frontier Texas, 1836–1900* (College Station: Texas A&M University Press, 1992), 153, 162; Chester R. Burns, "Health and Medicine," *Handbook of Texas Online*, http://www.tshaonline.org/handbook/online/articles/smhzc; Kevin B. Park, "St. Joseph Hospital," *Handbook of Texas Online*, http://www.tshaonline.org/handbook/online/articles/sbs10; Eleanor L. M. Crowder, "Nursing Education," *Handbook of Texas Online*, http://www.tshaonline.org/handbook/online/articles/shn01; Rebecca Sharpless, "'Us Has Ever Lived de Useful Life': African American Women in Texas, 1874–1900," in *Black Women in Texas History*, ed. Bruce A. Glasrud and Merline Pitre (College Station: Texas A&M University Press, 2008), 82–83; Winegarten, *Black Texas Women*, 159–62.

42. Cheryl Ellis Vaiani, "Galveston's Midwives in the Early Twentieth Century," *Houston Review* 19, no. 1 (1997): 39–41; Megan Seaholm, "Midwifery," *Handbook of Texas Online*, http://www.tshaonline.org/handbook/online/articles/sim02.

43. Downs, "Texas Women at Work," 320–21; Elizabeth Hayes Turner, *Women, Culture, and Community: Religion and Reform in Galveston, 1880–1920* (New York: Oxford University Press, 1997), 253–54; Ruth Hosey Karbach, "Ellen Lawson Dabbs: Waving the Equal Rights Banner," in *Texas Women: Their Histories, Their Lives*, ed. Elizabeth Hayes Turner, Stephanie Cole, and Rebecca Sharpless (Athens: University of Georgia Press, 2015), 181–82; Elizabeth Silverthorne, "Potter, Claudia," *Handbook of Texas Online*, http://www.tshaonline.org/handbook/online/articles/fpoeq; Elizabeth Silverthorne, "Herzog, Sofie Dalia," *Handbook of Texas Online*, http://www.tshaonline.org/handbook/online/articles/fheec; Cheryl Ellis Vaiani, "Women and Health," *Handbook of Texas Online*, http://www.tshaonline.org/handbook/online/articles/smwbn.

44. Emily Fourmy Cutrer, *The Art of the Woman: The Life and Work of Elisabet Ney* (Lincoln: University of Nebraska Press, 1988).

45. Winegarten, *Black Texas Women*, 134–36.

46. Lydia Mendoza, *Lydia Mendoza: A Family Autobiography*, ed. Chris Strachwitz (Houston: Arte Público Press, 1993).

47. Deborah Vargas, "Rosita Fernández: La Rosa de San Antonio," *Frontiers* 24, nos. 2 & 3 (2003): 168–84.

48. Elizabeth C. Ramírez, "Hispanic and Mexican American Women on the Texas Stage, 1875–1990," in Downs and Jones, *Women and Texas History*, 34–41.

49. Sylvia Ann Grider and Lou Halsell Rodenberger, *Texas Women Writers: A Tradition of Their Own* (College Station: Texas A&M University Press, 1997), 9.

50. Sarah Ragland Jackson, *Texas Woman of Letters: Karle Wilson Baker* (College Station: Texas A&M University Press, 2005), xiii.

51. Janis P. Stout, *Katherine Anne Porter: A Sense of the Times* (Charlottesville: University Press of Virginia, 1995).

52. Grider and Rodenberger, *Texas Women Writers*, 9–10.

53. Karen Kossie-Cherynyshev, ed., *Recovering Five Generations Hence: The Life and Writing of Lillian Jones Horace* (College Station: Texas A&M University Press, 2013), 1–9.

54. Winegarten, *Black Texas Women*, 143–44.

55. Acosta and Winegarten, *Las Tejanas* 281–82; Cynthia E. Orozco, "O'Shea, Maria Elena Zamora," *Handbook of Texas Online*, http://www.tshaonline.org/handbook/online/articles/fos21.

56. Manning, *Hill Country Teacher*, 90.

57. Judith N. McArthur and Harold L. Smith, *Minnie Fisher Cunningham: A Suffragist's Life in Politics* (New York: Oxford University Press, 2003), 22.

58. Barbara Bader Aldave, "Women in the Law in Texas: The Stories of Three Pioneers," *St. Mary's Law Journal* 25 (1993): 290–92; Downs, "Texas Women at Work," 320.

59. Mary Beth Rogers, Sherry A. Smith, and Janelle D. Scott, *We Can Fly: Stories of Katherine Stinson and Other Gutsy Texas Women* (Austin, TX: Ellen C. Temple, 1983), 10–23; Sherrie S. McLeRoy, *Texas Women First: Leading Ladies of Lone Star History* (Charleston, SC: History Press, 2015), 13–16.

60. Enstam, *Women and the Creation of Urban Life*, 80–82; Bianca Mercado, "Latinas in Dallas, 1910–2010: Becoming New Women," in Turner, Cole, and Sharpless, *Texas Women*, 306–8; Olga Bailey, *Mollie Bailey: The Circus Queen of the Southwest*, ed. Bess Samuel Ayres (Dallas: Harben-Spotts, 1943).

61. Jennifer Bridges, "Skiddy Street: Prostitution and Vice in Denison, Texas, 1872–1922" (master's thesis, University of North Texas, 2011), 7–12, 39–40; Amy S. Balderach, "A Different Kind of Reservation: Waco's Red-Light District Revisited, 1880–1920 (master's thesis, Baylor University, 2005), 32, 41.

62. Balderach, "Different Kind of Reservation," 42, 57.

63. Elizabeth Turner, *Women and Gender in the New South, 1865–1945* (Wheeling, IL: Harlan Davidson, 2009), 137; Bridges, "Skiddy Street," 13–15, 55–56; Thomas C. Mackey, *Red Lights Out: A Legal History of Prostitution, Disorderly Houses, and Vice Districts, 1870–1917* (New York: Garland, 1987), 353–87.

Chapter 8

1. Wilma Earl Colvin Edwards, in *Harder than Hardscrabble: Oral Recollections of the Farming Life from the Edge of the Texas Hill Country*, ed. Thad Sitton (Austin: University of Texas Press, 2003), 37.

2. Sitton, ed., *Harder than Hardscrabble*, 83; Rebecca Sharpless, *Fertile Ground, Narrow Choices: Women on Texas Cotton Farms, 1900–1940* (Chapel Hill: University of North Carolina Press, 1999), 146.

3. Quoted in Patsy Cravens, *Leavin' a Testimony: Portraits from Rural Texas* (Austin: University of Texas Press, 2006), 62; Rebecca Sharpless, "Women and Work during the Great Depression in Texas," in *Invisible Texans: Women and Minorities in Texas History*, ed. Donald Willett and Stephen Curley (Boston: McGraw Hill, 2005), 148.

4. Quoted in Cravens, *Leavin' a Testimony*, 42.

5. Sharpless, "Women and Work during the Great Depression,"149.

6. Harold L. Smith, "'All Good Things Start with the Women': The Origin of the Texas Birth Control Movement, 1933–1945," *Southwestern Historical Quarterly* 114 (January 2011): 253–85.

7. Sharpless, "Women and Work during the Great Depression,"148–49.

8. Sharpless, *Fertile Ground*, 234–37; Bernadette Pruitt, "'For the Advancement of the Race': The Great Migrations to Houston, Texas, 1914–1941," *Journal of Urban History* 31 (May 2005): 460; Bernadette Pruitt, *The Other Great Migration: The Movement of Rural African Americans to Houston, 1900–1941* (College Station: Texas A&M University Press, 2013), 15–53.

9. Julia Kirk Blackwelder, *Women of the Depression: Caste and Culture in San Antonio, 1929–1939* (College Station: Texas A&M University Press, 1984), 43–47 (quote on 45).

10. Sharpless, "Women and Work during the Great Depression," 149.

11. Judith N. McArthur and Harold L. Smith, *Texas through Women's Eyes: The Twentieth-Century Experience* (Austin: University of Texas Press, 2010), 82–83; Nancy Baker Jones and Ruthe Winegarten, *Capitol Women: Texas Female Legislators, 1923–1999* (Austin: University of Texas Press, 2000), 96–100; Darwin Payne, *Indomitable Sarah: The Life of Judge Sarah T. Hughes* (Dallas: Southern Methodist University Press, 2004), 78 (quote).

12. Diane Manning, *Hill Country Teacher: Oral Histories from the One-Room School and Beyond* (Boston: Twayne, 1990), 170 (first quote), 71 (second and third quote), 124 (fourth and fifth quote); McArthur and Smith, *Texas through Women's Eyes*, 83.

13. Manning, *Hill Country Teacher*, 10.

14. Sharpless, "Women and Work during the Great Depression," 153–54; McArthur and Smith, *Texas through Women's Eyes*, 88; Ruthe Winegarten, *Black Texas Women: 150 Years of Trial and Triumph* (Austin: University of Texas Press, 1995), 148.

15. Sharpless, "Women and Work during the Great Depression," 151.

16. McArthur and Smith, *Texas through Women's Eyes*, 82, 84.

17. Merline Pitre, "At the Crossroads: Black Texas Women, 1930–1954," in *Black Women in Texas History*, ed. Bruce A. Glasrud and Merline Pitre (College Station: Texas A&M University Press, 2008), 132–34 (quote on 133).

18. McArthur and Smith, *Texas through Women's Eyes*, 83–84.

19. Ibid., 82; Teresa Palomo Acosta and Ruthe Winegarten, *Las Tejanas: 300 Years of History* (Austin: University of Texas Press, 2003), 120.

20. Acosta and Winegarten, *Las Tejanas*, 129.

21. Ibid., 140–41.

22. McArthur and Smith, *Texas through Women's Eyes*, 86–87; Acosta and Winegarten, *Las Tejanas*, 143–45.

23. McArthur and Smith, *Texas through Women's Eyes*, 84–85; Patricia Evridge Hill, "Real Women and True Womanhood: Grassroots Organizing among Dallas Dressmakers in 1935," *Labor's Heritage* 5 (Spring 1994): 5–15.

24. Acosta and Winegarten, *Las Tejanas*, 212.

25. Winegarten, *Black Texas Women*, 197–98.

26. Sharpless, "Women and Work during the Great Depression," 150.

27. Joanne Rao Sánchez, "The Latinas of World War II: From Familial Shelter to Expanding Horizons," in *Beyond the Latino World War II Hero: The Social and Political Legacy of a Generation*, ed. Maggie Rivas-Rodríguez and Emilio Zamora (Austin: University of Texas Press, 2009), 74.

28. Paul Alejandro Levengood, "For the Duration and Beyond: World War II and the Creation of Modern Houston, Texas" (PhD diss., Rice University, 1999), 353–56.

29. Mary Potchernick Cook, "Angelina's Rosies: Women at War in World War II East Texas," (master's thesis, Stephen F. Austin State University, 1998), 5 (quote), 135.

30. Sandra Denise Harvey, "Working for Change: Wage-Earning Women in Waco, Texas Defense Industries during World War II" (PhD diss., Texas Tech University, 2009), 83–114.

31. Gary Rabalais, "Humble Women at War: The Case of Humble's Baytown Refinery, 1942–1945," *Houston Review* 2 (2005): 33–35.

32. Patricia Portales, "Tejanas on the Home Front: Women, Bombs, and the (Re)Gendering of War in Mexican American World War II Literature," in *Latina/os and World War II: Mobility, Agency, and Ideology*, ed. Maggie Rivas-Rodriguez and B. V. Olguín (Austin: University of Texas, 2015), 175–76; Maggie Rivas-Rodriguez, et al., *A Legacy Greater Than Words: Stories of US Latinos and Latinas of the WWII Generation* (Austin: University of Texas Press, 2006), 211–17.

33. Portales, "Tejanas on the Home Front," 176.

34. Cook, "Angelina's Rosies," 84–85.

35. Ibid., 87.

36. Harvey, "Working for Change," 13.

37. Cook, "Angelina's Rosies," 87.

38. Harvey, "Working for Change," 115

39. Ibid., 134.

40. Cook, "Angelina's Rosies," 83.

41. Rivas-Rodriguez, *Legacy Greater Than Words*, 213.

42. Rabalais, "Humble Women at War," 35.

43. Harvey, "Working for Change," 141.

44. Rivas-Rodriguez, *Legacy Greater Than Words*, 217.

45. Harvey, "Working for Change," 103–4.

46. Cook, "Angelina's Rosies," 116, 137.

47. Quoted in Harvey, "Working for Change," 42–45.

48. Levengood, "For the Duration and Beyond," 354.

49. Cook, "Angelina's Rosies," 134.

50. Rabalais, "Humble Women at War," 34–35.

51. Levengood, "For the Duration and Beyond," 367.

52. Ibid., 364.

53. Ibid., 358–59.

54. Ibid., 358–66 (quote on 365); Harvey, "Working for Change," 51–54.

55. Levengood, "For the Duration and Beyond," 353; Cook, "Angelina's Rosies," 118, 126; Harvey, "Working for Change," 51, 58, 91; Rabalais, "Humble Women at War," 36.

56. Sánchez, "Latinas of World War II," 77.

57. Ibid., 79.

58. Alice Fraser, "Be Thankful for a Ration Book," *Parents' Magazine*, February 1943, quoted in Sharon Ann Smith, "Female Home Front Soldiers and Their Food for Freedom Campaign during the Second World War" (master's thesis, Texas Woman's University, 1996), especially 49.

59. Ibid., 99.

60. Tracy McGlothlin Shilcutt, "The Bluebonnet Brigade: Women and War in Abilene, Texas: 1941–1945" (master's thesis, Abilene Christian University, 1993), 1–15.

61. Sánchez, "Latinas of World War II," 80.

62. David C. Humphrey, "Prostitution in Texas: From the 1830s to the 1960s," *East Texas Historical Journal* 33, no. 1 (1996): 34–35.

63. Tanya Krause Randall, "Texas Ranch Women Remember World War II," *Sound Historian* 13 (2011): 41, 42, 46.

64. Cindy Weigand, *Texas Women in World War II* (Lanham: Republic of Texas Press, 2003), 75.

65. Sánchez, "Latinas of World War II," 82.

66. Elizabeth Norman, *We Band of Angels: The Untold Story of American Nurses Trapped on Bataan by the Japanese* (New York: Random House, 1999), 279–82.

67. Kelli Cardenas Walsh, "Oveta Culp Hobby: Ability, Perseverance, and Cultural Capital in a Twentieth Century Success Story," in *Texas Women: Their Histories, Their Lives*, ed. Elizabeth Hayes Turner, Stephanie Cole, and Rebecca Sharpless (Athens: University of Georgia Press, 2015), 322–27.

68. Susan M. Hartmann, *The Home Front and Beyond: American Women in the 1940s* (Boston: Twayne, 1982), 31–35.

69. Weigand, *Texas Women in World War II*, 132 (first quote), 136, 167 (last quote).

70. Ibid., 21, 22.

71. Sánchez, "Latinas of World War II," 83–84; Rivas-Rodriguez, *Legacy Greater Than Words*, 185 (quote).

72. McArthur and Smith, *Texas through Women's Eyes*, 95–96; Pitre, "At the Crossroads," 139–40; Winegarten, *Black Texas Women*, 27–28.

73. Weigand, *Texas Women in World War II*, 43.

74. Hartmann, *Home Front and Beyond*, 39; Weigand, *Texas Women in World War II*, 183; Molly Merryman, *Clipped Wings: The Rise and Fall of the Women Airforce Service Pilots (WASPs) of World War II* (New York: New York University Press, 1998), 14; Dawn Letson, "Girl Pilots of Avenger Field: Sweetwater's Romance with the WASP of WWII," *Sound Historian* 13 (2011): 33–35.

75. Kathleen Cornelsen, "Women Airforce Service Pilots of World War II: Exploring Military Aviation, Encountering Discrimination, and Exchanging Traditional Roles in Service to America," *Journal of Women's History* 17 (Winter 2005): 115.

76. Harvey, "Working for Change," 138–39; *Lufkin Daily News* quoted in Cook, "Angelina's Rosies," 140.

77. Levengood, "For the Duration and Beyond," 358; Cook, "Angelina's Rosies," 140; Rabalais, "Humble Women at War," 36 (quote).

78. John Reddit, Rotary presentation, reported in *Lufkin Daily News*, October 4, 1943, quoted in Cook, "Angelina's Rosies," 146.

79. Harvey, "Working for Change," 139; Levengood, "For the Duration and Beyond," 358; Cook, "Angelina's Rosies," 140.

80. Walsh, "Oveta Culp Hobby," 327–33.

81. Levengood, "For the Duration and Beyond," 357.

82. Cook, "Angelina's Rosies," 147.

83. Harvey, "Working for Change," 148.

84. US Census 1940 and 1950 employment and labor force tables. Nationally the percentage of women in the workforce rose from 25.4 percent of women employed outside the home in 1940 to 33.9 percent in 1950.

85. Harvey, "Working for Change," 149.

86. Fane Downs, "Texas Women at Work," in *Texas: A Sesquicentennial Celebration,* ed. Donald W. Whisenhunt (Austin, TX: Eakin Press, 1984), 320–21.

87. Nancy E. Baker, "Hermine Tobolowsky: A Feminist's Fight for Equal Rights," in Turner, Cole, and Sharpless, *Texas Women,* 437.

88. Downs, "Texas Women at Work," 320.

Chapter 9

1. Nancy Rubin, *The New Suburban Woman: Beyond Myth and Motherhood* (New York: Coward, McCann & Geoghegan, 1982), 60–62.

2. Ruth Schwartz Cowan, *More Work for Mother: The Ironies of Household Technology from the Open Hearth to the Microwave* (New York: Basic Books, 1983), 195–201.

3. Matthew D. Lassiter and Kevin M. Kruse, "The Bulldozer Revolution: Suburbs and Southern History since World War II," *Journal of Southern History* 75 (August 2009): 697.

4. Ann Richards with Peter Kobler, *Straight from the Heart: My Life in Politics and Other Places* (New York: Simon and Schuster, 1989), 91, 98; Rubin, *New Suburban Woman,* 62–65.

5. Richards, *Straight from the Heart,* 98–99.

6. Kenneth T. Jackson, *Crabgrass Frontier: The Suburbanization of the United States* (New York: Oxford University Press, 1985), 241; Betty Friedan, *The Feminine Mystique* (New York: Norton, 1963).

7. Don E. Carleton, "McCarthyism in Houston: The George Ebey Affair," *Southwestern Historical Quarterly* 80 (October 1976): 167–69, 174.

8. Kristi Throne Strickland, "The Significance and Impact of Women on the Rise of the Republican Party in Twentieth Century Texas" (PhD diss., University of North Texas, 2000), 1–44.

9. Sam Roberts, "Bruce Alger, 96, Dies; Led 'Mink Coat' Protest against Lyndon Johnson," *New York Times,* April 28, 2015.

10. Irwin A. Tang and Yvonne Lim, "The San Antonio Chinese Community, 1880–1949," *Asian Texans: Our Histories and Our Lives,* ed. Irwin A. Tang (Austin: It Works, 2008), 126; Bruce A. Glasrud, "Asians in Texas: An Overview, 1870–1990," *East Texas Historical Journal* 39, no. 2 (2001): 14–16; Marilyn Dell Brady, *The Asian Texans* (College Station: Texas A&M University Press, 2004), 16, 20, 44.

11. Brady, *Asian Texans,* 7, 34, 65–67; Judith N. McArthur and Harold L. Smith, *Texas through Women's Eyes: The Twentieth-Century Experience* (Austin: University of Texas Press, 2010), 94–95; Irwin A. Tang, "The Filipino Texans," in Tang, *Asian Texans,* 168; Irwin A. Tang, Lucy Lee, and Michell Cho, "The Korean Texans," in Tang, *Asian Texans,* 207–11; Naoko Kato, "Japanese Texans after World War II," in Tang, *Asian Texans,* 257–60.

12. Tang, Lee, and Cho, "Korean Texans," 208, 211; Kato, "Japanese Texans," 257–59; Brady, *Asian Texans*, 68.

13. Tang, "Filipino Texans,"166; Tang, Lee, and Cho, "Korean Texans," 208; Kato, "Japanese Texans," 257–59; Brady, *Asian Texans*, 68.

14. Glasrud, "Asians in Texas," 14.

15. Merline Pitre, "At the Crossroads: Black Texas Women, 1930–1954," in *Black Women in Texas History*, ed. Bruce A. Glasrud and Merline Pitre (College Station: Texas A&M University Press, 2008), 149–53.

16. Ibid., 153.

17. Stephanie Decker, "Women in the Civil Rights Movement: Juanita Craft versus the Dallas Elite," *East Texas Historical Journal* 39 (Spring 2001): 33–42.

18. Stephanie Decker, "African American Women in the Civil Rights Era, 1954–1974," in Glasrud and Pitre, *Black Women in Texas History*, 162–63; Nancy Baker Jones and Ruthe Winegarten, *Capitol Women: Texas Female Legislators, 1923–1999* (Austin: University of Texas Press, 2000), 169 (quotes).

19. Yvonne Davis Frear, "Making the Invisible Visible: African American Women in the Texas Civil Rights Movement," in *Southern Black Women in the Modern Civil Rights Movement*, ed. Bruce A. Glasrud and Merline Pitre (College Station: Texas A&M University Press, 2013), 35.

20. McArthur and Smith, *Texas through Women's Eyes*, 155–56.

21. Quoted in ibid.

22. Decker, "African American Women in the Civil Rights Era," 162–63.

23. McArthur and Smith, *Texas through Women's Eyes*, 156–67.

24. Ibid., 157.

25. Ibid., 158.

26. McArthur and Smith, *Texas through Women's Eyes*, 158; Decker, "African American Women in the Civil Rights Era," 164–65; Randolph B. Campbell, *Gone to Texas: A History of the Lone Star State* (New York: Oxford University Press, 2003), 425–29.

27. Decker, "African American Women in the Civil Rights Era," 165–66.

28. Ibid., 166–67.

29. US Census, 1960 and 1970. In 1970, 58 percent of employed black women worked in private households or as service workers, while only 18 percent of employed white women did so.

30. Joanne Rao Sánchez, "The Latinas of World War II: From Familial Shelter to Expanding Horizons," in *Beyond the Latino World War II Hero: The Social and Political Legacy of a Generation*, ed. Maggie Rivas-Rodríguez and Emilio Zamora (Austin: University of Texas Press, 2009), 79, 80 (quote), 86–89.

31. Arnoldo De León, *Ethnicity in the Sunbelt: A History of Mexican Americans in Houston* (Houston: Mexican American Studies Program, 1989), 105, 156.

32. Henry A. J. Ramos, *A People Forgotten, a Dream Pursued: The History of the American G.I. Forum, 1948–1972* (n.p.: American G.I. Forum, 1983), 41; De León, *Ethnicity in the Sunbelt*, 129.

33. McArthur and Smith, *Texas through Women's Eyes*, 148–49; Arnoldo De León, *Mexican Americans in Texas: A Brief History* (Wheeling, IL: Harland Davidson, 1999), 117–18.

34. McArthur and Smith, *Texas through Women's Eyes*, 148–49; De León, *Mexican Americans in Texas*, 117–18.

35. McArthur and Smith, *Texas through Women's Eyes*, 149–50; De León, *Mexican Americans in Texas*, 115–16; Sara Moreno Posas interview, credited to South Texas Public Broadcasting System, 2002, in "Felix Z. Longoria: Private, United States Army," Arlington National Cemetery Website, http://www.arlingtoncemetery.net/longoria.htm (quote).

36. Posas interview.

37. Ramos, *People Forgotten*, 43; De León, *Mexican Americans in Texas*, 116.

38. Martha Cotera, *Diosa y Hembra: The History and Heritage of Chicanas* (Austin, TX: Information Systems Development, 1976), 107–8.

39. De León, *Ethnicity in the Sunbelt*, 196.

40. Evey Chapa, "Mujeres por la Raza Unida," *Caracol* 1, no. 2 (1974): 3–5, reprinted in *Chicana Feminist Thought: The Basic Historical Writings*, ed. Alma M. García (New York: Routledge, 1997), 178.

41. Ibid., 178.

42. Mary Ann Villarreal, "The Synapses of Struggle: Martha Cotera and Tejana Activism," in *Las Obreras: Chicana Politics of Work and Family*, ed. Vicki L. Ruiz (Los Angeles: UCLA Chicano Studies Research Center Publications, 2000), 288–89; Cotera, *Diosa y Hembra*.

43. De León, *Ethnicity in the Sunbelt*, 196–97.

44. Chapa, "Mujeres por la Raza Unida," 178–79.

45. Linda Lewis, "Young, Gifted, and Black," in *No Apologies: Texas Radicals Celebrate the '60s*, ed. Daryl Janes (Austin, TX: Eakin Press, 1992), 66, 69.

46. Harold L. Smith, "Casey Hayden: Gender and the Origins of SNCC, SDS, and the Women's Liberation Movement," in *Texas Women: Their Histories, Their Lives*, ed. Elizabeth Hayes Turner, Stephanie Cole, and Rebecca Sharpless (Athens: University of Georgia Press, 2015), 364–67; Richard Croxdale and Jim Cullers, *Stand Ins: Austin, Texas, 1960* (Austin: People's History in Texas, 2015), http://peopleshistoryintexas.org/projects-2/standins.

47. Smith, "Casey Hayden," 367.

48. Susan Torian Olan, "Blood Debts," in Janes, *No Apologies*, 14–20 (quote on 14).

49. Robert Pardun, "It Wasn't Hard to Be a Communist in Texas," in Janes, *No Apologies*, 56.

50. Ibid.

51. Olan, "Blood Debts," 20.

52. Laura Joplin, *Love Janis* (New York: Villard Books, 1992), 91.

53. Mariann Garner-Wizard, "The Lie," in Janes, *No Apologies*, 79–80.

54. Frieda Werden, "Adventures of a Texas Feminist," in Janes, *No Apologies*, 195.

55. McArthur and Smith, *Texas through Women's Eyes*, 204.

56. Sarah Weddington, *A Question of Choice* (New York: Penguin Books, 1993), 22–25.

57. Smith, "Casey Hayden," 368, 372.

58. McArthur and Smith, *Texas through Women's Eyes*, 203–4.

59. Garner-Wizard, "Lie," 90–91; Werden, "Adventures of a Texas Feminist," 199.

60. Werden, "Adventures of a Texas Feminist," 191, 193.

61. Smith, "Casey Hayden," 381–83; Casey Hayden and Mary King, "Sex and Caste:

A Kind of Memo," 1965, http://www.historyisaweapon.com/defcon1/sexcaste.html (first and second quote); Paul Spencer quoted in Doug Rossinow, *The Politics of Authenticity: Liberalism, Christianity, and the New Left in America* (New York: Columbia University Press, 1998), 306 (last quote).

62. Ruth Rosen, *The World Split Open: How the Modern Women's Movement Changed America* (New York: Penguin Books, 2000), 159–62.

63. Rossinow, *Politics of Authenticity*, 311–12.

64. McArthur and Smith, *Texas through Women's Eyes*, 202; Rossinow, *Politics of Authenticity*, 313–14, 322.

65. McArthur and Smith, *Texas through Women's Eyes*, 204–5; Rossinow, *Politics of Authenticity*, 310–15; Werden, "Adventures of a Texas Feminist," 205.

66. Rossinow, *Politics of Authenticity*, 312; Werden, "Adventures of a Texas Feminist," 200–201.

67. Darwin Payne, *Indomitable Sarah: The Life of Judge Sarah T. Hughes* (Dallas: Southern Methodist University Press, 2004), 95–100.

68. Nancy E. Baker, "Hermine Tobolowsky: A Feminist's Fight for Equal Rights," in Turner, Cole, and Sharpless, *Texas Women*, 445; Peter Wyden, "The Revolt of Texas Women," *Saturday Evening Post*, January 14, 1961, 25, 55–56.

69. McArthur and Smith, *Texas through Women's Eyes*, 213–16; Louise Ballerstedt Raggio with Vivian Anderson Castleberry, *Texas Tornado: The Life of a Crusader for Women's Rights and Family Justice* (New York: Citadel Press, 2003), 174–83; Baker, "Hermine Tobolowsky," 439–48; Jones and Winegarten, *Capitol Women*, 47–50.

70. Judie Gammage, "Quest for Equality: An Historical Overview of Women's Rights Activism in Texas, 1890–1975" (PhD diss., North Texas State University, 1982), 154–56.

71. Ibid., 156–58, 168–71; Rob Fink, "Hermine Tobolowsky, the Texas ELRA, and the Political Struggle for Women's Equal Rights," *Journal of the West* 42 (Summer 2003): 52–57.

72. McArthur and Smith, *Texas through Women's Eyes*, 198–201.

73. Gammage, "Quest for Equality," 173–76; Jones and Winegarten, *Capitol Women*, 279–80.

74. Gammage, "Quest for Equality," 171.

75. Weddington, *A Question of Choice*, 28–35.

76. Weddington, *A Question of Choice*, 47–174.

77. *The Spirit of Houston: The First National Women's Conference: An Official Report to the President, the Congress and the People of the United States* (Washington, DC: National Commission on the Observance of International Women's Year, 1978), 10.

78. McArthur and Smith, *Texas through Women's Eyes*, 217–18.

79. Jason Mellard, *Progressive Country: How the 1970s Transformed the Texans in Popular Culture* (Austin: University of Texas Press, 2013), 113–14; Ellen Pratt Fout, "'A miracle occurred': The Houston Committee of International Women's Year, Houston, 1977," *Houston Review* 1 (Fall 2003): 4–11 (quote on 4).

80. Oral interview with Dr. Nikki Van Hightower, June 11, 1999, University of Houston Women's Studies History Project, Women's Archive and Research Center, Special Collections and Archives, University of Houston Libraries, 1999, quoted in Fout "A miracle occurred," 5.

81. *Spirit of Houston*, 111, 140; Judith N. McArthur and Harold L. Smith, "Not Whistling Dixie: Women's Movements and Feminist Politics," in *The Texas Left: The Radical Roots of Lone Star Liberalism*, ed. David O'Donald Cullen and Kyle G. Wilkison (College Station: Texas A&M University Press, 2010), 150; Debbie Mauldin Cottrell, "National Women's Conference, 1977," *Handbook of Texas Online*, http://www.tshaon line.org/handbook/online/articles/pwngq.

82. Prudence Mackintosh, "The Good Old Girls," *Texas Monthly*, January 1978, 88, 151.

Chapter 10

1. Frieda Werden, "Adventures of a Texas Feminist," in *No Apologies: Texas Radicals Celebrate the '60s*, ed. Daryl Janes (Austin: Eakin Press, 1992), 204.

2. Arnold Garcia Jr., "Caucus Rule Cuts Male Candidates Out of Endorsements," *Austin American-Statesman*, June 26, 1991.

3. Melissa Ann Gohlke, "Out in the Alamo City: Revealing San Antonio's Gay and Lesbian Past, World War II to the 1990s" (master's thesis, University of Texas at San Antonio, 2012), 54–55; Karen Wisely, "The 'Dallas Way' in the Gayborhood: The Creation of a Lesbian, Gay, Bisexual, and Transgender Community in Dallas, Texas, 1965–1986" (master's thesis, University of North Texas, 2011), 70–71.

4. Molly Ellen Bundschuh, "Cowboys, 'Queers,' and Community: The AIDS Crisis in Houston and Dallas, 1981–1996" (master's thesis, University of North Texas, 2014), 24; Wisely, "'Dallas Way' in the Gayborhood," 66–67.

5. Ammie Vanson, "Letters," *Gay Austin* 2 (December 1977), 2, quoted in Eric Jason Ganther, "From Closet to Crusade: The Struggle for Lesbian-Gay Civil Rights in Austin, Texas, 1970–1982" (master's thesis, University of Texas at Austin, 1990), 109.

6. Ganther, "From Closet to Crusade," 73–78.

7. Bundschuh, "Cowboys, 'Queers,' and Community," 68; Wisely, "'Dallas Way' in the Gayborhood," 77; Ganther, "From Closet to Crusade," 158.

8. Judith N. McArthur and Harold L. Smith, *Texas through Women's Eyes: The Twentieth-Century Experience* (Austin: University of Texas Press, 2010), 201, 205.

9. Ganther, "From Closet to Crusade," 61–64.

10. Ibid., 153–54.

11. Werden, "Adventures of a Texas Feminist," 207–8; Wisely, "'Dallas Way' in the Gayborhood," 64–69.

12. Linda Lewis, "Young, Gifted and Black," in Janes, *No Apologies*, 69.

13. Velma Roberts with Ruby Williams, "Welfare Is a Right," in Janes, *No Apologies*, 116.

14. Kenneth W. Howell and James M. Smallwood, "Expanded Opportunities: Black Women in the Modern Era, 1974–2000," in *Black Women in Texas History*, ed. Bruce A. Glasrud and Merline Pitre (College Station: Texas A&M University Press, 2008), 186–87; Ruthe Winegarten, *Black Texas Women: 150 Years of Trial and Triumph* (Austin: University of Texas Press, 1995), 284–85.

15. Evey Chapa, "Mujeres por la Raza Unida," *Caracol* 1, no. 2 (1974): 3–5, reprinted in *Chicana Feminist Thought: The Basic Historical Writings*, ed. Alma M. García (New York: Routledge, 1997), 178–79.

16. Evey Chapa, "Report from the National Women's Political Caucus," in García, *Chicana Feminist Thought*, 174–77 (first quote on 174; last quote on 177).

17. McArthur and Smith, *Texas through Women's Eyes*, 226.

18. Ibid., 210.

19. Kristi Throne Strickland, "The Significance and Impact of Women on the Rise of the Republican Party in Twentieth Century Texas" (PhD diss., University of North Texas, 2000), 5, 190n8.

20. Strickland, "Significance and Impact of Women," 129.

21. Ibid., 6–7.

22. Ibid., 188–90, 212; Republican Party Platform of 1976, American Presidency Project, http://www.presidency.ucsb.edu/ws/index.php?pid=25843.

23. Phyllis Schlafly, "What's Wrong with 'Equal Rights' for Women?," *Phyllis Schlafly Report* 5, no. 7 (February 1972); Donald T. Critchlow, *Phyllis Schlafly and Grassroots Conservatism: A Woman's Crusade* (Princeton: Princeton University Press, 2005), 217.

24. Phyllis Schlafly, "What's Wrong with 'Equal Rights' for Women?"; Ruth Murray Brown, *For a Christian America: A History of the Religious Right* (Amherst, NY: Prometheus Books, 2002), 66–67.

25. Brown, *For a Christian America*, 65.

26. Lottie Beth Hobbs, "Pink Sheet," reprinted in Brown, *For a Christian America*, 40.

27. McArthur and Smith, *Texas through Women's Eyes*, 216; David W. Brady and Kent L. Tedin, "Ladies in Pink: Religion and Political Ideology in the Anti-ERA Movement," *Social Science Quarterly* 56 (March 1976): 564–75.

28. Janet K. Boles, *The Politics of the Equal Rights Amendment* (New York: Longman, 1979), 163.

29. Bonnie Cook Freeman, "Antifeminists and Women's Liberation: A Case Study of a Paradox," *Women and Politics* 3 (Spring 1983): 21–38.

30. Brown, *For a Christian America*, 111–17; McArthur and Smith, *Texas through Women's Eyes*, 213–20 (quote on 219).

31. Strickland, "Significance and Impact of Women," 231–34.

32. Ruth Rosen, *The World Split Open: How the Modern Women's Movement Changed America* (New York: Penguin Books, 2000), 291–94.

33. Maria Swall-Yarrington, "Texas Council On Family Violence," *Handbook of Texas Online*, http://www.tshaonline.org/handbook/online/articles/pwtfg; Joann M. Ross, "Making Marital Rape Visible: A History of American Legal and Social Movements Criminalizing Rape in Marriage" (PhD diss., University of Nebraska, 2015), 68.

34. Nancy Baker Jones and Ruthe Winegarten, *Capitol Women: Texas Female Legislators, 1923–1999* (Austin: University of Texas Press, 2000), 159–60, 163–64.

35. "Texas Association against Sexual Assault History," http://taasa.memberlodge.org/Resources/Documents/Board%20Website/TAASA%20History.doc; Texas League of Women Voters, "Domestic Violence and Spousal Rape," http://www.lwvtexas.org/Domestic_Violence.html.

36. McArthur and Smith, *Texas through Women's Eyes*, 227; Jones and Winegarten, *Capitol Women*, 159–60, 163–64, 170, 178.

37. Nancy Baker Jones, "Making Texas *Our* Texas: The Emergence of Texas Women's History, 1976–1990," *Southwestern Historical Quarterly* 120 (January 2017): 278–313; Ann Richards with Peter Knobler, *Straight from the Heart: My Life in Politics and Other Places* (New York: Simon and Schuster, 1989), 190 (quote).

38. National Coalition for Women and Girls in Education, *Title IX at 30: Report Card on Gender Equity* (Washington, DC: National Coalition for Women and Girls in Education, 2002), 1–5, 8, http://www.feminist.org/education/TitleIXat30.pdf; McArthur and Smith, *Texas through Women's Eyes*, 228–31.

39. McArthur and Smith, *Texas through Women's Eyes*, 231; *Title IX at 30*, 14–15; Sandra Davis Maddox, "Title IX of the Educational Amendments of 1972: Level of Implementation in Texas Public Schools" (PhD diss., University of North Texas, 1995).

40. *Title IX at 30*, 14; Donna Lopiano in "Prohibition of Sex Discrimination, 1975: Hearings Before the Subcommittee on Education of the Committee on Labor and Public Welfare on S. 2106 to Amend Title IX of the Education Amendments of 1972," US Senate, 94th Cong., 1st sess., 100, http://files.eric.ed.gov/fulltext/ED136136.pdf; Margy Duval in ibid., 56.

41. Lopiano, in "Prohibition of Sex Discrimination, 1975," 112–43; Meredith M. Bagley, "Playing Fair: The Rhetorical Limits of Liberalism in Women's Sport at the University of Texas, 1927–1992" (PhD diss., University of Texas at Austin, 2010), 173–88.

42. McArthur and Smith, *Texas through Women's Eyes*, 230–31 (first quote), Mary Jo Festle, *Playing Nice: Politics and Apologies in Women's Sports* (New York: Columbia University Press, 1996), xxvi–xxvii.

43. Fane Downs, "Texas Women at Work," in *Texas: A Sesquicentennial Celebration*, ed. Donald W. Whisenhunt (Austin, TX: Eakin Press, 1984), 319.

44. McArthur and Smith, *Texas through Women's Eyes*, 196–98.

45. Downs, "Texas Women at Work," 320–21; Jennifer Ross-Nazzal, "Mae C. Jemison: The Right Stuff," in *Texas Women: Their Histories, Their Lives*, ed. Elizabeth Hayes Turner, Stephanie Cole, and Rebecca Sharpless (Athens: University of Georgia Press, 2015), 457–80.

46. McArthur and Smith, *Texas through Women's Eyes*, 234; "Meet Local Legend: Nancy Dickey, M.D.," in *Local Legends: Celebrating America's Local Women Physicians*, US National Library of Medicine, National Institutes of Health, https://www.nlm.nih.gov/locallegends/Biographies/Dickey_Nancy.html.

47. Downs, "Texas Women at Work," 321.

48. Ibid., 322–23.

49. McArthur and Smith, *Texas through Women's Eyes*, 231–33; Laurie Coyle, Gail Hershatter, and Emily Honig, "Women at Farah: An Unfinished Story," in *Mexican Women in the United States: Struggles Past and Present*, ed. Magdalena Mora and Adelaida R. Del Castillo (Los Angeles: Chicano Studies Research Center Publications, 1980), 134 (quote).

50. McArthur and Smith, *Texas through Women's Eyes*, 231–34.

51. Marilyn Dell Brady, *The Asian Texans* (College Station: Texas A&M University Press, 2004), 79; Irwin A. Tang, "The Filipino Texans," in *Asian Texans: Our Histories and Our Lives*, ed. Irwin A. Tang (Austin: It Works, 2008), 169–71; Jessica S. Barnes and Claudette E. Bennett, "The Asian Population: 2000," Census 2000 Brief, US Census Bureau, February 2002, https://www.census.gov/prod/2002pubs/c2kbr01–16.pdf.

52. Tang, "Filipino Texans," 167–73; Irwin A. Tang, Sockalingam "Sam" Kannappan, and Rakesh Amaram, "The Indian Texans," in Tang, *Asian Texans*, 190; Irwin A. Tang, Lucy Lee, and Michelle Cho, "The Korean Texans," in Tang, *Asian Texans*, 207, 212; Brady, *Asian Texans*, 79.

53. Irwin A. Tang and Rebecca Teng, "The Chinese Texans, 1945–2005," in Tang, *Asian Texans*, 235–40; Jessica Chew, "Vietnamese and Chinese American Cultures: Destination Houston," *Houston History* 13 (Fall 2016): 21–24.

54. Brady, *Asian Texans*, 106; Thao L. Ha, "The Vietnamese Texans," in Tang, *Asian Texans*, 266–76; Bruce A. Glasrud, "Asians in Texas: An Overview, 1870–1990," *East Texas Historical Journal* 39, no. 2 (2001): 18.

55. Jan Jarboe Russell, "The Mommy War," *Texas Monthly*, June 1989, 78–81, 115–17; Dominique Browning, "Waiting for Mommy," *Texas Monthly*, February 1982, 124–31, 184–93, 198.

56. Jones and Winegarten, *Capitol Women*, 32, 271–72, 279.

57. Mary Beth Rogers, *Barbara Jordan: American Hero* (New York: Bantam Books, 1998), xi, 113; Jones and Winegarten, *Capitol Women*, 145–51.

58. McArthur and Smith, *Texas through Women's Eyes*, 224; Jones and Winegarten, *Capitol Women*, 153–56 (quote on 153); Stephanie Fields-Hawkins, "Frances Farenthold: Texas' Joan of Arc" (master's thesis, University of North Texas, 2012).

59. McArthur and Smith, *Texas through Women's Eyes*, 224–25; Jones and Winegarten, *Capitol Women*, 11–12, 272–75, 282.

60. Jones and Winegarten, *Capitol Women*, 56–57, 280.

61. Elizabeth W. Fernea and Marilyn P. Duncan, *Texas Women in Politics* (Austin, TX: Foundation for Women's Resources, 1977), ix; Janet K. Boles, "The Texas Woman in Politics: Role Model or Mirage," *Social Science Journal* 21 (January 1984): 88.

62. Henry Tatum, "Fickle Fate for Female Mayors," *Dallas Morning News*, May 15, 1991 (quote); Melissa Marschall, "A Descriptive Analysis of Female Mayors: The US and Texas in Comparative Perspective," in *Local Politics and Mayoral Elections in 21st Century America: The Keys to City Hall*, ed. Sean D. Foreman and Marcia L. Godwin (New York: Routledge, 2015), 35–36, 44.

63. Sonia R. García, et al., *Políticas: Latina Public Officials in Texas* (Austin: University of Texas Press, 2008), 7, 8; José Angel Gutiérrez, Michelle Meléndez, and Sonia Adriana Noyola, *Chicanas in Charge: Texas Women in the Public Arena* (Lanham, MD: AltaMira Press, 2007), 8; Arnoldo De Leon, "María Cárdenas: San Angelo Chicano-Era Activist," in *Invisible Texans: Women and Minorities in Texas History*, ed. Donald Willett and Stephen Curley (Boston: McGraw Hill, 2005), 226–36.

64. Quote in García, *Políticas*, 34.

65. García, *Políticas*, 135–37.

66. Elizabeth Hayes Turner, "Lion in the Texas House: The Political Performances of Senfronia Thompson," paper given at the Women in Texas History Luncheon, March 6, 2014, Texas State Historical Association (paper in possession of author); Winegarten, *Black Texas Women*, 297–99; Jones and Winegarten, *Capitol Women*, 266–67.

67. Terry L. Gilmour, "A Difference: Women in the Texas Legislature" (PhD diss., Texas Tech University, 1999), 15, 132–33; Jones and Winegarten, *Capitol Women*, 15–19.

68. *Austin American-Statesman*, September 11, 1993, quoted in Jones and Winegarten, *Capitol Women*, 240.

69. Sue Tolleson-Rinehart and Jeanie R. Stanley, *Claytie and the Lady: Ann Richards, Gender, and Politics in Texas* (Austin: University of Texas Press, 1994), 57–93, 98–103 (first quote on 71; second quote on 99; third quote on 101).

70. Tolleson-Rinehart and Stanley, *Claytie and the Lady*, 76–79; Jan Reid, *Let the People In: The Life and Times of Ann Richards* (Austin: University of Texas Press, 2012), 246.

71. Tolleson-Rinehart and Stanley, *Claytie and the Lady*, 113; Reid, *Let the People In*, 232–61.

72. Reid, *Let the People In*, 259, 268–69.

73. Tolleson-Rinehart and Stanley, *Claytie and the Lady*, 143; Reid, *Let the People In*, 288.

74. Tolleson-Rinehart and Stanley, *Claytie and the Lady*, 145–46; Reid, *Let the People In*, 276, 342–46.

75. Reid, *Let the People In*, 375–407.

76. Tolleson-Rinehart and Stanley, *Claytie and the Lady*, 77, 123.

Conclusion

1. Peter Weber, "Wendy Davis' Stunning Filibuster of a Texas Abortion Bill," *Week*, June 26, 2013, http://theweek.com/articles/462815/wendy-davis-stunning-filibuster-texas-abortion-bill.

2. Ibid.; Christy Hoppe, "After 12 1/2-Hour Filibuster, Senate Bill 5 Is Dead," June 25, 2013, *Dallas News*, http://archive.li/qamI1.

3. Weber, "Wendy Davis' Stunning Filibuster."

4. Manny Fernandez, "Abortion Restrictions Become Law in Texas, but Opponents Will Press Fight," *New York Times*, July 18, 2013.

5. Caitlin Gerdts, et al., "Impact of Clinic Closures on Women Obtaining Abortion Services after Implementation of a Restrictive Law in Texas," *American Journal of Public Health* 106 (May 2016), 857 (quote); Tara John, "Thousands of Texas Women Are Trying to Perform Home Abortions, Study Finds," *Time.com*, November 18, 2005, http://time.com/4118323/texas-home-abortions.

6. Alexa Ura, "US Supreme Court Overturns Texas Abortion Restrictions," *Texas Tribune*, June 27, 2016, https://www.texastribune.org/2016/06/27/us-supreme-court-rules-texas-abortion-case.

7. Michelle Goldberg, "The War on Texas Women," *Newsweek*, March 12, 2012, 26–29; Jordan Smith, "Rick Perry's War on Women," *Nation*, December 19, 2011, 19–21; Molly Redden, "How the War on Women Was Won," *Mother Jones*, September/October 2015, 28–36, 65; Amanda J. Stevenson et al., "Effect of Removal of Planned Parenthood from the Texas Women's Health Program," *New England Journal of Medicine* 374 (March 3, 2016): 853–60; Betsy Joles, "After Funding Cuts and Restructuring, Are Texas' Women's Health Programs Working?" *Texas Standard*, December 12, 2016, http://www.texasstandard.org/stories/will-the-restructuring-of-texas-womens-health-program-fix-its-problems.

8. US Census Bureau, American Fact finder, Table B24010, "Sex by Occupation for the Civilian Employed Population 16 years and Over," 2015 American Community Survey 1-Year Estimates, https://factfinder.census.gov/faces/tableservices/jsf/pages/productview.xhtml?src=bkmk; Fane Downs, "Texas Women at Work," in *Texas: A Sesquicentennial Celebration*, ed. Donald W. Whisenhunt (Austin, TX: Eakin Press, 1984), 320–23.

9. US Census Bureau, "Sex by Occupation"; Downs, "Texas Women at Work," 320–23; Kalpana Pai and Sameer Vaidya, "Glass Ceiling: Role of Women in the Corporate World," *Competition Forum* 4, no. 2 (2006): 421–26.

10. Institute for Women's Policy Research, Analysis of American Community Survey data (Integrated Public Use Microdata Series, Version 5.0); Misha Werschkul, Barbara Gault, Amy Caiazza, and Heidi Hartmann, *Women's Education and Earnings in Texas* (Washington, DC: American Association of University Women Educational Foundation, 2005), https://files.eric.ed.gov/fulltext/ED485719.pdf, 5–6; "The Gender Wage Gap by Occupation 2014 and by Race and Ethnicity," *Fact Sheet* (Institute for Women's Policy Research), April 2015, http://www.iwpr.org/initiatives/pay-equity-and-discrimination; Derek Lester, "Superintendent Salary Study: Is There Gender Equity in Texas?" *National Forum of Educational Administration and Supervision Journal* 31 (November 1, 2013): 38–54.

11. Legislative Reference Library of Texas, http://www.lrl.state.tx.us/.

12. Angela Howard, "A Woman's Place Is in the Dome: Examining the Campaign Strategies of Women Legislators in Texas," paper presented at the annual meeting of the American Sociological Association, Boston, July 31, 2008, http://citation.allacademic.com/meta/p239358_index.html.

Bibliography

Ables, L. Robert. "The Second Battle for the Alamo." *Southwestern Historical Quarterly* 70 (January 1967): 372–413.

Acosta, Teresa Palomo, and Ruthe Winegarten. *Las Tejanas: 300 Years of History*. Austin: University of Texas Press, 2003.

Aldave, Barbara Bader. "Women in the Law in Texas: The Stories of Three Pioneers." *St. Mary's Law Journal* 25 (1993): 289–99.

Allen, Raye Virginia. "An Image-Maker from Texas: Gordon Conway and a New Look for a New Woman." *Southwestern Historical Quarterly* 101 (July 1997): 17–57.

Alonzo, Armando C. *Tejano Legacy: Rancheros and Settlers in South Texas, 1734–1900*. Albuquerque: University of New Mexico Press, 1998.

Amberson, Mary Margaret McAllen, James A. McAllen, and Margaret H. McAllen. *I Would Rather Sleep in Texas: A History of the Lower Rio Grande Valley and the People of the Santa Anita Land Grant*. Austin: Texas State Historical Association, 2003.

Andreadis, Harriette. "True Womanhood Revisited: Women's Private Writing in Nineteenth-Century Texas." *Journal of the Southwest* 31 (Summer 1989): 179–204.

———. "The Woman's Commonwealth: A Study in the Coalescence of Social Forms." *Frontiers: A Journal of Women Studies* 7, no. 3 (1984): 79–86.

Bagley, Meredith M. "Playing Fair: The Rhetorical Limits of Liberalism in Women's Sport at the University of Texas, 1927–1992." PhD diss., University of Texas at Austin, 2010.

Bailey, Olga. *Mollie Bailey: The Circus Queen of the Southwest*. Edited by Bess Samuel Ayres. Dallas: Harben-Spotts, 1943.

Baker, Nancy E. "Hermine Tobolowsky: A Feminist's Fight for Equal Rights." In Turner, Cole, and Sharpless, *Texas Women*.

Balderach, Amy S. "A Different Kind of Reservation: Waco's Red-Light District Revisited, 1880–1920." Master's thesis, Baylor University, 2005.

Barnes, Jessica S., and Claudette E. Bennett. "The Asian Population: 2000." Census 2000 Brief (US Census Bureau), February 2002. https://www.census.gov/prod/2002pubs/c2kbr01–16.pdf.

Barr, Alwyn. *Black Texans: A History of African Americans in Texas, 1528–1995*. 2nd ed. Norman: University of Oklahoma Press, 1996.

Barr, Juliana. *Peace Came in the Form of a Woman: Indians and Spaniards in the Texas Borderlands.* Chapel Hill: University of North Carolina Press, 2007.

Barrett, Thomas. "The Great Hanging at Gainesville, Cooke Co., Texas." In Gallaway, *Texas*, 109–24.

Barthelme, Marion K. *Women in the Texas Populist Movement: Letters to the* Southern Mercury. College Station: Texas A&M University Press, 1997.

Bass, Patricia M. "A Gendered Search through Some West Texas Rock Art." In *New Light on Old Art: Recent Advances in Hunter-Gatherer Rock Art Research*, edited by David S. Whitley and Lawrence L. Loendorf, 67–74. Los Angeles: UCLA Institute of Archaeology Press, 1994. http://www.ruf.rice.edu/~raar/bassdoc.pdf.

Bernhard, Virginia. *Ima Hogg: The Governor's Daughter.* Austin: Texas Monthly Press, 1984.

Bess, Jennifer J. "Equal Rights for All and Special Privileges for None: Women's Participation in the Farmers' Alliance of Texas." Master's thesis, University of Houston, 1998.

Betts, Vicki. "'Everyone Has the War Fever': Anglo-Texan Women Prepare for Secession and War." In Liles and Boswell, *Women in Civil War Texas*, 17–36.

———, ed. "Public Voice of Texas Women." Scholar Works at UT Tyler, 2016. https://scholarworks.uttyler.edu/cw_newstopics/19.

———. "'A Sacred Charge upon Our Hands': Assisting the Families of Confederate Soldiers in Texas, 1861–1865." In *The Seventh Star of the Confederacy: Texas during the Civil War*, edited by Kenneth W. Howell, 246–67. Denton: University of North Texas Press, 2009.

Billingsley, Carolyn Earle. *Communities of Kinship: Antebellum Families and the Settlement of the Cotton Frontier.* Athens: University of Georgia Press, 2004.

Bishop, Harriet L., and Laurie Gudzikowski. "Ellen Viola Perry Wilson Anderson." In Massey, *Texas Women on the Cattle Trails*, 207–19.

Black, E. W. *A Pioneer Texas Family Follows Free Grazing.* New York: Carlton Press, 1967.

Black, Linda L. "Female Community Leaders in Houston, Texas: A Study of the Education of Ima Hogg and Christia Daniels Adair." PhD diss., Texas A&M University, 2008.

Blackwelder, Julia Kirk. *Women of the Depression: Caste and Culture in San Antonio, 1929–1939.* College Station: Texas A&M University Press, 1984.

Blücher, Maria von. *Maria von Blücher's Corpus Christi: Letters from the South Texas Frontier, 1849–1879.* Edited by Bruce S. Cheeseman. College Station: Texas A&M University Press, 2002.

Boles, Janet K. *The Politics of the Equal Rights Amendment.* New York: Longman, 1979.

———. "The Texas Woman in Politics: Role Model or Mirage." *Social Science Journal* 21 (January 1984): 77–90.

Boles, John. *The South through Time: A History of an America Region.* Upper Saddle River, NJ: Simon & Schuster, 1999.

Boswell, Angela. "Black Women during Slavery." In Glasrud and Pitre, *Black Women in Texas History*, 13–37.

———. "Harriet Perry: A Woman's Life in Civil War Texas." In Turner, Cole, and Sharpless, *Texas Women*, 105–27.

————. *Her Act and Deed: Women's Lives in a Rural Southern County, 1837–1873*. College Station: Texas A&M University Press, 2001.

————. "The Meaning of Participation: White Protestant Women in Antebellum Houston Churches." *Southwestern Historical Quarterly* 99 (July 1995): 27–47.

Bousman, C. Britt, Barry W. Baker, and Anne C. Kerr. "Paleoindian Archeology in Texas." In *The Prehistory of Texas*, edited by Timothy K. Perttula, 15–98. College Station: Texas A&M University Press, 2004.

Brady, David W., and Kent L. Tedin. "Ladies in Pink: Religion and Political Ideology in the Anti-ERA Movement." *Social Science Quarterly* 56 (March 1976): 564–75.

Brady, Marilyn Dell. *The Asian Texans*. College Station: Texas A&M University Press, 2004.

Brannon-Wranosky, Jessica S. "Southern Promise and Necessity: Texas, Regional Identity, and the National Woman Suffrage Movement, 1868–1920." PhD diss., University of North Texas, 2010.

Brannon-Wranosky, Jessica, and Bruce A. Glassrud, eds. *Impeached: The Removal of Texas Governor James E. Ferguson*. College Station: Texas A&M University Press, 2017.

Bridges, Jennifer. "Skiddy Street: Prostitution and Vice in Denison, Texas, 1872–1922." Master's thesis, University of North Texas, 2011.

Brindley, Anne A. "Jane Long." *Southwestern Historical Quarterly* 56 (October 1952): 211–38.

Brown, Norman D. *Hood, Bonnet, and Little Brown Jug: Texas Politics, 1921–1928*. College Station: Texas A&M University Press, 1984.

Brown, Ruth Murray. *For a Christian America: A History of the Religious Right*. Amherst, NY: Prometheus Books, 2002.

Browning, Dominique. "Waiting for Mommy." *Texas Monthly*, February 1982, 124–31, 184–93, 198.

Bundschuh, Molly Ellen. "Cowboys, 'Queers,' and Community: The AIDS Crisis in Houston and Dallas, 1981–1996." Master's thesis, University of North Texas, 2014.

Burnett, Georgellen. *We Just Toughed It Out: Women in the Llano Estacado*. El Paso: Texas Western Press, 1990.

Burns, Chester R. "Health and Medicine." *Handbook of Texas Online*. http://www.tsha online.org/handbook/online/articles/smhzc.

Calderón, Roberto R. "Unión, Paz y Trabajo: Laredo's Mexican Mutual Aid Societies, 1890s." In Zamora, Orozco, and Rocha, *Mexican Americans in Texas History*, 63–77.

Campbell, Randolph B. *An Empire for Slavery: The Peculiar Institution in Texas, 1821–1865*. Baton Rouge: Louisiana State University Press, 1989.

————. *Gone to Texas: A History of the Lone Star State*. New York: Oxford University Press, 2003.

Campbell, Randolph B., and Donald K. Pickens. "'My Dear Husband': A Texas Slave's Love Letter, 1862." *Journal of Negro History* 65 (Autumn 1980): 361–64.

Campbell, T. N., and T. J. Campbell. "Cabeza de Vaca among the Indians of Southern Texas." In *The Indians of Southern Texas and Northeastern Mexico: Selected Writings of Thomas Nolan Campbell*, edited by T. N. Campbell, 7–21. Austin: University of Texas, 1988.

Cantrell, Gregg. "The Bones of Stephen F. Austin: History and Memory in Progressive Era Texas." In Cantrell and Turner, *Lone Star Pasts*, 39–74.

————. *Stephen F. Austin: Empresario of Texas*. New Haven: Yale University Press, 1999.

Cantrell, Gregg, and Elizabeth Hayes Turner, eds. *Lone Star Pasts: Memory and History in Texas*. College Station: Texas A&M University Press, 2007.

Carleton, Don E. "McCarthyism in Houston: The George Ebey Affair." *Southwestern Historical Quarterly* 80 (October 1976): 163–76.

Carlson, Paul H. *The Plains Indians*. College Station: Texas A&M University Press, 1998.

Caro, Robert A. *The Years of Lyndon Johnson: The Path to Power*. New York: Alfred A. Knopf, 1982.

Carroll, Mark A. *Homesteads Ungovernable: Families, Sex, Race, and the Law in Frontier Texas, 1823–1860*. Austin: University of Texas Press, 2001.

Carter, Cecile Elkins. *Caddo Indians: Where We Come From*. Norman: University of Oklahoma Press, 1995.

Cashin, Joan E. *A Family Venture: Men and Women on the Southern Frontier*. Baltimore: Johns Hopkins University Press, 1991.

Caughfield, Adrienne. *True Women and Westward Expansion*. College Station: Texas A&M University Press, 2005.

Chapa, Evey. "Mujeres por la Raza Unida." *Caracol* 1, no. 2 (1974): 3–5. In García, *Chicana Feminist Thought*, 178–80.

————. "Report from the National Women's Political Caucus." In García, *Chicana Feminist Thought*, 174–77.

Chew, Jessica. "Vietnamese and Chinese American Cultures: Destination Houston." *Houston History* 13 (Fall 2016): 21–24.

Chipman, Donald E. *Spanish Texas, 1519–1821*. Austin: University of Texas Press, 1992.

Chipman, Donald E., and Harriett Denise Joseph. *Notable Men and Women of Spanish Texas*. Austin: University of Texas Press, 1999.

Christian, Stella L., ed. *The History of the Texas Federation of Women's Clubs*. Houston: Dealey-Adey-Elgin, 1919.

"Civil War Letters of John Samuel Shropshire." *Nesbitt Memorial Library Journal* 7 (January 1997): 61–70.

Cochrane, Michelle. "Educational Opportunities Available for Women in Antebellum Texas." Master's thesis, University of North Texas, 2006.

Coleman, Ann Raney Thomas. In Exley, *Texas Tears and Texas Sunshine*, 29–47.

Cook, Mary Potchernick. "Angelina's Rosies: Women at War in World War II East Texas." Master's thesis, Stephen F. Austin State University, 1998.

Cornelsen, Kathleen. "Women Airforce Service Pilots of World War II: Exploring Military Aviation, Encountering Discrimination, and Exchanging Traditional Roles in Service to America." *Journal of Women's History* 17 (Winter 2005): 111–19.

Cotera, Martha. *Diosa y Hembra: The History and Heritage of Chicanas*. Austin: Information Systems Development, 1976.

Cottrell, Debbie Mauldin. "National Women's Conference, 1977." *Handbook of Texas Online*. http://www.tshaonline.org/handbook/online/articles/pwngq.

————. *Pioneer Woman Educator: The Progressive Spirit of Annie Webb Blanton*. College Station: Texas A&M University Press, 1993.

Cowan, Ruth Schwartz. *More Work for Mother: The Ironies of Household Technology from the Open Hearth to the Microwave.* New York: Basic Books, 1983.

Coyle, Laurie, Gail Hershatter, and Emily Honig. "Women at Farah: An Unfinished Story." In *Mexican Women in the United States: Struggles Past and Present,* edited by Magdalena Mora and Adelaida R. Del Castillo, 117–43. Los Angeles: Chicano Studies Research Center Publications, 1980.

Cravens, Patsy. *Leavin' a Testimony: Portraits from Rural Texas.* Austin: University of Texas Press, 2006.

Crawford, Audrey. "'To protect, to feed, and to give momentum to every effort': African American Clubwomen in Houston, 1880–1910." *Houston Review* 1 (Fall 2003): 15–23.

Crimm, Ana Carolina Castillo. *De León: A Tejano Family History.* Austin: University of Texas Press, 2003.

Critchlow, Donald T. *Phyllis Schlafly and Grassroots Conservatism: A Woman's Crusade.* Princeton: Princeton University Press, 2005.

Crowder, Eleanor L. M. "Nursing Education." *Handbook of Texas Online.* http://www.tshaonline.org/handbook/online/articles/shn01.

Croxdale, Richard, and Jim Cullers. *Stand Ins: Austin, Texas, 1960.* Austin: People's History in Texas, 2015. http://peopleshistoryintexas.org/projects-2/standins.

Cummins, Light Townsend. *Emily Austin of Texas, 1795–1851.* Fort Worth: Texas Christian University Press, 2009.

Cutrer, Emily Fourmy. *The Art of the Woman: The Life and Work of Elisabet Ney.* Lincoln: University of Nebraska Press, 1988.

Cutter, Charles R. *The Legal Culture of Northern New Spain, 1700–1810.* Albuquerque: University of New Mexico Press, 1995.

Czuchry, Rebecca A. "In Defense of Their Families: African American Women, the Freedmen's Bureau, and Racial Violence during Reconstruction in Texas." In *Lone Star Unionism, Dissent and Resistance: Other Sides of Civil War Texas,* edited by Jesús F. de la Teja, 174–94. Norman: University of Oklahoma Press, 2016.

De La Teja, Jesus F. "Indians, Soldiers, and Canary Islanders: The Making of a Texas Frontier Community." *Locus* 3 (Fall 1990): 84–96.

———. *San Antonio de Bexar: A Community on New Spain's Northern Frontier.* Albuquerque: University of New Mexico, 1995.

De La Teja, Jesús F., Paula Marks, and Ron Tyler. *Texas: Crossroads of North America.* Boston: Houghton Mifflin, 2004.

De León, Arnoldo. *Ethnicity in the Sunbelt: A History of Mexican Americans in Houston.* Houston, Tex.: Mexican American Studies Program, 1989.

———. "María Cárdenas: San Angelo Chicano-Era Activist." In Willett and Curley, *Invisible Texans,* 226–36.

———. *Mexican Americans in Texas: A Brief History.* Wheeling, IL: Harland Davidson, 1999.

———. *The Tejano Community, 1836–1900.* Albuquerque: University of New Mexico Press, 1982.

———. *They Called Them Greasers: Anglo Attitudes toward Mexicans in Texas, 1821–1900.* Austin: University of Texas Press, 1983.

Decker, Stephanie. "African American Women in the Civil Rights Era, 1954–1974." In Glasrud and Pitre, *Black Women in Texas History*, 159–76.

———. "Women in the Civil Rights Movement: Juanita Craft versus the Dallas Elite." *East Texas Historical Journal* 39 (Spring 2001): 33–42.

Downs, Fane. "Texas Women at Work." In *Texas: A Sesquicentennial Celebration*, edited by Donald W. Whisenhunt, 309–25. Austin, TX: Eakin Press, 1984.

Downs, Fane, and Nancy Baker Jones, eds. *Women and Texas History: Selected Essays.* Austin: Texas State Historical Association, 1993.

Dugas, Vera Lea. "A Social and Economic History of Texas in the Civil and Reconstruction Periods." PhD diss., University of Texas, 1963.

Dunn, Patricia A., and Sara R. Massey. "Catherine (Kate) Malone Medlin." In Massey, *Texas Women on the Cattle Trails*, 25–35.

Dykes-Hoffman, Judith. "German Texas Unionist Women on the Civil War Home Front." In Liles and Boswell, *Women in Civil War Texas*, 181–202.

Dysart, Jane. "Mexican Women in San Antonio, 1830–1860: The Assimilation Process." *Western Historical Quarterly* 7 (October 1976): 365–75.

Edwards, Laura F. *Scarlett Doesn't Live Here Anymore: Southern Women in the Civil War Era.* Urbana: University of Illinois Press, 2000.

Enstam, Elizabeth York. *Women and the Creation of Urban Life, Dallas, Texas, 1843–1920.* College Station: Texas A&M University Press, 1998.

Exley, Jo Ella Powell. *Frontier Blood: The Saga of the Parker Family.* College Station: Texas A&M University Press, 2001.

———, ed. *Texas Tears and Texas Sunshine: Voices of Frontier Women.* College Station: Texas A&M University Press, 1985.

Faulk, Odie B. *The Last Years of Spanish Texas, 1778–1821.* London: Mouton, 1964.

Faust, Drew Gilpin. *Mothers of Invention: Women of the Slaveholding South in the American Civil War.* Chapel Hill: University of North Carolina Press, 1996.

———. *Southern Stories: Slaveholders in Peace and War.* Columbia: University of Missouri Press, 1992.

Federal Writers' Project: Slave Narrative Project, vol. 16, *Texas.* Washington, DC: Library of Congress, 1941.

"Felix Z. Longoria: Private, United States Army." Arlington National Cemetery Website. http://www.arlingtoncemetery.net/longoria.htm.

Fenton, James I. "Critters, Sourdough, and Dugouts: Women and Imitation Theory on the Staked Plains, 1875–1910." In Wunder, *At Home on the Range*, 19–35.

Fernea, Elizabeth W., and Marilyn P. Duncan. *Texas Women in Politics.* Austin: Foundation for Women's Resources, 1977.

Festle, Mary Jo. *Playing Nice: Politics and Apologies in Women's Sports.* New York: Columbia University Press, 1996.

Fields-Hawkins, Stephanie. "Frances Farenthold: Texas' Joan of Arc." Master's thesis, University of North Texas, 2012.

Fink, Rob. "Hermine Tobolowsky, the Texas ELRA, and the Political Struggle for Women's Equal Rights." *Journal of the West* 42 (Summer 2003): 52–57.

Foley, Neil. *The White Scourge: Mexicans, Blacks, and Poor Whites in Texas Cotton Culture.* Berkeley: University of California Press, 1997.

Ford, Ramona. "Native American Women: Changing Statuses, Changing Interpretations." In *Writing the Range: Race, Class and Culture in the Women's West*, edited by Elizabeth Jameson and Susan Armitage, 42–68. Norman: University of Oklahoma Press, 1997.

Fout, Ellen Pratt. "'A miracle occurred': The Houston Committee of International Women's Year, Houston, 1977." *Houston Review* 1 (Fall 2003): 4–11.

Frear, Yvonne Davis. "Making the Invisible Visible: African American Women in the Texas Civil Rights Movement." In *Southern Black Women in the Modern Civil Rights Movement*, edited by Bruce A. Glasrud and Merline Pitre, 29–43. College Station: Texas A&M University Press, 2013.

Freeman, Bonnie Cook. "Antifeminists and Women's Liberation: A Case Study of a Paradox." *Women and Politics* 3 (Spring 1983): 21–38.

Friedan, Betty. *The Feminine Mystique*. New York: Norton, 1963.

Gallaway, B. P., ed. *Texas: The Dark Corner of the Confederacy: Contemporary Accounts of the Lone Star State in the Civil War*. 3rd ed. Lincoln: University of Nebraska Press, 1994.

Gammage, Judie. "Quest for Equality: An Historical Overview of Women's Rights Activism in Texas, 1890–1975." PhD diss., North Texas State University, 1982.

Ganther, Eric Jason. "From Closet to Crusade: The Struggle for Lesbian-Gay Civil Rights in Austin, Texas, 1970–1982." Master's thesis, University of Texas at Austin, 1990.

García, Alma M., ed. *Chicana Feminist Thought: The Basic Historical Writings*. New York: Routledge, 1997.

García, Mario T. *Desert Immigrants: The Mexicans of El Paso, 1880–1920*. New Haven: Yale University Press, 1982.

García, Sonia R., et al. *Políticas: Latina Public Officials in Texas*. Austin: University of Texas Press, 2008.

Garner-Wizard, Mariann. "The Lie." In Janes, *No Apologies*, 72–99.

Garrett, Alan W. "Teacher Education." *Handbook of Texas Online*. http://www.tshaonline.org/handbook/online/articles/kdtsj.

Gauderman, Kimberly. *Women's Lives in Colonial Quito: Gender, Law, and Economy in Spanish America*. Austin: University of Texas Press, 2003.

Gelo, Daniel J., and Scott Zesch, eds. "Every Day Seemed to Be a Holiday: The Captivity of Bianca Babb." *Southwestern Historical Quarterly* (July 2003): 34–67.

"The Gender Wage Gap by Occupation 2014 and by Race and Ethnicity." *Fact Sheet* (Institute for Women's Policy Research), April 2015. https://iwpr.org/wp-content/uploads/wpallimport/files/iwpr-export/publications/C431.pdf.

Gerdts, Caitlin, et al. "Impact of Clinic Closures on Women Obtaining Abortion Services after Implementation of a Restrictive Law in Texas." *American Journal of Public Health* 106 (May 2016): 857–64.

Gilmour, Terry L. "A Difference: Women in the Texas Legislature." PhD diss., Texas Tech University, 1999.

Glasrud, Bruce A. "Asians in Texas: An Overview, 1870–1990." *East Texas Historical Journal* 39, no. 2 (2001): 10–22.

Glasrud, Bruce A., and Merline Pitre, eds. *Black Women in Texas History*. College Station: Texas A&M University Press, 2008.

Gohlke, Melissa Ann. "Out in the Alamo City: Revealing San Antonio's Gay and Lesbian Past, World War II to the 1990s." Master's thesis, University of Texas at San Antonio, 2012.

Goldberg, Michelle. "The War on Texas Women." *Newsweek*, March 12, 2012, 26–29.

González, Gabriela. "Jovita Idar: The Ideological Origins of a Transnational Advocate for *La Raza*." In Turner, Cole, and Sharpless, *Texas Women*, 225–248.

González, Jovita. *Life along the Border: A Landmark Tejana Thesis*. College Station: Texas A&M University Press, 2006.

Gould, Florence C., and Patricia N. Pando. *Claiming Their Land: Women Homesteaders in Texas*. El Paso: Texas Western Press, 1991.

Grider, Sylvia Ann, and Lou Halsell Rodenberger. *Texas Women Writers: A Tradition of Their Own*. College Station: Texas A&M University Press, 1997.

Griffith, William Joyce. *The Hasinai Indians of East Texas as Seen by Europeans, 1687–1772*. New Orleans: Tulane University Press, 1954.

Gutiérrez, José Angel, Michelle Meléndez, and Sonia Adriana Noyola. *Chicanas in Charge: Texas Women in the Public Arena*. Lanham, MD: AltaMira Press, 2007.

Hall, Jacquelyn Dowd. *Revolt against Chivalry: Jessie Daniel Ames and the Women's Campaign Against Lynching*. New York: Columbia University Press, 1993.

Hall, Sarah Harkey. *Surviving on the Texas Frontier: The Journal of an Orphan Girl in San Saba County*. Austin, TX: Eakin Press, 1996.

Hämäläinen, Pekka. *The Comanche Empire*. New Haven: Yale University Press, 2008.

Harris, Dilue Rose. "The Reminiscences of Mrs. Dilue Harris. II." *Quarterly of the Texas State Historical Association* 4 (January 1901): 155–89.

Hartmann, Susan M. *The Home Front and Beyond: American Women in the 1940s*. Boston: Twayne, 1982.

Harvey, Sandra Denise. "Working for Change: Wage-Earning Women in Waco, Texas Defense Industries during World War II." PhD diss., Texas Tech, 2009.

Hayden, Casey, and Mary King. "Sex and Caste: A Kind of Memo." 1965. *History Is a Weapon*. http://www.historyisaweapon.com/defcon1/sexcaste.html.

Helm, Mary Sherwood Wightman. In Exley, *Texas Tears and Texas Sunshine*, 19–28.

Hernández, Salomé. "*Nueva Mexicanas* as Refugees and Reconquest Settlers, 1680–1696." In *New Mexico Women: Intercultural Perspectives*, edited by Joan M. Jensen and Darlis A. Miller, 41–69. Albuquerque: University of New Mexico Press, 1986.

Hickerson, Nancy Parrot. *The Jumanos: Hunters and Traders of the South Plains*. Austin: University of Texas, 1994.

Hill, Jane Hallowell. Narrative. MS 288. Thomson Family of Texas Papers, 1832–1898. Woodson Research Center, Fondren Library, Rice University, Houston.

Hill, Patricia Evridge. "Real Women and True Womanhood: Grassroots Organizing among Dallas Dressmakers in 1935." *Labor's Heritage* 5 (Spring 1994): 5–15.

Hinojosa, Gilberto M. *A Borderlands Town in Transition: Laredo, 1755–1870*. College Station: Texas A&M University Press, 1983.

Howard, Angela. "A Woman's Place Is in the Dome: Examining the Campaign Strategies of Women Legislators in Texas." Paper presented at the annual meeting of the American Sociological Association, Boston, July 31, 2008. http://citation.allacademic.com/meta/p239358_index.html.

Howell, Kenneth W., and James M. Smallwood. "Expanded Opportunities: Black Women in the Modern Era, 1974–2000." In Glasrud and Pitre, *Black Women in Texas History*, 177–93.

Hudson, Linda S. *Mistress of Manifest Destiny: A Biography of Jane McManus Storm Cazneau, 1807–1878*. Austin: Texas State Historical Association, 2001.

Humphrey, David C. "Prostitution in Texas: From the 1830s to the 1960s." *East Texas Historical Journal* 33, no. 1 (1996): 27–43.

Institute for Women's Policy Research. "The Status of Women in Texas, 2015: Highlights." IWPR #R454. https://statusofwomendata.org/wp-content/themes/witsfull/factsheets/factsheet-texas.pdf.

Ivy, James D. *No Saloon in the Valley: The Southern Strategy of Texas Prohibitionists in the 1880s*. Waco, TX: Baylor University Press, 2003.

Jackson, Emma Louise Moyer. "Petticoat Politics: Political Activism among Texas Women in the 1920s." PhD diss., University of Texas, 1980.

Jackson, Jack. *Los Mesteños: Spanish Ranching in Texas, 1721–1821*. College Station: Texas A&M University Press, 1986.

Jackson, Kenneth T. *Crabgrass Frontier: The Suburbanization of the United States*. New York: Oxford University Press, 1985.

Jackson, Sarah Ragland. *Texas Woman of Letters: Karle Wilson Baker*. College Station: Texas A&M University Press, 2005.

Jameson, Elizabeth. "Women as Workers, Women as Civilizers: True Womanhood in the American West." In *The Women's West*, edited by Susan Armitage and Elizabeth Jameson, 145–64. Norman: University of Oklahoma Press, 1987.

Janes, Daryl, ed. *No Apologies: Texas Radicals Celebrate the '60s*. Austin, Tex.: Eakin Press, 1992.

Jaques, Mary J. *Texas Ranch Life, with Three Months through Mexico in a "Prairie Schooner."* College Station: Texas A&M University Press, 1989.

Johansson, M. Jane, ed. *Widows by the Thousand: The Civil War Letters of Theophilus and Harriet Perry, 1862–1864*. Fayetteville: University of Arkansas Press, 2000.

John, Tara. "Thousands of Texas Women Are Trying to Perform Home Abortions, Study Finds." *Time.com*, November 18, 2005. http://time.com/4118323/texas-home-abortions.

Johnson, Henry F. C., to Delilah Johnson. September 23, 1861, and April 10, 1863. MA83–19. Henry F. C. Johnson Civil War Letters. Texas/Dallas History & Archives Division, Dallas Public Library.

Johnston, S. M. *Builders by the Sea: History of the Ursuline Community of Galveston, Texas*. New York: Exposition Press, 1971.

Joles, Betsy. "After Funding Cuts and Restructuring, Are Texas' Women's Health Programs Working?" *Texas Standard*, December 12, 2016. http://www.texasstandard.org/stories/will-the-restructuring-of-texas-womens-health-program-fix-its-problems.

Jones, Nancy Baker. "Making Texas *Our* Texas: The Emergence of Texas Women's History, 1976–1990." *Southwestern Historical Quarterly* 120 (January 2017): 279–313.

Jones, Nancy Baker, and Ruthe Winegarten. *Capitol Women: Texas Female Legislators, 1923–1999*. Austin: University of Texas Press, 2000.

Joplin, Laura. *Love, Janis*. New York: Villard Books, 1992.

Jordan, Terry G. *German Seed in Texas Soil: Immigrant Farmers in Nineteenth-Century Texas.* Austin: University of Texas Press, 1966.

Karbach, Ruth Hosey. "Ellen Lawson Dabbs: Waving the Equal Rights Banner." In Turner, Cole, and Sharpless, *Texas Women*, 176–200.

Kattner, Lauren Ann. "The Diversity of Old South White Women: The Peculiar Worlds of German American Women." In *Discovering the Women in Slavery: Emancipating Perspectives on the American Past*, edited by Patricia Morton, 299–311. Athens: University of Georgia Press, 1996.

Kelley, Sean M. *Los Brazos de Dios: A Plantation Society in the Texas Borderlands, 1821–1865.* Baton Rouge: Louisiana State University Press, 2010.

Kerber, Linda K. *No Constitutional Right to Be Ladies: Women and Obligations of Citizenship.* New York: Hill and Wang, 1998.

Kilgore, Dan. "'Two Sixshooters and a Sunbonnet': The Story of Sally Skull." In *Legendary Ladies of Texas*, edited by Francis Edward Abernethy, 59–71. Denton: University of North Texas Press, 1994.

King, Kelley M. *Call Her a Citizen: Progressive-Era Activist and Educator Anna Pennybacker.* College Station: Texas A&M University Press, 2010.

Kirkland, Kate Sayen. *The Hogg Family and Houston: Philanthropy and the Civic Ideal.* Austin: University of Texas Press, 2009.

Kitch, Sally L. *This Strange Society of Women: Reading the Letters and Lives of the Woman's Commonwealth.* Columbus: Ohio State University Press, 1993.

Kleberg, Rosa. "Some of My Early Experiences in Texas." *Quarterly of the Texas State Historical Association* 1 (April 1898): 297–302.

Kosary, Rebecca A. "'To Punish and Humiliate the Entire Community': White Violence Perpetrated against African-American Women in Texas, 1865–1868." In *Still the Arena of Civil War: Violence and Turmoil in Reconstruction Texas, 1865–1874*, edited by Kenneth W. Howell, 327–51. Denton: University of North Texas Press, 2012.

Kossie-Chernyshev, Karen, ed. *Recovering Five Generations Hence: The Life and Writing of Lillian Jones Horace.* College Station: Texas A&M University Press, 2013.

Labadie, Cecilia. Diary. 1863. Folder 94–0004. Galveston and Texas History Center, Rosenberg Library, Galveston, Texas.

Lack, Paul D. "Slavery and the Texas Revolution." *Southwestern Historical Quarterly* 89 (July 1985): 181–202.

Lassiter, Matthew D., and Kevin M. Kruse. "The Bulldozer Revolution: Suburbs and Southern History since World War II." *Journal of Southern History* 75 (August 2009): 691–706.

La Vere, David. *Texas Indians.* College Station: Texas A&M University Press, 2004.

Leckie, Shirley Anne, ed. *The Colonel's Lady on the Western Frontier: The Correspondence of Alice Kirk Grierson.* Lincoln: University of Nebraska Press, 1989.

Ledesma, Irene. "Unlikely Strikers: Mexican-American Women in Strike Activity in Texas, 1919–1974." PhD diss., Ohio State University, 1992.

Lester, Derek. "Superintendent Salary Study: Is There Gender Equity in Texas?" *National Forum of Educational Administration and Supervision Journal* 31 (November 1, 2013): 38–54.

Letson, Dawn. "Girl Pilots of Avenger Field: Sweetwater's Romance with the WASP Of WWII." *Sound Historian* 13 (2011): 33–40.

Levengood, Paul Alejandro. "For the Duration and Beyond: World War II and the Creation of Modern Houston, Texas." PhD diss., Rice University, 1999.

Lewis, Linda. "Young, Gifted, and Black." In Janes, *No Apologies*, 62–71.

Lich, Glen E. *The German Texans*. San Antonio: University of Texas Institute of Texan Cultures, 1981.

Liles, Deborah M. "Not Your Typical Southern Belles: Women on the Western Frontier of Texas." In Liles and Boswell, *Women in Civil War Texas*, 259–81.

Liles, Deborah M., and Angela Boswell, eds. *Women in Civil War Texas: Diversity and Dissidence in the Trans-Mississippi*. Denton: University of North Texas Press, 2016.

Lincecum, Jerry Bryan, Edward Hake Phillips, and Peggy A. Redshaw, eds. *Gideon Lincecum's Sword: Civil War Letters from the Texas Home Front*. Denton: University of North Texas Press, 2001.

Lomas, Clara. *The Rebel: Leonor Villegas de Magnón*. Houston: Arte Público Press, 1994.

Loveland, Carol J. "Vertebral Anomalies and Degenerative Lesions in the Caddoan Skeletal Population, Kaufman-Williams Site, Red River County, Texas." *Bulletin of the Texas Archeological Society* 65 (1994): 161–81.

Lucko, Paul M. "The 'Next "Big Job"': Women Prison Reformers in Texas, 1918–1930." In Downs and Jones, *Women and Texas History*, 72–87.

Lundy, Benjamin. *The Life, Travels, and Opinions of Benjamin Lundy, including His Journeys to Texas and Mexico*. Philadelphia: William D. Parrish, 1847.

Mackey, Thomas C. *Red Lights Out: A Legal History of Prostitution, Disorderly Houses, and Vice Districts, 1870–1917*. New York: Garland, 1987.

Mackintosh, Prudence. "The Good Old Girls." *Texas Monthly*, January 1978, 88, 151.

Maddox, Sandra Davis. "Title IX of the Educational Amendments of 1972: Level of Implementation in Texas Public Schools." PhD diss., University of North Texas, 1995.

Malone, Ann Patton. *Women on the Texas Frontier: A Cross-Cultural Perspective*. Southwestern Studies Monograph 70. El Paso: Texas Western Press, 1983.

Manning, Diane. *Hill Country Teacher: Oral Histories from the One-room School and Beyond*. Boston: Twayne, 1990.

Maret, Elizabeth. *Women of the Range: Women's Roles in the Texas Beef Cattle Industry*. College Station: Texas A&M University Press, 1993.

Marks, Paula Mitchell. *Hands to the Spindle: Texas Women and Home Textile Production, 1822–1880*. College Station: Texas A&M University Press, 1996.

———. Introduction to *Surviving on the Texas Frontier: The Journal of a Frontier Orphan Girl in San Saba County, 1852–1907*, by Sarah Harkey Hall, xii–xix. Austin, TX: Eakin Press, 1996.

———. "Trials, Tribulations, and Good Times: Westering Women in Frontier Texas, 1821–1870." In Willett and Curley, *Invisible Texans*, 74–84.

Marschall, Melissa. "A Descriptive Analysis of Female Mayors: The US and Texas in Comparative Perspective." In *Local Politics and Mayoral Elections in 21st Century America: The Keys to City Hall*, edited by Sean D. Foreman and Marcia L. Godwin, 35–49. New York: Routledge, 2015.

Massey, Sara R. *Texas Women on the Cattle Trails*. College Station: Texas A&M University Press, 2006.

McArthur, Judith N. *Creating the New Woman: The Rise of Southern Women's Progressive Culture in Texas, 1893–1918*. Urbana: University of Illinois Press, 1998.

———. "Maternity Wars: Gender, Race, and the Sheppard-Towner Act in Texas." In Turner, Cole, and Sharpless, *Texas Women*, 249–76.

———. "Minnie Fisher Cunningham's Back Door Lobby in Texas: Political Maneuvering in a One-Party State." In *One Woman, One Vote: Rediscovering the Woman Suffrage Movement*, edited by Marjorie Spruill Wheeler, 315–32. Troutdale, OR: NewSage Press, 1995.

McArthur, Judith N., and Harold L. Smith. *Minnie Fisher Cunningham: A Suffragist's Life in Politics*. New York: Oxford University Press, 2003.

———. "Not Whistling Dixie: Women's Movements and Feminist Politics." In *The Texas Left: The Radical Roots of Lone Star Liberalism*, edited by David O'Donald Cullen and Kyle G. Wilkison, 133–56. College Station: Texas A&M University Press, 2010.

———. *Texas through Women's Eyes: The Twentieth-Century Experience*. Austin: University of Texas Press, 2010.

McCaslin, Richard B. *Tainted Breeze: The Great Hanging at Gainesville, Texas, 1862*. Baton Rouge: Louisiana State University Press, 1994.

McCord, Louisa S. "Woman and Her Needs." In *Louisa S. McCord: Political and Social Essays*, edited by Richard C. Lounsbury, 125–57. Charlottesville: University Press of Virginia, 1995.

McCoy, Ingeborg Ruberg. "Tales of the Grandmothers, II." In *Eagle in the New World: German Immigration to Texas and America*, edited by Theodore Gish and Richard Spuler, 212–20. College Station: Texas Committee for the Humanities by Texas A&M University Press, 1986.

McDonald, Dedra S. "To Be Black and Female in the Spanish Southwest: Toward a History of African Women on New Spain's Far Northern Frontier." In *African American Women Confront the West, 1600–2000*, edited by Quintard Taylor and Shirley Ann Wilson Moore. Norman: University of Oklahoma Press, 2003.

McElhaney, Jacquelyn Masur. *Pauline Periwinkle and Progressive Reform in Dallas*. College Station: Texas A&M University Press, 1998.

McKellar, Margaret Maud. *Life on a Mexican Ranch*. Cranbury, NJ: Associated University Presses, 1994.

McKenzie, Phyllis A. "Margaret Heffernan Dunbar Hardy Borland." In Massey, *Texas Women on the Cattle Trails*, 89–118.

McLeRoy, Sherrie S. *Texas Women First: Leading Ladies of Lone Star History*. Charleston, SC: History Press, 2015.

McMichael, Kelly. "'Memories Are Short but Monuments Lengthen Remembrances': The United Daughters of the Confederacy and the Power of Civil War Memory." In Cantrell and Turner, *Lone Star Pasts*, 95–118.

McMillen, Sally G. *Motherhood in the Old South: Pregnancy, Childbirth, and Infant Rearing*. Baton Rouge: Louisiana State University Press, 1990.

"Meet Local Legend: Nancy Dickey, M.D." In *Local Legends: Celebrating America's Local Women Physicians*. US National Library of Medicine, National Institutes of Health. https://www.nlm.nih.gov/locallegends/Biographies/Dickey_Nancy.html.

Mellard, Jason. *Progressive Country: How the 1970s Transformed the Texan in Popular Culture*. Austin: University of Texas Press, 2013.

Mendoza, Lydia, and Chris Strachwitz. *Lydia Mendoza: A Family Autobiography*. Houston: Arte Público Press, 1993.

Mercado, Bianca. "Latinas in Dallas, 1910–2010: Becoming New Women." In Turner, Cole, and Sharpless, *Texas Women*, 302–17.

Merryman, Molly. *Clipped Wings: The Rise and Fall of the Women Airforce Service Pilots (WASPs) of World War II*. New York: New York University Press, 1998.

Meschke, Amy. "Women's Lives through Women's Wills in the Spanish and Mexican Borderlands, 1750–1846." PhD diss., Southern Methodist University, 2004.

Mills, Betty J. *Calico Chronicle: Texas Women and Their Fashions, 1830–1910*. Lubbock: Texas Tech Press, 1985.

Monday, Jane Clements, and Betty Bailey Colley. *Voices from the Wild Horse Desert: The Vaquero Families of the King and Kenedy Ranches*. Austin: University of Texas Press, 1997.

Monday, Jane Clements, and Frances Brannen Vick. *Petra's Legacy: The South Texas Ranching Empire of Petra Vela and Mifflin Kenedy*. College Station: Texas A&M University Press, 2007.

Montejano, David. *Anglos and Mexicans in the Making of Texas, 1836–1986*. Austin: University of Texas Press, 1987.

Moore, Eudora Inez. In Exley, *Texas Tears and Texas Sunshine*, 142–53.

Moore, James Talmadge. *Through Fire and Flood: The Catholic Church in Frontier Texas, 1836–1900*. College Station: Texas A&M University Press, 1992.

Moore, Laura Jane. "Lozen: An Apache Woman Warrior." In *Sifters: Native American Women's Lives*, edited by Theda Perdue, 92–107. New York: Oxford University Press, 2001.

Murr, Erika L., ed. *A Rebel Wife in Texas: The Diary and Letters of Elizabeth Scott Neblett, 1852–1864*. Baton Rouge: Louisiana State University Press, 2001.

Myers, Lois E. *Letters by Lamplight: A Woman's View of Everyday Life in South Texas, 1873–1883*. Waco, TX: Baylor University Press, 1991.

Myres, Sandra L. Introduction to *A Cowman's Wife*, by Mary Kidder Rak. Austin: Texas State Historical Association Press, 1993.

———. *Westering Women and the Frontier Experience, 1800–1915*. Albuquerque: University of New Mexico Press, 1982.

National Coalition for Women and Girls in Education. *Title IX at 30: Report Card on Gender Equity* Washington, DC: National Coalition for Women and Girls in Education, 2002. http://www.feminist.org/education/TitleIXat30.pdf.

Newcomb, W. W., Jr. *The Indians of Texas: From Prehistoric to Modern Times*. Austin: University of Texas Press, 1961.

———. "Karankawa." In *Ethnology of the Texas Indians*, edited by Thomas R. Hester, 139–49. New York: Garland, 1991.

Norgaard, Carolyn Porter. "Women A-horseback, Side or Astride." In *2001: A Texas Folklore Odyssey*, edited by Francis Edward Abernethy, 172–85. Denton: University of North Texas Press, 2001.

Norman, Elizabeth. *We Band of Angels: The Untold Story of American Nurses Trapped on Bataan by the Japanese.* New York: Random House, 1999.

Norwood, Vera. "Crazy-Quilt Lives: Frontier Sources for Southwestern Women's Literature." In *The Desert Is No Lady: Southwestern Landscapes in Women's Writing and Art*, edited by Vera Norwood and Janice Monk, 74–95. New Haven: Yale University Press, 1987.

Olan, Susan Torian. "Blood Debts." In Janes, *No Apologies*, 12–48.

Oldham, Williamson S., and George W. White. *A Digest of the General Statute Laws of the State of Texas.* Austin, TX: John Marshal, 1859.

Olien, Diana Davids. "Domesticity and the Texas Oil Fields: Dimensions of Women's Experience, 1920–1950." In Downs and Jones, *Women and Texas History*, 116–26.

Orozco, Cynthia E. "Beyond Machismo: La Familia and Ladies Auxiliaries." *Renato Rosaldo Lecture Series* 10 (1994): 33–77.

———. "O'Shea, Maria Elena Zamora." *Handbook of Texas Online.* http://www.tshaonline.org/handbook/online/articles/fos21.

Pai, Kalpana, and Sameer Vaidya. "Glass Ceiling: Role of Women in the Corporate World." *Competition Forum* 4, no. 2 (2006): 421–26.

Pardun, Robert. "It Wasn't Hard to Be a Communist in Texas." In Janes, *No Apologies*, 49–61.

Park, Kevin B. "St. Joseph Hospital." *Handbook of Texas Online.* http://www.tshaonline.org/handbook/online/articles/sbs10.

Payne, Darwin. *Indomitable Sarah: The Life of Judge Sarah T. Hughes.* Dallas: Southern Methodist University Press, 2004.

Perry, Nellie M. *Woman of the Plains: The Journals and Stories of Nellie M. Perry.* Edited by Sandra Gail Teichmann. College Station: Texas A&M University Press, 2000.

Pitre, Merline. "At the Crossroads: Black Texas Women, 1930–1954." In Glasrud and Pitre, *Black Women in Texas History*, 129–58.

Portales, Patricia. "Tejanas on the Home Front: Women, Bombs, and the (Re)Gendering of War in Mexican American World War II Literature." In *Latina/os and World War II: Mobility, Agency, and Ideology*, edited by Maggie Rivas-Rodriguez and B. V. Olguín, 175–96. Austin: University of Texas Press, 2015.

Postel, Charles. *The Populist Vision.* New York: Oxford University Press, 2007.

Poyo, Gerald E., and Gilberto M. Hinojosa. "Spanish Texas and Borderlands Historiography in Transition: Implications for United States History." *Journal of American History*, 75 (September 1988): 395–416.

"Prohibition of Sex Discrimination, 1975: Hearings before the Subcommittee on Education of the Committee on Labor and Public Welfare on S. 2106 to Amend Title IX of the Education Amendments of 1972." US Senate, 94th Cong., 1st sess. http://files.eric.ed.gov/fulltext/ED136136.pdf.

Pruitt, Bernadette. "'For the Advancement of the Race': The Great Migrations to Houston, Texas, 1914–1941." *Journal of Urban History* 31 (May 2005): 435–78.

———. *The Other Great Migration: The Movement of Rural African Americans to Houston, 1900–1941.* College Station: Texas A&M University Press, 2013.

Pycior, Julie Leininger. "Tejanas Navigating the 1920s." In *Tejano Epic: Essays in Honor of Félix D. Almaráz, Jr.,* edited by Arnoldo De León, 71–86. Austin: Texas State Historical Association, 2005.

Quiroga, Miguel Gonzalez. "Mexicanos in Texas during the Civil War." In Zamora, Orozco, and Rocha, *Mexican Americans in Texas History,* 51–62.

Rabalais, Gary. "Humble Women at War: The Case of Humble's Baytown Refinery, 1942–1945." *Houston Review* 2 (2005): 33–36, 58.

Rabb, Mary Crownover. In Exley, *Texas Tears and Texas Sunshine,* 5–18.

Rable, George C. *Civil Wars: Women and the Crisis of Southern Nationalism.* Urbana: University of Illinois Press, 1989.

Raggio, Louise Ballerstedt, with Vivian Anderson Castleberry. *Texas Tornado: The Life of a Crusader for Women's Rights and Family Justice.* New York: Citadel Press, 2003.

Ragsdale, Crystal Sasse. "The German Woman in Frontier Texas." In *German Culture in Texas: A Free Earth: Essays from the 1978 Southwest Symposium,* edited by Glen E. Lich and Dona B. Reeves, 144–56. Boston: Twayne, 1980.

———. *The Women and Children of the Alamo.* Austin, TX: State House Press, 1994.

Ramírez, Elizabeth C. "Hispanic and Mexican American Women on the Texas Stage, 1875–1990." In Downs and Jones, *Women and Texas History: Selected Essays,* 34–41.

Ramos, Henry A. J. *A People Forgotten, a Dream Pursued: The History of the American G.I. Forum, 1948–1972.* n.p.: American G.I. Forum, 1983.

Randall, Tanya Krause. "Texas Ranch Women Remember World War II." *Sound Historian* 13 (2011): 41–57.

Raska, Ginny McNeill, and Mary Lynne Gasaway Hill, eds. *The Uncompromising Diary of Sallie McNeill, 1858–1867.* College Station: Texas A&M University Press, 2009.

Redden, Molly. "How the War on Women Was Won." *Mother Jones* (September/October 2015): 28–36, 65.

Reid, Debra A. *Reaping a Greater Harvest: African Americans, the Extension Service, and Rural Reform in Jim Crow Texas.* College Station: Texas A&M University Press, 2007.

Reid, Jan. *Let the People In: The Life and Times of Ann Richards.* Austin: University of Texas Press, 2012.

Reinier, Jacqueline S. "Concepts of Domesticity on the Southern Plains Agricultural Frontier, 1870–1920." In Wunder, *At Home on the Range,* 57–70.

"Reminiscences of James Williams Holt." *Nesbitt Memorial Library Journal* 6 (September 1996): 151–60.

Republican Party Platform of 1976. American Presidency Project. http://www.presidency.ucsb.edu/ws/index.php?pid=25843.

Reynolds, Phin W. "Chapters from the Frontier Life of Phin W. Reynolds." Edited by J. R. Webb. In Gallaway, *Texas,* 169–71.

Richards, Ann, with Peter Knobler. *Straight from the Heart: My Life in Politics and Other Places.* New York: Simon and Schuster, 1989.

Rivas-Rodriguez, Maggie, et al. *A Legacy Greater Than Words: Stories of US Latinos and Latinas of the WWII Generation.* Austin: University of Texas Press, 2006.

Roach, Joyce Gibson. "Introduction: Cowgirls and Cattle Queens." In Massey, *Texas Women on the Cattle Trails*, 8–22.

Roberts, Velma, and Ruby Williams. "Welfare Is a Right." In Janes, *No Apologies*, 108–19.

Rocha, Rodolfo. "Early Ranching along the Rio Grande." In Wunder, *At Home on the Range*, 3–18.

Rogers, Mary Beth. *Barbara Jordan: American Hero*. New York: Bantam Books, 1998.

Rogers, Mary Beth, Sherry A. Smith, and Janelle D. Scott. *We Can Fly: Stories of Katherine Stinson and Other Gutsy Texas Women*. Austin: Ellen C. Temple, 1983.

Rosen, Ruth. *The World Split Open: How the Modern Women's Movement Changed America*. New York: Penguin Books, 2000.

Ross, Joann M. "Making Marital Rape Visible: A History of American Legal and Social Movements Criminalizing Rape in Marriage." PhD diss., University of Nebraska, 2015.

Rossinow, Doug. *The Politics of Authenticity: Liberalism, Christianity, and the New Left in America*. New York: Columbia University Press, 1998.

Ross-Nazzal, Jennifer. "Mae C. Jemison: The Right Stuff." In Turner, Cole, and Sharpless, *Texas Women*, 457–80.

Rubin, Nancy. *The New Suburban Woman: Beyond Myth and Motherhood*. New York: Coward, McCann & Geoghegan, 1982.

Russell, Jan Jarboe. "Mommy War." *Texas Monthly*, June 1989, 78–81, 115–17.

Sáenz, Andrés. *Early Tejano Ranching: Daily Life at Ranchos San José and El Fresnillo*. College Station: Texas A&M University Press, 2001.

Sager, Robin C. *Marital Cruelty in Antebellum America*. Baton Rouge: Louisiana State University Press, 2016.

Sallee, Shelley. "'The Woman of It': Governor Miriam Ferguson's 1924 Election." *Southwestern Historical Quarterly* 100 (July 1996): 1–16.

Sánchez, Joanne Rao. "The Latinas of World War II: From Familial Shelter to Expanding Horizons." In *Beyond the Latino World War II Hero: The Social and Political Legacy of a Generation*, edited by Maggie Rivas-Rodríguez and Emilio Zamora, 63–89. Austin: University of Texas Press, 2009.

Schlafly, Phyllis. "What's Wrong with 'Equal Rights' for Women?" *Phyllis Schlafly Report* 5, no. 7 (February 1972), http://eagleforum.org/publications/psr/feb1972.html.

Schoen, Harold. "The Free Negro in the Republic of Texas, I." *Southwestern Historical Quarterly* 39 (April 1936): 292–308.

Schwartz, Marie Jenkins. *Born in Bondage: Growing up Enslaved in the Antebellum South*. Cambridge: Harvard University Press, 2000.

Seaholm, Megan. "Earnest Women: The White Woman's Club Movement in Progressive Era Texas, 1880–1920," PhD diss., Rice University, 1988.

———. "Midwifery." *Handbook of Texas Online*. http://www.tshaonline.org/handbook/online/articles/sim02.

Seed, Patricia. *To Love, Honor, and Obey in Colonial Mexico*. Stanford: Stanford University Press, 1988.

Sharpless, Rebecca. *Fertile Ground, Narrow Choices: Women on Texas Cotton Farms, 1900–1940*. Chapel Hill: University of North Carolina Press, 1999.

———. "'In Favor of Our Fathers' Country and Government': Unionist Women in North Texas." In Liles and Boswell, *Women in Civil War Texas*, 205–26.

———. "'Us Has Ever Lived De Useful Life': African American Women in Texas, 1874–1900." In Glasrud and Pitre, *Black Women in Texas History*, 73–98.

———. "Women and Work during the Great Depression in Texas." In Willett and Curley, *Invisible Texans*, 144–55.

Shilcutt, Tracy McGlothlin. "The Bluebonnet Brigade: Women and War in Abilene, Texas: 1941–1945." Master's thesis, Abilene Christian University, 1993.

Silverthorne, Elizabeth. "Herzog, Sofie Dalia." *Handbook of Texas Online.* http://www.tshaonline.org/handbook/online/articles/fheec.

———. "Potter, Claudia." *Handbook of Texas Online.* http://www.tshaonline.org/handbook/online/articles/fpoeq.

Sitton, Thad, ed. *Harder than Hardscrabble: Oral Recollections of the Farming Life from the Edge of the Texas Hill Country.* Austin: University of Texas Press, 2003.

Smallwood, James M., and Barry A. Crouch. "Texas Freedwomen during Reconstruction, 1865–1874." In Glasrud and Pitre, *Black Women in Texas History*, 38–72.

Smith, Harold L. "'All Good Things Start with the Women': The Origin of the Texas Birth Control Movement, 1933–1945." *Southwestern Historical Quarterly* 114 (January 2011): 252–85.

———. "Casey Hayden: Gender and the Origins of SNCC, SDS, and the Women's Liberation Movement." In Turner, Cole, and Sharpless, *Texas Women*, 359–88.

Smith, Jordan. "Rick Perry's War on Women." *Nation*, December 19, 2011, 19–21.

Smith, Sharon Ann. "Female Home Front Soldiers and Their Food for Freedom Campaign during the Second World War." Master's thesis, Texas Woman's University, 1996.

Smithwick, Noah. *The Evolution of a State; or, Recollections of Old Texas Days.* Austin, 1900.

Sneller, Judy E. "Saints, Hell-Raisers, and Other 'Typical Texans': Frontier Women and the Humor of Mollie Moore Davis." *Journal of the American Studies Association of Texas* 25 (October 1994): 14–31.

Sokolow, Jayme A., and Mary Ann Lamanna. "Women and Utopia: The Woman's Commonwealth of Belton, Texas." *Southwestern Historical Quarterly* (April 1984): 371–92.

The Spirit of Houston: The First National Women's Conference: An Official Report to the President, the Congress and the People of the United States. Washington, DC: National Commission on the Observance of International Women's Year, 1978.

Starr, Sarah Joyce Rutherford. "'Yours Heart and Hand': An Analysis of the Correspondence of James and Patience Crain Black, 1861–1865." Master's thesis, Baylor University, 1990.

Stephan, Scott. *Redeeming the Southern Family: Evangelical Women and Domestic Devotion in the Antebellum South.* Athens: University of Georgia Press, 2008.

Stevenson, Amanda J., et al. "Effect of Removal of Planned Parenthood from the Texas Women's Health Program." *New England Journal of Medicine* 374 (March 3, 2016): 853–60.

Stockel, H. Henrietta. *Chiricahua Apache Women and Children: Safekeepers of the Heritage.* College Station: Texas A&M University Press, 2000.

Stott, Kelly McMichael. "From Lost Cause to Female Empowerment: The Texas Division of the United Daughters of the Confederacy, 1896–1966." PhD diss., University of North Texas, 2001.

Stout, Janis P. *Katherine Anne Porter: A Sense of the Times.* Charlottesville: University Press of Virginia, 1995.

Strickland, Kristi Throne. "The Significance and Impact of Women on the Rise of the Republican Party in Twentieth Century Texas." PhD diss, University of North Texas, 2000.

Struve, Walter. *Germans and Texans: Commerce Migration and Culture in the Days of the Lone Star Republic.* Austin: University of Texas Press, 1996.

Stuart, David E. *Anasazi America: Seventeen Centuries on the Road from Center Place.* Albuquerque: University of New Mexico Press, 2000.

Stuntz, Jean A. *Hers, His and Theirs: Community Property Law in Spain and Early Texas.* Lubbock: Texas Tech University Press, 2005.

———. "Spanish Laws for Texas Women: The Development of Marital Property Law to 1850." *Southwestern Historical Quarterly* 101, no. 4 (April 2001), 542–59.

Swall-Yarrington, Maria. "Texas Council on Family Violence." *Handbook of Texas Online.* http://www.tshaonline.org/handbook/online/articles/pwtfg.

Tang, Irwin A., ed. *Asian Texans: Our Histories and Our Lives.* Austin: It Works, 2008.

Taylor, A. Elizabeth. "The Woman Suffrage Movement in Texas." *Journal of Southern History* 17 (May 1951): 194–215.

"Texas Association against Sexual Assault History." http://taasa.memberlodge.org/Resources/Documents/Board%20Website/TAASA%20History.doc.

Texas League of Women Voters. "Domestic Violence and Spousal Rape." https://my.lwv.org/texas/position/domestic-violence.

Thompson, Jerry D. *Vaqueros in Blue and Gray.* Austin, TX: State House Press, 2000.

Thompson, Jerry, and Elizabeth Mata. "Mexican Texan Women in the Civil War." In Liles and Boswell, *Women in Civil War Texas,* 151–79.

Tijerina, Andrés. *Tejanos and Texas under the Mexican Flag, 1821–1836.* College Station: Texas A&M University Press, 1994.

Tolleson-Rinehart, Sue, and Jeanie R. Stanley. *Claytie and the Lady: Ann Richards, Gender, and Politics in Texas.* Austin: University of Texas Press, 1994.

Tongate, Vicki Adams. *Another Year Finds Me in Texas: The Civil War Diary of Lucy Pier Stevens.* Austin: University of Texas Press, 2016.

Torget, Andrew J. *Seeds of Empire: Cotton, Slavery, and the Transformation of the Texas Borderlands, 1800–1950.* Chapel Hill: University of North Carolina Press, 2015.

Turner, Elizabeth Hayes. "Lion in the Texas House: The Political Performances of Senfronia Thompson." Paper presented at the Women in Texas History Luncheon, Texas State Historical Association, March 6, 2014.

———. "'White-Gloved Ladies' and 'New Women' in the Texas Woman Suffrage Movement." In *Southern Women: Histories and Identities,* edited by Virginia Bernhard, Betty Brandon, Elizabeth Fox-Genovese, and Theda Perdue, 129–56. Columbia: University of Missouri Press, 1992.

———. *Women and Gender in the New South, 1865–1945*. Wheeling, IL: Harlan Davidson, 2009.

———. *Women, Culture, and Community: Religion and Reform in Galveston, 1880–1920*. New York: Oxford University Press, 1997.

Turner, Elizabeth Hayes, Stephanie Cole, and Rebecca Sharpless, eds. *Texas Women: Their Histories, Their Lives*. Athens: University of Georgia Press, 2015.

Ura, Alexa. "US Supreme Court Overturns Texas Abortion Restrictions." *Texas Tribune*, June 27, 2016. https://www.texastribune.org/2016/06/27/us-supreme-court-rules-texas-abortion-case.

Vaiani, Cheryl Ellis. "Galveston's Midwives in the Early Twentieth Century." *Houston Review* 19, no. 1 (1997): 39–41.

———. "Women and Health." *Handbook of Texas Online*. http://www.tshaonline.org/handbook/online/articles/smwbn.

Vargas, Deborah. "Rosita Fernández: La Rosa de San Antonio." *Frontiers* 24, nos. 2 and 3 (2003): 168–84.

Viele, Teresa Griffin. *Following the Drum: A Glimpse of Frontier Life*. Foreword and bibliography by Sandra L. Myres. Lincoln: University of Nebraska Press, 1984.

Villarreal, Mary Ann. "The Synapses of Struggle: Martha Cotera and Tejana Activism." In *Las Obreras: Chicana Politics of Work and Family*, edited by Vicki L. Ruiz, 273–95. Los Angeles: UCLA Chicano Studies Research Center Publications, 2000.

Villarreal, Roberto M. "The Mexican-American Vaqueros of the Kenedy Ranch: A Social History." Master's thesis, Texas A&M University, 1972.

Wagner, Mathilda. In Exley, *Texas Tears and Texas Sunshine*, 107–23.

Walsh, Kelli Cardenas. "Oveta Culp Hobby: Ability, Perseverance, and Cultural Capital in a Twentieth Century Success Story." In Turner, Cole, and Sharpless, *Texas Women*, 318–37.

Weaver, Bobby D. *Oilfield Trash: Life and Labor in the Oil Patch*. College Station: Texas A&M University Press, 2010.

Weber, David J. *The Mexican Frontier, 1821–1846*. Albuquerque: University of New Mexico Press, 1982.

———. *The Spanish Frontier in North America*. New Haven: Yale University Press, 1992.

Weber, Peter. "Wendy Davis' Stunning Filibuster of a Texas Abortion Bill." *Week*, June 26, 2013. http://theweek.com/articles/462815/wendy-davis-stunning-filibuster-texas-abortion-bill.

Weddington, Sarah. *A Question of Choice*. New York: Penguin Books, 1993.

Weigand, Cindy. *Texas Women in World War II*. Lanham: Republic of Texas Press, 2003.

Welter, Barbara. "The Cult of True Womanhood: 1820–1860." *American Quarterly* 18 (Summer 1966): 151–74.

Werden, Frieda. "Adventures of a Texas Feminist." In Janes, *No Apologies*, 189–210.

Werschkul, Misha, Barbara Gault, Amy Caiazza, and Heidi Hartmann. *Women's Education and Earnings in Texas*. Washington, DC: American Association of University Women Educational Foundation, 2005. https://files.eric.ed.gov/fulltext/ED485719.pdf.

White, Deborah Gray. *Ar'n't I a Woman? Female Slaves in the Plantation South*. New York: W. W. Norton, 1985.

Willett, Donald, and Stephen Curley, eds. *Invisible Texans: Women and Minorities in Texas History*. Boston: McGraw Hill, 2005.

Wilson, Carol O'Keefe. *In the Governor's Shadow: The True Story of Ma and Pa Ferguson*. Denton: University of North Texas Press, 2014.

Wilson, Diane. "Division of Labor and Stress Loads at the Sanders Site (41LR2), Lamar County, Texas." *Bulletin of the Texas Archeological Society* 65 (1994): 129–60.

Winegarten, Ruthe. *Black Texas Women: 150 Years of Trial and Triumph*. Austin: University of Texas Press, 1995.

———. "From Ranchers to Reformers: South Texas Women in Texas History." *South Texas Studies* (1998): 71–86.

Wink, Amy L., ed. *Tandem Lives: The Frontier Texas Diaries of Henrietta Baker Embree and Tennessee Keys Embree, 1856–1884*. Knoxville: University of Tennessee Press, 2008.

Wintz, Cary D. "Women in Texas." In *The Texas Heritage*, edited by Ben Procter and Archie P. McDonald, 185–208. Wheeling, IL: Harlan Davidson, 1998.

Wisely, Karen. "The 'Dallas Way' in the Gayborhood: The Creation of a Lesbian, Gay, Bisexual, and Transgender Community in Dallas, Texas, 1965–1986." Master's thesis, University of North Texas, 2011.

Wooster, Ralph. *Civil War Texas: A History and a Guide*. Austin: Texas State Historical Association, 1999.

Wunder, John R., ed. *At Home on the Range: Essays on the History of Western Social and Domestic Life*. Westport, CT: Greenwood Press, 1985.

Wyden, Peter. "The Revolt of Texas Women." *Saturday Evening Post*, January 14, 1961, 25, 55–56.

Zamora, Emilio, Cynthia Orozco, and Rodolfo Rocha, eds. *Mexican Americans in Texas History: Selected Essays*. Austin: Texas State Historical Association, 2000.

Index